# Staff Development in Higher Education

An International Review and Bibliography

*Edited by*
**David C B Teather**
*Director, Higher Education Development Centre,*
*University of Otago*

Kogan Page, London/Nichols Publishing
Company, New York

First published in Great Britain 1979 by Kogan Page Limited,
120 Pentonville Road, London N1
ISBN 0 85038 178 9

First published in the United States of America 1979 by
Nichols Publishing Company,
Post Office Box 96, New York, NY 10024

*Library of Congress Cataloging in Publication Data*
Main entry under title:
Staff development in higher education.

Bibliography: p.
Includes indexes.

1. College teachers — Addresses, essays, lectures.
2. College teachers, Rating of — Addresses, essays,
lectures. 3. Universities and colleges — Faculty —
Addresses, essays, lectures. I. Teather, David C B
LB2331.7.S72     378.1'2     79—2141
ISBN 0-89397-060-3

Printed in Great Britain by Brown Knight & Truscott Ltd,
London and Tonbridge

# Contents

# Contributors

**Donald Bligh** has experience of further, higher and adult education. After studying at a college of education, he took degrees in geography, psychology and philosophy. He has taught students in art and technical colleges, WEA and extramural classes, a polytechnic and two universities. Before becoming Director of Teaching Services at the University of Exeter, Dr Bligh was a member of London's University Teaching Methods Unit. He has conducted research into the effectiveness of lectures and other teaching methods. His other publications include *Teaching Students* (with G J Ebrahim, D Jaques and D W Piper) and *Research into Teaching Methods in Higher Education* (4th edition) with Ruth Beard and Alan Harding.

*Address:* Teaching Services Centre, University of Exeter, Exeter EX4 4QJ, UK

**Professor John Clift** became foundation Director of the University Teaching and Research Centre, Victoria University of Wellington in 1973. This Centre, as well as teaching and conducting research into various aspects of tertiary education, provides a staff development service to the University. Prior to the Wellington appointment, he was Director of the Higher Education Research Unit, Monash University, Australia. His interests are in the areas of the process of staff development, learning and development in adolescence and adults, and evaluation strategies for the improvement of learning.

*Address:* University Teaching and Research Centre, Victoria University of Wellington, Private Bag, Wellington, New Zealand

**Joan Conrad** became Assistant Professor at the Institute for Studies in Higher Education, University of Copenhagen in 1972, and Associate Professor at the same Institute in 1976. Her main research interests are curriculum planning, course evaluation and processes of innovation in higher education.

*Address:* Institute for Studies in Higher Education, St Kannikestraede 18, DK 1169 Copenhagen K, Denmark

**Geoff Foster** taught mechanical engineering for 14 years at Queensland University before he took his present post in the Tertiary Education Institute (TEDI). As well as his involvement in many aspects of staff development, he has a keen interest in the ways in which computers can best be used in education.

*Address:* TEDI, University of Queensland, St Lucia, Australia 4067

**Jerry Gaff** studied social psychology and taught both psychology and sociology. While teaching in an experimental college, he became interested in evaluating the consequences of its innovations. This interest in research led him to the University of California, Berkeley, where at its Center for Research and Development in

Higher Education he studied and wrote about college students, faculty, and structures. Recently he has tried to apply his ideas about educational improvement by directing action projects of the Society for Values in Higher Education. The three-year Project on Institutional Renewal through the Improvement of Teaching terminated in 1978, and his current work dealing with the improvement of general education began.

*Address:* Project on General Education Models, 1818 R Street NW, Washington, DC 20009, USA

**Professor Dr Bernd Gasch** studied psychology at the Universities of Erlangen and Hamburg. After working as an *Assistent* at the Psychological Institute of the University of Erlangen, he became Head of the *Hochschuldidaktisches Zentrum* at the University of Augsburg. He was then appointed head of a research group established by the German Assembly of Ministries of Law to evaluate models of legal education. He also founded a 'Team for Psychological Management' for the in-service education of managerial staff in industry and administration.

In 1978 he spent six months as a Visiting Fellow in the Office for Research in Academic Methods at the Australian National University, Canberra. He is now Professor of Psychology of Education at the Pädagogische Hochschule Ruhr, Dortmund. His main interest is in the psychology of teaching and learning.

*Address:* Fachbereich III, Pädagogische Hochschule Ruhr, Postfach 380, 4600 Dortmund 50, Federal Republic of Germany

**Professor Marcel L Goldschmid** has been the Director of the Chair of Higher Education and Psychology at the Swiss Federal Institute of Technology in Lausanne, Switzerland since 1973. A psychologist by training (PhD, University of California, Berkeley), his former appointments include a professoriate at UCLA and the directorship of the Centre for Learning and Development, McGill University, Montreal, Canada. His research interests focus on student learning, peer teaching, individualized instruction and the evaluation of courses.

*Address:* Chaire de Pédagogie et Didactique, Ecole Polytechnique Fédérale de Lausanne, Centre Est, CH-1015 Lausanne, Switzerland

**Harriet Greenaway** has been assistant academic registrar at the Polytechnic of North London since 1972 where her work is concerned mainly with professional support for decision-making bodies. She had been administrator of the Society for Research into Higher Education for three years and previously a local government officer. She undertook the first national survey of training of British university teachers in 1971. Since then she has been actively involved in staff development of academic and administrative staff in polytechnics. Her recent research interests are staff development policies and academic government. For five years she was a member of a London borough council and has been Vice-Chairman of the SRHE since 1975.

*Address:* The Polytechnic of North London, Holloway, London N7 8DB, UK

**Bradford W Imrie** is a senior lecturer in the University Teaching and Research Centre, Victoria University of Wellington. Brad Imrie joined the Centre in 1975 after a period of 11 years as a lecturer in the Department of Mechanical Engineering, University of Leeds, England, with previous technical college teaching and industrial experience. During 1973-75 he had a UGC Research Fellowship to consider the training of university teachers recruited from industry to university departments of (Applied) Science. Current interests include professional development processes for staff (including evaluation), small group methods, independent learning and assessment of learning.

*Address:* University Teaching and Research Centre, Victoria University of Wellington, Private Bag, Wellington, New Zealand

**Geoff Isaacs** taught mathematics at the University of New South Wales for a number of years. He then moved (via a large science curriculum evaluation project) to a lectureship in the newly established Tertiary Education Institute and has been there since early 1974. He spent the latter half of 1977 on study leave in the Netherlands. His main concern is improving teaching and learning within the University of Queensland; he is currently conducting a large-scale longitudinal study of mature age entrants to the University.

*Address:* TEDI, University of Queensland, St Lucia, Australia 4067

**Hans Jalling** left the University of Stockholm where he was the Director of Studies of the English Department in 1970 to become the first Director of Staff Development in the Office of the Chancellor of the Swedish Universities. He has served as an expert in a number of public commissions on higher education, most recently in the 1974 Commission on the Training of Teachers and the 1975 Commission on the Swedish University Reform.

*Address:* National Board of Universities and Colleges, Box 45501, S-104 30 Sweden

**Ray McAleese** is a lecturer in education in the University of Aberdeen with responsibility for staff development work. He is editor of the journal *Programmed Learning & Educational Technology* and co-author of the *Encyclopaedia of Educational Media, Communications and Technology*. His doctoral dissertation was in the area of staff development. During 1979 he is Visiting Fellow in the Centre for the Study of Higher Education, University of Melbourne.

*Address:* Department of Education, University of Aberdeen, Aberdeen AB9 2UB, Scotland

**Professor Dr sc Horst Möhle** holds the Chair of University Pedagogics at the Karl Marx University, Leipzig. Originally a chemist, in 1958 he became Deputy Vice-Chancellor for Study Affairs, and from 1968 to 1975 was First Deputy Vice-Chancellor of the University.

Professor Möhle is the author of some 200 papers on political and pedagogical issues in higher education and on problems of chemistry teaching. He has organized several international conferences on aspects of higher education, has lectured in many countries, and since 1966 has participated in a number of UNESCO projects and conferences. Current research interests include the development of the student's creativity in independent academic work, aspects of distance and post-experience education and training, and educational technology.

*Address:* Chair of University Pedagogics, Karl-Marx-Universität, Karl-Marx-Platz 9, 701 Leipzig, German Democratic Republic

**Derek Mortimer** is Head of the Educational Development Unit at the Polytechnic of Central London. He has taught in schools, a college of education and two polytechnics. His main interests are in course development and the institutionalization of staff training and development. He serves on a number of committees of the Council for National Academic Awards, co-directs a research project on school-focused initial and in-service training, and between 1974 and 1977 served as Chairman of the Standing Conference on Educational Development Services in Polytechnics.

*Address:* Educational Development Unit, Polytechnic of Central London, 309 Regent Street, London W1R 8AL, UK

**Professor John Nisbet** has held the Chair of Education in the University of Aberdeen since 1963. He has been editor of the *British Journal of Educational Psychology,* Chairman of the Educational Research Board (SSRC, London), Chairman of the Scottish Council for Research in Education, and President of the British Educational Research Association. He took part in the first British courses on university teaching methods in 1963, and initiated courses in Aberdeen in 1965.

*Address:* Department of Education, University of Aberdeen, Aberdeen AB9 2UB, Scotland

**Professor Ernest Roe** established the Tertiary Education Institute at the University of Queensland in 1973, having previously been foundation Professor of Education at the University of Papua New Guinea since 1967. He worked with Professor (Sir) Fred Schonell in the 1950s and then taught at the University of Adelaide. A particular focus of his interest in teaching and learning in universities is on the efficiency of use of both print and non-print materials, and on library and study skills. Among his many publications are three books, *Teachers, Librarians and Children* (1965; new edn 1972), *Some Dilemmas of Teaching* (1971), and *Using and Misusing the Materials of Teaching and Learning* (1975).

*Address:* TEDI, University of Queensland, St Lucia, Australia 4067

**Bruce M Shore** is an Associate Professor of Education in the Centre for Learning and Development and the Department of Educational Psychology and Sociology, McGill University. During 1978-79 he is Acting Director of the Centre, Canada's first university instructional development unit. His main professional and research interests are intellectual giftedness and learning styles, and exceptional teaching and learning in higher education.

*Address:* Centre for Learning and Development, McGill University, 814 Sherbrooke Street West, Montreal, Quebec, Canada H3A 2K6

# Acknowledgements

Plans for this book were made during late 1977 and early 1978 while I was on study leave at the Centre for Communication Studies, University of Liverpool, England. I am indebted to the Director of that Centre, Mr Geoffrey Leytham, and to staff of other units in the UK which I visited at that time, for much productive discussion. Particular thanks go to Dr Christopher Matheson, Co-ordinating and Research Officer of the Co-ordinating Committee for the Training of University Teachers, for discussion on staff development in the UK and elsewhere, and for many useful contacts.

The report on pp 248-54 is reproduced by kind permission of Mr F S Hambly, Secretary of the Australian Vice-Chancellors Committee. Mr M G F Hall, Secretary of the University Authorities Panel (UK), permitted the reproduction of the text of the UAP/AUT agreement. I should also like to thank Janet Healey for translating the *Wieckenberger Thesen,* and my wife, Dr Elizabeth Teather, for preparing the comprehensive author and subject indexes. Jocelyn Diedrichs, Elaine Murray and Katrina Trevella typed the script; they and other staff of my Centre dealt efficiently with the Centre's daily business while I completed the final stages of editing this book. DCBT

# Introduction

Higher education institutions throughout the western world are under challenge. Six years ago a report to the Australian Vice-Chancellors Committee[1] stated:

> There is now, more than ever before, pressure on [university] administrators to examine their institutions critically — their objectives and processes — and to effect changes where these are deemed necessary. There is pressure on teachers to improve their courses of studies; to develop effective ways of facilitating students' learning; and to evaluate their own performance as well as that of their students.
>
> The present concern is in response to conditions which challenge universities everywhere, conditions such as:
>
> — the increased number and diversity of students
> — the critical and often articulate student body
> — the explosion of knowledge
> — the changing community values and expectations
> — the changing requirements of professions, of employers of graduates, and of governments
> — the institutional characteristics of some universities, their size and emphasis on activities other than teaching.

Shortly after this report was written, the economic repercussions of the oil crisis heralded the end of an era of unprecedented expansion of higher education in the western world. Governments were left with higher education systems which depended for their continuance on the consumption of higher proportions of GNP than ever before. For this and for many other reasons, higher education is today of great importance to the politician and to the public alike.

Adjustment of old institutions to new needs was not easy even in times of plenty. In nineteenth-century England, Oxford and Cambridge had to be outflanked by the creation of parallel institutions because of the dysfunction between the ancient universities and the higher education priorities of English society. Among more recent examples of alternative tertiary institutions are the polytechnics and the Open University in Britain, and the colleges of advanced education in Australia. Difficult though change is for traditional institutions in times of plenty, adjustment in times of comparatively scarce resources and immobile staff would seem to pose immeasurably greater problems.

Paradoxically, however, the 'steady state' — and for some traditional institutions a declining estate, both *vis à vis* the newer foundations and in absolute terms — may create just the conditions necessary to bring about change. Expansion of existing institutions too often meant more of the same, with little heed to the nature of the provision. To meet new needs (or old needs which have assumed higher priority, such as those of adult and continuing education) with limited institutional resources requires greater ingenuity and resourcefulness; this may in turn promote more fundamental reappraisals of institutional goals and processes.

Central to the response of higher education institutions to changing conditions is their willingness to study themselves — in the words of the Australian Report quoted above, 'to apply the processes of scientific inquiry to their own institutions'. This theme recurs in a number of the chapters of this book, together with encouraging evidence that higher education institutions are indeed becoming increasingly willing to engage in such self-appraisal.

During the 1970s, in the process of this self-appraisal, a cluster of useful concepts has come to prominence. Among these are *staff development, instructional development* and *organizational development.* Each draws upon a different intellectual tradition;[2] yet in practice all overlap and form different facets of the same response.

This book is about *staff development,* defined as:

> a systematic attempt to harmonise individuals' interests and wishes, and their carefully assessed requirements for furthering their careers with the forthcoming requirements of the organisation within which they [are] expected to work (Piper and Glatter, 1977).

Applied in higher education this definition covers, for example, the development of the abilities of academic staff in the areas of teaching and examining, research and research supervision, consultancy and administration; it also applies to administrative, technical and clerical staff.

Though it is a useful starting point, it would be wrong of me to imply that such a definition is universally acceptable without qualification or change of emphasis. Indeed it would be surprising if this were otherwise, for this decade has seen a rapid growth of what is, in higher education, a comparatively new field. Staff development programmes have been set up, centres established, and attempts at international co-operation have been initiated.[3] Workers in different countries have entered the 'higher education research and development centres' from diverse backgrounds, and this diversity of background, together with the diverse institutional and social contexts in which they work, is reflected in their thinking. One of the main aims of this book is to capture something of this rich diversity of experience, so that the reader may explore the concepts and practices of staff development as these are perceived by leading workers in different countries.

Each chapter takes the form of a self-contained and up-to-date review of staff development in higher education in the country concerned. Each has been specially commissioned for this volume and all are written by academics of international standing, directly involved in the field. The outstanding value of such a comparative approach is that, partly at least by virtue of their different contexts, each contribution serves to throw into sharp relief particular and often different aspects of staff development. One effect of this is to sensitize the reader to those unstated assumptions which underlie current practice in his or her own context.

Most of the contributions are from western countries, to which the generalizations in the first paragraphs of this introduction undoubtedly apply — though even here they are superimposed upon a range of higher education traditions. Other contributions relate to contexts in which the social, educational and/or institutional conditions differ greatly; the contributions from eastern Europe (Chapter 6), the developing countries (Chapter 7) and the British polytechnics (Chapter 2b) are cases in point. But these particular contributions serve to stress, only in rather more extreme form, the fact that each contribution should be read against its national and institutional context.[4]

In recent years much of the concern about the competencies of academic staff in higher education has centred on their function as teachers, and most of the contributors have chosen this aspect as their main focus. I say 'chosen' advisedly, since each was free to approach the subject in whichever manner he or she considered most appropriate. In inviting contributions I did, as editor, cite Piper and Glatter's definition of staff development (quoted above), but apart from that and a suggested length, constraints on the contributors were reduced to a minimum. Such an editorial policy has its shortcomings, but any other would have introduced unnecessary bias and risked defeating the main purpose of the book.

Now that the chapters are to hand, it is tempting to write a précis or distillation of salient points, particularly of those which have been raised independently by several of the authors. One might, for example, refer to the inherent differences between the notions of 'training' and 'development', and to the shift which appears to be occurring towards a more comprehensive view of 'development'; note the link between *Hochschuldidaktik*[5] (and its counterparts in other countries) and wider movements for higher education reform; or compare the programmes and activities of the variously named higher education research and development centres, about which a wealth of data is presented. This would only be the start of my own personal selection — but far better for each reader to form such a synthesis in the light of his or her particular concerns.[6]

Perhaps, however, one generalization is in order. When discussing the idea for this book some 12 months ago, an eminent Canadian colleague — not, I might add, one of the present contributors — counselled me to write an introduction which stressed the importance of staff development for the future of higher education. With the benefit of hindsight, this has proved to be unnecessary. There is more than sufficient evidence in the chapters which follow — from accounts of major government-funded projects to operations on shoestring budgets — to demonstrate to all but the most doubtful that the concept, the 'technology',[7] of staff development has much to offer in higher education — and that higher education has need of it. Furthermore it is clear that systematic provision for staff development, in the form of both policies and supporting services, is becoming an accepted feature of higher education institutions. Such provision will come to be expected not only by the rising generation of academics and administrators, but also by that much larger number now in mid-career whose early aspirations are being tempered by the pressures of the times.

*David C B Teather*
*University of Otago, New Zealand*
*January 1979*

## Notes

1. The text of this report is reproduced on pp 248-54.
2. Discussed in Chapter 12.
3. In this volume, for example, Bligh writes from experience as a visiting consultant in a foreign country (Section 7.2) and Jalling discusses bi-national and tri-national courses (Section 10.6); this book is itself an example of international co-operation and, one hopes, will foster more.
4. Also to assist the reader in the search for context, biographical notes are provided on each of the contributors (pp 7-10).
5. For a discussion of the meaning of *Hochschuldidaktik* see p 112.
6. While each chapter is self-contained, ample indexes are provided to assist cross-referencing (pp 321 ff).
7. In the sense used by Gaff, p 245.

# 1: Australia — in service, lip service and unobtrusive pragmatism

Geoff Foster and Ernest Roe

## 1.0 Introduction

Because the proportion of the population entering higher education is relatively large in Australia, the number of academic staff who are potential candidates for development is substantial. In 1978 Australia, with a population of over 14 million, had 19 universities with a total of over 160,000 students and about 80 colleges of advanced education with a total of nearly 150,000 students. The total number of academic staff in these two sectors of higher education probably exceeds 25,000. Precise figures are difficult to determine because definitions of 'college of advanced education' and of academic, research, administrative, etc staff vary.

A third sector of higher education, technical and further education, has been omitted from this review. Colleges in this sector are undergoing considerable growth, change and development at present, and an adequate picture of staff development activities is unobtainable. The TAFE sector, as it is known, might also be omitted by definition. It is one of three sectors of *tertiary* education (a term in common use in Australia, meaning 'post secondary') but may not meet some definitions of 'higher' education.

Interest in academic staff development in Australia has been centred on the teaching role. Teaching in that statement includes examining/ assessment which, at least in theory, is an integral part of teaching though often regarded as a separate entity. There has been little activity in Australian higher education institutions towards making academic staff better researchers, committee men or administrators. It is generally assumed that research skills are fully acquired before appointment to the staff of a higher education institution; and that to function effectively on a committee or as a head of department depends on experience, on skills learned on the job, perhaps even on personality, but that in any case there is nothing to be taught or 'developed'.

No figures are available on how many of the 25,000 or so academic staff in Australian universities and colleges of advanced education have *directly* participated in staff development activities. However, the proportion is undoubtedly small. Participation is voluntary, and the majority of staff do not see themselves as in need of development. Some pressures exist; for example, on new staff to attend various kinds of induction courses; but no institution has staff development as a major preoccupation.

Much larger numbers of staff experience and may be influenced by *indirect* varieties of staff development; by, for instance, illuminative research carried out within their institutions, and by a steady flow of information coming to them both as reports on such research and as material about teaching, assessment, learning, course development and evaluation filtered to them from elsewhere.

The information services, the illuminative research and the direct staff development activities in Australian higher education are generally in the hands of the research and development units which exist in most universities and in some colleges. These units go by a wide variety of names and their activities vary considerably, most of all in emphasis.

Some institutions which do not have units have 'teaching development committees', known by various names, composed of (sometimes senior) academics who organize on the institutions' behalf seminars, workshops and courses on teaching and assessment, and often invite outside experts to conduct them. Some institutions have both units and committees, and the committees then tend to be advisory to the unit director rather than in control.

A few units, concerned with institutional research or staff development or both, came into existence in Australian universities in the 1960s and more at the beginning of the 1970s. They received their first official blessing in the fifth report of the Australian Universities Commission (1972, p 102) in these words:

> Teaching Research Units. Units concerned with improving the effectiveness of university teaching and learning and with conducting research into problems of higher education have been established at nine universities and three universities are proposing to establish them in the 1973-75 triennium. The Commission supports the establishment of such units. Student representatives who met the Commission stressed repeatedly their belief in the importance of such units as contributing to improved teaching. The Commission believes that all universities should operate such units. Their cost is not great in relation to total expenditure on teaching and research and there is evidence that considerable benefits flow from them.

Three years later, in its sixth report, the Commission repeated (p 62) 'There is evidence that the existence of such units has contributed to the effectiveness of universities' teaching during the triennium.' It reiterated its 'strong support', listed the universities which had established units since its last report, and noted 'with approval' that others were proposed during the 1976-78 triennium (p 113-14).

At the beginning of 1973 there were six such units actually operating. In 1978 there were 14 units in Australia's 19 universities and plans to establish a unit have been shelved in some of the others because of financial stringency.

The proportion of units in colleges of advanced education is much smaller. One reason for this is that many were formerly teachers' colleges and their staffs are assumed to be in no need of development as far as teaching skills are concerned. The largest and most active of the units in the college sector are in institutes of technology.

The total number of units in universities and colleges is approximately 40. 'Approximately' because there are occasionally problems of definition concerning whether a unit's activities can be properly described as either research and development or teaching research. Some are one-person enterprises. The number of units which are large, well staffed, and have a substantial 'staff development' presence in their institutions, is certainly only a small proportion of the total. It is, however, a reasonable assumption that all 40 sets of activities have *something* to do with staff development, even if marginally and indirectly. More precise information about the activities of research and development units will be found in the following sections.

Our earlier remarks about the lack of attention paid to the administrative skills of academic staff should not be taken to imply that administrative staff in universities and colleges have been left without organized development programmes. The Australian Vice-Chancellors Committee has for some years been sponsoring courses for university administrative staff, and the Victorian Universities and Colleges Committee has been similarly active in that state; running, for example, a three-day residential seminar for junior management staff in tertiary education institutions at La Trobe University in 1978. Many training sessions are conducted at a local level; to take a few examples from the University of Queensland, these have included induction courses for new administrative and secretarial staff, seminars on safety for laboratory managers and courses for supervisors of sections on interpersonal communication skills.

## 1.1 A context for staff development

In order to provide a framework for the account which follows we have chosen a number of categories which amount to a list of services upon which teaching staff can call.

These services may, as in many Australian universities and colleges, be provided by a specialist body, such as an educational research and development unit, or by several agencies within one institution. In either

Table 1.1 Staff development services in Australian universities

| | A 0 | B | C | D | E | F 3 | G | H | J | K | L | M | N 0 | P | Q | R | S | T 0 |
|---|---|---|---|---|---|---|---|---|---|---|---|---|---|---|---|---|---|---|
| 1. Information clearinghouse | | | * | | | | | | | | | * | | | | | | |
| 2. Library for local use | | | * | | | | | | | | | * | | | | | * | |
| 3. Newsletter publication | | | * | * | * | * | * | | * | * | | * | | | * | * | | |
| 4. Student study skills | | | | | | | | | | | * | | | | * | | | |
| 5. Formal courses for credit | | *1 | * | | *1 | *4 | | | | | | | | | | | | |
| 6. Short courses | | * | * | * | * | * | * | | * | * | * | * | | | | * | * | |
| 7. Seminars, workshops | | * | * | * | * | *2 | * | | * | * | * | * | | * | * | * | * | |
| 8. Packaged materials | | * | | * | * | * | * | | * | * | * | * | | * | * | | | |
| 9. Individual consultation | | * | * | * | * | * | * | | * | * | * | * | | * | * | * | * | |
| 10. Evaluation of teaching | | * | * | * | * | * | * | | * | * | * | * | | * | * | * | * | |
| 11. Course planning | | * | * | * | * | * | * | | * | * | * | * | | * | * | * | * | |
| 12. Policy advice | | | | | * | * | * | | * | * | * | * | | | * | | * | |
| 13. Descriptive research | | * | * | * | * | * | * | | * | * | * | * | | * | * | * | * | |
| 14. Theoretical research | | | * | * | * | * | * | | * | * | * | * | | | | | | |

0. No information available
1. As a component of BEd courses
2. Run by volunteer committee
3. Established as a research unit — may expand later
4. DipTertEd (correspondence)

Table 1.2 Staff development services in Australian colleges of advanced education

| | 1 | 2 | 3 | 4 | 5 | 6 | 7 | 8 | 9 | 10 | 11 | 12 | 13 | 14 | 15 | 16 | 17 |
|---|---|---|---|---|---|---|---|---|---|---|---|---|---|---|---|---|---|
| | | | | | 0 | | | 0 | | | | | | 0 | | | |
| 1. Information clearinghouse | | * | | | | | | | | | | * | | | | | * |
| 2. Library for local use | | | * | | | | | | | | | | | | | * | * |
| 3. Newsletter publication | | * | * | * | | | | | | | | * | | | | * | |
| 4. Student study skills | * | | * | | | * | | | | | | | | | | * | |
| 5. Formal courses for credit | | | | * | | | | | | | | | *1 | | | | |
| 6. Short courses | | * | * | | | | | | | | | | | | | | * |
| 7. Seminars, workshops | * | * | * | * | | | | | | | | * | | | | * | * |
| 8. Packaged materials | * | * | * | | | | | | | | | | * | | | * | * |
| 9. Individual consultation | * | * | * | * | | * | | | | | | * | | | | * | * |
| 10. Evaluation of teaching | * | * | * | * | | | | | * | * | * | * | | | * | * | * |
| 11. Course planning | * | * | * | * | | * | * | | * | | | | | | * | * | * |
| 12. Policy advice | * | * | * | | | * | * | | | * | | * | | | | * | * |
| 13. Descriptive research | * | * | * | * | | * | | | | * | * | | | | | * | |
| 14. Theoretical research | | * | | | | | | | | | * | | | | | | |

0. No information available
1. DipEd (correspondence)

case they may be thought of as indicating the institutional context within which staff development has the potential to take place.

The headings we shall use have been adapted from those proposed by Shore (1976) and are:

1. clearinghouse for information
2. library for local use
3. newsletter publication or other information dissemination
4. reading, study skills and other training for students
5. formal courses leading to qualifications
6. short informal courses
7. seminars, workshops and discussions
8. packaged materials, such as self-instructional programmes
9. consultations with individual members of staff
10. evaluation of teaching and of subjects and courses
11. assistance with course and curriculum planning
12. advice on policy matters
13. descriptive research
14. theoretical and experimental research.

Some of these items (such as courses, workshops, seminars and self-instructional programmes) are very direct and are obvious ways of addressing staff development. Others are less obvious and direct, and comprise instead (as we have said above) a context in which staff (self?) development may occur. In particular, the first three items are concerned with the creation of an environment rich in information, without which attempts at development can be easily frustrated.

Tables 1.1 and 1.2 give an indication of the provisions for staff development services in Australian universities and colleges. We do not claim that our information is complete and, to save embarrassment (ours and theirs) we have not identified the institutions except to class them as universities or colleges of advanced education.

Entries in the tables are based almost entirely on the evidence which the institutions or units themselves regard as worthy of mention. Examples of such evidence are a mention in an annual report, a description in a newsletter article, a notice of a coming event, and a report of research completed. As an additional prompt, we wrote to each establishment seeking information and stating the purpose for which we wanted it.

Although an entry in the tables does not indicate any defined *amount* of provision of a particular service, it seems a reasonable assumption that no entry represents a token or gesture only. It would have been possible to fill every cell in the tables by making strenuous attempts to find at least one instance of each service in each institution, or of services provided for on paper, as plans or otherwise intended, but this would not have been a useful exercise. Entries therefore depend upon explicit, public evidence. It should be noted, however, that absence of explicit, public evidence of staff development activity does not necessarily mean absence of staff development.

### 1.1.1 Clearinghouse for information

To some extent, any person who has an interest in teaching and learning in higher education can act informally as a clearinghouse, enabling colleagues and others with whom contact is made to find out what is going on elsewhere, what others are doing.

Unfortunately, this must be a rather limited and uncontrolled process unless, on the one hand, some attempt is made to systematize the exchange or, on the other hand, the contact between these interested people is enhanced or intensified.

In Tables 1.1 and 1.2 we have recorded only those tangible cases in which some catalogue publication, designed to be comprehensive and systematic, has been established.

The *Labyrinth* service, provided by TEDI (the Tertiary Education Institute) at the University of Queensland, is an example. This is a well-indexed collection, in loose-leaf form, of references to the potentially useful output of the research and development units in Australian and New Zealand universities and colleges.

Better contact between interested people is one of the functions of societies like the Higher Education Research and Development Society of Australasia, or the Australian Association for Research in Education and, in particular, of the conferences arranged by these societies. It has become a cliché that more benefit is often obtained by delegates at a conference during informal contact than during the formal programme. Similar effects are achieved by research and development units which have cross-fertilization as one of their aims, and which maintain contact with one another through meetings of their directors and by correspondence, as well as through conference attendance.

Any such contact may take place within a broad 'higher education' context or may be confined to specific areas, either in a geographical sense (ie within a single institution) or in a subject-matter sense (for instance, in a society concerned with, say, medical education or programmed learning). There is a trade-off between depth and breadth.

### 1.1.2 Library for local use

Units with small, specialized libraries usually provide not only the usual monographs and journals but also copies or microcopies of selected single articles, together with locally produced materials which might be of insufficient general interest for wider publication. Articles are acquired in several ways: during a literature search on a specific topic undertaken for a specific client of a development unit, from routine scanning of journals or by the use of computerized searches. (Some units, for instance, subscribe to the ERIC service of the National Library in Canberra.)

Such specialized libraries are either self-contained collections or branches of the main library, with their catalogues integrated into the overall system.

### 1.1.3 Newsletter publication or other information dissemination
Some newsletters are produced by research and development units to cover matters concerned with their own interests in teaching and learning. Other units contribute articles to a general newsletter produced for the educational institution as a whole. In either case this provides a valuable medium for modest articles on topics relevant to staff development, for advertising forthcoming courses, workshops and seminars, for putting in contact people of similar interests, and for raising awareness of educational issues amongst its readership. As well as regular productions of this kind, occasional papers and research reports are published by many units or institutions. Frequency of newsletters ranges from two or three issues a year to as much as one issue a week.

### 1.1.4 Reading, study skills and other training for students
These services have an obvious direct value for those students who use them. They can also have, through their contribution to staff development, an indirect benefit to all students, whether they use them or not.

Study skills courses are indirectly useful in a number of ways. They are a laboratory for the identification, isolation and treatment of learning difficulties; they provide an opportunity for the staff of specialist units, who may no longer be practising teachers (or may never have taught), to keep in touch with students so that they are aware of their current needs, expectations and attitudes; they are a mechanism by which a balance may be preserved between teaching and learning, between the needs of both the teacher and the student. In this way, concern with study skills in research and development units provides a valuable corrective to excessive preoccupation with the instruction aspects of teaching.

Organizational arrangements have an effect here. If the study skills programme is run by the same body which is responsible for staff development (as is the case at Murdoch University, for instance) liaison is easy. If the student programme is the responsibility of a separate body, such as a counselling service (a more typical situation in Australia), both bodies have to make efforts if they wish to maintain a useful collaboration.

### 1.1.5 Formal courses leading to qualifications
Formal qualifications for tertiary teachers are not common in
Australia and to date have made little impact. There has never been, as
far as we know, any proposal to make them a requirement for new or
existing staff in universities or in most colleges of advanced education,
although posts in school teacher education have usually been restricted
to those with schoolteaching qualifications.

Darling Downs Institute of Advanced Education in Queensland
currently offers a diploma in tertiary teaching, to be taken part-time
or externally over two or three years. In Victoria, where colleges of
advanced education are linked through a state-wide organization, the
Hawthorn State College provides a diploma. At other institutions it is
possible for academic staff to attend certain lecture courses forming
part of Bachelor or Diploma of Education programmes and to receive
credit for these.

### 1.1.6 Short informal courses
These are more common and widespread than formal courses for
qualifications. Many research and development units devote a
substantial proportion of their resources and effort to mounting a
range of courses.

These take a variety of forms from set courses, repeated regularly, to
impromptu events arranged to suit the needs of a particular group or
department.

They may be offered in concentrated form over a few days at the
beginning of the academic year, acting partially as induction courses
for new staff, or they may take the form of regular sessions spread over
several weeks during term or semester time. Evening or weekend
sessions do not seem very popular in Australia though they are
occasionally used, especially by medical faculties.

As numbers involved get fewer and topics become more *ad hoc*, this
category merges into the next.

### 1.1.7 Seminars, workshops and discussions
The purposes of these sessions, whether pre-planned or impromptu,
are many; for example, to provide information, to impart skills, to
raise awareness and to exchange ideas. In the absence of a pattern
which can be taken as typical, all one can say is that there is wide
scope for variety in this category, and much activity can be classed
under this heading.

### 1.1.8 Packaged materials, such as self-instructional programmes
A one-page checklist is the simplest form of self-instructional material.
Others which have been produced in Australian higher education

institutions range through synchronized tape and slide programmes and videotapes to computer-aided instruction programmes on how to write computer-aided instruction programmes.

This category is one of the services which is potentially transferable from place to place, institution to institution, perhaps best via the medium of the clearinghouse (see Section 1.1.1).

Kinds of 'package' which have been transferred successfully between institutions include 16mm film, with notes (eg the Trigger Film series produced by the Tertiary Education Research Centre at the University of New South Wales [Boud and Pearson, 1979]), tape-slide programmes (such as one on making tape-slide programmes devised by Dr I Brewer of the University of Sydney), and 'Jackdaw Files', collections of print material on particular topics put out by the Tasmanian College of Advanced Education.

### 1.1.9 Consultations with individual members of staff
This is an especially intangible category, first because its definition is hazy, and second because many consultations are confidential and personal.

It should be stressed, nevertheless, that this type of staff development activity is widely seen as crucially important, and the provision of opportunities for consultation within an institution is regarded as a major step towards achieving real, if intangible, benefits in teaching and learning.

Often a simple query, perhaps on the technique of overhead projection, leads to a mutually profitable association between an academic client and the staff of a research and development unit.

### 1.1.10 Evaluation of teaching and of subjects and courses
There is a wide variety in practice, ranging from the provision of short checklists for a staff member to use, to microteaching laboratories with elaborate videotape facilities, where experienced staff can offer constructive advice. Questionnaires used for students' evaluation of teaching or of courses are often drawn up for a particular situation by an individual teacher in consultation with a development unit. Unit staff help the teacher to avoid some of the elementary pitfalls of questionnaire construction, offer alternative formats and suggest topics to cover. At the other end of the range an institution may provide standard questionnaires and a computer-based interpretation service, such as the system using optically scanned sheets at the Tertiary Education Research Centre (University of New South Wales).

The availability of services of this sort and the presence of a group of interested but unbiased colleagues in a development unit can encourage staff to accept scrutinization by self and others. Similarly, if one's colleagues regularly submit to student evaluation and criticism, there is at best a desire, or at worst a pressure, to follow suit.

This is a sensitive area. Staff of research and development units steer a careful course, maintaining a prudent balance, being helpful to the teacher, without infringing his/her jealously guarded academic autonomy. They try to avoid the Scylla of being seen as an inspectorate, in the pay of the institution's administration, and the Charybdis of being used merely as a means of obtaining tenure, or promotion or prestige.

### 1.1.11 Assistance with course and curriculum planning
The situation at Griffith, a fairly new university (first undergraduate entry in 1975), presents one extreme of involvement of a special unit in the planning process. The Centre for the Advancement of Learning and Teaching there was established before teaching began, and Centre staff took part in the work of course-planning teams almost from the outset. They continue to be routinely involved in planning discussions and in curriculum committee meetings about new courses in each of the University's four schools, as well as in evaluation and review of existing courses.

This is not typical. At many institutions, unit staff are never included in course planning (perhaps sometimes there is no course planning?) and at others they are called in as an afterthought. Many teaching departments continue to behave as they did before specialist units were available.

It would be a pity if such low reliance on 'outsiders' were to persist. There is a tendency, when departments or even individuals are working in a vacuum, for new courses to be modelled on old, for practices to be perpetuated simply as a matter of ingrained habit. There seems to be, at least in some Australian universities, a surprising lack of consultation between colleagues about the implementation and detailed content of subjects, which are often the responsibility *in toto* of one person. The staff development implications here are important.

### 1.1.12 Advice on policy matters
In this category also, there is a wide divergence in practice. In some institutions the director or other members of research and development unit staff are, *ex officio* or by selection, members of key committees. In others they are never consulted.

When research projects have been conducted (as is described in Sections 1.1.13 and 1.1.14), it has often been realized that the authors of the research report or the head of the unit possess valuable data, and this has prompted consultation on policy decisions. In other cases, of course, members of units already have reputations and expertise upon which key committees and administrators are ready to draw.

Occasionally administrators will commission studies for the express purpose of obtaining data for policy-making, but these also have value in contributing to the environment of information in which staff development takes place. Examples of this type of study include student workload surveys and a recent investigation into the working of the semester calendar which, a few years ago, replaced the term calendar at Queensland University.

### 1.1.13 Descriptive research
By this we mean the sort of research which is not hypothesis testing, not 'experimental', but simply intended to be illuminative, to describe the current reality of what is happening in the college or university.

Studies of the performance of students, of student workload and of patterns of library use fall into this category, and are all valuable in helping to provide a firm data base for decision-making at all levels, to replace the 'common knowledge' and folklore which has often been the only information available.

### 1.1.14 Theoretical and experimental research
The statements under the preceding heading were not meant to imply that properly conducted, meticulous, scientific research is undesirable, nor to imply that it has no relevance to staff development. If it can be shown in a controlled study that one method of presentation produces significantly better learning than another, then this is valuable too. It is a sad fact of life, however, that it is difficult (if not impossible) to conduct studies of this sort without seriously perturbing the day-to-day life of the department or the students involved. The number of such projects that result in clear-cut conclusions is fewer than, ideally, one would have hoped for. Comparatively few Australian research and development units are willing to devote resources to this kind of research.

## 1.2 Resources of research and development units

In that description of the context in which staff development takes place in Australian universities and colleges, most of the specific references have been to the activities of research and development units. In this section there is more information about the roles and the resources of these units.

Research and development units in higher education in Australia are often both academic departments and service departments, and this is an uneasy alliance. On the one hand, they belong with the library, the computer centre and the counselling services, meeting the expressed needs of others, providing a selfless service. On the other hand, their staffs are expected to behave like other academics, to conduct research, to publish, to demonstrate scholarship, to feather their own nests. The conflict for conscientious individuals is difficult to resolve.

Some units, in addition to the kinds of responsibilities already noted, also run the institution's audiovisual services. This is a mixed blessing. Audiovisual services add to the strength of the unit, particularly in staff numbers; technical staff tend to be a majority of the total staff of the unit. It can also be argued that the combination of research and development unit with audiovisual services is logical, since the latter are important in teaching, particularly in its more innovative aspects. On the other side, audiovisual services are sometimes seen as dominating the unit to the detriment of other activities, and reinforcing a somewhat narrow preoccupation with the improvement of teaching at the expense of staff development in a broader sense.

It has already been noted that research and development units in Australian universities and colleges vary a great deal in size. The Centre for the Study of Higher Education (CSHE) at Melbourne University has a total establishment of 27, comprising the director (an appointment at professorial level), five senior lecturers or lecturers, three research fellows, three graduate research assistants, six administrative/secretarial staff and nine technical staff.

The University of Queensland's Tertiary Education Institute (TEDI) is smaller, having three academic staff — the director, with professorial status, and two lecturers, augmented by six research and clerical staff. There are no technical staff since TEDI, unlike CSHE, has no responsibilities for audiovisual services. At the University of Queensland there is a separate department fulfilling these functions.

Some units in universities have three or less staff. The largest unit in a college appears to be the Education Unit at Royal Melbourne Institute of Technology. This has 24 staff — six teaching staff, including the head of unit at principal lecturer grade, 13 technical staff and five administrative and clerical staff.

A middle of the range unit is represented by the Educational Research and Development Unit (ERDU) at the Queensland Institute of Technology. This has a head, an information officer, an educational research officer, a secretary, a graphic designer and a technician — six staff in all.

Even from these few examples, a considerable diversity in type of staff is apparent. As noted at the beginning of this section, there is sometimes ambiguity about the academic status of unit staff; some have explicitly academic status, others have equivalence, for example in salary, but are classed as administrative staff, and others still (such as research assistants and technical staff) are explicitly non-academic.

Australian universities are hierarchical institutions. Unit staff who are explicitly academics and/or are senior in status may command more respect from staff in teaching departments than others without these attributes. It may be that the few units whose director is a professor of the university have a particular advantage. Against that, it is sometimes argued that academic staff who are defensive about and/or seek help in their teaching are more willing to expose themselves to relatively junior staff than to high-status figures.

## 1.3 Some special services

Tables 1.1 and 1.2 summarized the direct and indirect staff development activities of research and development units. It is obviously impossible in this review to provide a comprehensive picture of all the activities of all the units. In this section, we shall fill out the picture a little more by noting a few uncommon services which have generally been developed in response to specific circumstances or needs.

### 1.3.1 Tertiary teachers from South-East Asia

At the University of New South Wales the Tertiary Education Research Centre (TERC) has been operating the Indonesian University Lecturers Scheme since 1970. This scheme is funded by the Australian Government and enables a number of lecturers (ten in 1977) to come to Australia from Indonesia each year for a year's course consisting of project work plus attendance at classes, visits to departments teaching their own disciplines, seminars and conferences. The programme 'is designed to provide, for each participant, experience in the development of an appropriate education programme for the training of undergraduates and graduates both in specialised departments and in a particular school' (extract from the 1977 report for the scheme).

In 1977 the Higher Education Advisory and Research Unit (HEARU) at Monash University initiated a somewhat similar but shorter programme for tertiary teachers from Thailand, who spent about two days a week for four months attending a formal course based on a component of the Diploma in Education for Tertiary Teachers. In this case too, the Australian Government provided most of the funding.

### 1.3.2 Secondment of staff to units from academic departments

The Tertiary Education Institute (TEDI) at the University of Queensland and HEARU at Monash both have arrangements which allow teaching staff to spend some time, ranging from two months to a year, at the unit. The staff member undertakes a project or programme which has received prior approval from his/her department and the unit, and while seconded is relieved of all departmental duties so that he/she can concentrate on the task in hand. Funds are provided to the department so that part-time or other help can be acquired to compensate for the staff member's absence.

This arrangement has proved beneficial both to the seconded academics and their departments and to the research and development unit. As a bonus, the association commonly leads to a lasting contact and a consequent improvement of *rapport* between the parties. An ex-secondee becomes a valuable liaison person, giving the unit a measure of entrée into his/her department.

### 1.3.3 Collaboration between neighbouring units

In South Australia, the Advisory Centre for University Education (ACUE) at Adelaide University and the Educational Research Unit (ERU) at Flinders University have recently decided to pool their resources. Not only will they join forces in mounting a programme of minicourses on specific areas for staff of both universities but, subject to demand, they will also make their facilities available to staff from colleges of advanced education in the area. Collaboration will extend into research activities as well. This sort of rationalization is seen by those involved to be desirable, both for efficiency and to ensure viability of the units concerned, in a time of contracting resources.

### 1.3.4 Funds for teaching development

Individuals or departments at the University of Queensland can apply to the Tertiary Education Institute (TEDI) for funds to support experimental, innovative or developmental projects in teaching and learning. The total sum available was about $6000 in 1978. Although in a large university this is a modest amount, a few hundred dollars have often meant the difference between shelving a bright idea and giving it a fair trial.

Some examples of projects supported in this way range from the purchase of a freezer for storing pigs' mandibles for an experimental method of teaching periodontal procedures in dentistry, to the modification of an overhead projector to allow the acetate roll to be moved by remote control, computer programming assistance and equipment for an interactive simulation to teach leaf physiology in botany, and transport costs to bring schoolchildren in from outlying schools for microteaching in human movement studies.

### 1.3.5 Minicourses

Several units run small courses on a range of topics for academic staff. A typical example is the Centre for the Advancement of Teaching (CAT) at Macquarie University, which runs two parallel series of minicourses (Meyer, 1979) for, on the one hand, teachers at that university and, on

31

the other hand, school and college teachers from the surrounding areas of the state.

Topics dealt with include:

- using aims and objectives in developing a course of studies at tertiary level
- small group teaching at tertiary level
- lecturing techniques for university and college
- the overhead projector in tertiary teaching
- making and using 35mm slides for university and college classes
- audio-tutorial techniques for university and college.

### 1.3.6 Bulletins and outlines on selected topics
Macquarie's CAT and the Higher Education Research and Services Unit (HERSU) at the University of Newcastle are representative of units which provide series of booklets as quick guides to selected topics in teaching and learning. Some titles in the HERSU *Bulletin* list are:

- *Illustrating the lecture*
- *Examinations*
- *Instructional TV*
- *Personalized systems of instruction*
- *Peer teaching.*

Titles from the list of CAT *Guidelines* include:

- *Thoughts for new teachers*
- *How to prepare an audio-tutorial lesson*
- *Types of small groups*
- *Are lectures really necessary?*
- *Team teaching.*

A complete list of these and further series published by other units may be found in *Labyrinth.*

### 1.3.7 An educational radio station
Several radio stations are supported by universities and colleges in Australia.

Until recently one of these, 3RMT-FM, was actually conducted by a research and development unit, the Education Unit at Royal Melbourne Institute of Technology. This was run by a full-time staff based in the Education Unit together with students from the RMIT Radio Association and other volunteers. It offered an educationally oriented programme of wide general interest which included a variety of 'non-mainstream' music.

## 1.4 Discussion

The information contained in this chapter about staff development in Australian tertiary institutions can be used to justify almost any conclusion, optimistic or pessimistic. If the criterion is an active concern for staff development throughout Australian universities and colleges and both vocal and material support from the corridors of power, local and national, there is not much cause for us to be self-congratulatory. If the criterion is widespread, though usually small-scale, activity together with substantial achievement by relatively small groups of active and enthusiastic people, then it might be claimed that Australia has made its mark in this field. It is, however, a peculiarly difficult time for pronouncing judgements and there is no clear future trend.

It was noted in the introduction to this chapter (Section 1.0) that only a small minority of staff in Australian universities and colleges participate directly in staff development activities. It is, of course, easy to list the formidable difficulties in the way of staff development and the situation in Australia is probably similar to that in a number of other countries.

The staff of Australian universities have not traditionally been 'trained' to teach. Teaching skill is seen as a by-product of, or even as a natural accompaniment to, scholarship and competence in research; and as such is either possessed fully grown by those joining a university staff or will come easily with a little experience. Some academic staff have their doubts, but their numbers are not large enough for any pressure group favouring teacher-training for academics to be formed. The situation is somewhat different in colleges of advanced education, but the end result is much the same. Many of them were formerly teachers' colleges and the teaching expertise of their staffs is therefore taken for granted. Furthermore many of the colleges, including those which were *not* formerly teachers' colleges, aspire to most of the characteristics of universities, and for that reason excessive concern about teaching skill (excessive, that is, as compared with the concern in universities) might be seen as degrading to their status.

Also, since staff development tends to be narrowly viewed as the improvement of teaching, it is possible for academic staff to see staff development activities as being *in opposition* to research. Australian academics tread the familiar paths of research-publication-academic respectability-promotion/advancement, a sequence to which teaching is irrelevant. Much lip service is paid to its importance, but Australian academics tend to be cynical about the rewards likely to be forthcoming for time devoted to teaching over and above what is 'normal' discharge of an accepted responsibility.

That statement seems to apply primarily to universities. The situation in colleges of advanced education must, on the face of it, be different because there is not the same responsibility for research in the colleges. In practice, however, as already noted, many colleges try to imitate the ways of universities; research is strongly encouraged, particularly in the larger, more prestigious colleges. There may therefore be comparatively little difference between the university and the college view of how academic respectability is to be achieved. Furthermore, in colleges as in universities, the rewards tend to be available more readily to those who excel in other areas, for example, in scholarship, in professional reputation, rather than in teaching.

In general, then, staff development activities are to be admired (nobody denies teaching is important) rather than pursued ('But I can't spare the time from my research . . .'). There are reasons for non-involvement other than the one just cited, which is in any case not necessarily made explicit. They range from the crude excuse that anyone can teach and it is silly to make a fuss about it, to extended arguments, forcefully put, that teaching is a personal matter, that there is little agreement as to what its nature is or what skills are essential, that there is no evidence to justify confidence in those who conduct staff development (improvement of teaching) courses and that the courses, workshops and seminars are of doubtful value.

Staff in research and development units find the attitudes behind some of these reasons difficult to combat. Improvement of teaching tends to be associated in the minds of many academics with the activities of departments of education. Such departments do not always enjoy the highest of reputations in universities. A realistic acceptance of the somewhat ambivalent attitudes of other academics to 'educationalists' is a factor in the general (but not universal) practice in Australia, by which research and development units are not part of departments of education and are often entirely unconnected with them.

Finally there are the inevitable psychological difficulties experienced by staff in universities and colleges as a barrier to staff development activities. Any proposal to develop staff or improve teaching implies that there is room for development and improvement. It is difficult for many academics, as for other human beings, to admit an inadequacy.

Those who staff research and development units are fully aware of these problems. One result of this awareness is that in some units direct attention to staff development is of token proportions only. Unit staff, for example, either share or are at least acutely conscious of the attitudes of their colleagues in teaching departments towards research. If research is the royal route to academic respectability for the latter, then it is so for the former. They too, therefore, concentrate on research and hope to exert a useful influence through both their research activity *per se* and their findings. This is indirect staff development.

Staff of units are also apprehensive of any official sponsorship of their staff development activities, and rightly so. Any element of compulsion, for example, to tie tenure or promotion in some way to participation in staff development courses, would be generally resisted by the staff of units as well as by other academic staff. Many academics in universities would include within their concept of academic freedom the freedom to remain undeveloped.

For reasons which have probably become obvious from the preceding pages, it is difficult to evaluate what has so far been achieved in staff development in Australian higher education. What are the criteria of success? What defines a high level or a low level of staff development activity? Which is more significant, quantity or quality? Is advance on a narrow front but in depth 'better' than small advances on a wide front?

Quantitative measures are available, such as the number of research and development units and of the personnel staffing them. The total number of courses, workshops, seminars offered and the total number of academic staff contacted, either through such staff development events or privately, could be computed. But such figures would tell us very little about the nature of the programmes or the impact, temporary or lasting, on those who participate in them. It is particularly difficult even to estimate the effects of *indirect* staff development activities, and these are at least present in Australian higher education on a significant scale. Large numbers of academic staff are reached; touched, however lightly, without in many cases even being conscious of this.

Thus staff development is to an unknown extent dependent on acts of faith and the operation of intangibles. The majority of Australian academic staff would not respond to direct approaches. Nevertheless, most units persist in direct staff development programmes, for two main reasons: one, to cater for the keen or willing minority; and two, because they hope for substantial indirect effects from direct programmes; for example, those who attend courses talk to others who do not; a member of staff who has 'developed' may influence others in his department who have not.

To sum up, we incline towards an optimistic view. It seems that staff development activities, though on the whole somewhat narrowly conceived (that is, confined to the improvement of teaching), have become a feature of the higher education scene in Australia, and that this has occurred over a short period of time. In particular, it is likely that *indirect* staff development through the diverse activities of research and development units, though its effects are virtually impossible to assess, is of considerable significance.

## 1.5 Future prospects

Further progress in staff development appears to depend on changes in attitude by the (potential) client staff and on changes in the current climate.

Whether there will be changes (and if there are, whether they will be in the right direction) was in 1978 the great unanswered and then unanswerable question. A gloomy view would be that staff development is a likely casualty of financial stringency. Since the substantial majority of academic staff, though accepting that improvement of teaching is or would be 'a good thing', are unwilling to give it a high priority among their personal concerns, they are likely to regard it as expendable. Money for research, money for equipment, are examples of essentials; money for something so nebulous as the importance of teaching can, with much regret of course, be cut.

The cheerful view is that financial stringency means accountability, means the necessity for greater efficiency, means convincing a sceptical public that 'their' money is being well spent. The major responsibility of tertiary institutions in the eyes of the community is to teach, to do everything possible to see to it that John and Mary Citizen's sons, daughters, brothers and sisters, prosper through success in university or college careers. Thus universities and colleges will come under increased pressure to monitor their own procedures. They will need to demonstrate that they are concerned about their teaching and intend to do better, and so staff development activities will come into their own.

There is a cheerful factor on the psychological side also. Now that tertiary institutions in Australia have stopped expanding, the major way in which academics have obtained job satisfaction in the last 20 years is no longer available. Academic staff can no longer expect rapid promotion either within their own institutions or by moving to another. Many will have to remain in the same institution at the same status for most of their working lives. In these circumstances it may be that an abiding interest in teaching and a continual concern for self-improvement in the skills of teaching will be one of the most readily available sources of job satisfaction.

Nobody can yet say whether the cheerful view is a fantasy view. Universities and perhaps the newer tertiary institutions too are prone to inertia. Even under unpleasant financial restrictions, everything may go along much as it did before, rather more slowly, and this may be the future of staff development in Australia. Something will continue, at a modest level, a gesture of conscience by institutions rather than enthusiastic commitment, with significant achievements here and there about which nobody will know very much. It is one of the ironies of staff development activities that not even the participants necessarily know that they have been engaged in something important.

The views of the staff in research and development units reflect some of the current uncertainty by similar optimistic/pessimistic vacillations. The optimism tends to be associated with excessive expectations about what their role in the institution *ought* to be: in an ideal higher education world they would occupy a central, high-prestige role in their institution, and everything would revolve around them. The pessimism comes with despair about ever achieving that eminence and soon plunges to deep gloom about the future and whether they will be permitted even to exist.

Yet it really appears quite a simple matter to create conditions in which staff development could 'take off' in Australia. One clue is in the Australian Universities Commission references to teaching research units. It is impossible to assess the precise effects of the commendations included by this powerful body in its fifth and sixth reports. Many universities were already committed to establish research and development units and several already had them, so maybe the AUC was responding to a trend rather than creating one. It seems likely today, however, when accountability is creating considerable anxiety in tertiary institutions, that a strong official lead would have notable effects. It is particularly likely if the Tertiary Education Commission recommended, and the Government implemented, a proposal to put money into staff development. This or some other kind of official sponsorship with no hint of compulsion would probably provide just the leadership that is needed. More academic staff might come to accept that increased professionalism in the major aspects of their job need not negate their autonomy and that staff development to turn the gifted amateur into the competent professional is nothing to be feared.

# 2a: Britain (universities) — growth, consolidation, and now a new phase?

John Nisbet and Ray McAleese

## 2a.0 Recent developments

### 2a.0.1 Pre-1964

In retrospect the publication in 1964 of the Hale Report, *University Teaching Methods,* can be seen as a watershed in the provision for staff development in British universities. Before that, progress towards systematic provision was uphill and slow. Interest in the training of university teachers began to emerge more than 30 years ago. The widely read author, Bruce Truscot (1943), argued that we ought 'to subject all would-be lecturers to a specific course of lecturing', even suggesting 'the normal full year's course for the training of teachers' (see below, p 39). The Association of University Teachers (AUT) first raised the question of training in 1945. But despite contacts between the AUT and the Committee of Vice-Chancellors and Principals (CVCP) in 1954 and in 1961, it was not until the setting up of the Hale Committee that the idea of training university teachers began to be authoritatively promoted. After 1964 there was a marked increase in provision and a general acceptance of the need for such provision. There was no immediate flood of innovation, but a trickle of ideas has gathered strength over the years and seems now to be flowing quite strongly.

The Hale Report itself was not necessarily the cause of the change. The Robbins Committee, appointed to review the whole field of higher education, had reported in the previous year, and the following year saw the publication of another important report on teaching — the Brynmor Jones Report, *Audiovisual Aids in Higher Scientific Education.* The work of the Robbins Committee had focused attention on many issues in higher education, among which students' performance and the quality of the teaching they received were not the least important. Units for research into higher education had been established in the University of Essex and in the London School of Economics in 1963; and in 1964 scholars from a variety of disciplines joined in forming the Society for Research into Higher Education. With these and similar developments, higher education came to be viewed as a legitimate area of study, and thus the ground was prepared for a more systematic approach to general questions of teaching and learning in universities.

Why did this happen at this time? Previously there had been only occasional voices raised to question the assumption that the work of the university teacher was his private concern. For example, Truscot (1943) wrote:

> It seems to be assumed that anyone with a first class degree and an inquiring mind is capable of lecturing and teaching . . . without any sort of technical preparation . . . Universities are amateurish bodies which have never faced up to certain elementary facts . . . The only effective remedy is . . . to subject all would-be lecturers to a specific course of lecturing.

In the 1950s there was a growing concern over student failure (see, for example, Malleson, 1954a, 1954b, 1957, 1958, 1959). The awareness of student study problems, however, was not the principal cause for an interest in teaching and learning; two external factors contributed more.

First, there was the expansion of higher education, and the consequent need to recruit many new staff whose inexperience was more evident than in the pre-war years when the appointment of a new lecturer in a university department was a rare event. There were in 1978 46 universities and about a quarter of a million students (261,250). The number of staff has risen from 10,675 (1961) to 31,381 (1976). The present student to staff ratio is therefore about 8 : 1 (10 : 1 in 1961).

The Robbins Report (1963) was a major element in this expansion, but it came *after* a decade of growth in which the number of universities in Britain increased from 15 to 25. It was envisaged also that expansion would mean the enrolment of many new students from sectors of society which had not previously had experience of higher education, and the principle of equal opportunity required that the process of teaching these students should be opened up to investigation. Thus, initially, the movement focused on improving methods of university teaching and the title of the Hale Report illustrates this emphasis. Among the first formal courses of training for university teachers in Britain was a two-week course organized in 1963 for teachers in the field of engineering sciences in the Manchester College of Science and Technology by the Vice-Principal, Professor Morton, who had attended a similar course in the United States (see Hartley, 1964 for details of the Manchester courses). He invited university teachers from all over Britain (including one of the present authors) to contribute to this course, which included many of the features of current courses, such as the recording of short lectures for subsequent play-back and criticism. In other universities there was a less formal provision of guidance on request. Wright, a member of the Hale Committee, tells of the Committee questioning a professor of education on why he had not offered courses of training to his colleagues: 'I wait till I am asked' was the answer.

The second influential factor in the early 1960s was the impact of technology, in the form of aids to teaching and learning. This particular emphasis is illustrated by the title of the Brynmor Jones Report. This was the high season of popularity for programmed learning, and the use of the slide projector by university teachers was limited and often painfully incompetent. Television had at last reached the stage where its equipment could be made available to educational establishments, but the cost was substantial and the techniques were obviously difficult to master. It was not just a matter of providing training, but rather of staff development and possible reorganization of the whole system.

Underlying both these factors was a more general change in the intellectual climate. Higher education was seen as a form of national investment, and it began to borrow concepts from business management, such as manpower planning, cost effectiveness, analysis of objectives, and rationalization of production. The social sciences had grown in status and, in the opinion of some, offered a body of knowledge or didactic from which courses of instruction and a process of staff development might be drawn.

### 2a.0.2 Post -1964

Universities responded quickly to the recommendations of the Hale Report by instituting short courses on university teaching methods. In 1965 London University instituted a Teaching Methods Unit, which was soon offering courses nationally. But other universities appointed committees which organized their own courses, and these attracted quite substantial numbers of staff, including experienced lecturers as well as new recruits. The courses, however, often took the form of formal lecture sessions which were more effective in demonstrating the need for change than in providing a solution. The years to 1970 saw a growing acceptance of the idea of staff development, but equally a dissatisfaction with the unimaginative, haphazard and unco-ordinated provision which was being offered.

A questionnaire sent out by the Association of University Teachers in 1968, four years after Hale, showed that only some 50 per cent of universities made any provision for training, and this was mostly audiovisual in content. In 1968 a Select Committee set up by the Government included in its examination a review of the quality of teaching in universities:

> The evidence we have received does not encourage us to believe that the maximum is being done to make teaching by lectures as effective as it could be ... We believe that newly appointed staff should receive some form of organised instruction on how to teach.

This was the year in which student unrest reached a climax. It was also the period when the National Board for Prices and Incomes (NBPI) made the then outrageous suggestion that universities should make a discretionary payment to staff for good teaching, judged partly on the basis of student ratings (National Board for Prices and Incomes, 1968, 1970). Although this was an abortive idea, the awareness of the issue continued to grow. When the Society for Research into Higher Education conducted a survey in 1970 (Greenaway, 1971), it showed that 'training of some kind is provided in 41 universities.'

In 1971 the Committee of Vice-Chancellors and Principals set up a working group to define what had been achieved. As a result a new national committee was established in 1973, the Co-ordinating Committee on the Training of University Teachers, with a full-time co-ordinating officer. The pace of development quickened. The University Grants Committee, as a 'pump-priming' exercise, sponsored 19 projects, at a cost of £130,000, to develop and evaluate a variety of training procedures. In 1974 an important agreement was made between two bodies, the University Authorities Panel and the Association of University Teachers, which instituted a system of probation for newly appointed lecturers (see Section 2a.1.3 below).

Parallel to these formal organizational developments, there has been a noticeable growth of interest within universities in methods of teaching and assessment, in the content of courses and in the effective use of technical aids. The Nuffield Foundation set up a Group for Research and Innovation in Higher Education who published a series of publications (1975, 1976) on innovations in university teaching, which reviewed over 100 examples. The Society for Research into Higher Education, in addition to a quarterly journal of abstracts of research into higher education, has produced some 50 pamphlets or books, and commercial publishers have begun to find a ready market for books on the topic of university teaching, of which Bligh's *What's the Use of Lectures?* (1972) is probably by far the best seller.

This preliminary review, however, would be misleading if it suggested that the 1970s had ushered in a phase of rapid growth. As will be evident from the next section, the total investment in training is still only a fraction of 1 per cent of total expenditure; training tends to be interpreted in a narrow way; there are still many sceptics, possibly even a majority among university teachers; and there are fundamental issues to be resolved about the nature and scope of training or staff development — for example, is the concept of 'training' acceptable? We return to these issues in the final section of this chapter.

## 2a.1 The present position

### 2a.1.1 The extent of training

Virtually all the universities make some kind of provision for staff development or training. This usually takes the form of structured short courses for new lecturers, sometimes including an induction element — an introduction to the university which the newcomer is joining — as well as a general coverage of initial training The length of such courses ranges from a morning to ten days. They usually cover the full range of university subjects and are not designed to deal with teaching in specific disciplines or departments. The university itself is the unit, though a few universities have arrangements with other institutions for joint training and most would not stand in the way of their staff attending courses at other institutions.

There is also a growing provision beyond this initial stage, in the form of short courses or seminars on specific topics, consultancy and course development work within specific departments, and co-operation on a regional or national scale within disciplines, for the discussion of issues in teaching and examining. This growth is still rather unorganized, being dependent mainly on initiatives by individuals rather than following any prepared plan.

It is customary also for universities to stress the informal training provided within departments by the experience of working alongside colleagues. In some departments this is a genuine and important element, extending even to training postgraduate students who act as demonstrators in laboratory classes; but in the majority of departments provision of this kind, if it is made at all, is so informal and unorganized that it does not fall within the scope of the present review.

In as many as one third of the 46 universities in Britain, the responsibility for organizing training rests with a central service unit. These units have varying titles (Centre for Educational Technology, Centre for Educational Practice, etc). Most of them have been established within the past three or four years.

Twenty of the universities have made appointments, ten full-time, ten part-time, of persons with designated responsibility to carry out training or to co-ordinate arrangements within the university (see pp 268-70).

In support of these designated personnel, whether in a centre or working individually, there is a committee at senate level or its equivalent in all but four of the universities. The committee structure serves a double function, both to keep the overall supervision of training under the control of the regular academic staff, and also to involve senior members of staff in a responsible role in the provision of training, giving the designated personnel (who are usually not in the heart of the power structure) some slight leverage and some friends at court.

The figures quoted above give a misleading impression, in that they grossly underestimate the true involvement of other staff in training, many of whom give services voluntarily and informally, contributing to courses as tutors, lecturers, demonstrators or chairmen. A more realistic figure would certainly exceed 750 in any one year: for the session 1976-77, about 1000 members of staff in universities were involved in staff development work. This represents, however, only some 3 per cent of the 32,000 full-time staff in post.

It is difficult to estimate the investment of funds in staff development. The amount directly allotted to training activities in 1976-77 was less than £50,000 for the whole of Britain, a tiny fraction of the £581m in the total UGC grant. Most of the expenditure on training is hidden cost, but even on the most generous of estimates, the total of direct expenditure must be judged to be small. The range of expenditure among universities, from £100 per annum to over £13,000 in one case, suggests the varying concern for training.

Thus the present provision of training is still very patchy. However, within the past four years, its claim on resources has more than doubled and there has been a comparable increase in the range of systematic organization for training over this period. A doubling of effort is relatively easy, perhaps, if the initial figure is small enough.

### 2 a.1.2 The Co-ordinating Committee for the Training of University Teachers

An important development in recent years has been the setting up of the Co-ordinating Committee for the Training of University Teachers (CCTUT). This committee is composed of representatives of the Committee of Vice-Chancellors and Principals (CVCP), the University Grants Committee (UGC) and the Association of University Teachers (AUT), with the Vice-Chancellor of Nottingham University as chairman. It now includes an observer from the corresponding committee of polytechnics (SCEDSIP — see Section 2b.1.4). At its first meeting in July 1972 the National Union of Students (NUS) was invited to join the committee. The CCTUT declared a need for a full-time officer to service the committee and play a co-ordinating role in relation to staff development in universities. Early in 1973 the UGC provided an ear-marked grant for this purpose, for an initial two-year period of funding.

In general the terms of reference of the CCTUT are to keep itself informed of the needs of university teachers for training; to promote training at national and regional levels; to offer advice on training; and to disseminate information on staff development and training methods. Two co-ordinating officers have serviced the committee, the current officer being Dr C C Matheson who is on part-secondment from the

University of East Anglia. The co-ordinating officer is responsible for organizing, on behalf of the committee, a range of regional, national and international activities. As the committee meets only three or four times a year, he maintains the day-to-day impetus of its work. The CCTUT has been criticized recently by some active staff developers who feel it is remote from the pressing problems of training. However, it has accomplished a great deal in making teachers and trainers aware of the needs of staff development.

## 2a.1.3 Probation

A major development was the agreement on probation, which originated from a review of salaries in 1971 when the universities gave an undertaking that they would take a closer look at training and development. As a result of extended discussions between the AUT and the University Authorities Panel (the 'management' side in salary negotiations), an agreed document was drafted. (The full text of this agreement is reproduced on pp 255-8.)

In 1974-75 most universities took action to implement the agreement. This introduced a period of probation and an obligation on the universities to make formal provision for staff development. Since 1975 new lecturers in British universities who have no teaching experience have been appointed for a three-year probationary period. At the end of this period they are considered for a permanent appointment. This, said the agreement, must be *a positive act of decision* by the university (a phrase emphasized in the original). The period of probation may be extended for a fourth year but no longer.

The 1971 salaries settlement stated:

> *Lecturers*: Probationary period to be three years with possible extension to four years in doubtful cases. Training procedures to be improved with thorough review prior to confirmation on the basis of revised and improved procedures and criteria.

The 1974 agreement included several passages about the provision of training:

> It is incumbent on universities to provide training for the probationer of a helpful and comprehensive nature. Advice and guidance by a senior colleague nominated for this task, and encouragement to attend formal courses of instruction should be included.

> The probationer should receive a co-ordinated development programme which lasts throughout his probationary period.

And if the probationer is not confirmed, the university

> should be able to show (a) that training in university teaching was made available, and (b) that continuing advice and help towards improvement were offered.

In retrospect this document may yet be seen as the major institutional stamp of approval that training needed. Yet at the time the situation was far from clear. The interpretation of the document was imprecise and some universities were slow to implement the detail (if not the spirit) of the agreement. An Association of University Teachers survey in 1976 showed that 'as many as seven [universities] had not yet implemented the agreement' (Committee of Vice-Chancellors and Principals, 1976), while several universities were unaware of the 'mandatory nature' of the agreement. One of the troublesome features seemed to be the nature of departmental responsibility and the role of the 'senior colleague'.

The requirements for training are still by no means uniform throughout the universities. Probably few would even claim to have realized the ideal of a three-year co-ordinated development programme for probationers; and the impression is that most probationary lecturers receive only a short initial course (which they are encouraged, not compelled, to attend) and thereafter supervision by the head of department is nominal. The CCTUT has performed a useful function in organizing conferences to discuss implementing the agreement, having realized that advice and information would be welcomed by universities. These conferences have brought together the people in each university who are concerned with training; and thus they have begun to create a specialist group with an awareness of an identity, a common task, an aspiration unlikely to be realized, some shared technical skills and the beginnings of a literature, and a jargon of their own — all the elements necessary for a new subject specialism.

During the period of rapid expansion, initial training facilities were stretched by the recruitment of new inexperienced lecturers. This flood has receded and the concern in training has shifted to include later follow-on courses and staff development generally.

### 2a.1.4 Staff development
Though systematic provision for staff development is still at a very early stage, there is a great deal of informal work of this kind. In research, the universities have long provided continuing opportunities for a staff member to advance his knowledge and skill. Indeed, they have required this as a condition of promotion, have given time and resources to encourage it, and have developed systematic provision in the form of departmental seminars, support to attend conferences, help with publication, and so on. In the field of teaching, there is more informal work to improve courses than is generally realized. University teachers have relatively light teaching loads, and many courses are now organized as a team effort, so that there is consultation and experimentation and mutual support on the topic of how best to teach a course. Staff discussions on examining and assessment procedures, on objective tests and computer marking, on assignments and tutorials, on

new courses and the revision of old ones, are standard features of university life. The introduction of television services and of technicians specially gifted in photography or graphics has led to a new awareness of the importance of presentation of material.

This is as yet unorganized 'staff development'; and in some cases, perhaps, it is all the better for that. In other cases, the lack of formal provision means that there is nothing to make staff aware of inadequate teaching, or to press them to do something about it. The term, 'training of university teachers', tends to be interpreted narrowly. Perhaps this is why the word 'training' continues to be used, in spite of frequently voiced objections to it. (Or is the use of 'training' the cause of the narrow interpretation?) There are signs of changing attitudes and growing awareness — for example, in training for administration. Since many primary and secondary school heads now receive courses of training in administration and office management, it is not surprising that universities have begun to experiment with similar courses for heads of department. Training in research is also under scrutiny and the weakness of the traditional PhD route continues to be a topic of discussion. Staff supervision of research is criticized and the need for training in supervision is now being argued.

The present position may thus be summarized as follows:

- ☐ *Initial training:* generally available, short (one-week) courses, usually specific to the university, including an induction element.
- ☐ *Formal provision for experienced staff to develop their teaching:* beginning to grow, still mainly in the form of short conferences for discussion, often within a single discipline, regional or national.
- ☐ *Informal provision within universities* (often within departments): well-established for research, quite extensive for teaching, but not organized, and wide variations.
- ☐ *Other aspects* (training and supervision of research students, courses in administration): beginning of awareness of a need.

It is difficult to generalize, because of the wide variations, not only between institutions, but also between faculties and departments. Though it is difficult to produce firm evidence, it appears that concern over teaching and interest in training is stronger in medicine and science and less evident in arts and social science.

## 2a.2 Current trends

### 2a.2.1 Staff development
It is tempting to suggest that, just as the Hale Report in 1964 marked the acceptance of the idea of training, so the AUT/UAP agreement in

1974 initiated a new phase in which a wider concept — staff development rather than training — came to be adopted. This may prove to be the case, but it is too early as yet even to claim that we are now in a new phase. What has happened is that the process of expansion in higher education was checked in 1974: the Government White Paper of 1973, forecasting three-quarters of a million students in higher education by 1981, half of them in universities, was the high peak of optimism, and was followed almost immediately by severe financial cuts. The present period is one of consolidation, with very limited growth, and the pressure to train new recruits is no longer there. Indeed, the 1978 Government Green Paper, *Higher Education into the 1990s*, was concerned with how the universities should cope with possibly declining numbers in ten years' time.

A period of 'steady state' may be one in which innovative practices are securely rooted, when plans for future development are prepared, and when resources (especially trained personnel) and administrative structures are made ready for the time when they will be needed. Or it may be a period in which momentum is lost, enthusiasts are discouraged and ideas once exciting now seem stale. Our present state, thus, is either a period of stabilization or of stagnation, depending on one's point of view.

There is little hard evidence to say which point of view is the more accurate. The pace of events in staff development has slowed and many of us find this disappointing. There is, however, no sign of a 'backlash' from those who felt hostility but were not previously prepared to declare it openly; and progress is being made towards establishing an administrative structure, or at least a network of communication among those who are concerned with staff development. There is already a new generation of university teachers who are familiar with the need for training, who may even take it for granted, and who will perhaps claim a right to devote time and resources to the continuing improvement of the syllabuses they teach and their own teaching skills. If this does happen, we can expect a new movement fairly soon towards a wider concept of staff development. But such a move will not occur by itself, and it will not gather strength unless we actively prepare for it now.

What kind of preparation is most appropriate? We do not know precisely, but we can be sure that we need to develop courses or other frameworks for development, to identify relevant skills and explore appropriate content material for courses, to establish structures of organization and channels of communication, and possibly to build a professional grouping of persons and ideas as a core to staff development activities. These are the topics considered in the remainder of this chapter.

### 2a.2.2 Courses and programmes

The courses, conferences and seminars being offered in different universities have a degree of similarity. They are settling into a standard form. It may be that this is the 'correct' pattern, the style of provision which meets the special needs of the times; once that has been found, there is no merit in changing for the sake of change. This rosy view is dubious, for there is little evidence of efforts to diagnose the training needs of university staff, or even to survey the market.

In the meantime, the standard pattern for a course of initial training is one which includes lecture/discussion sessions on lecturing, small-group teaching and assessment, and videotape recording of each course member in action in a lecture. The videotape recorder is a central element in many courses, though it may not be presented as such; and we suspect it is the element which attracts many of those enrolling. In our experience it is always the most approved element in the course. There are few signs of radical innovation here, such as taking the tape recorder to the lecturer's own class instead of bringing him to the machine, or working in a consultancy relationship with new lecturers, or with departments — though these are being done.

Seminars and conferences have a sharper focus: small-group work, objective tests, individualized instruction, and so on. There is the beginning of a move to organize meetings within disciplines regionally (see Section 2a.2.3), but most 'short course' units seem to deal with cross-disciplinary aspects, possibly to raise sufficient numbers.

There is a strong tendency to play down the technical element in training. Course organizers like to point out that their courses are *not* about audiovisual aids, and those who attend courses are quick to grumble if they are given simple instructions on the use of equipment like the overhead projector. Technology is one of the factors forcing the pace in course construction — partly because of the influence of the Open University whose television programmes, printed workbooks and well-organized lists of resource material, are all public. Each year better quality reprographic techniques come on the market; but staff need support services and training (for example, in design and layout) if they are to use them most effectively. Perhaps we all have an ambivalent love-hate attitude to all the technology which we are coming to depend on (and to resent because of the constraints which it imposes on us).

Educational technology is of course not just aids to learning but rather the systematic organization of teaching and learning. New modes of structuring learning — especially individualized learning, such as the Keller Plan or audio-tutorial programmes — have aroused particular interest in recent years and promise to maintain their impetus of innovation.

## 2a.2.3 National and regional organization of staff development

If we are right in seeing the present time as a period for consolidating the recent advances and building up for the next push, then the emergence of a national structure is an important event for staff development and training in universities. The CCTUT and its co-ordinating officer provide a potential national organization. In itself, and with such limited staffing, it is bound to appear ineffectual, remote and slow. What it requires is a supporting structure at a lower level of organization. It is difficult to decide the form of this lower-order organization. Should the national committee work through a series of regional committees? The problems for this model include persuading universities to co-operate regionally (economy of travel?) and establishing a communication system, so that the central body can be responsive to the regional groups and each may play its agreed part in the system. In Britain we have only begun to consider such matters.

Hitherto, each university has tended to make its own arrangements independently. Because of the autonomy of each institution, co-operation between universities in Britain is difficult to arrange in any field of action, except at the level of national groups (like the CVCP) which meet (usually in London) on equal terms to inform, discuss and align policies. Since initial training courses usually include an induction element, they are all the more likely to be local. However, there is co-operation even for this kind of provision: for example, in Scotland, Dundee, Heriot-Watt and Stirling form a syndicate for initial courses. When we turn to staff development as distinct from initial courses, the need for inter-university collaboration is more evident. This is particularly so if we accept that staff development is more likely to be acceptable and effective if it is subject-based. Thus the development of teaching skills in, say, modern languages cannot be managed within a single institution, and there are already regional and national subject organizations and contacts which could be helped to foster this kind of professional activity.

There is also an informal organization emerging which may in the long run be more important than the committees and conferences. This is the awareness of a new specialism, and of a sense of belonging to it, or even a missionary feeling of creating it, among those who have been appointed on a full-time or part-time basis to training or development posts. In a subsequent discussion (see Section 2a.3.2) we shall consider whether or not this is a good thing. It is a process of institutionalization, a professionalizing of an activity, with all the paraphernalia of conferences, books and journals, a society, office-bearers, a council, and so on. The Society for Research into Higher Education provides a potential support service of this kind, but it has a wider remit and is open to all who are interested. Usually a professional group of this kind is supported also by a structure of qualifications; and there have been some attempts to institute diploma courses covering aspects of higher education. At present, it is questionable how successful these will be. It is perhaps premature, because of uncertainty about the material content of teaching for the diploma and about the competencies to be used as criteria for award. This issue requires fuller discussion and is taken up in the next section (2a.3.1).

## 2a.3 Issues

### 2a.3.1 Training or development? Art or Science?
The term 'training' has been used extensively in describing the professional requirements of university teachers in Britain. It is agreed that the word is an unfortunate choice. What is envisaged is something much wider than training; but though 'staff development' is commonly understood in business and industry, it is not yet a generally accepted term in the British university context. The AUT/UAP agreement resolves the dilemma by using both words: 'to provide training for the probationer of a helpful and comprehensive nature' and 'the probationer should receive a co-ordinated development programme which lasts throughout his probationary period.' Those who have the task of organizing support for teaching are uncertain what to call themselves: they are not trainers or developers or supervisors, though they might be staff development officers (too pompous?) or advisers, consultants or counsellors (a suggestion of helping those in trouble?), or training technologist (too manipulative?) or adaptive interventionist (too clever?). They may have to invent a term: PROST (Person Responsible fOr Staff Training, (McAleese, 1978b) or *deveacher* (Bligh, 1978). But there is more to it than words. 'Training' implies that there is a body of knowledge or a set of skills to be imparted to the novitiate, and it has the connotation of a limited and even unquestioning acquisition of an accepted practice. 'Staff development' shifts the onus from a trainer to the staff member himself: it is his task to develop his own competence and understanding, and it has the connotation of personal growth and maturity.

Behind this question is a deeper issue. Is there a field of knowledge here, which might one day be developed into a coherent area of theory? Is this the direction in which we should be moving? The alternative view is that there are skills, but training in these skills is most useful when it is content-specific. The 'mainstream social scientists', according to Bernstein (1976), hold that 'the improvement of practice involves the application of empirically-verified theory' (Pinar, 1978). Others, however, hold the view that theory is not essential to the improvement of practice and may indeed prove an obstacle, because theory is often at variance with actual practice. This may occur even when the principles have been abstracted from experience, because it is the context which gives validity to a practice, and when a principle is abstracted from its context, it loses its meaning. Those who are involved in the argument between school-based and college-based teacher education will be familiar with this issue.

Although at first sight this may appear to be an abstruse philosophical digression, it is, we think, of fundamental importance in deciding the nature of 'training' or 'development', whichever term is used. It applies to training in research even more obviously than to training for teaching. In British universities it is rare to find formal training courses in research methodology for graduate students (except, significantly, in the social sciences). The research student learns his skills by doing research, alongside a skilled researcher. Similarly, the new university teacher will not expect to receive any formal training in research, though his promotion may depend on his doing research. It is assumed that the very general skills (reading, information retrieval, even thesis writing) are already mastered, and the specialist techniques are learned on the job.

To return to the matter of training for teaching, the offer of a course implies that there is a body of knowledge or skill to transmit. This applies particularly to a course in 'university teaching methods', where new lecturers from various disciplines join together for a systematic programme, as is commonly the practice in induction courses in British universities. The alternative view is expressed in the idea, endorsed by the AUT/UAP agreement, of help from a 'senior colleague' working alongside the inexperienced lecturer. (The agreement avoids the issue by approving both styles.) A common element in initial training courses is the use of videotape to record and play back for criticism a specimen lecture by each of the participants. This also may be interpreted as relying directly on practical and experiential training, without any intervening theory to confuse or even mislead the practitioner.

How does one decide what should be the content of an induction course, and what part should theory play in such a course, or in subsequent courses for experienced teachers in their programme of self-development? Perhaps the question is better phrased in terms of the task facing those of us who have an interest in development work. Should we aim primarily to provide a service, as a support to our colleagues; or should we aim to build up a body of theory, empirically verified, a structure of knowledge which will generate new hypotheses and new experiments in order to illuminate the whole field of higher education?

Sanford (1964), in *The American College,* wrote:

Practice in higher education, as in politics, remains largely untouched by

51

the facts and principles of science. What our colleges do tends either to
be governed by tradition, or to be improvised in the face of diverse —
and usually unanticipated — pressures.

The remedy he suggests is to build up 'a science of higher education',
based on 'the notion that the field may ultimately be constituted as a
body of fact and theory, a discipline of sorts, in which individuals
become specialists'. In Britain this view would be rejected by the
majority of university teachers, though perhaps it has more adherents
now than 15 years ago, when a group of some 250 university teachers
gathered to form the Society for Research into Higher Education.

The controversy might be described as between those who are
process-oriented, and those who are product-oriented, or (less
impartially) between the professionals and the amateurs. Those who
are process-oriented wish to develop understanding of the psychological
and philosophical issues which run through the variety of practical
problems, returning like Plato's philosopher-kings to settle the practical
problems by reference to overriding principles. Their opponents propose
to get on with training 'good' teachers, or at least to remove the worst
of the indisputable bad practices in present-day teaching, and to exploit
what seem to them the obvious advantages of technical aids. Thus there
is a tendency for separate groups to emerge for medical education and
science education, each with its own journal, and with a strong
representation of practitioners (and often a strong antipathy to social
scientists, and university departments of education in particular). An
influential factor in determining attitudes is the traditional autonomy
of universities, and especially of university departments. The authority
of professors and the independence of subject specialists have already
been eroded by the growth of the administrative and other ancillary
services in the university; and now even their teaching seems likely to
be exposed to interference by a new breed of non-specialist staff.

### 2a.3.2 Who and how? Compulsory or voluntary?

These wider philosophic differences underlying training or
development are directly relevant to questions of who should do it
and how it should be done. Each university has worked out its own
answers to these questions. It is the exception rather than the rule for
the university department of education to be given the responsibility
for providing courses of training for university staff. In some
universities, media specialists in service centres have been given
responsibility for staff training and development; but where this is so,
the director of the service centre himself has academic qualifications
and status and experience of university teaching prior to his present
post. The usual arrangement is that responsibility is placed with an
academic committee representing a variety of respectable disciplines.
Such a committee, though it may not be particularly well disposed to

the social sciences, may use the social science departments to implement their policies. (Indeed, perhaps the most effective way for the social scientist to operate is under the 'protection' of such a group).

Whether the job is seen as initial training or as staff support, inevitably the provision of the actual services has tended to devolve on a small group — sometimes only one or two in the university — who work full-time or part-time on this activity and so begin to develop specialisms and expertise. Perhaps it is equally inevitable that these specialists should develop not only expertise but also a territorial attitude of possession over their area of responsibility. There is a danger in this attitude, if the result is to discourage close collaboration between such specialists in method and teachers who consider themselves as specialists in their own disciplines. The experience of curriculum development work in the fields of primary and secondary education has shown how important it is for methods (or curriculum) specialists to establish a close collaborative relationship with teachers. In the university context, there is little likelihood that lecturers will be made to feel incompetent by the professionalism of those who claim to be specialists in the areas of methods and curriculum design. Appropriate lip service is paid to collaboration and mutual respect, but there are few universities without some tension or ambiguity about roles, and attempts by one of the parties to take over the other's role. As long ago as 1931, Curtis argued for the creation of a cadre of experts in the field of research on science education:

> It must be undertaken *only* by education specialists with specific training for this work, or by capable workers under the personal direction of such specialists in educational research. The scientist, trained only for research in pure science, and the teacher, equipped only with the facilities and willingness to engage in educational 'research', must alike be discouraged from attempting educational investigation; there have already been too many worthless or even . . . harmful results of such 'investigation'.

But this attitude of 'keep off the grass' results only in the failure of training and research to affect teaching practice; yet there is a danger at the other extreme that some of our present subject specialists use their own versions of popular psychology or their own images of progressive education as a substitute for rigorous analysis of their ideas. We have not yet worked out the most effective division of labour; and until there is a clearer understanding of the nature of knowledge in this field of inquiry, it is unlikely that agreement can readily be found.

The problem of structuring a training course is usually 'papered over' by combining theory with a mixture of methods, practical hints, workshops, videotape recordings, etc. Most courses are a rag-bag of such offerings. This may be the only practical solution, since participants will choose which sessions to attend, but the practical solution is not necessarily the best solution, for practitioners base their choice on values

and assumptions which they bring to the courses offered. The staff
member attending the course is not necessarily best placed to assess his
requirements or the likely benefits of different parts of the course. In
1906, Paulsen wrote:

> Some of the imperfections of bad lecturing are not just technical
> imperfections in a technical operation. Many critics of lecturing give this
> wrong impression when, for example, they complain of inaudibility, or
> faults in using the blackboard, and go on to recommend attendance at a
> teachers' training college. Technical training may be needed, but what is
> more needed (and more difficult to contrive) is a turning outwards of a
> personality that is inclined to be turned inwards. Speech that is inaudible
> or slovenly or inarticulate is not just a defective instrument; it is a symptom
> of a defective point of view, defective in relation to the actual need to
> communicate effectively with other people.

On this view, it is not training or development that lecturers need, but
psychotherapy! In induction courses the elements of attitude change
and confidence-building must be considered seriously. Other stages of
education, primary, secondary and tertiary, include personal
development and maturity high among their aims; and this 'quaternary'
provision should acknowledge the relevance of a mature personality.

There have been demands from students, politicians and others for
compulsory induction courses for new lecturers. University teachers are
opposed to compulsion and still adhere to the principle of a scholar's
privilege to teach as he chooses. Staff members are also sceptical about
the courses offered: what evidence is there that the 'trainers' know how
to train? (Indeed, the cynics are quick to point to examples of 'trainers'
who do not practise what they preach.) Most university teachers in
Britain would accept that courses and advice *must* be available to new
lecturers, and that the lecturers *should* be encouraged and helped to
improve their teaching skills; but probably a substantial majority
would oppose the introduction of compulsory training.

### 2a.3.3 When and why?

Initially the improvement of university teaching was seen as a matter of
training, in pre-service courses, in terms of transmitting the accumulated
experience of senior staff to new recruits. There has been a move
towards interpreting the task as one of staff development, through in-
service courses and by building up a coherent body of knowledge from
which scholars can draw as they do from the scientific theories of their
own disciplines. But no revolution in attitudes has yet occurred and
there remains a degree of indifference, if not hostility, to the very notion of
training. Conversely, discussion groups between university teachers on
teaching methods and course content and opportunities to acquire
administrative skills point to gradual change and, perhaps, presage the
establishment of some co-ordinating machinery.

Similarly, to the initial idea of doing an existing job better has been added the aim of innovation and experiment. In the early 1960s, innovation was interpreted mainly in terms of audiovisual aids; but as educational technology developed to recognize the importance of systems, there has been a growing recognition that staff development is the means to a more fundamental innovation. For many university teachers, the implicit aim of training is to maintain the *status quo*, by ensuring that established procedures of teaching and examining are carried out effectively. Others, however, see staff development as implying reform and pursue 'systems engineering', not 'systems maintenance'. Whatever the organizers have as their purpose, what they are able to do will be decided by the attitudes of their client-colleagues; and it is not over-pessimistic to state that in British universities the 'systems maintenance' aim is still the dominant one.

## 2a.3.4 The organization of staff development
One of the issues which has been resolved in different ways in different universities is the role of media services, especially television, in staff development. Should staff development be linked with the services which provide technical support for teaching, or is this an arrangement which limits development by placing emphasis on the wrong aspect? In practical terms, this means establishing in a university a centre which provides television and other audiovisual and reprographic services, and training in the effective use of these facilities, and also has the wider responsibility of encouraging innovation and experiment as well as mounting general pre-service courses. Though this form of organization tends to find favour in other countries, it has been resisted by the majority of British universities. Indeed, the principle of autonomy for departments is so strong that the centralization of technical support facilities is limited in most universities to the most expensive technology such as television, or to old established services such as the university library.

At a national level, an unresolved issue is what kind of organization is required. The answer depends on what function is envisaged for a national organization. The present structure of a co-ordinating committee (CCTUT) with one full-time officer, relies almost exclusively on exchange of information and ideas, through conferences and bulletins, and its only source of power is through its direct link to the Committee of Vice-Chancellors and Principals. The British university system would not be compatible with a directive or interventionist role for a national committee. Instead the university system is managed informally through the control of finance by the University Grants Committee. On this basis, staff development must rank low in priority, for it receives only a minuscule financial provision. Increases will not be made until the need for and objectives of staff development have been demonstrated. The University Grants Committee was quick to respond when such a need was apparent, in the 'pump-priming' exercise of 1971.

### 2a.3.5 The role of the person responsible for staff development

The clumsy title of this section reflects the confusion of the present situation. We do not even have a name for the officers in 20 of the 46 British universities responsible for staff development. (See pp 268-70.) It is difficult to be precise as to their number: some of those employed in technical support services have a similar responsibility, and some senior staff members perform staff development functions informally.

The previous sections have outlined a number of unresolved issues in staff development. In the absence of a clear definition of the nature and purpose of development or training, it is inevitable that the role of the staff development officer should be uncertain. He is organizer, teacher, researcher, consultant, counsellor and facilitator. He mounts formal courses, carries out research studies on teaching and learning in higher education, adopts a consultancy relationship with those of his colleagues who approach him, and tries to establish himself in decision-making in areas concerning the management of teaching and learning. His strategies are various: the long siege, the commando attack, the leaflet raid, the calculated alliance, the fifth column, the wooden horse. His central problem is the ambivalence between active intervention and non-directive support, and his approach must be sensitive to the work undertaken and the problems encountered (McAleese, 1978b).

In the event, his choice of role depends on how he perceives the nature of staff development, and on his personal resolution of the issues reviewed in this section. In particular, he needs to consider, more deeply than any of us has yet done, whether there is, or could be, a theory of higher education which would give a unity and coherence to his work.

*Acknowledgement*
The authors are grateful to Dr C C Matheson for his help in preparing the data in section 2a.1.1. Dr Matheson is Co-ordinating and Research Officer of the Co-ordinating Committee for the Training of University Teachers.

# 2b: Britain (polytechnics) — a case of rapidly evolving institutions

Harriet Greenaway and Derek Mortimer

## 2b.0 The formation of the polytechnics

In the United Kingdom about half the higher education provision exists outside the universities. Since the late 1960s an increasing proportion of this public sector provision has been located in the 30 newly established polytechnics in England and Wales, one new polytechnic in Northern Ireland and 14 'central institutions' in Scotland. The remainder is located in the 'colleges of education' (formerly known as 'teachers' colleges'), the 'colleges and institutes of higher education' and in a number of specialist and general 'technical colleges'. Although this chapter is concerned primarily with the polytechnics, occasional reference will be made to the other types of institution. As the polytechnics are relatively new and rapidly evolving organizations, it is appropriate to comment on their formation and major characteristics before considering concepts, strategies and organizational structures associated with staff development.

The polytechnics in England and Wales were established between 1969 and 1973 in accordance with the 1966 Government White Paper, *A Plan for Polytechnics and Other Colleges.* The plan was to develop a strong and distinctive sector of higher education complementary to the universities by merging a number of existing colleges of art and design, commerce and technology which were already providing degree and other advanced level courses. Following consultation with the local education authorities, the Government created 30 polytechnics from about 70 existing institutions. They are funded by the new local education authorities and, apart from the Inner London Education Authority, no authority is responsible for more than one.

The 1966 White Paper and the subsequent Administrative Memorandum 8/67 (Department of Education and Science, 1967) set out defining characteristics for the polytechnic sector of higher education. Of central importance was that the polytechnics should provide a comprehensive range of courses. This would include courses of various levels and modes of attendance. They range from sub-degree to doctoral level and are full-time, sandwich (ie including industrial experience) and part-time day and evening. The polytechnics would develop as mixed communities of full-time and part-time teachers and students which, compared with most universities, would have closer and more direct links with industry and the professions. While polytechnics were to be 'primarily teaching institutions', provision should be made for research essential to the proper fulfilment of the teaching function and the development of close links with industry, particularly local industry, so as to promote rapid application of results of research to industrial problems. Polytechnics should, in addition, be ready to undertake *ad hoc* research projects on behalf of industry or under contracts from research councils.

The defining documents also made a number of references to the intended internal organization of the polytechnics. Academic authority would not be vested in the college principal, as in the former colleges, but in an academic board. Staff of all levels, and students, were to be involved in polytechnic government. Furthermore, academic staff should have adequate opportunities for keeping abreast of new knowledge in their fields and should be given adequate opportunities for doing so through private study, attending conferences and working for higher degrees.

Although the colleges from which the polytechnics were formed were all well-established institutions, there were considerable differences between them in respect of age, proportion of advanced and degree-level work, range of subjects offered and amount of consultancy and research work undertaken. Some, through the University of London external degree system, had been involved in degree-level teaching for longer than many universities, while others were still building up a range of degree level courses. Most had very close relationships with local industry and commerce but only a few had well-established research activities.

Whereas the colleges were, on the whole, well placed to develop polytechnic functions on the basis of subject expertise and experience, they were not so well placed with regard to academic government and staff development structures. Many decisions affecting even day-to-day matters were taken outside the institutions by local education authorities and by university and professional validating bodies. Opportunities for academic staff to keep up to date in their subject and professional areas were relatively limited and again were usually controlled from outside the institution.

The initial organizational and staff development needs of the polytechnics were considerable. For most there was the immediate need to merge two or more institutions often well separated geographically and with very different traditions. Within each there was the need to set up new governmental and management structures. A vast amount of curriculum development was necessary, initially to rationalize similar courses inherited from the merging colleges and subsequently because of the wish and (from 1972 when the University of London external degree system for institutions ended) the need to change from university validation to validation by the Council for National Academic Awards (CNAA). This body was established in 1964 to award degrees and diplomas to those successfully completing approved courses in public sector instititions. Its attraction was that it gave institutions considerable freedom in the design and control of their own courses. Besides course development, major efforts were also made to establish new research and consultancy activities and to improve contacts with local industry and commerce.

Long before these initial development tasks were completed new pressures were brought to bear upon the polytechnics. In the 1972 White Paper, *Education — A Framework for Expansion,* the Government, 'impressed by the speed and vigour' with which the polytechnics 'have assumed and pursued their innovative task', indicated that they would have a key role to play in the expansion of higher education during the 1970s. The same White Paper also made first reference to a further major reorganization of the non-university sector of higher education in order to assimilate the colleges of education more closely into that sector. This matter was taken up in DES Circular 7/73 since which time some 40 colleges of education have been involved in a variety of amalgamations with 23 polytechnics. In one or two instances amalgamation was achieved relatively simply by a college becoming a faculty of a nearby polytechnic. In other cases, however, amalgamation involved the creation of a new institution, a new academic structure and formal application by staff for posts in the new institution.

By the late 1970s the polytechnics have grown into major institutions of higher education. They are large by United Kingdom standards, with many polytechnics having more than 500 academic staff. In terms of students they vary between 2500 and 7000 on full-time and sandwich courses, with 15 of the 30 polytechnics having more than 4000 such students. As far as part-time students are concerned, all but two polytechnics have over 1000 while in four cases the number exceeds 5000 students. The recently published *Polytechnic Courses Handbook* sets out a very wide range of full-time and sandwich courses at sub-degree, degree and postgraduate level, while research reports of many individual polytechnics indicate that significant progress has been made in the area of research and consultancy. It would appear that, in the short time since their formation, the polytechnics have gone a long way towards establishing the 'distinctive' sector referred to in the 1966 White Paper.

## 2b.1 Academic staff

### 2b.1.1 Concepts of staff development

The decade following the publication of the 1966 White Paper has been a period of tremendous pressure for the academic staff of the polytechnics. Many of those who had been in post in the previous colleges found themselves with new roles and functions virtually overnight. Whereas before they had simply managed courses designed and controlled externally, they now became fully involved in the government of the institution and in the development and control of its courses. Some found academic work changing around them without any effort being made to match their existing skills to new needs. Many new staff joined the polytechnics with experience of industry, commerce and the professions or having recently qualified by study and research in the universities. All these groups faced enormous challenges in the rapidly developing institutions. Perhaps at no time in the development of English and Welsh higher education has there been a greater need for a planned staff development programme firmly linked to the development of particular organizations. Unfortunately, the concept of staff development was not well understood in higher education institutions in the early 1970s, although it is true that many of the activities which would now be included in that term did exist albeit in a limited and unco-ordinated manner.

The concept of staff development was brought to the attention of the polytechnics and other colleges by the report of a joint Working Party of the Association of Colleges for Further and Higher Education and the Association of Principals of Technical Institutions entitled *Staff Development in Further Education* (ACFHE/APTI, 1973). While it did not distinguish the needs of staff in polytechnics from those of staff in other non-university post-school institutions, it did act as an important focus of attention in polytechnics in their deliberations on staff development.

The report defined staff development as 'identifying the professional needs of individual teachers and devising programmes to meet those needs'. This is an individual or teacher-centred concept of staff development which would now be regarded as very limited. However, in 1973, it served its purpose well because, by referring to 'professional needs', it allowed the inclusion of functions not directly related to teaching to be considered as part of staff development. Thus staff development methods, which it quoted, included not only initial and in-service professional training and attendance at courses and conferences but also a variety of other approaches including research, consultancy and service with professional organizations.

In the same year, one of the members of the ACFHE/APTI Working Party, speaking on 'Staffing and staff development — the present position' at the Further Education Staff College (Bristow, 1973), elaborated a management-centred view of staff development. He saw its purpose to be to examine a teacher's functions, to consider present and future roles and to formulate a training programme to meet the needs of the institution. He argued that staff appraisal would form an essential part of staff development activity in any institution.

The issue as to whether staff development should be teacher-centred, management-centred or should involve the best of both in a partnership approach has featured prominently in the spate of papers which have appeared since 1973. The rationale and implications of each approach have been set out in a stimulating review article (Yorke, 1977). It would appear from the increasingly complex definitions of staff development now appearing in the literature that the trend is clearly towards the partnership model. Piper (1975), for example, defined staff development as 'a systematic attempt to harmonise the individual's interests and wishes, his carefully assessed requirements for furthering his career and the forthcoming requirements of the organisation within which he is expected to work'.

Evidence that the partnership approach was gaining ground in non-university institutions of higher education was provided by Billing (1977). Speaking at a conference on staff development organized by the Society for Research into Higher Education in December 1976, he reported on replies received from 42 institutions operating CNAA courses. They pointed to

> a clear agreement at a general level over what should be encompassed within a definition of staff development: individual and institutional needs should both be recognised as should present and future orientations, programmes to satisfy these needs must resolve any conflicts, should be continuing and should derive from identification and appraisal of needs.

Such an all-embracing definition of staff development involves the individual and the institution in a mutual process of change.

Discussion about the range of activities which should be included within the concept of staff development still continues in the polytechnics. There has, however, been a marked trend towards increasing the range of activities involved. Until about 1970 many held the view that staff development was no more than study leave, sabbatical leave and secondment. Following designation many polytechnics, conscious no doubt that they were to be 'primarily teaching institutions' and that most of their staff were not teacher-trained, established staff development programmes with teaching methods as their sole focus. Then in 1973 the ACFHE/APTI report extended the concept to include research, consultancy and service with professional organizations.

The inclusion of these activities, which were already established in their own right, within the concept of staff development might not have been taken too seriously in the polytechnics had it not been for the publication of a major report by the CNAA in 1974. The CNAA is a major force in the polytechnics. It is the body which validates their proposed courses leading to first degrees, postgraduate degrees and diplomas. Its relationship with institutions is symbiotic but, in a sense, it is the host plant which has the power to give or deny life to a course. Consequently its major policy statements are landmarks in institutions' routes to their own policy determination.

In the report entitled *Resources for Research in Polytechnics and Other Colleges* (Council for National Academic Awards, 1974) the CNAA stated 'In approving courses of study leading to first degrees and even more in the case of masters' degrees, the Council expects colleges to provide opportunities for staff to undertake research, advanced study and scholarship, appropriate consultancy and related forms of staff development.' Staff development is here placed in association with research, advanced study and scholarship and consultancy — a quite different approach from that related to study leave and training in teaching methods.

Another activity which is being seen increasingly as important for staff development is course design and curriculum development. This is a feature of academic life in the polytechnics which has provided almost all staff with a traumatic experience. This process is complex and continuous. It involves design, internal validation, submission to the external validating body, and (if approved) monitoring and evaluation while the course is running and preparation for re-submission, normally after five years. This type of work is carried out not only for CNAA courses but also for sub-degree level, college-designed courses for the awards of the Business and Technician Education Councils. It is, therefore, difficult for any polytechnic teacher to avoid being caught up in curriculum development.

It does appear that over the last decade there has been an increase in the number of activities which are perceived to contribute to staff development, at least amongst those who have written about the subject. However, the recent survey by Greenaway and Harding (1978) has shown that not only is there little general agreement in the polytechnics about what constitutes staff development but also interesting perceptual differences between respondents in polytechnics and universities. They found that while a similar proportion of polytechnics and universities (39 per cent : 35 per cent) understood staff development to be focused on initial training in teaching methods, the proportion of polytechnic respondents giving it a wider interpretation to include 'growth' of established staff was double that of university respondents (43 per cent : 22 per cent). Conversely the proportion of polytechnic respondents associating research with staff development was significantly smaller than for the universities (6 per cent : 22 per cent).

The percentages given for the polytechnics appear to be disappointingly low in the light of the previous discussion. However, it must be remembered that the responses relate to perceptions of staff development, not to the existence of specific activities. Although it is very difficult to collect hard evidence about the level of activity in these fields (institutions seeming to be unusually reticent), information available from a variety of sources would suggest that much has happened in recent years. The next section of this chapter will report some of the policy decisions made and some of the activities which exist within the polytechnics.

### 2b.1.2 Policies and staff development activities

In their survey Greenaway and Harding noted 'some evidence of a move in polytechnics towards developing comprehensive institutional policies on staff development'. Of the 20 polytechnics responding to their questionnaire, 11 indicated the existence of an approved policy, while another four had the matter under active consideration. Available documents show a number of approaches to staff development figuring prominently. These include induction, initial and in-service training in teaching methods; conferences, short courses and study leave; consultancy, research and publication. Several documents, however, include rotation of administrative tasks and/or positions of responsibility and formal procedures for staff appraisal and/or self-evaluation. Consideration will now be given to established activities in each of these main categories.

INDUCTION, INITIAL AND IN-SERVICE TRAINING
IN TEACHING METHODS

Most polytechnics provide an *induction* course for new members of staff whether they are trained, experienced or not. Both Harding (1974) and Trickey (1977) have described such courses. They are usually held at the beginning of the academic year before teaching starts and vary in duration from one day to about a week. The courses aim to introduce staff to the philosophy, organizational structure and facilities of the particular institution. Topics covered include academic and administrative structures and procedures, support facilities such as library, media services, computer services, and staff and student affairs. Most courses consist of lectures, discussions, tours and visits to specialist facilities.

At about the same time most new staff would receive some sort of induction to their teaching department. Usually this will be a less formal experience involving a single new member of staff and a course or section leader. Understandably it is likely to focus fairly directly upon the role which the new member will undertake within the institution. If the member of staff is new to teaching, support may be available either from a senior colleague in a related subject area acting as mentor or, in an increasing number of institutions, from an educationalist acting as a professional tutor.

There is at present no national pre-service *initial training* requirement for teachers in the polytechnics, nor indeed for teachers in any other type of institution offering courses of higher education in England and Wales. In Scotland, however, the situation is rather different. Although teachers in its central institutions are not required to train, their colleagues in other post-school institutions, as a result of pressures from the General Teaching Council of Scotland, are obliged by their institutions to train.

Courses of training for teachers in post-school public sector institutions are provided in England and Wales at five specialist centres — Garnett College London, Bolton College of Education, Huddersfield Polytechnic, Wolverhampton Polytechnic, and jointly at University College and the University of Wales Institute of Science and Technology in Cardiff. In Scotland, Jordanhill College of Education, Glasgow has a national remit under the Teacher Regulations (Education, Training and Registration, Scotland) 1967. The main training course at each of these centres leads to a Certificate in Education. Generally it is available in a variety of modes including full-time, sandwich and part-time. Most teachers joining the polytechnics and central institutions do not enrol for these courses. There is usually no expectation and no pressure from their institution for them to do so. There is also a widely held perception among teachers in higher education that the courses are not well suited to their needs — a view which has been expressed by some participants in courses at two of the centres.

A survey by Whitburn, Mealing and Cox (1976) found that only about 25 per cent of polytechnic staff had a recognized teaching qualification. Unfortunately the type of qualification was not reported. It is highly likely, however, that only a small proportion of staff had a teaching qualification specifically related to higher education. Most are likely to have qualified as school teachers and moved into the polytechnics at the time of their major expansion, either as subject teachers or quite specifically as teacher-trainers.

The absence of a national pre-service training requirement has led to a wide variety of local initiatives in individual polytechnics. The establishment of in-house courses in teaching methods is perhaps the most significant training development. A survey of this provision in 1972-73 by Harding (1974) found that 18 polytechnics ran such courses. A follow-up survey in 1974-75 by Mortimer (1976) indicated a marked growth in the volume and status of this provision over the two-year period. The number of polytechnics providing courses had risen to 24 and the amount of time allocated to training had increased. Whereas in 1972-73 many of the courses occupied only a few days at the beginning of the academic year, by 1974-75 most courses consisted of an initial short block followed by regular weekly or fortnightly contact through the first year of appointment. In fact seven of the courses provided between 72 and 108 hours' contact and six exceeded 108 hours in duration.

Trickey (1977) analysed the content of these teaching method courses. He found that they were remarkably similar, including such topics as the nature of learning; choice of teaching methods; use of audiovisual aids; methods of examination and assessment. In every case an attempt was made to relate the topics to the practical experiences of the students. Formal presentation of theory was at a minimum.

The status of these in-house courses changed markedly between 1972-73 and 1974-75. Whereas in 1972-73 only two polytechnics required newly appointed staff, without a teacher-training qualification and with no or limited teaching experience, to attend such a course, by 1974-75 12 did. Also by 1974-75 a number of polytechnics were exploring ways in which their courses might gain credit as part of a formal qualification. Indeed by this time the five polytechnics within the Inner London Education Authority area were able to send their staff on an induction course provided for all staff joining post-school institutions, a course which constituted the first stage of a course leading to a Certificate in Education. (However, they did not all in fact send staff to the course.)

The whole question of initial training for polytechnic teachers was under active consideration during 1978 following the issue of DES Circular 11/77 with an attached report from the Advisory Committee on the Supply and Training of Teachers. The report, which was concerned with the training of teachers in further education (ie teachers in all post-school public sector institutions), recommended that all new entrants who have not had pre-service training and who have had less than three years' full-time equivalent teaching experience should take a systematic induction training course involving release for the equivalent of one day a week throughout one academic year, together with a period of block release equivalent to not less than four weeks. The report recommended that a training requirement in this sense should be introduced, if possible before 1981. It further recommended that opportunities should be available for perhaps one-third of untrained new entrants to receive an additional year's induction training on the same scale as they would receive in their first year. Together with the first year's training such a course might lead to a formal qualification. In Circular 11/77 the Secretary of State asked the Regional Advisory Councils for Further Education to submit plans for the implementation of the proposals in their regions. By late 1978 most had done so and a policy statement on whether, and if so when, an induction training will be mandatory is awaited.

The effect of the circular and its attached report on training arrangements within the polytechnics has already been considerable. This is partly because some polytechnics have wished to improve training provision for their own staff and partly because a number of the regional plans have given polytechnics a role within their locality in respect of the training of non-polytechnic further education staff. Whatever the reason the effect has been the same. Many new courses have been designed which incorporate an initial teaching methods course to be taken in a first year of appointment which, if the individual member of staff wishes, may be continued in a second year leading to a formal teacher qualification. In many cases this has brought together staff previously concerned with running initial in-house courses for the staff of the particular polytechnic with those responsible for the part-time course validated by the City and Guilds of London Institute, which for many years has provided a training mainly for teachers in non-advanced further education. It must be said, however, that while some polytechnics have moved quickly into these new arrangements, others have held back believing that polytechnic staff can be better provided for with courses designed specifically and solely for teachers in higher education. Already several such courses exist, involving three universities and one polytechnic. Thus while it is highly likely that there will be significant developments in initial training for polytechnic teachers in the next year or two, the exact direction of that development is not yet certain.

In recent years there has been increasing interest in the provision of *in-service training* programmes for established staff within most polytechnics. This has arisen in part as a natural extension of the initial provision and in part as a result of the limited or no-growth situation in which most polytechnics now find themselves. This has both increased the need for in-house training of experienced staff and made available the services of specialist staff, originally recruited to run induction courses, to organize it. Trickey (1977) found a wide range of topics on offer mostly in the form of seminars, workshops or short courses. Topics included lecturing, small-group teaching, course design and analysis, interviewing, personal tutoring, evaluation and assessment and a wide variety of topics associated with audiovisual presentation. A number of polytechnics have programmes of between ten and 20

major 'public' lectures each year given by their own specialist staff or
eminent outsiders on a range of topics of general academic or
educational interest.

CONFERENCES, SHORT COURSES AND STUDY LEAVE
Attendance at conferences and short courses is perhaps one of the
simplest ways for a member of the academic staff to become acquainted
with recent developments in a specialized field and to meet colleagues
from other organizations who work in related fields. Unfortunately,
however, there are no data available on the number of staff involved,
the frequency of their attendance or the benefit to either individuals or
institutions. In most polytechnics it would appear that these matters
are dealt with at the level of the teaching departments. General
experience would suggest that both the scale of provision and of
involvement are increasing.

Rather more information is available concerning study leave (also
called sabbatical or staff development leave). This is probably the oldest
and most readily accepted and understood method of staff development
in the polytechnics. It is a facility which has long been available to all
teachers in the public sector and, in cases where a member of staff has
attended a course of study leading to a formal qualification, a cost-
sharing arrangement between local education authorities has operated.
The extent to which each polytechnic has control over study-leave
resources and allocation varies. In some cases the local authority makes
a sum of money available, leaving the individual polytechnic to
adjudicate applications and make awards, while in other cases the
applications are processed outside the polytechnic by the local
authority. The number of staff released for study each year ranges
from a mere one or two to about a dozen, or in percentage terms
from near zero to about 3 per cent of the full-time teaching
establishment.

Historically, study leave was intended for further study leading to
further qualification in the staff member's own discipline. This is still its
main use. However, as polytechnic staff become more highly qualified
at entry this limitation will be less appropriate. Already an increasing
number of staff are seeking leave to qualify in pedagogic fields such as
educational technology and curriculum development. Several polytechnics
awarding study leave give equal priority to a variety of other activities
including further professional and industrial experience, academic
research and the development of learning resources. Greenaway and
Harding (1978) analysed critically the policies and procedures
associated with study leave.

CONSULTANCY, RESEARCH AND PUBLICATION
Many staff in polytechnics are now involved in consultancy, research

and publication. These activities have been seen to be important in their own right but are rarely seen to be directly related to staff development. From a staff development point of view the significant questions are how many staff are involved in these activities, to what extent, and with what developmental return to themselves and to the institution. Unfortunately, there is little evidence available on these matters.

Research is certainly the most highly regarded of these activities and in most polytechnics there is a high-level committee concerned with its promotion. In spite of the severe restrictions placed upon research in the polytechnics by the founding documents and by resources controls, which do not allow full-time staff more than three hours a week release from teaching to undertake research and do not allow maintenance grants to be spent on research, a considerable amount of research does take place.

Whitburn, Mealing and Cox (1976) questioned 20 per cent of the staff of the polytechnics about research in 1972-73. They found that 59 per cent of their sample engaged in research, of which 23 per cent were working for a higher degree and 44 per cent for publication. Perhaps more significantly they found that staff doing research devoted only five hours a week to it and that there was no significant difference in teaching and administrative loads between those doing research and those not. Research for most appeared to be an extra. This survey also found that a higher proportion of the younger staff was involved in research. While this may reflect the higher qualifications and research experience of recent entrants, it may also reflect aspirations to a career outside the polytechnics. The survey showed that staff aspiring to university posts spent far longer on research than other staff. This limited evidence would suggest that the level of research being undertaken, in 1972-73 at least, was far from adequate if it is to be seen as an effective staff development strategy.

STAFF APPRAISAL AND SELF-EVALUATION
Since 1975 about half a dozen polytechnics have developed policy in the area of staff appraisal and self-evaluation. Most of the procedures in operation are voluntary in the sense that any individual member of staff need not participate in them. Most involve meetings each year between a member of staff and the head of department or some other nominated person. The purpose is to review the staff member's activities during the past year and to exchange views over possible developments during the next year. One polytechnic expects that over a period of years each member of staff will engage in some developmental activity in each of the four areas — teaching, research, consultancy and administration. Another expects the outcome of the meeting to be the identification of a specific developmental programme for the member of staff involved.

Warren (1977) provided an interesting case study of the arrangements in one polytechnic. He reported that one-third of the staff opted to participate in the scheme. Of developmental activities identified, research figured most frequently. There are many difficulties, perceived and real, in operating schemes of appraisal and evaluation — instanced by the frequency with which appraisal is denied in descriptive documents. Most polytechnics with schemes in operation attempt to create a situation in which a member of staff can engage in self-evaluation. Whether this can be achieved when a superior in direct line-management terms is involved in the essential procedure is a moot point. Such schemes may, however, provide a means by which the needs of the individuals and of the institution can be more closely matched.

### 2b.1.3 Organizational structures

In this section a little will be said concerning organizational structures existing in the polytechnics to support staff development. Responsibility normally resides in one or more committees of the academic board usually under the chairmanship of a member of the directorate who has day-to-day executive responsibility. The formulation of policies is discussed in some detail by Greenaway and Harding (1978).

In the early 1970s many polytechnics appointed full-time staff to be responsible for the organization of certain aspects of staff development. In some cases single posts were created with, say, responsibility for running an induction course in teaching methods. In other cases one or more units were established to cover a range of support services in, for example, educational technology, curriculum development, staff training and development.

Information about these units is contained in the register of the Standing Conference on Educational Development Services in Polytechnics (SCEDSIP, 1976). Of the 24 polytechnics contributing information to the register, 20 had a unit or person with duties embracing educational technology and staff development while another three polytechnics had established two separate units in these fields. The number of academic staff involved in these units varied from one to five. More recently, as Trickey (1977) has reported, there has been a marked improvement in staffing levels in many units following recent mergers of colleges of education and polytechnics.

### 2b.1.4 Collaboration

Since 1972 many staff working in the field of staff development in the polytechnics have met in conference twice yearly. In 1974 the Standing Conference on Educational Development Services in Polytechnics (SCEDSIP) was formally established with a brief to improve the effectiveness of educational development services by:
  — collecting and disseminating information

— providing a regular forum for discussion of aspects of educational development services
— encouraging collaborative activities among members of staff in the polytechnics in the field of educational development
— maintaining regular contact with the Committee of Directors of Polytechnics (CDP).

To this end SCEDSIP publishes bulletins four times a year, a register and occasional papers; arranges workshop conferences twice yearly (originally aimed at those working in educational development, but since 1976 one conference is arranged each year to bring educational development staff and a particular group of subject staff together); arranges regional meetings; produces teaching/learning packages collaboratively and has developed formal relationships with CDP, the Council for Educational Technology (CET) and the Co-ordinating Committee for the Training of University Teachers (CCTUT — see Section 2a.1.2).

## 2b.2 Administrative staff

### 2b.2.1 Identification
Staff in polytechnics are thought of as academic and non-academic but, compared with the universities' acceptance of the academically related role of administrators, librarians and a few other categories, there is no clear term separating non-teaching staff in polytechnics whose roles are dominated by their being performed in a higher education institution from those who are merely in a large institution. It is therefore necessary to make a distinction for the purpose of this book and, in making it, to try to draw attention to the reason for the absence of a suitable term for 'academically related' staff in polytechnics.

The colleges of whose legal ashes the polytechnics are the phoenix were run on systems which needed only a low level of administration. Typically their administrative head was the secretary, and he had few 'professional' administrators in his command. There was no need for such people as the method of government and management was relatively autocratic and routine.

Most polytechnics are legally constituted as colleges under the direct maintenance of a local education authority.[1] Their non-teaching staff are employees of the local education authority; they therefore enjoy the same conditions of service as local government officers. This has an important bearing on attitudes to staff development.

Firstly, it is not easy to identify polytechnic administrators as a group. Local authorities need not consider their conditions of service any differently from those of other employees. As conditions of service are negotiated nationally for all local authorities except the Greater London Council and Inner London Education Authority (which have their own negotiating machinery), there is little likelihood of polytechnic administrators being an identifiable group.

Secondly, there is no link between the conditions of service of administrative and academic staff. This is an important contrast with universities. The lack of use of the term 'academically related' with reference to polytechnic administrators probably derives in part from the fact that there is no administrative reason why their jobs should be thought of as related to those of academic staff.

Thirdly, as non-academic staff (apart from technicians) are lumped together for salary bargaining purposes, it is not easy to think separately about the needs of those staff whose jobs are related to the academic function and those whose jobs are not. Where the administrative component of work, compared with the clerical part, was low before the designation of polytechnics, and consequently the number of administrative staff was small, there could not be an identifiable group of administrative staff whose development needs could be considered. This was in major contrast to universities. The extent to which any polytechnic has acquired a cadre of para-academic administrators since about 1970 has depended on the age profile and turnover of the inherited staff and the foresight of the senior administrators.

In the course of time, staff recruited to registry/secretariat work have come to resemble their non-teaching university counterparts and their staff development needs are similar. Staff in academic support services (computer, educational development service, library) similarly share a professional identity irrespective of type of institution. (For ease of reading, henceforth all these staff will be generally included in the term 'administrative'.)

### 2b.2.2 Concept of staff development

The basic concept of staff development for administrative staff is no different from that for academics. There is, however, an important difference in approach. This has been explained by Greenaway and Harding (1978) as follows:

> The greatest difference between non-teaching staff and their academic colleagues' needs is not in identifying objectives but in providing the means for fulfilling them. For instance, it takes longer to perfect many teaching and administrative skills than it does to learn many manual and clerical tasks. Each skill is as important to the role of the member of staff but the time-scale for its achievement differs. As the time-scale varies so does the nature of the training programme.

> Perhaps the greater difference is created by the loneliness of teaching compared with the interactive group nature of most non-teaching work.

Teaching involves mostly a single teacher meeting a group of students. Non-teaching work normally relies on the performance of various tasks by several people each contributing part of a single activity. The product is identifiable and can usually be measured and assessed. The opportunity for each to learn from the other while actually doing the job is therefore much greater.

Much staff development for administrative staff takes place on the job. The concept of teamwork is strong, so it is relatively easy for skills to be learned while performing new tasks with more experienced colleagues. It could be argued that there is little need for the identification of a 'senior colleague' to act as mentor because this situation is impossible to avoid.

This would be to deny, however, the extreme loneliness of certain administrative posts. As polytechnics have recognized the need for a professional approach to, say, their public image, they have appointed specialist administrators who are not always well-integrated into a team in an administrative department. The need for the institution to ensure that such people develop their skills and mode of working in line with the polytechnic's plan is even greater than it is in the case of the individual teacher.

One of the most isolated non-teaching jobs of all is that of the sole academic in an educational development service who has neither the role and status of a teacher nor the professional camaraderie of administrators. Those whose whole function relates to staff development have been the most neglected of all.

### 2b.2.3 Collaboration
There is no national collaborating body for administrative staff development. The Committee of Directors of Polytechnics has not addressed itself to this topic, which is a matter for regret but not of surprise. There are no national staff development programmes or activities for polytechnic administrators but some regional efforts exist.

There is, however, national collaboration at a specialist level. The desire to find out how similar functions were performed elsewhere was strong in the early 1970s. The resultant growth of 'functional groups', normally recognized by the Committee of Directors of Polytechnics, has made a significant beginning in a collaborative process which can, of itself, become staff developmental.

The Conference of Polytechnic Secretaries (COPS) comprises the chief administrative officers. Of all the functional groups it is the least developmental in nature as its purpose is not to improve the relationship between its members and their institutions but to compare and develop the work for which they have responsibility. Its interest is not how the individual officers do their work but what that work comprises.

The Polytechnic Academic Registrars Group (PARG) and the Polytechnic Finance Officers Group (PFOG) have, however, taken an interest in the development of their staff as well as of themselves. The finance officers have acted as a professional corporate voice to outside bodies on the manner in which their work is performed. Indeed, they have so successfully collaborated in an exercise on unit costing in polytechnics that they have caused anxiety among the Committee of Directors of Polytechnics on how to react academically to the implications of the accounting progress shown.

The finance officers' relationship with the professional accountancy bodies has important implications for the development of the specialized profession of higher education finance officers. In 1976 the accountancy bodies recognized experience in polytechnic finance offices as suitable for the practical training requirement of their courses. The potential importance of this decision for future recruitment and development of staff is enormous.

The librarians and computer staff have collaborative bodies which represent them as a national voice but most extra-mural staff development takes place through the activities of professional bodies. Computer staff belong to the British Computer Society and their heads meet in the Association of Computer Units in Colleges of Higher Education. Similarly, librarians' professional needs are catered for by the Library Association with the Council of Polytechnic Librarians acting as the specialist group. The latter has, in fact, been active on behalf of its own staff and occasionally organizes training activities specifically for polytechnic librarians.

The most difficult group of non-academic staff is that of the generalist administrators. Those performing registry or secretariat work have no professional body; there is no separation of identity between their profession and their job. Their whole function is to serve the needs of the institution and those needs have only recently been identified. The history of polytechnics, in their present form, is short so those administrative staff who have come into polytechnic work since the designation of their institutions include some of the most flexible people in higher education. The problem is how to satisfy the needs of staff for skill training and absorption into the thinking of higher education, when the pressures on them are severe. The administrative staffing in polytechnics has not been as generously provided as in universities with a resultant workload and attitude problem. Even in those polytechnics with an enlightened head of the relevant administrative section, it is often difficult for junior staff to secure release from urgent work to attend outside activities which will, in the long run, add to their professional understanding.

This pressure also means that plans for collaborative training activities are shelved and good intentions forgotten. In Greater London there are enough polytechnics to make it feasible to organize one- or two-day training programmes on such topics as committee servicing and interviewing. Both those were run in 1977 but pressure of work for those organizing them has led to a diminution of activity. The motivation for the organizers has to be very high for them to be prepared to devote overtime to staff development.

In fact, in London the picture is not quite so dark. One reason for the loss of enthusiasm for a polytechnics-only staff development programme was the success of another enterprise in which those same organizers were involved. The Meeting of University and Polytechnic Administrators in London (MUPAL) embraces staff from both types of institution. This reinforces the professional identity of administrators and broadens the opportunities for understanding the needs of higher education as a whole system. MUPAL organizes a termly meeting on a specified topic and has, so far, spawned one specialist group on staff development. Others on admissions and examinations administration are planned.

## 2b.3 Conclusion

The position outlined in this chapter shows a limited level of activity and understanding of staff development but, nevertheless, great strides have been made since the designation of the polytechnics. However much a mismatch exists between the thinking of those active in promoting staff development and staff at large, most polytechnics have the institutional framework for the generation of staff development activities, policies and procedures.

The next step will be the need to evaluate these strategies and programmes. Thus it may be possible to plan for the future. As British higher education moves into a more static period the greatest task will probably be to match the needs of institutions with those of individuals. This will not be easy.

To identify the needs of institutions will require clarity of purpose. Individuals will need both flexibility of attitude and the provision of means to enable new and changing needs to be met. However, the development of the polytechnics so far gives hope that they — both corporately and as collections of individuals — will continue to adapt to their position as major institutions of higher education.

Note
1 The exceptions are the five in Inner London and Ulster Polytechnic. The Inner London polytechnics are legally limited companies and therefore directly responsible for their own management although the majority, if not all, of their

income derives from the Inner London Education Authority. Ulster Polytechnic is directly funded by the Northern Ireland Department of Education.

# 3: Canada
# — an emphasis on instructional development

Bruce M Shore

## 3.0 Background

Canada is a confederation of ten provinces, each of which jealously guards its responsibilities in education. The federal government provides some of the finance and is responsible for schools in the far north, but tertiary education is a provincial matter. Policy-making depends on factors operating at a provincial level and staff development programmes, if they exist, vary accordingly. Thus there are inevitably exceptions to the general points made in this chapter.

There are essentially two classes of institutions of higher education in Canada. There are universities, some small ones similar to American four-year colleges, and some larger ones, typically with American-style undergraduate programmes (meaning courses and credits) and graduate schools strongly influenced by Scottish and German universities with very few courses and a research thesis requirement. This distinction applies to both English and French institutions, all of which are North American more than anything else. The second class of institutions are community colleges, offering liberal arts and technical programmes, usually in competition with the universities.

In largely Francophone Quebec, college graduation is a prerequisite of university entrance, but the total number of years of schooling required to obtain a BA is much the same across the country.

Universities tend to be staffed by PhDs or their equivalents, and colleges by masters in their crafts or holders of degrees below doctorate level. Also, college teachers' salaries and working conditions are more closely tied to those of public servants and schoolteachers; these, incidentally, are very favourable in world terms. All the colleges and universities, whatever their historical origins as private, church, or public institutions, receive considerable public subsidies, resulting in low annual tuition fees, from zero to well below $1000, and an essentially public system of higher education. Despite the ensuing bureaucratic encroachment, there is still almost complete academic freedom. The universities have almost complete curricular control and the colleges have considerable powers of definition within a broadly delineated framework.

This background is important in understanding what kinds of staff development are likely to be required or desired, and at what level it is likely to be instituted. The key points are that Canadian institutions of higher education are fairly autonomous but public, never rich but never poor because of the public purse, independent but united in strong provincial lobbies to deal with monolithic ministries of education. They provide formidable exercises in tight-rope walking.

## 3.1 Is it really staff development?

Staff development refers to improving the skills and knowledge of the faculty. This is only part of the story of improving learning and teaching in a college or university. Some improvements can be made by changing the reward system for good teaching, upgrading it *vis-à-vis* the publishing, committee, and administrative achievements which are, in practice, the main criteria for tenure and promotion. Other improvements can be effected by providing better media services, heating classrooms in late October, and spending money on the library. This was an early realization in Canadian universities where, largely because of status, faculty and faculty associations were unlikely to be told that they were under-prepared to teach well, or could do better if processed through one kind of in-service refresher course or another. A few professors without doctorates secure leave to obtain them, but knowledge of one's discipline or subject matter is only a part of staff development. The improvement of teaching skills is more palatable — however necessary — if it is seen in a broader context. As will be described, most staff development in Canadian universities has been within this larger context of improving the instructional system. Variations have come in the means taken to achieve this. Canadian colleges have tended more to opt for staff development or pedagogical consulting, perhaps as a result of the typically less-than-maximum academic credentials of staff, perhaps because of stronger administrative control, but most likely — at least as far as acceptance if not imposition is concerned — because the first commitment of community college faculty is to teaching, and this is taken as seriously as scholarly contribution is in the universities. It is not a case of mutual exclusion at all, merely relative position.

Pedagogical services are found in colleges and universities across Canada and nearly half of these are in Quebec, although all provinces are represented. The question that universities and colleges have to answer is how they will provide for instructional development. Some leave it to chance. Some set up committees or ask a seemingly appropriate unit, such as a counselling service, to operate workshops.

A few assign an individual co-ordinating responsibilities. The persons responsible for these services include directors of services, vice-presidents and deans of universities, chiefs of staff development, co-ordinators of research and experimentation, institutional research and development personnel, planning animators, and counsellors. Some colleges and universities which do not list pedagogical services or personnel have committees on instructional development instead. Finally, a growing number of institutions have established pedagogical service units of various sizes, charged with relatively broad ranges of instructional development activities.

Audiovisual and media centres are usually excluded from definitions of instructional development in Canada. Their exclusion might be only partly justifiable, but it is based on the degree of initiative exercised by the centre in carrying out its mandate. Media centres tend to be exclusively responsive to requests. Although they will frequently counsel an instructor about the appropriateness of a medium he or she has selected, in general if the instructor wants slides (or whatever) and provides an active account number, slides will be produced. Instructional development centres are also designed to be responsive to instructors' requests, but not exclusively. They frequently take much more initiative in selecting whom they will serve and in what way. They are also relatively free of commitments to either hardware or any specific set of instructional techniques (eg television or computer-assisted instruction). They would, however, counsel an instructor in the effective use of any of these, and probably be involved in their development and validation on the campus.

In the remainder of this chapter I present the growth of these pedagogical services in Canada from four points of view: first, the obvious growth in numbers; second, the range of activities being undertaken; third, the growth of a community of instructional development centres; and finally, the future of such services in this country.

## 3.2 The spread of instructional development agencies

The first established instructional service in Canada was that of the Southern Alberta Institute of Technology in Calgary. In the early 1960s, the position of director of instruction was created to help new instructors adapt to the educational and instructional policies of the institute. York University established a counselling and development centre in 1960 which was student-oriented but included a programme on the development of teaching skills and effectiveness. The earliest college organizations to develop were those of the *Centre de Recherche* at Cap Rouge, Quebec in 1968 and the Division of Professional Development in Humber College, Toronto, Ontario which began in

1969 to provide training for new teachers through an orientation session and weekly seminars. The Centre for Learning and Development (CLD) at McGill University was given the mandate to improve instruction at the university in 1969. Attempts to provide for staff development by organizing pedagogical services have been a product for the most part, therefore, of the early 1970s.

By the spring of 1974, there were formal agencies or standing committees at more than 13 universities and 65 colleges, plus two created to serve several campuses. This is undoubtedly an underestimate and does not take account of dozens of individuals with other titles who fulfilled some of these functions, nor agencies serving only single faculties. In 1973 CLD polled every college, university, and relevant government and association office across the country. The product was a 41-page first version of an *Index to Pedagogical Services in Canadian Universities and Colleges* containing over 270 names of offices and concerned individuals. A follow-up request for more information was sent out in April 1974, and an annotated second version was prepared.

The most striking feature of the growth of these services was its irregularity. Here are some examples. First, community colleges expanded more quickly than universities in providing formal instructional development services; services are found in colleges in every province. Second, colleges are more likely than universities to appoint an official to co-ordinate these activities. They have titles such as Director of In-Service Training, Staff or Educational Development Officer, and *Directeur des Services Pédagogiques*. Universities still tend to have committees, and several of these are planning committees considering the formation of centres rather than actually providing services. A third irregular feature is the regional disparity in the extent to which the idea has caught on. Quebec had pedagogical services in its four largest universities before any other university in the country, though the Atlantic Institute of Education in Halifax, Nova Scotia preceded three of them, with its instructional development services to colleges and universities being only one part of an extensive mandate.

Ontario had a few units, but took its first big step with the founding of the Ontario Universities Programme for Instructional Development in 1973. Very little has happened at the universities west of the Great Lakes. There are active individuals, for example, on most western campuses, but centres and even service committees exist at only about a half-dozen institutions.

What are the reasons for this irregular growth in numbers, and the hesitancy to take the step of institutionalizing instructional development? We can begin by rejecting a few possible answers.

The first is that the provision of such services invades academic freedom. There are certainly grounds for suggesting such an answer. Colleges have moved much more quickly than universities in establishing formal services, and college instructors have a narrower range of responsibilities than university professors. Put another way, teaching is a smaller part of the total work of the average university than of the college instructor, whatever might be regarded as average or typical. The other activities of university professors, in particular, are endowed with a heritage of freedom of choice and inquiry. The demand for such things as mission-oriented or mission-relevant research, taken up by some granting agencies, is seen as enough of an encroachment. 'At least leave me alone with my teaching', is not an unheard rejoinder. Nevertheless, most professors are sufficiently impressed by the demands of teaching large and heterogeneous groups of students to be willing more than merely to tolerate assistance in pedagogy. There have also always been many professors who take great pride in their teaching and are eager to add to their teaching skills. As long as using instructional development services is voluntary, as it is in Canada, no threat to academic freedom exists.

Neither does lack of concern in one region or another explain the irregular growth. There are people on every campus in the country, and in organizations from the Canadian Association of University Teachers and the Association of Universities and Colleges of Canada to Statistics Canada, who are committed to the improvement of teaching and learning in higher education.

There are really only two significant reasons. The first is internal politics, and the second is money. Let us deal with the question of finance first. What does it cost to mount a formal instructional development service?

Our experience is that to achieve a minimum critical mass, the equivalent of two full-time workers and some clerical help is required. Initial outlay would be at least $60,000, enough to deter some universities, not because it is a large expense *per se*, but because it would necessitate cuts in other departments.It is a lot of money to a chairman told he cannot fill that vacancy in his department. This is where we come to politics.

Where instructional development centres and committees exist, they are new and hence the proverbial low-men on the totem pole. The provision of pedagogical services in Quebec, in fact, has achieved a unique sign of its development, namely the first loss of a pedagogical service in one of the colleges. Where services do not exist they face similar competition for drying up dollars. This explanation fits the facts very well. In Quebec, where enrolments have continued to climb and are now only levelling off rather than declining, and where a financing formula less totally tied to enrolments has prevailed, services have mushroomed. In addition, and most important, the senior academic officers have themselves been convinced of the value of such services. Any campus hoping to start a service very much needs a guardian angel in the front office. In the absence of a guardian angel, a vice-principal will do.

The fact that there are more instructional development services in the community colleges than in the universities also fits this money and politics hypothesis. Community colleges were an educational priority in all parts of Canada during the early 1970s. The boom is over, but they are here to stay and thrive. Proponents of instructional development services have ridden that boom successfully.

We have so far left out one part of the money/power equation with which we will conclude our discussion of numerical growth. This variable is student activism. Student pressure was important in securing changes in Canadian universities in the late 1960s. This desire for involvement and opportunities for personal development has since been manifest in the community colleges. Times are again quiet in the universities to a large extent. If such things are cyclical (an open question), then students may again help those who are trying to get institutions to commit hard cash to improving the main product the students are receiving.

## 3.3 Instructional development activities

There are many different kinds of instructional development services. The emphasis is less on their organization and more on what they actually do in the name of instructional development. Of course, the two are not entirely independent — organization does, thankfully, follow purpose, or perhaps in some cases the other way around! Canadian pedagogical services vary in size from one to 20 persons. Their status ranges from senate and faculty committees to formal organizations resembling academic departments.

Instructional development agencies primarily provide the following services, in various combinations:

- clearinghouse for information on various topics
- library for local use, eg on innovation
- information dissemination, eg publishing a newsletter
- reading and study skills training to students
- ongoing (formative) evaluation of courses
- assistance with course and programme planning
- production of 'packaged' course materials
- staff workshops on instructional methods
- course and teaching evaluations (final or summative)

— applied research on learning in higher education
— theoretical research
— advising administrators on educational policy, such as changes
in the reward system for good teaching.

A general purpose centre such as McGill's CLD is active in almost all of these. Smaller centres, particularly in community colleges, tend to specialize in a small cluster of activities, for example, the first few (generally information dissemination) or evaluation and staff workshops. Size is only one of the criteria against which differences in approach may be identified.

Another basis of differences in services provided is the nature of the staff. Members of teaching staff involved in instructional development are more often found doing the services at the beginning and end of the list, namely the library and research services. Maybe these have some kind of special appeal to academics. When the centres are staffed by administrators or technical personnel, the middle services (workshops, course design, and evaluation) seem to be the main services provided. It might be that only such persons, free of the other pressures on academics, are able to devote themselves to the repetitive application required by these services. A general purpose centre most likely requires a differentiated staff. On the other hand, a campus may need more than one centre.

In order to provide an idea of how this differentiation of services exists across the country, here are some brief examples of other units, their basic organizations, and the main services they provide.

At Grande Prairie Regional College, Alberta, the Professional Development Committee is responsible for collecting and disseminating information on seminars and conferences and the like, organizing in-service seminars, and administering the Professional Growth Fund. At Algonquin College of Applied Arts and Technology in Ottawa, the Department of Staff Development (two people) organizes workshops, circulates articles, and consults with individuals on request. Dawson College in Montreal has a documentation centre which acts as a clearinghouse for information on educational innovations. It is also considering a separate centre for personal development of students. The *Service Pédagogique* at the *Université de Montréal* and the *Service de Pédagogie Universitaire* at *Université Laval* are each organized around specialists assigned to specific services, such as measurement and testing, course evaluation, and instructional design. Not all their core members are academic members of staff. At *l'Université de Montréal,* only the first director was. In all four Quebec university services, though, the core staff are academically trained and research figures in all of their organizations to varying degrees.

These examples illustrate two points: first, the differences of approach at various campuses, and second, the grouping of these activities as discussed above. It is especially important to note that no one set of activities is best. An instructional development centre must serve locally appropriate needs most directly.

The last activity in the list given earlier — namely, seeking changes in the reward system for effective teaching — seems to be getting the least attention. This is probably because it is such a difficult problem to resolve. The problems are compounded when colleges and universities take negative steps first, such as using course evaluation results to fire or not promote people. It is very difficult to convince an instructor to be evaluated in any way for the purpose of improvement when he knows a promotion and tenure committee has recently refused a promotion to a colleague for low ratings on some questionnaire. And that even assumes participation in the evaluation is voluntary. There is a dire need to turn such procedures to positive ends, and one way to accomplish this might be to assign responsibility for all such evaluative procedures to instructional development centres which, independent of the bureaucracy, could refuse to apply them to anything but positive uses. CLD has made a couple of dents at McGill with the acceptance by the University of two programmes of leave fellowships for instructors to work on the development of some aspect of their teaching. The centralized Ontario programme also gives considerable attention to observing teaching innovations in operation at other campuses and financing them locally.

There is, fortunately, growing awareness of this idea across the country. It is reflected, for example, in some of the deliberations of the Teaching Effectiveness Subcommittee of the Canadian Association of University Teachers. The latter is preparing a handbook on demonstrating teaching effectiveness which should be ready in early 1979. This handbook will be accompanied by approaches to administrators concerning the recognition of such demonstration. This is very important because there is no point in asking instructors to offer evidence of quality of teaching (evidence that was previously used to demonstrate the lack of quality!) if those who will make the decisions about tenure, promotions, or merit pay are not prepared (in both senses of the word) to accept it. Such recognition of demonstrated competence is, of course, the first part of any effective incentive system.

In summary, then, no one involved in instructional development in Canadian higher education claims to have the cure-all for every teaching and learning problem we might encounter. A variety of approaches is being followed. They vary according to the size and nature of the institutions and according to what they see as their most pressing local needs. There is an obvious awareness — observed in contacts with many of the people involved — that there are larger issues. Rewards for good teaching are one example of a larger issue that can take many forms, from supportive and confidential applications of evaluations, to public statements by administrators, to promotions and pay raises. An important strength in Canadian efforts at staff development and instructional development is that the financing is through regular college and university funds, as well as special ministry appropriations. There is virtually no dependence on temporary grants, public or private.

## 3.4 The evolution of an instructional development community

The community has expressed itself most formally in three sectors — Quebec and Ontario universities, and the colleges. All the universities of Quebec plus the Universities of Ottawa and Moncton comprise the *Comité Interuniversitaire des Services de Pédagogie.* The Committee provides a forum for discussion and serves as a consultative agency to the Conference of Rectors and Principals. Indeed, the Committee rendered obsolete the Conference's Subcommittee on Teaching Methods and, in return for the opportunity for consultation, the Conference provides the secretariat for the Committee. It was very active in 1976, but may be receding into formality as established units 'get on with the job'. The Ontario programme will probably serve a similar unifying function once services on individual campuses are strengthened. Instructional development, for reasons alluded to earlier, cannot be carried out in a vacuum. At the very least, one needs the solace of colleagues. The Canadian Community College Association has also provided a forum for collegial instructional development officers to get together. Psychologists teaching at college level also met at recent Canadian Psychological Association meetings to focus their concerns for the teaching of psychology.

The community extends across international boundaries as well. A Special Interest Group on Instructional Development in Higher Education within the large American Educational Research Association was founded in 1978 on the initiative of McGill's Centre, and another on Instructional Evaluation also brings many practitioners together.

Finally, in addition to traditional learned journals and associations concerned with higher education, a number of new ones are emerging dedicated primarily to the work of change agencies in higher education.

Instructional development in Canada reflects a realization by the higher education establishment (in the good sense of that word) that devoting a share of available resources to formal instructional development is a reasonable expenditure. The people involved in instructional development are often lone voices in the wilderness of their own institutions, but have the reassurance that there are others elsewhere with similar problems and successes. Sometimes this sense of community is the only thing that keeps us going when frustrations pile up, as they do from time to time. There is an element of crusading in the whole enterprise, and certainly a lot of proselytizing. The hard part is keeping in mind the admonition to tread gently.

## 3.5 The future of instructional development

In Canada the progress so far has been good, and as good as anywhere else in the past ten years. This is especially true at college level. There are still too many universities where there is no one for a teacher to approach for pedagogical help. There are still too many colleges with only one beleaguered professional development officer trying to do the whole job without a secretary or even the money to hire temporary help when needed.

Despite the problems, the outlook is good. First steps tend to be shaky; surefootedness and agility come later. We share in this country a variety of thriving pedagogical services. Governments and institutions are very sensitive to the demands of students for effective teaching. There is growing concern that educational outputs (eg learning) as well as inputs (eg costs) should be looked at. This last point is one of the main distinctions between instructional development agencies, on one hand, and more traditional departments of higher education and institutional research units on the other. The improvement of evaluation techniques is an important part of the ability to examine educational outputs at all. These two approaches to the study of higher education are very much complementary.

In short, then, the importance of accountability in higher education, budget limitations or not, should augur well for the continued but slow growth of instructional development in Canada. And the biggest winners will, one hopes, be students and teachers.

## 3.6 But what do you do?

I have taken the risk of not describing in detail any particular projects or activities in staff or instructional development in Canadian higher education. They are not unique, and may probably be found in other chapters.[1] The uniqueness of the Canadian experience is in its relatively early start, and its institutional adaptation to political realities. The development and history of these services, in an immense country with but 23 million inhabitants 'next door' to the USA for 6000 kilometres, will, one hopes, have been a more interesting inspection tour for the visitor. Canadians like to think that while we look like our neighbours to the south, we are really different underneath. It may be partly true in staff and instructional development.

*Note*

This chapter draws extensively on an earlier article by the author (1974): Instructional development in Canadian higher education. *Canadian Journal of Higher Education,* 4 2 : 45-53. There are also three brief excerpts from Donald, J G and Shore, B M (1976) *Annotated Index to Pedagogical Services in Canadian Colleges and Universities.* Centre for Learning and Development: McGill University, Montreal .

[1] Most services publish annual reports. The Centre for Learning and Development at McGill University, Montreal will gladly provide a copy of current or past reports, all listing many projects in detail, and also assist in making contact with other centres or offices in Canada.

# 4: Denmark — the state of the art and the need for a change

Joan Conrad

## 4.0 Introduction

The focus of this chapter was predetermined and this should be an advantage to the author. Describing 'the state of the art of staff development' in a geographical region as limited as Denmark ought not to pose insurmountable difficulties. To anyone employed in teaching or education in general, however, it is a well-known fact that it is extremely difficult to acquaint oneself with the inner workings of institutions other than one's own, be it another university or just the department next door. Some knowledge of other institutions may be obtained from statistics, statutes, articles, etc but frequently one is left with a rather diffuse overall picture which fails to pinpoint the influences at work in any institution. These influences might tentatively be listed under such headings as 'the inner climate of the institution'; 'indigenous tradition'; 'student and teacher attitudes'; 'management policies'. Put into words, these factors often carry unintentional connotations and one is left without accurate grounds on which to base any reasonable evaluation.

All these difficulties are, of course, more easily overcome in a domestic than an international context. In the latter, an immediate understanding of given facts is hampered by linguistic as well as cultural incommensurability, and it is not always easy to determine where to begin and where to end.

### 4.0.1 The aims of this chapter
The term 'staff development' poses a number of initial problems. Directly translated into Danish this term has no meaning, but in our higher education institutions we do have activities that are reasonably covered by the definition sent to each contributor prior to the writing of these chapters:

> Staff development is a systematic attempt to harmonize individuals' interests and wishes, and their carefully assessed requirements for furthering their careers with the forthcoming requirements of the organization within which they [are] expected to work (Piper and Glatter, 1977).

Table 4.1
Number of students and teaching staff (full-time) at institutions of higher education,
1 October 1975 (Statistisk Aarbog, 1977)

| | Students | Full professors | Assistant and associate professors |
|---|---|---|---|
| University of Copenhagen | 28286 | 234 | 1143 |
| University of Arhus | 15125 | 113 | 633 |
| University of Odense | 3838 | 36 | 160 |
| Alborg University Centre | 2158 | 35 | 225 |
| Roskilde University Centre | 1454 | 29 | 91 |
| Technical University of Denmark | 3355 | 76 | 419 |
| Academic School of Engineers in Copenhagen | 1084 | 23 | 141 |
| Royal Veterinary and Agricultural College | 1536 | 57 | 199 |
| Dental College of Copenhagen | 933 | 12 | 41 |
| Dental College of Arhus | 543 | 11 | 30 |
| Danish School of Pharmacy | 681 | 10 | 58 |
| The Copenhagen School of Economics and Business Administration | 6767 ⎱ | | |
| Arhus School of Economics and Business Administration | 2894 ⎰ | 41 | 145 |
| The Royal Danish School of Educational Studies | 1437 | 22 | 86 |
| *Total* | 70091 | 699 | 3371 |

However, I must hasten to add yet another qualification: this chapter will deal solely with activities at Danish educational institutions that *we* (ie the Danes) call 'institutions of higher education', meaning institutions administering university-level courses where all full-time educators are obliged to devote around 50 per cent of their working hours to scientific research. The consequences of this delimitation will be made clear below, and Table 4.1 specifies which types of institutions are covered. This is only to stress the fact that the term 'higher education' is not unequivocal in an international context.

There are two staff categories at these institutions, the educators and the technical/administrative staff. This chapter will mainly be concerned with activities pertaining to the development of the 'educator' category, and exclusively with the development of educators as teachers. The internal activities aimed at the development of educators as scientists are not as yet 'developed' to the same degree, and the external activities organized by professional unions, for example medical doctors, physicists, etc, will not be mentioned here. The development of activities for the technical/administrative staff is at a very early stage, too.

The scope of this study is to describe the activities encompassed by the above definition of 'staff development'. Furthermore, it has been my intention to analyse the changes these activities have undergone in order to discuss possible directions that 'staff development' might take in the near future.

To understand fully a specific development of a practice or activity within an educational system, however, one must possess some knowledge of the organizational framework peculiar to that particular practice. This entails a certain knowledge of the historical factors which initiated this development — and should also include some knowledge of how interests (public and private) in this particular activity have fluctuated.

The first part of this chapter, Section 4.1, will describe the system of higher education in Denmark. Developments since 1960 will be stressed since the idea of 'staff development' originates from this period.

## 4.1 Higher education in Denmark

### 4.1.1 Administration and management
Universities and colleges in Denmark are all government institutions administered by the Ministry of Education, with the exception of the Royal Academy of Music and the Royal Academy of Architecture and Fine Arts, which are administered by the Ministry of Cultural Affairs. These institutions are somewhat atypical and will not be dealt with here.

Normally, preparation for the final examination within higher education requires from five to seven years of study. The entrance examination for institutions of higher education is the Danish *Examen Artium* (resembling the German *Arbitur*) or an equivalent examination.

University studies normally lead to a 'Candidate's Degree'. The academic titles are Latin abbreviations, eg 'Cand Med' (*Candidatus/a medicinae*) and 'Cand Mag' (*Candidatus/a magisterii*). In addition to these degrees, mainly designed to qualify graduates for specific jobs as physicians, teachers, etc, there are three categories of research degrees in higher education: the 'magister' degree, the 'licentiate' degree and the 'doctor's' degree.

The institutions of higher education enjoy a wide degree of autonomy. The total amount of money at the disposal of each university is provided for in the national budget, but the allocation of these funds within the universities is, to a large extent, left to the governing bodies of the institutions themselves.

The institutions are governed by the Act on Administration of Institutions of Higher Education, an act based on the principle of an equal say for *all* involved, and this includes *all* teachers, *all* students and *all* technical/administrative staff.

The management of each institution is carried out by the Vice-Chancellor (Danish: *Rektor*) in collaboration with the central governing body (the *Konsistorium*), the Faculty Boards, Institute Boards and Study Boards. The Vice-Chancellor and the Deputy Chancellor are elected for two-year and three-year terms respectively. Those eligible are the professors and associate professors (senior lecturers) of the institution.

The *Konsistorium* is the sovereign collegiate committee of the institution and rules on all matters concerning the institution as a whole. The *Konsistorium* at the University of Copenhagen numbers 40; 20 teachers (including the Vice-Chancellor, the Deputy Chancellor and the five Deans of the Faculties), ten students and ten members of the technical/administrative staff.

Education and research take place within main departments or faculties, the administration of which comes under a Faculty Board, elected according to principles similar to those of the *Konsistorium*. Each faculty comprises a number of institutes, each representing a specific subject and research field. The institutes are directed by Institute Boards.

The Study Board consists of an equal number of teachers and students, four or six members in all. The members are elected by the teachers and the students within the appropriate subject area. The Study Board rules on matters regarding the content of courses, organization of instruction and examinations, and appointment of assistant lecturers. Also it has a say in the appointment of tenures (professorships, lectureships) and in judging the *educational qualifications* of applicants to such posts.

*All* full-time teachers in higher education are obliged to teach, to carry out research, and to take part in the administration of their institute. The average distribution of time should be 50 per cent to teaching, 40 per cent to research and 10 per cent to administration. In addition to this, the institutes also rely on part-time teachers to a great extent. Normally, these teachers are employed elsewhere, and at the institute their only task is to teach.

The Act on Administration of Institutions of Higher Education dates from 1973. It meant a radical departure from the structure which had hitherto left formal decisions on all matters affecting the institutions as a whole in the hands of the full professors. This act was one of the results of the extensive debate on problems of higher education that took place in Denmark from the mid-1960s to the beginning of the 1970s.

### 4.1.2 The expansion in higher education

Denmark, like so many other countries, has experienced a general expansion of higher education in the past two decades. In 1970 the higher education budget constituted nearly a quarter of total education expenditure whereas, in 1960, it had only amounted to about one seventh.

In Denmark children must attend school for a compulsory nine years, usually from the age of seven to the age of 16. In 1970, however, almost 30 per cent of the generation aged 18 to 19 were enrolled in post-secondary, non-compulsory education. By 1970 around 53,000 students were enrolled in institutions of higher education, compared with about 18,000 in 1960 (*Nationaløkonomisk Tidsskrift,* 1972).

Up till 1976, anyone having passed the *Examen Artium* was entitled to enrol at any university and faculty he/she might choose. Consequently, the pressure on the universities was especially high compared with other institutions of higher education, but all institutions went through a considerable expansion, and many new ones were established.

The institution to undergo the most remarkable expansion was the University of Copenhagen (Table 4.2); indeed, the expansion was such that a total breakdown at times seemed imminent.

The University of Copenhagen is the largest of all Danish institutions of higher education. It accounts for more than 40 per cent of the Danish student population, ie about 30,000 students in 1977 (Table 4.3).

Table 4.2

**Number of students enrolled in the University of Copenhagen 1960-70**

*(Aarbog for Koebenhavns Universitet, 1960-70)*

| Faculty | 1960 | 1962 | 1964 | 1966 | 1968 | 1970 |
|---|---|---|---|---|---|---|
| Arts | 1853 | 3011 | 5066 | 6572 | 8122 | 9976 |
| Medicine | 1832 | 2303 | 3195 | 3781 | 4061 | 4220 |
| Law and Social Science | 1451 | 1940 | 3233 | 4141 | 4196 | 4821 |
| Theology | 253 | 286 | 341 | 420 | 411 | 418 |
| Science | 915 | 1395 | 2059 | 2624 | 3035 | 3395 |
| Faculty unspecified | 393 | 249 | 568 | 726 | 695 | 617 |
| *Total* | 6697 | 9184 | 14402 | 18264 | 20820 | 23447 |

Table 4.3

Number of students, full professors and lecturers in the University of Copenhagen,
October 1977

| Faculty | Number of students | Full professorships | Assistant and associate professors |
|---|---|---|---|
| Arts | 13743 | 68 | 395 |
| Medicine | 3987 | 83 | 211 |
| Law and Social Science | 5687 | 27 | 61 |
| Theology | 578 | 10 | 12 |
| Science | 5214 | 66 | 450 |
| Total | 29214 | 254 | 1329 |

### 4.1.3 Educational controversy in the 1960s

This decade of vast expansion also caused controversy between the different groups of people involved. It was accepted that the development of modern industrial society called for extensive changes in the qualifications of the labour force in so far as the industrial development of a country must go hand in hand with educational development. The general awareness of this relationship notwithstanding, politicians, educational planners, teachers and students seemed to lack a shared and integrated conception of the development of society, and consequently of the development of the educational system, including higher education. The debate was influenced by a number of novel approaches, eg democratic organization, humanistic values in general and full participation in decision-making by the individuals involved.

The old structures, however, were not easily moved. At times it seemed nearly impossible to change anything in the old system of higher education — even to the planning committees appointed by the Ministry of Education (as early as 1962). Indeed not until the end of the 1960s, when the verbal skirmishes between the universities and their students culminated in open violence and revolt, did the barriers collapse. The time had come for a different kind of innovation.

## 4.2 Staff development activities — how it all began

Why was a need for these activities felt — and by whom? *Who* wished 'to harmonize individuals' interests and wishes, and their carefully assessed requirement for furthering their careers with the forthcoming requirements of the organization within which they [are] expected to work'? — to recount the initial definition.

Historical outlines of this sort are always a precarious undertaking. Somehow, a certain bias tends to prevail; how do you determine exactly when an interest in an activity such as 'staff development' starts to appear? Some disagreement on the reasons for such an interest is hardly avoidable. For the time being, I shall abstain from an attempt at resolving *why?* and concentrate on the *when?*

Systematic deliberations on activities covered by the above definition first surfaced in Denmark at the beginning of the 1960s. The interest appeared in several places simultaneously, but worth mentioning are — among others — the discussions that took place under the auspices of the Scandinavian Summer University.

The Scandinavian Summer University is an independent organization of graduates and students from the five Nordic countries (Denmark, Norway, Sweden, Iceland and Finland). It was founded in 1950 in an attempt to widen the perspective of the different university subjects by promoting insights into the common basic problems of science and by encouraging research across the traditional scientific divides.

The participants at these seminars met in the different university cities throughout the winter in preparation for the summer two-week plenary session held in one of the Scandinavian countries. The main topic at these winter sessions in 1964, 1965 and (partly) 1966 was 'University problems today and tomorrow'. A few groups concentrated on 'University teaching'. In 1964-65 the Copenhagen group was chaired by the Professor of Chemistry, Thor A Bak. He later became *Rektor* of the University of Copenhagen (1972-76). These activities are dealt with in the journal *Nordisk Forum* (Thomsen, 1967).

In 1966 a group of teachers at the Technical University decided to arrange a course under the heading 'University teaching'. The teaching staff at this course came mainly from the Royal Danish School of Educational Studies where they had either taught or graduated. This meant that all had done research in either psychology or educational studies. The subjects dealt with at this course were the psychology of learning, instructional planning, teaching methods, and audiovisual media. It lasted four days.

In the years that followed, this course model was emulated by the Copenhagen School of Economics and Business Administration, by the dental colleges in Copenhagen and Arhus — and by Arhus University as well.

The course intensity was rather modest — a maximum of a couple of courses a year at each institution. Roughly the same teaching staff were used at the courses of each institution, although soon it was thought wise to include in the group of course teachers one or two scientific experts from the institution in question.

To begin with, the impetus for these course activities came from a small group of interested teachers, but by the end of the 1960s nearly all higher education institutions had also established 'didactic committees' (as they were often called) under the governing body of the institutions. These were supposed to deal with matters concerning educational practice at the institutions, including the setting up of courses for teachers. This in a way marked the overall acceptance of such course activity. The plight of these committees will be dealt with later (Section 4.4).

The institutions mentioned above are all relatively small. What happened at the largest educational institution, the University of Copenhagen?

## 4.3 Setting up an educational centre at a university

In January 1967 the Vice-Chancellor of the University of Copenhagen decided to set up a preliminary committee 'to consider under which form the University most feasibly might provide guidance and educational assistance to its teachers in carrying out their educational tasks'.

The initiative behind these terms of reference came from the Students' Council at the University, but it is beyond doubt that the Vice-Chancellor had a genuine interest in these problems as well (Fog, 1968). Four full professors (Chemistry, Philosophy, Classical Philology and Law), one associate professor (Psychology) and two representatives from the Students' Council were invited to participate in the work of this committee. The chairman was a holder of a scholarship, granted for research in the field of higher education. In August 1967 the committee submitted a *Report on Pedagogical Guidance and Assistance to University Teachers (Koebenhavns Universitet,* 1967). Their proposal was to establish an educational centre with the following functions: (a) research and development in the field of higher education, (b) documentation services, (c) advisory assistance, (d) providing information, and finally (e) setting up courses in pedagogy for university teachers.

The immediate reaction from university teachers was not unequivocally positive, although they were becoming increasingly conscious that it was necessary to do something.

At the same time, a group of medical doctors from the medical faculties and the Medical Association were working on reform in education in their field. The group pointed out that the implementation of reform would require as a corollary changes in the method of teaching at the universities and subsequent preparation of the teaching staff.

On the initiative of the Vice-Chancellor and a number of teachers from the Faculty of Medicine, the chairman of the committee launched two courses for teachers in medicine and one for teachers at the Institute of Chemistry. These courses were oriented towards the following subjects:

- the systems approach to education. Analysis and formulation of educational objectives (six hours)
- students' characteristics (two hours)
- the psychology of instruction and learning (six hours)
- course planning and instructional methods (12 hours)
- programmed instruction (two to four hours)
- audiovisual aids in education (four hours)
- educational evaluation (six to eight hours)
- voice test
- an attempt at establishing a syllabus for the participants' teaching

in the ensuing semester. Presented and discussed at a seminar
(four hours)
— course evaluation.

Résumés from these courses were published in a number of articles
(Nerup *et al,* 1968, 1972; Güttler *et al,* 1969; Thomsen, 1969, 1971).
The participants were generally satisfied with the outcome, but other
university teachers were sceptical, many doubted whether the courses
were any use at all, and some considered the very idea ridiculous.

In spite of these controversies among the teachers, the Institute for
Studies in Higher Education was set up in 1969 following a decision by
the *Konsistorium.* The Institute began its work in January 1970, and it
remains the only organization of its kind within higher education in
Denmark.

The aims of the Institute are as follows:

— The Institute for Studies in Higher Education will assist and
  guide teachers and governing bodies at the University of
  Copenhagen in educational matters.
— The Institute will arrange courses for university teachers,
  provide advice and information, and maintain a library on
  university teaching. The Institute staff will carry out research
  and development work related to the teaching activities of
  universities and colleges.

The staffing establishment of the Institute is as follows:

☐ 1 full professorship (vacant)
☐ 5 assistant/associate professors
☐ 3 part-time lecturers (The number of part-time teachers may be
  expanded.)
☐ 1 librarian (assisted by two students)
☐ 2 secretaries.

Until March 1974, the Institute was responsible directly to the Vice-
Chancellor and the *Konsistorium* with no intermediary faculty. Since
then the Institute has been placed under the Faculty of Arts. This does
not entail any changes in the goals or the function of the Institute,
although some co-operation between the Institute and the Institute for
Educational Theory has been initiated.

In March 1978 the *Konsistorium* submitted a recommendation to the
Ministry of Education concerning the future of the two hitherto
independent institutes of education, namely that in April 1979 the two
institutes should merge into one institute of education. It was suggested
that teachers at the new institute must carry out research and teach
students in the field of education. As a supplementary purpose the
institute must provide advisory services for teachers of the different

university departments and arrange pedagogical courses for the teachers as well.

## 4.4 Teaching activities for university teachers

The following is a short description of activities for teachers which have been offered at the Institute for Studies in Higher Education so far. Somewhat similar courses are held at other institutions of higher education, but there are many more courses at the Copenhagen Institute than at other institutions.

I have mentioned above how the governing body of the various institutions appointed a didactic committee — usually for a one-year period. This committee was to take care of the courses for teachers at the institution in question. However, the committee members had neither the time nor the money needed for in-depth study of the specific problems related to courses of this kind, and the lack of continuity in the committee's work was obvious. Not surprisingly in these circumstances, it was difficult for the committee members to maintain an interest in the courses, and this led to most of these didactic committees being abandoned or forgotten.

At the dental colleges in Copenhagen and Arhus and at the Copenhagen School of Economics and Business Administration there are departments with teaching tasks similar to those of the Institute for Studies in Higher Education. These departments are obliged to do research and teach in other subjects as well, but they may offer one or two basic courses in teacher education every year, in addition to occasional special courses, and they try to develop new educational courses as well.

In principle three types of courses are offered by the Institute for Studies in Higher Education:

- A basic course in higher education focusing on aims and objectives, instructional planning, learning psychology, audiovisual media, teaching methods, and evaluation. The basic course is usually offered to specific institutes or faculties (participants with common background). It will normally run over a period of two or three months, with half-day meetings, once or twice a week; about 50 hours in total.
- Special courses concentrating on one special subject, such as aims and objectives, curriculum construction, evaluation, group teaching methods, etc. These courses vary from 12 to 36 hours.
- Full-year courses in higher education in general. These are open to university teachers from all faculties. The participants meet for four hours a week and to a large extent they plan the courses themselves.

Table 4.4 Courses offered by the Institute for Studies in Higher Education, University of Copenhagen, autumn 1977

| | *Number of participants* |
|---|---|
| A. *Basic courses:* | |
| — For teachers from the faculty of medicine (two groups) | 15 + 11 |
| — For teachers from the faculty of science and engineering (two groups) | 17 + 16 |
| — For teachers from the faculty of social science (particularly for teachers of law) | 18 |
| — For teachers in pharmacology | 15 |
| — For teachers in botany and geology | 13 |
| B. *Special courses:* | |
| — Small-group teaching | 10 |
| — Student counselling (two groups) | 19 + 22 |
| — Communication, running meetings and committee skills (for the technical/administrative staff) | 12 |
| — Teaching methods (two groups) | 18 + 11 |
| — Project-oriented studies A | 13 |
| — Project-oriented studies B | 10 |

Approximately 1400 people have so far participated in the courses offered by the Institute. Several teachers have taken more than one course. Full-year courses were organized in the academic years 1972-73, 1973-74 and 1975-76 but with very few participants, less than 20 in total.

It is apparent from the 1977 plan of courses that there are no basic courses for teachers from the Faculty of Arts. This is a characteristic picture. Different groups of teachers at university show different degrees of interest, and teachers from the Faculty of Arts are not frequent visitors. Some do, however, participate in courses like group teaching, project organized studies, etc.

The Institute has prepared plans for (a) a fully fledged Diploma Course in Higher Education and (b) a course specifically for new teachers at university. The plans for both courses have been presented to the Faculty Board and the *Konsistorium*; still there are doubts about whether the suggestions will be accepted. At the moment the University of Copenhagen is unlikely to expand its activities in the field of courses for university teachers.

## 4.5 The state of the art of staff development

The governing bodies of the universities and of other institutions of higher education are unlikely to expand course activities for their teachers at present. But why is this so? What has prompted the radical change of attitude regarding these activities over the last ten years? Participants still sign up for the courses, but the interest among teachers as a whole is declining. What can be done about this state of affairs? In a critical situation such as this, institutions working with the development of these activities might very well ask themselves: should these kinds of courses be offered at all?

It is impossible to give definitive answers to these questions. However, if one feels a genuine interest in the teaching function at university level and its improvement, discussion of questions such as these is imperative as a first step towards determining 'the state of the art' and, eventually, towards resolving this critical situation. Here I should like to offer a few contributions to such a discussion.

### 4.5.1 The dual function as expert and teacher
In the initial definition the term 'staff development' was defined as the attempts made to harmonize teachers' interests and wishes with the requirements and norms of the organization within which they are to work.

According to the Act on Administration of Institutions of Higher Education, the major functions of these institutions are to provide society at large with teaching, research and other services. Although there is a general consensus as to these functions, a great deal of controversy persists about their relative importance, judging from the teachers' and the governing bodies' interests in courses relating to education.

As part of their evaluation of university instructors, Rotem and Glasman (1977) devised a model aimed at presenting a systematic approach to the discussion of the questions posed above. The model is abstract, but of high illustrative value since it employs an individual perspective for examining a given practice in a social organization which has governed staff development activities up till now — not only in Denmark, but also in other countries all over the world. Using our concrete experiences as a starting point, I shall now discuss the adequacy of this perspective.

The model is built on the assumption that people, in performing their tasks, have some notion of what they want to achieve and what they can actually accomplish. A discrepancy occurs when an individual perceives a gap between intentions and outcomes. When the individual wants to eliminate this discrepancy, this will be experienced as a need. The degree of importance attached to this elimination is a function of the extent to which it violates his/her internalized standards, aspirations and self-interest.

The gap can be closed or reduced in two ways, either by lowering the level of aspirations or by trying to improve the achievements. If the domain in which the discrepancy appears is not of great interest to the individual, it is likely that the aspiration level will be reduced. If the domain is important, he/she is more likely to try to improve the outcome. The probability of responding to a given discrepancy is a function of a need to do so and an awareness of opportunities available (Rotem and Glasman, 1977).

The authors use this model to explain the teachers' interest in the teaching process, or lack of interest as the case might be. They state that university teachers are unlikely to perceive any discrepancies in their teaching performances and thus do not experience a need to improve them. Although teaching is a major activity, it is not a major concern. The teachers' domain for excellence and competence is research. Therefore research is also the field where university teachers feel they must legitimize their membership of the organization.

According to the model, improvement in university teaching is impossible unless two requirements are fulfilled, namely (a) that the organization recognizes the dual function of the teacher as scientist and educator and expects him to be competent in both functions, and (b) that opportunities for teacher-training are established.

Before we leave this model it is important to point out that the individual is always affected by external influences. Thus 'discrepancies' of the above kind may also be pointed out by others. In this case the need to eliminate such discrepancies may still become important to the individual, even though it did not originate from 'within'.

### 4.5.2 Course strategies in Denmark

Let us return for a moment to the time when staff development activities began to take form, ie at the end of the 1960s. Higher education was troubled by dissent and unrest. Universities were being criticized because of their inefficient structure — too much time was wasted and too many students dropped out. Also the curriculum was criticized for being too extensive and irrelevant compared with the direction of the courses of study. Teachers were accused of being too authoritarian and of supporting the patriarchal relationship between the university administration (the professors) and the students. Most people agreed that something had to be done, but the extent of the criticism was so far-reaching that it was not immediately resolvable, even though the politicians, to a great extent, were in sympathy with student dissatisfaction at the age-old formal structure of the university and the university disciplines. However, it was all-important that immediate changes were made and a number of problems of more limited scope were debated.

One obvious issue was the university teacher as educator. The situation was tense, and it was not difficult to imbue teachers with 'an experience of need' — or a sense of guilt! The main question became: 'How do we teach university teachers to be better educators?' In relation to the model above the requirements needed for improving university teaching were present.

Arranging courses and offering guidance was one obvious way of going about this. These courses for university teachers were influenced by many different thoughts and ideas. At first the approach was definitely 'behaviouristic'. The different course objectives were carefully stated in terms of behavioural change — meaning that the participants were to be trained in 'correct behaviour'. As an example I shall cite one statement of course objectives from the 'Basic Course in Pedagogy for Teachers at the Faculty of Medicine', May 1971:

> At the end of the basic course, the participant should be able, *with reference to the analysis and formulation of instructional objectives,*
> — to define his standpoint concerning demands for formulating instructional objectives
> — to assist in analysing and formulating objectives for entire courses of study
> — to analyse and formulate instructional objectives for his own subject with special reference to curriculum plans and similar material
> — to propose ways in which students and teachers can co-operate in specifying instructional objectives.

Later, these behavioural goals were replaced by statements of a more overall nature, such as: 'It is our purpose to provide the individual with a background conducive to his qualification in the role as teacher and to develop his/her educational competence.' At the same time, the discussions during the course started to focus on the everyday situation of each teacher. Through these discussions, the goal was to acquaint the participants with a few theories and a frame of reference enabling them to analyse their own situation with a view to changing it.

## 4.6 A changed perspective of staff development

Nevertheless, all courses, whether they were 'behaviouristic' or 'developmental', were aimed at changing the behaviour of the individual teacher. The aim was to make the entire educational institution better by improving the individual teacher.

Participants generally rated these courses favourably, but when the teachers returned to their respective departments the value of what they had learned often seemed limited. What appeared to satisfy the individual teacher's needs did not always prove beneficial to the organization as a whole.

Changing habits and procedures is not always merely a question of providing knowledge and information, nor is it exclusively an intellectual matter. It is also a question of working on attitudes rooted in normative structures, intra-institutional expectations and relations, as well as the relations between the institution and the surrounding world. The change of attitudes towards pedagogical courses is probably to be understood as the result of a widespread realization of the somewhat limited potentiality of these courses, rather than as any diminished interest in educational problems on the part of the teachers.

In order to change a given practice, it is necessary to take the entire organization into account. This does not mean the whole university all at once, but it *is* important to work on smaller parts of the organization such as departments, individual subjects or even smaller units, like the first year of a specific course of study.

The collective educational practice at a given institution is not only a result of the behaviour of individual teachers, it is also a function of the organization as a whole, ie its goals, group interests, structure of disciplines, decision-making processes, norms and values of the system.

Norms and requirements in an organization or in parts of it are determined by the overall goals of the organization, but these are continually changing and cannot be unequivocally stated once and for all. It is by no means evident that the *actual* goals of an organization are in every respect congruent with the official goals of that same organization. This aspect often hampers efforts at harmonizing interests and wishes. Institutions of higher education are social units where the goals of the various interest groups may differ. They are institutions where viewpoints may clash and where ideas, values and expectations at times seem irreconcilable.

Changing any practice within an organization which is governed by democratic ideas must involve several parties. In educational institutions, the teachers, the students and the administration should all participate. At the core of any change must lie a clarification of the common norms. This should be a first step towards identifying inherent conflicts in the organization as well as resolving them. The situation in Denmark regarding staff development requires renewed evaluation. The social system affected by and affecting these activities is immensely complex, and nearly every question touching upon factors determining human behaviour must be viewed from a perspective of totality.

Perhaps the teachers have a special kind of responsibility for the outcome of the teaching-learning process, but they also have to learn to involve the other parties in the solution of educational problems, and the other parties have to understand their responsibility for the entire educational institution.

Those who previously arranged and taught educational courses should now devote their time to trying to resolve these problems: together with the different parties of the organization they might as consultants help in the formulation of the problems at hand, thus facilitating collation of data, testing of ideas and evaluation. This process should be repeated until an (intermediate) solution has been found.

The role of consultant requires a different kind of expertise from that of a teacher at courses such as the ones described above. An extensive knowledge of the inner workings of the institution in question is crucial, as is knowledge of its relation to society. Furthermore, it is imperative that the 'consultant' possesses some knowledge of the psychological mechanisms pertinent to different groups of individuals striving to co-ordinate their activities and interests, in order to function as an institution of education and research. It is necessary for 'the consultant' to identify himself with the teacher's situation, in his dual function as researcher and teacher. The 'qualifications' are probably best attained if the designated consultants or educators in 'education' are obliged to do research of their own in the field of higher education.

We need research aimed at finding the key characteristics or qualities concerned with the functioning of the total organization. We need, for example, to know something about how the structure of the subjects influences the relation between the teachers, and how the relations between teachers influence teacher-student relations or student-student relations.

Rotem and Glasman's model makes it clear that two conditions have to be fulfilled before any 'improvement in university teaching' can be expected:

- realization of the teacher's double function as educator and researcher
- acceptance that somebody at the institution in question must be responsible for training the teachers of that institution.

These qualifications, however, do not seem altogether sufficient. The realization of the double function as researcher and educator must also entail an acceptance that teachers will need to approach problems of education from the research point of view. This means viewing educational problems systematically in a way similar to the way in which scientific problems are treated. It is not a question of 'training', not to any serious extent, at least. In an institution like, for instance, a university, it is necessary to have a group of people with the responsibility not only of educating teachers, but also of working as consultants to teachers and other parties trying to solve educational problems in the manner hinted at above.

## 4.7 Closing remarks

The starting point of this chapter was the definition of *staff development* given to all contributors. This definition is wide-ranging, but not exhaustive. It only encompasses the attempts at harmonization between individual needs and organizational demands, and the thought behind it seems to be that by improving each individual you automatically improve the organization as a whole. Furthermore, this definition does seem rather static in so far as it does not include resistance to planned changes or innovations within the organization, or within parts of it. One might very well question the term 'staff development'. Does this term have connotations incompatible with its intention?

We all want changes, but if the term 'development' is conceived as change leading to a final, static product rather than as a continuing process always leading towards something better, then the term should be replaced.

# 5: The Federal Republic of Germany — a successful synthesis of method, content and theory?

Bernd Gasch

## 5.0 Introduction

In writing a review on the state of staff development in higher education, an author faces some objective problems as well as obvious subjective constraints. The first of the objective difficulties is the impossibility of acquiring all the necessary data, a task which is not easy even for official organizations. As an example: a questionnaire sent out recently to 40 Advisory Centres for Tertiary Education in Germany by the most important Association in this field (*Arbeitsgemeinschaft für Hochschuldidaktik*) was answered by only 19 of the centres (Holtkamp, 1977b). Another problem is the great diversity of aims, content, methods and opinions in this field. Any general statement (and a review of this length has to generalize) cannot give an accurate account of all these variations. A further difficulty is that of definition: how are we to define 'higher education' in the particular educational system of modern West Germany? What should be understood by 'staff development'? A word-by-word translation is of no use here; what is required is a more or less vague, perhaps even partly intuitive, interpretation.

This leads naturally into the subjective problems. It is not to be expected that one person will be competent in every branch of staff development in every field of higher education, because his view is limited by his experience, the people he has contact with, and even his ideological standpoint.

In this situation, the only solution is to restrict the range of the subjects discussed in detail to those within the experience of the writer and to emphasize the subjectivity of this process. Figure 5.1 illustrates how it was done in the present case.

The major section of this review (5.2) discusses staff development by education with respect to the improvement of university teaching (see parts of Figure 5.1 in heavy boxes). But this obviously forms only a small part of the whole pattern of staff development in higher education, which is briefly treated in Section 5.1.

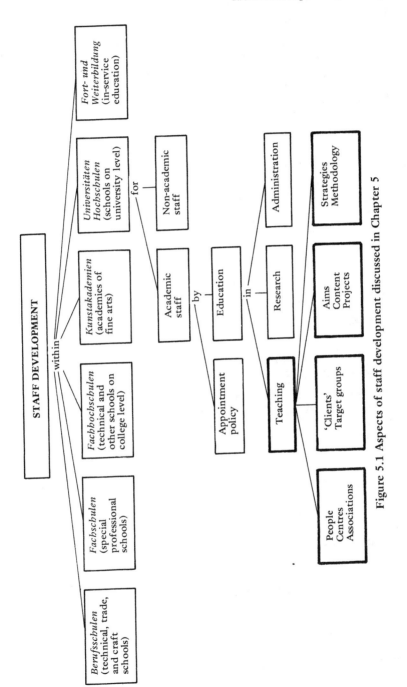

Figure 5.1 Aspects of staff development discussed in Chapter 5

## 5.1 The wider context of staff development

The German educational system has become increasingly complex over the last 15 years; there has been a proliferation in both the types and the numbers of schools and educational institutions. If we take 'higher education' to be education that follows compulsory schooling, the following types of institutions should be included (see also Figure 5.1).

*Berufsschulen* (technical, trade and craft schools): These schools train apprentices, normally for one day per week over two or three years. The rest of their time is spent in workshops or factories where they acquire practical experience.

*Fachschulen* (special professional schools): These are special schools for those who wish to enter certain professions, such as nurses, social workers or technicians. Education here is mostly a combination of courses and practical work.

*Fachhochschulen* (technical and other schools on 'college' level): These schools can be located on the level beneath universities. There are, however, some new institutions which combine the functions of the *Fachhochschule* and the university (Zweite Kasseler Hochschulwoche, 1976). These schools mainly offer the engineering disciplines, but also economics, design, etc.

*Kunstakademien* (academies of fine arts): Schools of music, painting, graphics, sculpture and so on provide a very specialized education, according to the subjects they teach.

*Fort- und Weiterbildung* (in-service education): There is a great variety of activity in this field, in trade and industry (Thomas, 1974), the public service, and welfare organizations. Even a few universities, for example Augsburg and Hagen (Kochs and Dandl, 1978), have recognized its value. There are also many private individuals and 'teams' who offer their services on a commercial basis to companies and to the public. Further development of this kind of education can be predicted in the future.

It is impossible to report generally on staff development in these schools as they vary so widely in their aims and approaches, and efforts are mostly localized within individual institutions. Two broader approaches have been developed at the *Berufsschule* and *Fachhochschule* levels. Firstly, some years ago a very unusual method which could be called 'staff development by regulation' was introduced in the *Berufsschulen*. An official regulation was passed requiring that everyone teaching in this field had to prove 'pedagogical ability', which could be acquired either through special courses or by demonstrating some years of experience on the job. Secondly, most of the *Fachhochschulen* have made one teacher responsible for all questions of teaching; and some

German states have also established centres to be responsible for teaching issues in all *Fachhochschulen* in the state.

Given a concentration on universities, the next limiting factor in the discussion is the distinction between academic and non-academic staff. Section 5.2 is concerned almost exclusively with academic staff. But of course administrative, clerical and technical staff members need development programmes as well. Here too, however, there is no general or systematic concept. Specialized individual courses exist, for the operation of new data processing units for example, but they are all initiated for single and particular practical purposes, and do not follow a general concept.

With respect to academic staff members within universities, three methods of staff development can theoretically be distinguished:

(a) the planning, establishment and definition of posts
(b) the selection and/or placement of candidates and applicants
(c) the 'education' of current staff members in the form of information, training and advice about teaching.

Section 5.2 is devoted to a detailed discussion of (c), but a few remarks should be made about (a) and (b).

(a) There was an almost unbelievable increase in the number of university posts from World War II to the mid-1970s. All German governments allocated large funds for this purpose. Then, with the change in the economic situation, the number of university posts stopped growing, although student numbers were still increasing. As their contribution to solving this problem, the German Assembly of University Presidents decided recently to concede an overload of students, compared with the normal facilities of their universities, for a limited time — namely till the end of the 1980s when it is predicted that student numbers will decline. This means that the issues of economical and effective teaching methods will become still more important in the near future.

This whole development can be ironically interpreted as a very sophisticated programme, including phases of tension and easing, increase and decrease, to keep university staff (and also students) flexible. But to be honest, the conclusion can only be that the specific factors of a systematic planning of university posts, such as teacher:student ratios, the importance of any one discipline for the future, or even coherent ideological aims in regard to university development, can only be taken into account within the limitations of the money available. This main decision is, of course, more related to the economic situation and the political aims, needs, and powers in general than to any other factor.

109

(b) It might be argued that if there is no possibility of staff development through the establishment of new posts, then the alternative is at least to select the right applicants for the posts that do exist. To examine this approach, it might be useful to describe the normal procedure for academic appointment in Germany: an advertisement is placed in the specialist journals, and a university committee, elected by the faculty, ranks the incoming applications, invites a few selected applicants to give a lecture and to be interviewed, and finally prepares a short list, usually of three names. This list has to be approved by the department and/or faculty, and is then sent to the appropriate governmental ministry which usually (though not always) offers the position to the first person on the list. The subsequent negotiations between the ministry and the applicant are successful or not, depending on the applicant's previous position, personal preferences and special requirements. If negotiations break down, the second candidate is approached. It is obvious that this procedure leaves so much room for personal, social, political, and various other pressures to influence the final decision that it can hardly be the most effective way of promoting systematic staff development.

With the discussion narrowed down to staff development by education within universities and for academic staff, it remains to decide which academic staff duties should be considered. These duties can be divided into the three main categories of teaching, administration and research. Teaching will be treated in Section 5.2 and some brief comments about administration and research follow.

*Administration:* It should be surprising (but, on the contrary, it is taken for granted) that an academic career always requires the performance of tasks for which a university education does not provide any preparation. The most striking example is, of course, 'teaching'; but there are also many administrative requirements, such as office organization, correspondence, or handling a budget. Basic skills in using technical equipment may be expected, even to the extent of operating electronic data processing units. Leadership and communication skills may be necessary for working with clerical staff and colleagues, and within committees and boards. It is always when something goes wrong that the importance of these abilities becomes obvious; it is then that people realize that this kind of work can influence the atmosphere and effectiveness of a unit or institution far more than does the purely 'professional' work. Obviously, staff development is very necessary in this area; but it does not occur.

*Research:* Research is seen as the most important role of an academic in Germany; indeed a successful academic career depends far more on research than on, for instance, teaching ability. But research methods are tailored to the individual discipline and are generally integral to its curriculum, so that a general educational programme originating outside the discipline would usually be inappropriate. One problem which might be open to a broader approach is that of the ethical responsibility entailed in research. This is certainly an important question, but it has not yet been the theme of broad discussion in staff development programmes. Another is the attempt to link research more closely with teaching processes: the method known as 'action research' (Moser, 1977a and 1977b) tries this by suggesting that the 'artificial' separation of the 'object and subject of research', and of the 'teacher and student', should be abolished. This is an extreme and highly controversial position; but a related method, 'project study', is less extreme and currently the subject of some interest. Some new universities, for instance Bremen and Kassel, have even tried to establish it as a formal part of their programme (Hering and Hermanns, 1978; Brauner, Hering and Zalfen, 1976). The basic idea of the method is that instead of the usual lectures and seminars, teachers and students agree on a project which they plan, design and carry out together. It is a matter of dispute whether it has proved successful and whether it can be adapted to all phases and all disciplines of university education. If it does become more popular, it will present a challenge for staff development programmes, because it will require special skills and abilities from the university teacher.

## 5.2 Improving university teaching

In this section the improvement of teaching in universities will be discussed. The term 'universities' denotes all institutions at this level, including those which are not actually called 'universities', such as *Technische Hochschulen* (technical universities), *Pädagogische Hochschulen* (universities of teacher education), and so on. Other arguments aside, the need for an improvement of teaching is indicated by the fact that while primary teachers, and to a certain extent secondary teachers as well, have been educated to teach, this is not the case with teachers at the tertiary level. Becoming a university teacher depends much more on research ability, and on some other factors not directly related to pedagogical skills.

It is, of course, true that some people are naturally gifted teachers, but in most cases those with no other source of experience tend, quite understandably, simply to imitate the teaching techniques they themselves experienced as students. This is the main reason why change or improvement in university teaching is so difficult to achieve: the system is a closed and rigid one, which continually reproduces itself. In the absence of strong outside pressures, very few advances can be made. One instance of such external pressure in West Germany was the so-called student revolt of the late 1960s. Although its primary cause was certainly not dissatisfaction with teaching, one of its consequences was that 'teaching methods became a live issue', and a number of units were established to address themselves to it (Spindler, 1968).

The central concept is carried out in the term *Hochschuldidaktik*, and here we encounter a problem of translation. The word-by-word rendition, 'university didactics', is too academically conservative to convey the sense of the German word, while 'methodology of university teaching' is too technocratic, because *Hochschuldidaktik* embraces not only the methodological aspects but also problems of course content, aims, and curricula, and the attempt to establish a theory. The expression *Hochschuldidaktik* will therefore be used below untranslated to refer to this form of staff development.

### 5.2.1 People, centres, associations

PEOPLE

A rather naive approach to the improvement of teaching is the suggestion that problems of teaching should be discussed with a colleague. There is no doubt that this has been and is being done, but by a very small proportion of teachers and in relation to a very small proportion of problems. An impetus from outside is required to stimulate this kind of activity, like the impetus that was generated by the student revolt of the 1960s. In this instance, some of the *Assistenten* (the most junior of the academic staff of universities) aligned themselves with the students, and they were followed by some of the professors, mostly the younger ones. It was an intrinsic feature of that situation that a distinction was drawn not so much between 'experts' and 'clients' as between 'interested' and 'uninterested' persons. A shift occurred when Hochschuldidaktik became, to some extent at least, institutionalized. Having now an opportunity to do this job professionally, those who were deeply committed decided to do it professionally. This is one reason why nowadays the disciplines of those working in this field are wide: former secondary teachers, economists, physicists, psychologists, sociologists, political scientists, and even theologians.

The immediate question in view of this very heterogeneous population is whether Hochschuldidaktik is, or can ever be, an autonomous discipline. Apart from the question of whether the contents and methodology lend themselves to the structure of a single discipline, the present mixture of disciplinary backgrounds in the field certainly does not give an impression of homogeneity or uniformity, and it is unlikely that the immediate future will see the establishment of an autonomous curriculum to produce professional 'Hochschuldidaktiker'. Furthermore, even if this were to happen, it would appear that such 'professionals' would require a double qualification, namely in both Hochschuldidaktik and in the special academic field in which they want to improve teaching. Finally, one must ask whether there are sufficient career opportunities available for those who might wish to pursue this course. At present, it seems that there are not; on the contrary, some have argued that if no further consolidation takes place, talented people will begin to leave the field.

Some of the established centres of Hochschuldidaktik try another approach. They have rotating posts, which means that one of the staff members of a department or faculty can spend one or two years at the *Hochschuldidaktisches Zentrum*, and thus have the opportunity to train in the field through the technique of 'learning by doing'. The problem with this concept, on the face of it a good one, is that not many young academics want to take advantage of the opportunity, because they fear that they will lose contact with their original discipline and with developments within it, and in the present university career structure they cannot expect that any resulting improvement to their teaching will compensate for this loss of time. Moreover, the institutions where Hochschuldidaktik is professionally practised are neither numerous, well equipped nor prestigious, so that there is neither the opportunity nor the incentive for a young university staff member to leave his/her original discipline and remain in Hochschuldidaktik. Staff developers are faced with the irony that their own establishment and development is one of their greatest developmental problems.

CENTRES AND UNITS

It has already been mentioned that at least some centres or units for Hochschuldidaktik have been established. The name given to them is generally *Hochschuldidaktisches Zentrum*. ('HDZ'; word for word, 'Centre for Hochschuldidaktik'; in English-speaking countries they have such titles as Advisory Centre for Tertiary Education, or Centre for the Improvement of Learning and Teaching). But it cannot be claimed that this process of establishment has been steady and undisputed. Although there is much demand for further centres, and some are at the planning stage, there is also a strong tendency to halt this development, and even to abolish some of the existing units. The attitudes of both universities and ministries to this issue have varied widely in the past, and continue to do so. Some have an accurate perception of the real problem of improving university teaching, especially in times when teaching tasks are increasing (see the development mentioned in Section 5.1 concerning a period of 'overload'); others hope or fear that centres of Hochschuldidaktik might gain control of universities and limit their autonomy; a third group is made up of those who look to such units as a basis for a revolutionary change in the whole educational system and are, therefore, according to the individual's ideological standpoint, either strong supporters or powerful opponents.

In addition to these basic questions, there are many associated organizational and bureaucratic problems:

— Should centres/units of this kind be established within a department (preferably the department of education), or as independent centres connected to the administration or directly to the president of the university?

— Referring back to our previous question of whether Hochschuldidaktik can be an academic discipline, is it possible, or even necessary, to create 'chairs' or to appoint 'professors' of Hochschuldidaktik, or should the staff consist of clerical personnel? Related to this is the question of whether such centres should engage primarily in 'service' or 'research' or both? And can you expect a professor to perform a 'service' function? Or can you allow, expect or demand 'research' from a clerical worker?

— Another problem that has been touched on before is that of the teaching duties of the Hochschuldidaktik staff: should teaching be compulsory, optional, or forbidden? If teaching does take place, what should be taught and to whom?

— Finally, how should the tasks of such centres be defined in relation to the work of other 'service' centres, such as audiovisual centres, student counselling and advisory centres, or planning units?

(For discussion of these questions, see Herz, Huber and Walther, 1970; Häberlein and Nieschmidt, 1973; Röhrs, 1973; Behrend and Schürmann, 1974; *Hessischer Kultusminister,* 1977a and 1977b; Heinz, 1977.)

Given these very diverse problems, it is no wonder that all kinds of centres exist today. Holtkamp (1977b) lists 40 of them, though the last official list published showed only 30. But all these figures change very fast: the present Chairman of the German Association for Hochschuldidaktik states that the list of closed centres and centres under threat is almost longer than that of permanent ones. Those engaged in Hochschuldidaktik also fear that a new commission, cited in the *Hochschulrahmengesetz* (Structure of Universities Ordinance) called the *Studienreformkommission* (Commission for Study Reform), which is in the process of being established in all *Länder* (states), might take over some of the main functions of the centre for Hochschuldidaktik (*Kultusministerkonferenz,* 1977, pp 245ff).

As far as the situation of the existing centres is concerned, Holtkamp's report (1977b) gives a good description of it. Although his results are based on the responses of only 19 centres to a questionnaire (and of these one replied simply that it had been closed), one can probably generalize from them as follows:

    1. Most of the existing centres are directly responsible to the

president of the university, and therefore do not belong to a faculty or department. The remainder are located in several faculties, but *none* is in a medical school/faculty.

2. More than half the centres do not have a full complement of tenured staff.

3. Only two of the centres have more than ten posts for academic staff (Hamburg and Frankfurt-am-Main); one has five posts, seven from three to four and seven from one to two.

4. The budgets (excluding salaries) range from over DM 100,000 to less than DM 5000 per annum.

5. Descriptions in official papers of tasks and aims for these centres are sometimes in marked conflict with their resources. For example, a centre with four staff and DM 7720 per year is expected to carry out the following catalogue of tasks (cited from the university statutes):
   - improvement of teaching
   - improvement of in-service education
   - systematic and continuous examination of objectives and curricula
   - observation of teaching and effectiveness of education
   - scientific analysis of the conditions of learning and teaching and of the effectiveness of education
   - systematic testing of new methods of teaching
   - supplying information to teaching staff about practical results of research into teaching.

And all this is supposed to be 'essentially based on existing scientific results'. (See also *Arbeitsgemeinschaft für Hochschuldidaktik*, 1977; Zuber, 1976.)

ASSOCIATIONS

The largest general association for all people interested in the improvement and development of university teaching is the *Arbeitsgemeinschaft für Hochschuldidaktik* (Association for Hochschuldidaktik). This association co-operates with similar associations in other countries, such as the *Österreichische Gesellschaft für Hochschuldidaktik* (Austria), the *Kommission für Studienreform der Schweizerischen Hochschulkonferenz* (Switzerland), the Society for Research into Higher Education (Britain), and the European Association for Research and Development in Higher Education. There are also many informal links with similar organizations elsewhere.

The AHD (*Arbeitsgemeinschaft für Hochschuldidaktik*) was founded in 1967 and financially supported by the *Stiftung Volkswagenwerk* (a foundation of the Volkswagen Company to support research and science). When this support ran out in 1972, the AHD changed its status and became an independent association relying on the membership of individuals and institutions (Ritter and Thieme, 1974). The most recent figures (June 1978) show 150 institutional members, mainly university institutes, libraries, and scientific organizations, and 850 individual members. The structure of the individual membership reflects the history of Hochschuldidaktik in Germany. On the one hand, there are interested university staff members who are looking for some benefit for their own discipline; on the other hand, there are those who became professional Hochschuldidaktik staff in the course of the process described earlier; and the AHD is also open to student members.

In fact, there is a very curious mixture of 'doctors and patients' or of 'consultants and clients', which makes the AHD a combination of scientific association, professional association and, as explained below, publishing company and political pressure group.

Recently an internal discussion has broken out about the proportion of professors within the total membership, and several suggestions have been made about attracting more of them (Thieme, 1977; AHD-Vorstand, 1977; Eckstein, 1978; Klüver, 1978). Underlying this discussion is the question of whether the AHD should promote university reform by political means, or concentrate on practical aspects of the daily work of university staff. It is difficult to say which of these represents the present orientation of the AHD; one group perceives it as too political, the other as too technocratic.

But this basic dichotomy notwithstanding, the AHD has done, and is doing, a great deal of useful work. It concentrates on three main activities (Huber, 1977):

— publications: the AHD edits four series of publications, *Blickpunkt Hochschuldidaktik* (49 issues to September 1978); *Hochschuldidaktische Materialien* (65 issues); *Hochschuldidaktische Forschungsberichte* (6 issues); and *Informationen zür Hochschuldidaktik* (several issues per year)
— conferences and meetings, with themes such as new forms of teaching and learning in daily university life, the relation of study and practice, opening up the universities, etc
— promoting membership, in order to achieve a multiplier effect in the improvement of teaching.

### 5.2.2 'Clients', target groups
Since nobody anticipates the establishment of compulsory teacher education for university staff in the near future, the effort has to be directed towards voluntary motivation. There is, however, evidence to suggest that this is a very complex problem. For instance, if university teachers are asked by a questionnaire whether they think that courses for the improvement of teaching are useful, many of them say that they do (84 per cent in an inquiry by Meyer, Gasch *et al,*

1973). But if they are invited to participate in actual courses, the response is generally very poor (for example, see Scholz in Ritter and Rieck, 1977 — of 185 persons invited, there were six participants in a course). However, other reports indicate that *if* they can be persuaded to take part, they display a very high level of commitment in discussing their own problems and those of others (Metz-Göckel, in Huber, 1978).

It appears to be very difficult to arrive at an explanation which covers all these facts. Studies by Flechsig (1975) and Huber (1978) offer some clues. They suggest, for example, the following reasons why university teachers are reluctant to take Hochschuldidaktik seriously:

*Prejudice against Hochschuldidaktik itself* and against those engaged in it. This prejudice is not in fact without basis. In the earlier days particularly, the radical political opinions associated with Hochschuldidaktik, combined with an incomprehensible professional jargon, could easily be perceived as a threat.

*The amount of work involved.* It takes a considerable personal effort to engage honestly in the improvement of one's own teaching, and some 'clients' might question whether it is worthwhile.

*Lack of positive reward.* Those who do take part in these activities do not benefit in either salary, workload, prestige, or career opportunities, and intrinsic motivation cannot always be relied upon.

*Other priorities.* There has been a big increase in recent years in some university staff duties (for example, administration, committee work, and teaching). In some cases this is a genuine reason for lack of involvement, but in others it provides a welcome excuse.

To turn to those who do concern themselves about the topic (those who, for example, attend courses), Scholz (in Ritter and Rieck, 1977, No 4/78) found that they fall into three categories:

— people who experiment independently and only wish to discuss their own experiences
— people who are genuinely well-disposed and interested, but inexperienced; they accept the limited findings of the research done in this field very gratefully
— people who attend for various external reasons but are rigidly unwilling to accept any suggestions or to change their attitudes.

In addition, there is a fourth type: people who are seeking a simple recipe for solving all teaching problems at once, and for saving time and effort on the part of the teacher as well. When this is not forthcoming, they decide that the whole approach is obviously worthless.

To look at the 'clientele' from another perspective, it is generally agreed

117

that support comes from the middle and lower levels of university staff (*Assistenten*), rather than from the level of full professor. With respect to individual disciplines, Holtkamp's study (1977b) gives a rank order of the departments/faculties with which the centres surveyed were working. Economics, natural sciences, and teacher education headed the list.

A further target group which is of interest, although some people doubt whether they should be classified as academic staff, consists of the tutors. Tutoring programmes vary from university to university (and from department to department) in their extent, their objectives, and their quality. But they should be mentioned here because some universities or departments have introduced quite efficient training courses for their tutors, including not only information about subject matter but also the development of basic psychological skills in handling groups or individual students (Behrend, 1969; Ritter and Diepold, 1975; Götz-Marchand and Götz, 1976; *Marburger Autorenkollectiv*, 1977; Leuthold, Zechlin *et al*, 1977). A study of some of these attempts to educate tutors to teach can sometimes convey the surprising (or not so surprising) impression that these tutors are better prepared for their teaching tasks than are the 'real' academics.

Finally, one of the most important target groups consists of the students. If university education is a communication process, then the improvement of teaching is only half the story — the other half is the improvement of learning. The techniques of teaching and of learning should complement each other to improve the whole process, and with this end in view some Hochschuldidaktik staff offer, for example, courses for students in learning and studying techniques. Some universities have separate centres for this purpose, and here there is a need for a high degree of co-operation between the two sides of the enterprise. Students are also important in another respect — as very necessary subjects of almost all research done in the field of Hochschuldidaktik. Most centres therefore try to maintain good relations with the students and to involve them in their work as far as possible.

### 5.2.3 Aims, content, projects
It is also clear from the foregoing that there is no straightforward answer to the question of what Hochschuldidaktik should aim for, or what the content of this 'semi-academic' discipline should be. In theory, it is true, the problem could be solved by research. For instance, it would be possible to investigate the desires and expectations of the different groups involved, such as 'the clients', 'the students' or 'the educational experts'. Another possible approach, common in the field of industrial psychology, would be the analysis of 'under-achievers' (in

this case, recognized bad university teachers), 'over-achievers' (recognized good teachers), and 'critical incidents' (problem situations in university teaching) (see Schott, 1973). But the actual development of a discipline rarely conforms to a previous pattern, so it is necessary to approach the aims and content of Hochschuldidaktik from another angle.

There have, of course, been various papers setting out how (in the opinions of the editors at least) we should proceed. Of these, the best-known are the *'Wieckenberger Thesen'* (AHD-Thesen, 1973), reproduced in English translation on pp 259-63. But as these statements might be criticized as reflecting a past situation, we refer here to a more recent paper of the AHD (1977, p 21) which says that Hochschuldidaktik has the task of

> research-based work on teaching, learning and assessment in universities. Hochschuldidaktik therefore links educational research with scientifically based study reform. Hochschuldidaktik thus includes:
> - research-based investigation, criticism and reform of study goals and content according to the criteria of academic, social, and professional relevance
> - analysis and development of methods of teaching, learning and examining: within these, methods of learning by research and project studies are of particular importance
> - collection, interpretation and evaluation of proposed teaching reforms, as well as initiation, support and assistance with experiments in teaching reform
> - advising teachers and students, and in-service education of teachers and tutors.
>
> *(Author's translation)*

It is impossible to say to what extent a statement like this will influence everyday practice; but before looking at what is actually happening, further discussion is needed of another problem which has already been touched on briefly: whether Hochschuldidaktik can or should be an academic discipline in its own right. This is a very difficult and delicate question, because it entails not only the definition of a philosophy of research and its criteria, but also various other problems of terminology, legal regulations, and political feasibility; even personal privileges and subjective hopes and fears enter into it. Moreover, it is usually difficult, even impossible, to distinguish the basis of argumentation. Even within the AHD there are differences of opinion: thus Klüver (the present chairman) recently wrote that 'Hochschuldidaktik is perhaps a professional occupation, but by no means an autonomous academic discipline' (Klüver, 1978, p 82; author's translation), whereas his predecessors in 1977 had said that 'Hochschuldidaktik too, like every other discipline, requires research which concentrates on the basic elements of teaching and learning in the university' (AHD, 1977, p 21; author's translation). These two statements are not necessarily totally contradictory, but they do indicate the complexity of the problem.

It is relevant at this point to note that the largest German research foundation *(Deutsche Forschungsgemeinschaft)* has supported several research projects in the field, carried out by both scholars in particular disciplines and professional staff of centres for Hochschuldidaktik; this suggests that the foundation finds no difficulty in recognizing Hochschuldidaktik as an academic discipline *(Senatskommission,* 1976).

Clearly the focus of discussion should be not whether staff development through Hochschuldidaktik should be based on research or not, but whether this research should be carried out by those who develop the resulting educational programmes. But who will do it if these people do not?

Leaving this question unanswered, we should look at what actually happens which is, of course, education *and* research: indeed, it is sometimes hard to draw the distinction. The following account is based on the author's subjective experience of six years of professional work in the field, and on three more or less 'empirical' studies: a survey by the *Deutsche Forschungsgemeinschaft (Senatskommission,* 1976), a study by Brandt (1978) of themes and topics for courses for the education of university teachers, and the Holtkamp survey (1977b) of the objectives and resources of advisory centres for tertiary education. According to these sources the main fields of work are:

*The psychology of learning and teaching at university level:* This is a natural area of interest. There are, however, many problems arising from the fact that most findings in, for example, the psychology of learning are based on laboratory experiments, and are hard to transfer to real-life situations (see Schott, 1973; Gasch and Schick, 1975). (The publications quoted in the following are offered only as examples, and do not represent a complete survey of the literature.) A special problem that some authors have focused on is that of student motivation (Heckhausen, 1970; Herz, Reif and Sader, 1972), but they have, of course, the same problems as in the psychology of learning.

*Curriculum theory and research:* Again, this is an obvious field of interest (Quitzow, 1973). But as it is closely related to the specific disciplines, it can only be carried out in co-operation with experts in these disciplines (Flechsig, 1974).

*Teaching methods and media:* This very broad heading covers various sub-themes, ranging from the preparation of slides (Meyer-Hartwig *et al,* 1975), the preparation of written materials (Gasch, 1974; Mattl, 1973), programmed and/or computer-assisted instruction (Georgi, 1977), audiovisuals (Hoffman and Eickhoff, 1977), case studies (Grochla and Thom, 1975), to simulation games (Friedrich and Tschersig, 1978), project studies (Hering and Hermanns, 1978), and self-directed learning systems such as the Keller Plan.

*Small-group teaching:* Several approaches have been taken to small-group teaching. As well as accounts of applying theoretical findings in group psychology, some universities have developed courses in sensitivity training, group dynamics, and T-grouping (Scholz, 1975; Vopel, 1972). In this area the distinctions between content, aim, and method are naturally fluid.

*Socialization and performance of students:* Besides overall reviews which treat the topic in a more general way (Bargel, Framheim *et al*, 1975; Bargel and Bürmann, 1977; Schmid, 1976), this topic includes studies of the transition from school to university (Schott and Schott, 1975; Klüver and Schmidt, 1977; Rauch, 1978), as well as rates and causes of student attrition (Selle, 1977), and career performance after graduation.

*Examinations:* This is a permanent issue for discussion. The AHD mounted its own research programme on examinations (Prahl, 1976), and some informal groups are working on the various functions of examinations (Daxner, 1978). Some universities also offer courses for examiners and students on appropriate examination preparation and behaviour (Ritter, 1977).

*Evaluation:* The term evaluation covers a wide range of activities, from the application of standardized questionnaires about the performance of individual lecturers to the investigation of curricula, faculties, and even complete educational systems. The importance of evaluation becomes obvious if one takes into consideration that there are not less than 71 officially acknowledged and financially supported models and experiments in education currently running in the Federal Republic of Germany (Modellversuche, 1978). Clearly, however, the question of whether an evaluation is carried out at all and if so, who should do it, and whether it is thought of as a task of Hochschuldidaktik, requires special investigation.

*Tasks of the future:* Some trends are emerging which will affect university teaching in the future, and will therefore come within the province of staff development. One of these is the projected decrease in student numbers in the 1990s. This could result in a swing in university teaching towards part-time students, in-service education, and non-degree courses, which would in turn require specialized teaching abilities. A related development, which is equally relevant to the present student population, is the trend towards individualized, or at least group-specific, modes of instruction. Principles of fitting the right teacher to the right student must be developed. Finally — and this is a favourite hobby-horse of mine — university teaching could and should move towards the encouragement of divergent and creative thinking, independent of any one discipline. This is a task for which very few of today's teachers are prepared.

### 5.2.4 Strategies, methodology

As far as broad strategies of Hochschuldidaktik are concerned several styles can be distinguished, but nearly all of them can be located on a spectrum ranging from controversial/fighting/revolutionary at one extreme to co-operative/yielding/reformative on the other. There is, of course, no blanket solution to this fundamental polarity, which has already been outlined in the section dealing with associations; nor can one strategy alone be recommended. The question probably depends less on Hochschuldidaktik itself than on the personalities of those involved. It is likely that success can be achieved using approaches both at the extremes of the range and at all intermediate points. Generalized application of one strategy, which was successful under particular circumstances, to all other situations is the only danger.

The more specific methodology of Hochschuldidaktik (apart from the research methods which are excluded for the reasons cited above) employs three main approaches: information by printed material, courses and seminars, and personal consultations.

PRINTED MATERIAL

This is not the most important method, because it depends on whether the individual 'client' makes the effort to find, select and read the relevant papers; and even if he does make the effort, there is no guarantee that he will modify his behaviour or attitudes. Moreover, there is no official or broadly distributed publication series or journal for Hochschuldidaktik in Germany. Plans for a journal have been discussed for some years, but publication has been postponed each year for financial reasons, and as yet no commercial publishing company has ventured into the field. Thus the AHD publications already mentioned, although not originally designed for broader educational purposes, have become the most relevant literature. Apart from these, there are very few 'real' books, only various kinds of informal papers (institutional reports and the like) which go by the rather apposite title of grey literature. This type of literature, however, is circulated only to 'insiders'.

COURSES AND SEMINARS

These are the most important methods today. However, they too have their problems, beginning with the procedure for inviting people to attend. A circular, for instance, appears to be a good deal less successful than a personal invitation or a personally addressed letter.

General experience suggests that the number of participants in these courses should not exceed 25 (Brandt, 1978). (For some courses, however, to attract even half that number represents an achievement.) Bürmann (1978) reports the feeling of a number of people who run such courses that a compact form is best, lasting from two to five days, and preferably held off campus, for instance in a well-equipped country hotel, which should have some recreation facilities to promote a stress-free environment. Of course, the question of cost arises in this case; but this is not as important as one might suppose because universities and other official organizations are frequently more willing to support single enterprises than to provide funds for Hochschuldidaktik in general. Furthermore, the participants are often willing to pay a fee on the basis of the unstated assumption that what costs nothing is worth nothing. No answer has been found to the question of whether participants should come from the same discipline or a group of disciplines, or whether a heterogeneous combination is preferable. There are advantages and disadvantages either way.

With respect to the methodology of the courses themselves, the organizers are naturally under a moral obligation to follow their own precepts. Consequently, in almost all cases, they start with a discussion of the aims and objectives of the course, and then adapt various kinds of instructional and training methods and audiovisual and media techniques (simulation games, case studies, written summaries, change from plenary to small-group work, etc). The basic principle is constant change of phase from information to training to application (Brandt, 1978).

A special type of course is that which deals with group dynamics, sensitivity training, communication training and the like. (At the moment the method of R Cohn, 1974 and 1976, seems to be gaining popularity.) A few years ago, this method (or content?) was thought by some people to be a wide-spectrum antibiotic for all diseases of university teaching. Today, however, attitudes are more realistic, and people seem better able to judge where the undoubted value of the method lies and where it does not.

CONSULTATIONS

One method of consultation, which could be mentioned also under 'courses', is microteaching, and some universities have made efforts to make it a more or less regular feature of their institutions. Given enough time and genuine interest on both sides, it is probably one of the most effective methods of improving teacher performance.

Other kinds of consultation or counselling are probably employed quite often, either with individuals or with groups; but it is very difficult to reach general conclusions about their degree of success, because the specific circumstances strongly influence content, style and outcome. It may be only an instinctive judgement, and one not susceptible of proof, but here, especially in these one-to-one situations, a lot of useful work is done which understandably does not become public knowledge. Consultation with groups and committees becomes more difficult the more official they are, and its effectiveness seems to depend more on whether the group acknowledges and respects the adviser as a person than on the force, accuracy or brilliance of his arguments. In this context, Hochschuldidaktik appears to be more an emotional and social activity than an argumentative and logical one.

## 5.3 Conclusion

The final answer to whether staff development in higher education is successful in the Federal Republic of Germany is both yes and no. As a glass of water can be perceived as half-empty or half-full, any conclusion of this kind depends on your subjective standpoint. You can of course argue that teaching has increasingly become a topic for discussion, and that this could be seen as a success; on the other hand, the effect in terms of an overall improvement of teaching certainly remains unsatisfactory. As to the people engaged in Hochschuldidaktik, they display an admirably high level of activity and commitment. But the criticism can also be made that this takes place mainly within a closed circle who publish for each other, read each other and communicate with each other, thus counterfeiting a success based only on their own internal activities.

The glass of Hochschuldidaktik is neither half-full nor half-empty; the only permissible statement is 'between empty and full'. The potential exists for the evaluation of effective and widely adopted methods of staff improvement, but the process is only in its initial stage and the rate of progress cannot be predicted.

*Acknowledgements*
The author finished this chapter during a visiting fellowship at the Office for Research in Academic Methods, Australian National University, Canberra.
I should like to express my thanks especially to Janet Healey, who was a great help in formulating the final English version, to Allen Miller for his useful advice and to Joan Rowe for typing.

# 6: The German Democratic Republic — staff development in a socialist setting

Horst Möhle

## 6.0 Introduction

The main task of the German Democratic Republic (GDR) is to ensure that 'the country's material and cultural standard of living is improved on the basis of a fast rate of development in socialist production, greater efficiency, scientific and technological progress and increased productivity' (Programme of the Socialist Unity Party of Germany [SED], 1976). The fulfilment of this task is of decisive importance for the continuation of the GDR's socialist revolution and the further evolution of its developed socialist society. In this connection, the main emphasis is being placed on the acceleration of scientific and technological progress. The GDR's institutes of higher education have a particular contribution to make in research and in the training of highly qualified graduates.

The task higher education has been set serves humanist ideals as well as furthering progress, and its successful fulfilment is influenced by the work of academic personnel, both junior staff members (*wissenschaftliche Mitarbeiter*) and senior faculty members (*Hochschullehrer*). At the beginning of the academic year 1978-79, Professor H -J Böhme, Minister for Higher Education in the GDR, stressed this very point: 'Greater achievements in the sphere of higher education depend above all else on the political stance of the academic staff, their knowledge and abilities in their specialist disciplines and in the field of Marxism-Leninism, their pedagogical skill and their social commitment' (Böhme, 1978).

For this reason the main foci of our investigations are as follows:

1. The demands made on staff establishment and development as a result of social, scientific and political developments.
2. The corresponding qualifications of the teaching staff with regard to politics, ideology, specialist disciplines, university pedagogics and management techniques.
3. The main stages of a planned, long-term qualification process.
4. The purposeful planning and management of staff development.

125

The solution of this task is complex and for want of space this chapter will deal only with its basic aspects.

## 6.1 The demands made on academic staff resulting from social, scientific and political developments

As early as the beginning of the 1950s when the basis for socialism was being laid in the GDR, scholars and university educators were set important tasks. The higher education system of the GDR, which at first comprised only eight traditional universities and colleges, was expanded considerably. There are now 53 state institutes of higher education including seven universities, 18 technical colleges, three medical academies, ten teacher-training colleges and ten schools for the arts. (There are no private educational establishments in the GDR.) This development paved the way in the first instance for a quantitative increase in academic capacity. In 1976 there were 31,832 academic members of staff at the 53 higher education institutes of the GDR, which represents an improvement in the staff : student ratio to a figure of 1 : 4 (UNESCO-CEPES, 1978).

The academic staff structure has been modified as part of our 1968 higher education reform. In accordance with the Regulations concerning the Appointment of Faculty Members of 6 November 1968 (Official Gazette of the GDR, Part II, 1968), the staff consists primarily of the *Hochschullehrer,* ie ordinary, extraordinary and honorary professors and university and honorary lecturers. Ordinary professors hold a chair, whereas extraordinary professors are senior faculty members who are appointed to a professorship in recognition of their teaching and research work, but for whom no chair is made available. University lecturers *(Hochschuldozenten)* hold a lectureship. Honorary professors and lecturers do university teaching as a subsidiary appointment in addition to their normal professional work.

Also included as part of the academic personnel are the *wissenschaftliche Mitarbeiter,* junior staff members involved principally in teaching. The Regulations concerning University Staff *(Mitarbeiterverordnung)* of 6 November 1968 (Official Gazette of the GDR, Part II, 1968) place in this category assistants on fixed length and permanent contracts, senior assistants, lectors *(Lektoren,* generally holding a doctor's degree) and teachers with a university appointment *(Lehrer im Hochschuldienst).* Assistants on permanent contract to a university or college are recruited from among those assistants with a contract limited to four years. This system ensures that new, capable blood is constantly being added to the staff. Permanent assistants have normally obtained the degree of Doctor of an Academic Discipline *(Doktor eines Wissenschaftszweiges),* known as Promotion A, which is the second academic grade after the bachelor's degree (Official Gazette of the

GDR, Part II, 1969). As distinct from senior assistants, who teach and do research, lectors are primarily involved in post-experience higher education. Teachers with a university appointment normally have a heavy load of seminars and other classes (20 hours a week) which they give under the supervision of a senior faculty member.

The IX Party Conference of the Socialist Unity Party of Germany (SED), the leading social force in the GDR, provided a new orientation for higher education. Because of growing social needs in the sphere of higher education, it was decided that the time was ripe to call for greater achievements from an academic corps now numerically strong. This orientation is rightly appreciated as being of strategic importance for the academic world.

New and more rigorous academic standards demand better quality staff at all levels in the academic structure. Senior faculty members must delve more deeply into the inter-reactions between politics, economics, science, technology and culture and develop an overall view of the role that their particular academic disciplines play in the acceleration of scientific and technological progress. This enables senior faculty staff to function effectively as teachers and to relate their research activities to the imperatives of social progress. The findings of Marxism-Leninism form the methodological basis for the senior faculty member's academic work and determine his/her standpoint when confronted with ideas that represent obstacles to progress. At the same time, knowledge of Marxism-Leninism enables him/her to answer students' political and ideological questions in a positive, sound and convincing manner.

As the advanced socialist society in the GDR evolves still further, the general demands on the creativity of all working people increase accordingly. This particularly applies to the creative talents of scholars. Thus it is logical to concentrate on increasing the creativity of students, young academics and the whole teaching staff. In this respect, the standard of the third academic grade, Doctor of Sciences (*Doktor der Wissenschaften,* referred to as Promotion B), which is the qualification required for appointment as senior faculty member, has been raised again (Official Gazette of the GDR, Part II, 1969). The aim is to make scientific discoveries and to evaluate them with precision. Promotion B candidates strive to produce top-class work on a par with research anywhere else in the world. Their doctoral theses ought to represent an original contribution to scientific, technological and social progress. In this respect, the ability to do inter-disciplinary work and to co-operate in international research projects is an important factor.

Members of staff are expected to keep themselves fully informed of the latest developments in their respective disciplines by studying foreign journals and taking an active part in international academic life. For this reason, Promotion B candidates must satisfy the examiners that they have an active command of two foreign languages. To this end, arrangements are made for them to study abroad for at least five months, usually in another socialist country.

Equal importance is attached to acquiring a masterly understanding of the progression — basic research, applied research, putting the results of the research into practice and adapting them to the production process. Hence we set more and more value on Promotion B graduates gaining at least one year's practical experience of production immediately after their studies, so that they become aware of society's needs in their particular branch of learning. In this way, they learn how to detect practical problems, how to formulate them scientifically, and how to solve them to the best of their ability. This practical training also encourages co-operation between university scientists and the working people involved in the production process, which is an important precondition for arriving at new scientific findings and putting them into practice.

The task of our universities and colleges is to educate and train highly qualified socialist cadres. Clearly there is a need for senior faculty staff with teaching ability to fulfil this task. To obtain the teaching qualification, the *facultas docendi,* they must demonstrate their ability in a practical teaching examination and a colloquium. In particular, they must show that they can make creative use of both schemes of study and syllabuses, using their knowledge of university pedagogics and psychology as a foundation. It is worth stressing at this point that these training dossiers, which have been prepared in the past few years by groups of leading academics, form the basis for the successful shaping of the teaching and study process throughout the higher education system. They have proved their worth, but in the final analysis successful teaching depends on the overall qualifications of the teacher. His/her fundamental task is to teach students how to do responsible, original and creative work.

Finally, in accordance with the development of scientific work, we now set more store by the need for senior faculty members to learn how to lead teams of specialists, because not only does research work call for co-operation among experts, but also teaching makes collective preparation and widespread agreement necessary. Senior staff must demonstrate their proficiency in group management skills as part of Promotion B.

Under the conditions of the socialist order, we see that social requirements harmonize more and more with the personal interests of university staff. This is because the aim of academic work in socialism is to serve social progress.

Seen in this context, the requirement that university staff should be highly qualified becomes a genuine challenge to their sense of responsibility and an incentive to them in their pursuit of further knowledge. They are aware of the complicated tasks they have been set and are striving to complete them.

This need for all academic personnel, especially professors and lecturers, to have ever better qualifications inevitably has consequences for the training of capable young members of staff. Gifted and talented young scholars must be recognized at an early stage and encouraged. One of the specific duties of every senior faculty member is to pick out those students from the first year onwards who have a particular aptitude for academic work and systematically to develop their abilities.

As for the training of junior academic staff, the emphasis is placed on a broad, scientifically grounded education. In this way, versatility is guaranteed. The qualification process focuses on certain important themes and these will be discussed in the next section (6.2). The separate stages of this long-term, planned training programme will be described in Section 6.3.

Because the average age for appointment as senior faculty member is at present too high, there is a need to compress various stages and elements of the qualification process or else combine them intelligently. For instance, further training in foreign languages can be concentrated to good effect in intensive courses. Or the dissertation can be written during the spell of practical training or the period of study abroad. By departing from the customary sequence in this way, time is saved. Thus, although higher qualifications are asked for, the training programme can be speeded up.

## 6.2 Staff qualifications in politics, ideology, specialist disciplines, university pedagogics and group management

The education and training of academic staff concentrates on important socio-political and specialist themes as well as dealing with university pedagogics and methodology and group management. Whatever the subject, theory is never separated from practice. Training in each case involves study of the principal contents of the subject, an organizational and methodological approach to it and consideration of the specific needs of the trainees.

### 6.2.1 Socio-political qualifications
Staff training in social sciences is a continuation of the social sciences foundation course all university and college graduates have taken. The full training programme consists of several stages, the most important

of which are at the level of the doctorands' seminar *(Doktorandenseminar)* and the Marxist-Leninist Evening School.

The doctorands' seminar serves to widen and deepen the participants' knowledge of social sciences. The doctoral candidates, who are preparing their Promotion A degree, study important theoretical questions from philosophy, political economy, scientific communism and the history of the workers' movement, with emphasis on the dialectical links between them. The studies are related to the candidates' academic disciplines and their teaching and research work. For this reason, seminars are organized on a departmental basis. The key element in the seminars is the doctorands' private study. They present papers or lead discussions. Candidates who have not presented a seminar paper must take a final examination, the results of which count towards the degree.

The knowledge which the doctorands acquire is used particularly in their work as assistants or as academic supervisors to their students and is also useful when they conduct seminars.

In the mid-1960s, the Marxist-Leninist Evening School was founded at universities and colleges in the GDR. It serves to provide both junior and senior academic staff with in-service training in the social sciences. This institution thus meets the needs of senior faculty members for deeper socio-political knowledge. Lectures on selected, topical themes from philosophy, political economy and scientific communism are given, either by specialists who are active in these fields or by representatives of our State. Lively discussions follow. Other debates may centre on fundamental decisions taken by the SED or on laws and ordinances which concern higher education. The course, which lasts for more than a year, includes several week-long intensive courses for which the participants prepare by studying selected literature. During these intensive courses, visits to leading industrial and agricultural enterprises are organized. Participants are particularly interested to learn how new socio-scientific findings can be applied to their own teaching and research work.

In this way, the social and academic activities of the course participants are furthered and the socio-scientific foundation of their work as leaders of teaching and research teams is laid.

### 6.2.2 Specialist qualifications

The attainment of qualifications in specialist fields serves social requirements at the same time as satisfying the individual academic's thirst for knowledge. Each university or college graduate has already demonstrated his ability to do independent academic work at the time of preparing his first degree dissertation *(Diplomarbeit)*. The participation of each member of staff in the main field of research of his university or institute of higher education, his department or his sub-department also serves to increase his specialist knowledge.

It is true to say that the greater the theoretical demands of the research subject (which should be of social and practical significance) and the more ambitious the researchers, the more considerable is the increase in creative academic capacity. Participation in research projects also trains academics for collective, inter-disciplinary work. This may involve links with outside firms and co-operation on an international level.

Participation in collective research work is normally combined with individual preparation for the Promotion A and B degrees. In this respect, it is important to see exactly how the work of each doctoral candidate contributes to the main research programme.

Since there is this connection between team research and individual postgraduate work, the content and schedule of the research programme dictates to a large extent the nature of the doctorand's specialist qualifications and the length of time it will take him to obtain them. The doctorand can complement his research work by attending departmental colloquia and academic conferences as well as by completing examinable or non-examinable courses of postgraduate study. The main aim of these postgraduate studies is to acquire additional knowledge and skills which will be needed to solve research problems.

Building on this basis, junior staff members go on to participate in academic life. Particular emphasis is placed on personal contributions to colloquia and conferences, but supervision of academic student circles and conferences is also a source of useful experience.

The acquisition of specialist qualifications ensures above all else that there will be a continual increase in teaching and study standards.

### 6.2.3 Qualifications in university pedagogics and methodology

Because the main task of universities and other institutes of higher education is to prepare qualified socialist graduates, the main concern of academic staff is for higher educational standards and greater efficiency. In this respect, training in university pedagogics is an indispensable prerequisite for the staff. In the light of the increasing importance of pedagogical training, it would be appropriate at this point to discuss it in some detail.

The training course in university pedagogics will be introduced in the academic year 1979-80. Using the results of nearly 20 years of extensive research and development, it will consist of two integrated stages supplemented by additional special classes. The first stage is a course entitled 'Introduction to University Pedagogics'. This is followed by postgraduate or postdoctoral study of the subject.

The introductory course is intended for junior members of staff at the beginning of their teaching career who have received no previous training in pedagogics. The aims of the course are:

☐ to impart a minimum of basic teaching knowledge of such quality and in such quantity as to meet the present and future professional needs of the member of staff (with particular reference to the specific needs of the assistant) and

☐ to impart a basic stock of pedagogical knowledge and skills which the course participants can use as a foundation for further private study after the course and which will also serve as a basis for later postgraduate studies.

The specific educational tasks of the assistants consist of:

☐ preparing, giving and evaluating classes such as seminars, exercises and laboratory practicals. Although under the supervision of a senior faculty member, the assistants organize their classes largely on their own initiative on the basis of pre-established schemes of study and syllabuses

☐ training the students to work scientifically on their own initiative and

☐ performing special educational functions, such as acting as academic supervisor to seminar groups.

In line with the assistants' needs, the introductory course concentrates on major themes. A total of 36 hours is available to deal with the following topics:

☐ the nature of the pedagogical process in higher education
☐ the aim and manner of educating students and developing their personalities
☐ the educational work of academic staff
☐ the work of the seminar group adviser and tasks relating to the development of socialist student collectives
☐ educational work with first-year students
☐ some basic views on the teaching and study process
☐ the planning and preparation of classes
☐ conducting seminars, exercises and practicals
☐ the use of teaching and study materials and
☐ conducting assessments of university and college students.

It is hoped that the choice of course topics will arouse the interest of the participants in teaching problems at higher education level. The particular aim of the course is to make participants appreciate the importance of a sound theoretical basis for practical teaching work. A further objective is to pass on concrete recommendations on the shaping of the teaching and study process.

The course takes the form of lectures followed by seminars. Although the participants have only limited teaching experience, they should be made to take an active part in the seminars. Private study of selected literature is stimulated, with emphasis placed on *An Introduction to University Pedagogics (Einführung in die Hochschulpädagogik)* (Autorenkollektiv, 1977) and articles in the magazine *Higher Education (Das Hochschulwesen)* with its supplement *University Pedagogics in Theory and Practice (Aus Theorie und Praxis der Hochschulpädagogik)*. Course participants listen to talks which serve as a starting point for an exchange of views based on their own teaching experience. In order to gain more experience, they sit in on classes in their own discipline given by senior faculty members. They also prepare a written lecture which they deliver in the presence of a senior member of staff and which is then evaluated. Participants who complete the course successfully are awarded a certificate.

The second stage of the training programme in university pedagogics comprises postgraduate or postdoctoral study of the subject. It is designed for members of staff who have already taken the introductory course and have had several years' teaching experience. Most of the second stage participants are working towards their teaching qualification, the *facultas docendi*.

Hence the aim of the postgraduate studies is to deepen, complement and extend in a systematic way the knowledge and skills which were acquired during the introductory course and which have been enriched by considerable teaching experience.

The course should enable the participants to carry out their tasks of educating and training socialist graduates at a high standard and with optimum efficiency. This means imparting to the participants in the course pedagogically substantiated theoretical views as well as tried and tested practical recommendations that are relevant to:

- ☐ promoting the development of the student's personality
- ☐ teaching, especially delivering lectures
- ☐ stimulating and helping the students to do creative academic work on their own initiative as well as associating them with research projects and
- ☐ guiding the students in the practical application of academic knowledge.

This planned in-service training course ought to encourage members of staff to study by themselves the latest findings in the field of university pedagogics and to share with other academics the knowledge they have gained as a result of their teaching experience.

The postgraduate or postdoctoral study of university pedagogics is organized according to an integrated, five-part timetable with a total of 124 hours of lectures and seminars:

- ☐ the fundamentals of university pedagogics (eight hours)
- ☐ the application of psychological findings to higher education (30 hours)
- ☐ pedagogical findings regarding the development of socialist personalities (16 hours)
- ☐ didactical findings regarding the shaping of the teaching and study process in higher education (40 hours) and
- ☐ the study of methods of teaching special subjects at university and college level (30 hours).

Without going into details, it should be noted that importance is attached to laying a psychological foundation for the educational process and that specialist course content, pedagogical principles and subject methodology are studied, with emphasis on the dialectical links between them. Our constant aim is to present the theory of university pedagogics, psychology and methodology in close relation to the practice of teaching and training in higher education.

From a didactical point of view, the demands of the postgraduate course on course lecturers, that is to say university and college pedagogues, are great. They must continually consider, for example, the theoretical level and the effectiveness of the classes, as well as the applicability of the subject matter.

The course, which is organized as a series of classes, consists primarily of lectures and seminars combined with exercises and attendance at lectures given by senior faculty members. The course teachers rely on private study and the practical experience of the participants as well as their active involvement. Hence the basic format of the seminars is a talk given by one of the course participants followed by discussion and exchange of views. Participants also sit in on classes given by successful lecturers as well as on one another's classes. Another useful teaching technique is to make a video-recording of a lecture and evaluate it in a group discussion afterwards.

For the methodological part of the course, participants from related disciplines must be grouped together. The classes are held by university teachers in collaboration with experienced lecturers of the corresponding university departments who are qualified in university pedagogics.

At the end of the course there is a three-part examination. Firstly, there is a complex oral examination to test the candidate's knowledge of basic university pedagogics and the theory of education. Then, in a practical teaching examination, he must demonstrate that he can apply the knowledge and skills he has acquired. The third part of the examination is an essay related to the candidate's teaching work.

Successful candidates are awarded a certificate. The second and third parts of the examination are the requirements for the award of the teaching qualification, the *facultas docendi.*

### 6.2.4 Qualifications in group management

In connection with the implementation of our principle that scholarly inquiry and education should be approached in a scientific manner, we attach great importance to staff members receiving instruction in management techniques. So, for example, candidates for the Promotion B degree must demonstrate that they can lead teams of academics.

Academic staff receive their management training principally at conferences and residential courses. For instance, the Ministry of Higher Education organizes a conference at the beginning of each academic year for university and college rectors on the management and planning aspects of the main tasks in the areas of education, research and staff development.

In addition, special courses on questions of academic policy are held at the Ministry's in-service training centre for senior staff at Merseburg. These courses, which last for four weeks, are attended by rectors, prorectors, administrative directors and heads of department as well as their deputies. They focus principally on issues related to the guidance of the main higher education processes, such as education, research and staff development. Course lecturers include leading State and university officials and senior faculty members.

Involvement in the guidance process at universities and colleges ensures that senior staff also gain management experience in the field.

## 6.3 The main stages of planned staff development

There are several main stages in the planned development of university and college staff. The first stages cover the recruitment of graduates to the staff. The next stages serve to prepare junior academics for their appointment as senior faculty members, and in the final phase senior staff undergo periods of in-service training.

### 6.3.1 The selection and advancement of 'best students'

The selection and promotion of the most socially active and academically outstanding students, called 'best students', is of decisive importance for the development of a qualified teaching staff. The main task is to pick out at an early stage those students with exceptional gifts and talents who are eager and able to achieve notable results. The main responsibility for talent spotting falls on the shoulders of academic personnel, both senior faculty members and junior scholars. Particular attention is paid to women and candidates from the working and peasant classes.

'Best students' are selected at the end of the first year or at the beginning of the second; at that point they may begin to work according to individual plans of study at a level which is higher than that foreseen in the prescribed training dossiers. In training 'best students', we follow the principle of active encouragement in return for substantial achievements; in other words, the best students are set exacting tasks but receive our support in carrying them out. Hence we encourage the best students to join in scholarly debates and motivate them to produce excellent results in their academic work. This applies both to their regular studies (in particular annual course work, practical training and degree theses) and to their optional participation in academic student circles and conferences and in student rationalization and construction groups. When working on socially and academically important problems and tasks, 'best students' should be constantly trying to develop their ability to work creatively on their own initiative — perhaps by presenting seminar papers and contributing to academic discussions, or perhaps by tackling difficult scientific tasks in conjunction with outside firms. 'Best students' often display their work at local and national exhibitions, where they may receive awards and prizes in recognition of their special achievements.

'Best students' may also be taken on as auxiliary assistants to help with teaching and research work. We also think it important for best students to gain management experience by leading small student collectives in social and academic activities.

We take care to ensure that the advancement of outstanding students is always combined with the work of the rest of the class. On the one hand, this policy has a positive influence on the general progress of student collectives; and on the other hand, co-operation between staff and students is the basis for the selection and swift development of the most able students.

### 6.3.2 The development of research students
The Ordinance concerning Research Studies (*Anordnung über das Forschungsstudium*) (Official Gazette of the GDR, Part II, 1970) introduced research studies for graduates of institutes of higher education. The studies are designed to train capable young scholars swiftly and rationally to Promotion A standard within three years.

Research students normally concentrate on their department's main fields of research but are also expected to prepare for their later teaching career. To prove their academic ability, they have to write a dissertation. It must be an original piece of work which adds to society's stock of knowledge and it has to be defended in public. Additionally, they must demonstrate their knowledge of foreign languages and satisfy the examiners that they have deepened their knowledge of Marxism-Leninism. They are also expected to work actively for society, normally within the framework of the youth organization. Research students receive a grant of 500 marks per month as well as an annual book allowance.

After they have obtained the degree of Doctor of an academic discipline, junior academics may be kept on as permanent assistants.

### 6.3.3 Further education for assistants within the framework of Promotions A and B

Preparation for the Promotion A degree can also proceed on planned lines in the course of a four-year assistantship. The principal duties of an assistant are to conduct seminars, exercises and laboratory practicals. They also act as advisers to seminar groups. A proper foundation for this, the assistant's first teaching work, is provided by the introductory course in university pedagogics (Section 6.2.3).

Assistants also take part in research work, primarily basic research on important subjects, but also applied research where they are involved in putting the results of research projects into practice. In this connection, it is important to see research training as part of the overall process of becoming qualified and to integrate it as far as possible with the preparatory work for Promotion A.

Towards the end of their Promotion A studies, assistants may be relieved of most of their teaching duties in order to concentrate on research and other work necessary for their Promotion.

The Promotion B degree can be prepared within the framework of a permanent appointment, either as an assistant or as a senior assistant. As a rule, candidates must have obtained their Promotion A in the same discipline and are expected to have published papers in the meantime serving as evidence of their progress as scholars. To obtain the highest academic degree, that of Doctor of Sciences, candidates are required to produce a thesis with research findings which help to set new standards in that particular discipline. It is expected that candidates will have had many years' experience either as successful leaders of a teaching and research collective or as departmental managers of a firm.

The candidate's advanced education in selected fields of Marxism-Leninism should, in most cases, take the form of outstanding contributions to the solution of social tasks.

Promotion B candidates who also wish to obtain the teaching qualification must successfully complete the postgraduate course in university pedagogics.

Thus, by means of a co-ordinated programme of studies, the conditions are met for promotion to senior faculty member — in the first instance, as a lecturer.

137

### 6.3.4 The opportunity for graduates already in employment to gain further qualifications as part-time or full-time 'aspirants'

On the basis of the Ordinance concerning Aspirants in Higher Education *(Anordnung über die wissenschaftliche Aspirantur)* (Official Gazette of the GDR, Part II, 1972), graduates can go on and obtain further qualifications either as part-time students *(Aspiranten)* who combine their studies with their professional activity or as full-time students who study on leave from their job. These students have proved their academic ability and have distinguished themselves both professionally and socially. During their period of study, which is referred to as the *Aspirantur*, they prepare a thesis (either for Promotion A or B) which is of theoretical and academic importance and of practical significance for their firm. In this way, a close link is established between professional activity and academic training, especially in the case of part-time students.

Past experience has shown the value of agreements between the institute of higher education and the graduate's firm concerning his return to the institute at a later stage as a student. These arrangements are best made as soon as the graduate joins the firm. Other graduates may return to higher education to obtain further qualifications while working as assistants. Hence, there is often an exchange of staff between the university or college and the firm — graduates leave the university to gain practical experience in the firm, the employees of which return to university as students or assistants.

An *Aspirantur* leads to either the Promotion A or B degree. Full-time students take three years to complete their Promotion A, and part-time students a year longer. As another alternative, students can take a shortened course of study known as a partial *Aspirantur* *(Teilaspirantur)*.

Full-time postgraduate students receive a grant amounting to 80 per cent of their regular net wage. Thus, thanks to State support, students can continue with their academic training free from material burdens.

### 6.3.5 Further education of senior faculty members

The personal commitment of each and every senior faculty member to add to his knowledge in the fields of politics, ideology, university pedagogics and group management, as well as in his own specialist subject, is also rooted in the Regulations concerning the Appointment of Senior Faculty Staff *(Hochschullehrerberufungsverordnung)* (Official Gazette of the GDR, Part II, § 16).

Our general socially determined need for life-long education on the part of our citizens is particularly applicable in the case of senior academic staff.

Further learning is associated first and foremost, of course, with personal teaching and research work and the publication of scholarly papers and books. Because teaching and research are planned, learning too proceeds to a certain extent along planned lines. The completion of tasks connected with the further education of graduates directly presupposes that professors and senior lecturers will become more qualified in their own specialist subjects. This is achieved principally by private study of relevant literature and by participation in academic life.

Whereas senior staff add to their specialist knowledge on this individual basis, further education in social sciences and university pedagogics is provided as organized in-service training. Professors and senior lecturers take one-year courses at the Marxist-Leninist Evening School, the subjects of which are endorsed by the rector of the university or college.

Special courses are also organized to discuss certain topical aspects of university pedagogics. For example, in the academic year 1978-79, the Karl Marx University is arranging special courses on the development of creativity in students by providing them with the ability to do scientifically creative work. A collective publication is planned detailing the positive experiences of the course participants in this field. Similar in-service training opportunities for senior academic staff exist at other institutes, in particular at those 18 universities and colleges with departments of university pedagogics.

Extended courses are also organized for teachers of certain important subjects and others engaged in particular modes of study, such as distance education. For instance, teachers of the foundation course in social sciences can obtain their special further qualifications in a five-month course at the Franz Mehring Institute of the Karl Marx University. Some of the lectures are given by experienced guest lecturers. Teachers of Russian can also receive further specialist training at the Karl Marx University: courses are organized for them by the Institute for the Advanced Training of Russian Teachers with the help of guest lectors from the Soviet Union. Finally, the Academy for Further Medical Training provides opportunities at national and regional level for doctors to receive in-service training.

The Central Office for Higher Distance Education in Dresden has a centralized system of pedagogical training for teachers engaged in distance education at higher level. Lecturers are issued with teaching recommendations and briefings are held on how to supervise distance studies in a methodical way.

Ordinary professors and holders of chairs can take up to 12 months' academic leave every five to seven years in order to concentrate on

139

further training. This sabbatical year provides an opportunity for periods of study abroad.

## 6.4 The planning and management of staff development

Staff development is an integral part of the planning and management of higher education because it is of decisive importance for social and academic development. Under the aegis of the Ministry of Higher Education's Advisory Committees for the main academic disciplines, long-term development strategies for these disciplines have been elaborated and endorsed. The strategies include proposals for staff development and extend beyond 1980. They are being implemented in stages as part of the five-year and annual plans of the educational institutes involved, with particular responsibility being assumed by rectors, staff development and training directors and heads of department. They work out staff development strategies and plans. Responsibility is also shared by the holders of chairs of academic and staff development, and it is their duty to pay special attention to staff from the working and peasant classes, women, and teachers who have studied for a length of time abroad.

Each university department in the GDR has staff development programmes for its junior academics and advancement plans for its best students which are drawn up on the basis of thorough analyses.

Questions such as long-term staff development, the securing of academic development by means of staff training, ways of overcoming any difficulties, and so on, are often subjects for discussion at the university convocation, at management meetings and at meetings of academic advisory bodies. For instance, in 1977 the convocation of Karl Marx University addressed itself to the question of junior staff development.

The trades union organizations at universities and colleges and in their various departments make responsible use of their right to a say in all matters concerning staff development.

## 6.5 Summary

In the above review we have stressed that in the GDR staff development, and in particular development of teaching staff, is of prime importance for the further evolution of the advanced socialist society and the sytematic implementation of academic and higher education policies. Staff development can be summed up as follows.

Staff development at universities and colleges is a planned, unified process geared to the implementation of academic and higher education policies. The main intention is that members of the academic staff should become more qualified in the fields of politics, ideology, university pedagogics and group management as well as in their own specialist subjects. Each scholar's training consists of a number of integrated stages and the whole process of qualification depends above all for its success on the unity of personal and social interests.

# 7: The Indian Sub-Continent — a problem of resources

Donald Bligh

## 7.0 Introduction

### 7.0.1 Separate paths from a common heritage

In addition to the reservoir of knowledge and physical resources, a major resource of any educational system lies in its history and traditions. Education changes slowly. India, Pakistan and Bangladesh shared a common history under British colonial rulè. It was during this period that the first universities were established. While Nepal pursued a policy of isolation in the 100 years before 1950, its higher education also experienced Anglo-Indian influence. In the past 30 years the extent and administration of higher education in these four countries has steadily diverged.

The methods have not. They are the same as may be found in many parts of the world. All four countries have recently been taking very different steps to improve the quality of their teaching. The growing contrasts reflect their differing administrative and educational outlooks. Many of their problems are the same, yet their solutions will be different because the problems lie in different cultures and contexts. The training of university teachers is only one aspect of these solutions.

### 7.0.2 Common problems

Eight common problems are inter-related, frequently in vicious circles: poverty, lack of equipment for teaching and research, insufficient research to revitalize teaching, an inadequate knowledge base of research into higher education, out-dated curricula, higher education as the privilege of an urban and wealthy élite, diverse language backgrounds and undue respect for authority and rote learning at the expense of independent thought.

Unlike most of the other countries discussed in this book, none of these four countries can be described as wealthy in terms of per capita income. Within a national economy education is a service industry which does not immediately earn foreign currency. There is a poverty of general education too. Nepal has been estimated as having 15 per

142

cent literacy and the rate for Bangladesh is little different.

In this context, is university education a luxury? Is schooling not the educational priority? What is the justification for spending money on research when it appears to be done better by western countries? Does the knowledge gained repay the expense? But what happens to university teaching when there is no longer a research atmosphere? Worse still, does the development of university education for the few who can afford it, not increase the differences between the wealthy educated élite and the poor? You may say 'No' if the élite use their education with a sense of service to the poor; but exploitation is more common than service. Neglect is most common. Though overpopulated, these are predominantly rural countries; the effect of universities is to draw the educated elite to the towns where there are responsible jobs, cultural activities, like-minded people and luxuries (eg electricity and commerce) to support the kind of life the privilege of university education has led them to expect. Rural areas are drained of intellect and remain backward.

All this may seem a far cry from development in university teaching. It is not. Consider curriculum development. Through aping western countries it is assumed that medical training should be hospital based and that future doctors should be shown the latest and best techniques and equipment. 'Surely', it is said, 'if you want medical services to improve, trainee doctors must be shown the latest developments. How else can knowledge be disseminated? They will soon be out of date anyway; why make it worse by teaching out-of-date techniques?' But once trained in this way, a doctor will naturally wish to use his training. Rural areas have few hospitals and little equipment. These are found in the towns. Thus the best intentions in curriculum planning leech new blood from rural medicine, thereby depleting medical services.

What this example illustrates is that the development of university teaching on the Indian sub-continent, and probably everywhere else, is not merely a matter of polishing a lecturer's image on a student rating questionnaire; it is part of national development.

The problem of out-dated curricula has several causes. Many university teachers do no research. Obtaining foreign journals to keep up to date costs foreign currency. There is no incentive to redesign courses. Western universities are prestigious. Lecturers are often appointed because they have qualifications from Britain or North America and proceed to give pale shadows of the courses they received. It is easier that way. They know nothing else and do not have the resources or knowledge to work out anything different. The result is courses that are irrelevant and soon out of date, yet western and prestigious.

How can it be, after 30 years of independence, that universities on the Indian sub-continent are still intellectually dominated by Europe and North America? It is not surprising. The same may be true of universities in Australia and parts of South Africa and South America which do not suffer from comparable poverty. There is an additional factor. In common with many other non-western countries, particularly the Islamic world, there is a great respect for authority. This is reflected not only in the nature of students' work, their dependence on teachers, their gross over-emphasis upon rote learning, and their neglect of critical, original, creative or almost any kind of independent thought, but also in the hierarchic nature of university government. It is difficult for young teachers to innovate. The pressures to teach in traditional ways are too great for the young teacher. When he is established he is already encrusted with tradition.

It is not so much that western nations have wealth or power or ideological leadership — it is questionable how far they have these political things — but there is an intellectual dependence on the West because of its research and publications. It is from western sources that most lecturers obtain their material. For this reason, and because there is no common native language in any of these four countries, English is the common language of intellectuals. Although Pakistan universities are changing to Urdu, English is usually the language of instruction. It is out of the question to translate or rewrite university textbooks in all the languages of the Indian sub-continent. Thus students must learn through English. This may be their second or third language. Consequently, even if the quality of teaching could be said not to suffer through being conveyed in a foreign language, the quality of learning does and this is sufficient to require developments in teaching.

With this background it would be surprising if there was a sufficient knowledge base of research into higher education from which developments in teaching could arise. Thus the development of university teaching will need to be a shoestring operation using limited resources, possibly with outside help. Of the four countries only India has not sought foreign expertise.

## 7.1 India

### 7.1.1 The size of the problem
Any consideration of developing teaching in India must take account of the enormous size of the task. In 1947 there were 19 universities, 636 colleges and a total enrolment of 258,000 at the post-matriculation stage. By the mid-1970s there were over 100 universities, about 4000 affiliated colleges and a total post-matriculation enrolment of 4 million, of which about 1.7 million are at the intermediate stage and

2.3 million are taking degree-level courses at universities or their affiliated colleges. In 1975 the 102 universities shared 350,000 students while their affiliated colleges enrolled 2 million. These figures show that the average university has 3500 students while the average affiliated college has only 500. Indeed, the 1975 Conference of Vice-Chancellors reported that over half the affiliated colleges of arts, science and commerce had less than 400 students.

The Indian authorities are well aware that these figures must raise questions about the standards of teaching. Can colleges with less than 400 students be sufficiently well staffed and equipped to offer a range of courses at a suitably high standard without being grossly over-expensive? With rare exceptions it is quite clear that they cannot. It has been difficult for the Government to control the establishment of affiliated colleges, but the rate has slowed from 292 in 1970 to 80 in 1975. There has also been a steady decline in the growth rate of the enrolment of new students from 14.5 per cent in 1970 to 3 per cent five years later.

The only way universities have been able to control the quality of courses has been by playing a vital role in examining. This has taken a large amount of the university teachers' time, has earned them good fees, and made them reluctant to relinquish this income or to permit enterprising innovations in courses, curricula and teaching in the affiliated colleges.

However, any attempt to curtail the growth of affiliated colleges and create fewer larger institutions favours the urban élite at the expense of the rural poor. The Indian Government is well aware of this problem. It expects the total post-matriculation student population to increase to 8 million in the next 15 years and has suggested that only 50 per cent of the additional enrolment should be in full-time courses, 20 per cent in evening courses, 20 per cent in correspondence courses and 10 per cent in private study. It has been argued that the introduction of non-formal and non-full-time courses should provide an opportunity for restructuring not only these courses, but the formal and full-time courses in universities. This process should include the establishment of evaluation systems.

What is remarkable in the context of this book is not the high proportion of the Indian population that receives higher education for a developing nation, nor that a developing nation is seen to be trying to cut back, rather than expand, its over-extended educational provision. It is the recognition that this cut-back necessitates curricula innovations and consequently staff evaluation. However, what is disappointing is that the faculty improvement programmes are primarily conceived in terms of developing teachers' academic knowledge. The importance of teaching skills is only recognized in exceptional cases. Perhaps for this reason, faculty improvement is almost wholly directed at teachers in the affiliated colleges, not at university teachers. It is as if, as in western countries, university teachers wear a danger label saying 'Academic freedom! Don't touch!' which administrators dare not disobey.

### 7.1.2 Faculty improvement programmes

In the fifth five-year plan the University Grants Commission (UGC) provided necessary support for eight types of programme for raising professional competence of teachers in affiliated colleges to be implemented simultaneously to produce a multiplying effect.

UNIVERSITY LEADERSHIP PROJECTS
During the fifth five-year plan every university with more than 25 affiliated colleges was invited to take up a university leadership project in subjects where it had strong viable departments. The purpose was to bring about the reform of the syllabus as well as of examinations at the undergraduate level, together with the improvement of the curriculum and other materials required for better teaching. It was also hoped that the channels of communication between university and college teachers would be improved.

It was hoped that 40 additional projects would be initiated in science subjects and a similar number in humanities and social sciences. The university was to take responsibility for bringing about the improvement of professional competence of teachers in affiliated colleges through the organization of seminars, symposia, summer institutes, workshops and actual participation by university teachers in the reform of the curricula and examination systems of the affiliated colleges. This was to include the preparation of textbooks, manuals, monographs and other instructional materials for the new curricula. The UGC was willing to give up to half a million rupees ($US 60,000) to each leadership project for a period of three years.

Now as soon as we see that the instruction is to be carried out by university teachers, the reasons for the limitation of the project to affiliated colleges are all too evident. University teachers can instruct their inferiors in their subject, but they dare not instruct each other and they do not have the competence to give advice about teaching. These things can only be provided by outside experts and they would be more difficult to organize and finance.

In short, the UGC is doing what it can. It is not attempting what it cannot. But the question of whether an opportunity to improve teaching is being lost remains.

REFRESHER COURSES AND SHORT-TERM INSTITUTES
It is the refresher courses and short-term institutes that are meant to

take this opportunity. They are particularly directed towards improvement of curricula, teaching methods and examination reforms· proposed by the universities. Although the universities are free to organize such institutes at any convenient time, it was expected that they would commonly last six to eight weeks during the summer vacation. It was expected that universities might offer one institute in the science subjects and one in social science subjects for up to 150 teachers each. Rather than picking one teacher from each college to attend it was hoped that as many teachers as possible from a single college would attend a given course so that there would be a sufficient body of common opinion and experience to implement new ideas.

The UGC expects the performance of all participants in these courses or institutes to be evaluated at the end of the course, and the evaluation, whether satisfactory or not, to be sent to the participants' college principals. In turn the refresher course itself would be evaluated by the participants, probably on a specially prepared form.

### IN-SERVICE, POST MA OR MSc DIPLOMA COURSE THROUGH CORRESPONDENCE IN MAJOR SUBJECTS

The purpose of this course is to raise the level of competence in academic subject matter of teachers in undergraduate colleges through correspondence. It is conceived as a one-year course covering eight semesters, plus the completion of an independent project. As in other countries, it has been thought wise to supplement correspondence material with two four-week contact classes and laboratory work organized by each of the participating universities. Although it was anticipated that several universities might co-operate in producing a correspondence course, it was expected that one should take overall responsibility for co-ordination in each subject. The courses were not thought to be viable where there were less than 250 teachers in a particular state.

### ALL-INDIA ADVANCED LEVEL AND ENGLISH LANGUAGE TEACHING INSTITUTES

The purpose of the All-India advanced level institutes was to create opportunities for teachers from universities or colleges to learn about the latest developments in their subject through lectures, seminars, discussions and project work for six weeks at selected university departments with a reputation in specific fields. It was expected that attendance at any given six-week course would be about 50. The majority of participants would be teachers from postgraduate colleges and less than a quarter would be from universities.

The English language teaching institutes also last for six to eight weeks and are specially organized to benefit teachers of English in colleges. Like the All-India advanced level institutes, these are organized on a national, not a State, basis.

147

TEACHER FELLOWSHIPS AND NATIONAL ASSOCIATESHIPS
Teacher fellowships are intended to provide opportunities for teachers to work towards an MPhil, MLitt or a PhD. Teachers under the age of 35 are preferred for the long-term fellowships of up to three years, while teachers below the age of 45 are given preference for the short-term fellowships of one year's duration. Teachers over the age of 45 will be considered on merit, but understandably the UGC wishes to ensure that the teaching profession will obtain years of benefit from their investment. Teachers receiving fellowships may be required to serve their current university for at least five years on their return. The fellowships take living expenses into account and may recompense the university for the absence of their teachers.

A national scheme permitting teachers in affiliated colleges or universities to visit universities or research institutions with specialized facilities in their area of research for 8 to 12 weeks is also being generously financed.

SEMINARS, SYMPOSIA, WORKSHOPS, CONFERENCES ETC
The UGC is also willing to finance seminars and workshops of between one and two weeks on an All-India or a regional basis. Universities, colleges or any other institutions seeking to set up any of these programmes simply apply to the UGC for support.

The effort, imagination and finance being devoted to improving Indian teachers is to be admired. The faculty improvement programmes should go some way towards raising the quality of Indian graduates. The question remains: is the right balance and integration between teaching skill and academic knowledge being promoted?

## 7.2 Bangladesh

The eight problems mentioned in the introduction (Section 7.0.2) occur in a staggering way in Bangladesh. Bangladesh appears to be a textbook example of Malthusian stagnation. At the turn of the century its people were relatively well fed, but now its population of 75 million, scattered amongst 65,000 villages, struggles to survive on a scarcely altered agriculture. After a period of repressive government and war involving India's intervention, the nation was founded in 1972 and immediately experienced floods, famine, disease, rampant corruption and unrest.

Higher education is provided by six universities, 34 government and about 252 private degree colleges, together with several specialist colleges. Dacca University is by far the largest university with 15,000 students and is the only one to have been founded before 1947. Two of the remaining universities specialize in engineering and agriculture respectively, and Jahangirnagar University is of recent origin having fewer than 1000 students. The universities, government colleges and private colleges have about 25,000, 70,000 and 220,000 students respectively. One-fifth of university students are women, and although this proportion may be less than would be found in other countries, the attitudes towards women in a traditional Islamic society should be borne in mind.

In Pakistan and Bangladesh several factors have led to the introduction of a semester system together with increasing attention to university teaching methods. Universities have been the traditional source of political unrest and disruption. This was sometimes because of frustration with the poor quality of teaching and the lack of books and other alternative resources to compensate for it. The semester system, which imposes modular courses and half-yearly examinations, allows students less respite for sustained political agitation. By creating an atmosphere of working for examinations, cheating and the resignation of an Islamic fatalism have been reduced.

In August 1975 there was a political revolution, an army takeover of power and the assassination of Sheik Mujib, the dictator who three years earlier had been the people's hero during the struggle against Pakistan. It may seem a strange set of priorities that by Easter of the following year the University Grants Commission had organized a seminar on university teaching methods and invited two British academics, Mr Colin Flood Page and myself, to conduct workshops on university teaching methods and to advise on the training of university teachers. We made the following recommendations:

☐ That a second workshop, for senior staff this time, should be held in the near future. For reasons of prestige and parity, it was thought necessary that it should again be organized by 'experts from England'.

☐ Participants in this second workshop were to be selected as possible personnel to staff future teaching service units in Bangladesh universities. If willing, the persons selected would begin a research project on a topic of their choice relevant to Bangladesh universities. They would then come to England in pairs; first, to finish their research project, possibly for an academic qualification; second, to acquire a detailed background knowledge of research into teaching and learning in higher education; and third to carry out and practise consultancy skills and the organization of workshops with academic staff.

☐ The participants were to be selected to visit Great Britain in pairs on the basis of the quality of their research, and their observed ability to organize workshops for university staff in Bangladesh. For this latter purpose British experts would again visit Bangladesh to observe and supervise their work.

☐ The first teaching service unit in Bangladesh would be established under the auspices of the Bangladesh University Grants Commission, but in the long term such units might be established in each university and perhaps ultimately in each faculty. Until such units were established, senior staff were to be encouraged to discuss teaching problems with younger teachers. They should do this from a standpoint of equality; discussion from a standpoint of authority is inappropriate and likely to be counter-productive.

☐ There is a great need for the dissemination of information both in the subjects taught and in the methods of education. Booklets on teaching methods, examination techniques, etc based upon experience elsewhere, but specifically adapted to Bangladesh needs and written in Bengali, should be encouraged by the University Grants Commission and perhaps initially overseen by it. The research and development studies to be carried out by prospective members of teaching services units could be published in this form.

☐ The University Grants Commission might seek the co-operation of professional bodies in disseminating academic information relevant to their fields.

On our first visit the striking feature was the superficiality of thinking about university teaching by university teachers themselves. At the seminar organized by the University Grants Commission, many of the proposals were quite impracticable. This seemed surprising in a country where practicalities make themselves felt at every moment of every day.

Similarly, participants at one of the workshops completed a questionnaire. Both the responses themselves and the inability of some participants to recognize inconsistencies in their replies, suggested that they had not thought deeply about their work. For example, virtually every participant agreed that 'the *main* purpose of universities is to encourage students to think independently' but most participants did not think that 'university students should be encouraged to disagree with their teachers.' Furthermore, they strongly affirmed that 'the *main* purpose of universities is to give students knowledge' and without exception believed that 'I am quite clear what my purposes in the university are.' When asked to state on the other side of the paper what their purposes in the university were, it was clear that almost no one had given the matter any thought and that they had great difficulty in expressing any abstract principles they had not previously learned from a textbook. On the whole participants did not believe that 'it is the teachers' responsibility to ensure that university students pass their examinations', but with one exception they were unanimous in believing that 'teachers should spend extra time with students who seem likely to fail.'

A good proportion of participants had difficulty in recognizing the inconsistencies in their responses even when these were pointed out to them. This suggested that the capacity to think is a skill not well developed even in those people who perform particularly well in the Bangladesh university system. Any development of university teaching in Bangladesh must pay attention to this problem.

These proposals are now being implemented with the assistance of the British Council. In 1978 Colin Flood Page visited Bangladesh for a third time and two Bengali academics are expected to spend the whole of 1979 based at Exeter University Teaching Services. These pages give little more than an interim report.

## 7.3 Pakistan

Pakistan cannot be described as an industrial country, but compared with the other three countries in the Indian sub-continent it has a relatively industrial economy. Before the secession of Bangladesh in 1972 there was a net flow of capital towards 'East Pakistan'. When this flow stopped, more money was available for educational development.

Expenditure upon higher education more than trebled during the first half of the 1970s. By 1975 there were 12 universities and 275 degree colleges in the country with a total of over 12,000 teachers. Inevitably such a rapid expansion brought difficulties. The most prominent of these was the shortage of adequately qualified and properly trained teachers. There was a considerable brain drain of senior academics to other countries which created a vacuum and exacerbated the imbalance between experienced and inexperienced staff. Consequently the rapid expansion of higher education resulted in a considerable deterioration of standards, which was in danger of being passed down through the whole educational system.

These factors clearly imply the need for training of university teachers. But there are other factors. The availability of capital promoted a more industrial and commercial economy with an increasing demand for professional and technical expertise. Thus the demand upon higher education switched towards a more goal-oriented curriculum at a time when educational theory was emphasizing the specification of objectives. At the same time there were innovations in teaching methods including those made possible by the increasing availability of electrical power and equipment. The salary scales of university teachers had been very poor, but they were suddenly revised to be comparable with the Civil Service. This financial recognition brought with it the expectation of higher professional standards.

All these factors combined with greater government control of universities than would normally be expected in western universities, led the Pakistani University Grants Commission to take active steps towards the training of university teachers. Conferences, in-service seminars and summer institutes had previously been organized by individual universities, but the University Grants Commission had the authority and power to demand co-ordinated consideration of the provision of training. It established study groups on 'problems of teachers' and 'improvement of education and research in the universities'. They both recommended the establishment of a national academy which would provide pre-service and in-service training for university and college teachers. This proposal was strongly supported in September 1975 by the Inter-provincial Education Conference presided over by the Federal Minister of Education. The academy was to be at Islamabad on the premises of the University Grants Commission itself. The University Grants Commission listed the academy's objectives and functions as follows:

*Objectives*
— to promote good teaching and high research standards in the universities and institutes of higher learning
— to help motivate the teaching community to improve its efficiency and its continuous professional growth through training and retraining.

*Functions*
— to provide pre-service training to the teachers selected for university or college service into the practices, innovative concepts and ethics of the teaching profession
— to provide more systematic and effective in-service training and orientation to working teachers and to keep them abreast of current trends and developments
— to provide a common platform for teachers from different universities and colleges to discuss and deliberate upon improving the teaching-learning process in the institutions of higher learning
— to conduct continuous study of research in curriculum development and in teaching methods and techniques and make it available to the colleges and universities of the country
— to arrange seminars, conferences, educational workshops, symposia, lectures and meetings for improving the quality of teaching and research in various subjects
— to provide an effective information service for the universities and other institutions of higher learning by maintaining an up-to-date reference library and documentation service
— to maintain a register of the teachers of colleges and universities in order to provide information regarding their qualifications, experience, movement and publications

— to publish regularly information booklets, monographs, dissertations, research reports and journals.

ORGANIZATION OF THE ACADEMY
The academy was to work under the supervision and control of the University Grants Commission but would have its own governing body, a director and sufficient administrative staff to organize its various sub-units.

Academic staff who run courses were to be employed on a contractual basis to ensure economy, varied available expertise and recent experience of university teaching.

PRE-SERVICE ORIENTATION COURSE
It was envisaged that the pre-service orientation course for college and university teachers would last three months from September to November. The following topics were to be considered:

— newer teaching methods and learning procedures
— modern instructional technology
— preparation of lectures, assignments and tests
— evaluation techniques and assessment procedures
— ethics and norms of university and college life
— dealings with students, colleagues and seniors
— administration, statutes, rules and regulations
— management of laboratories, libraries and seminars
— information and documentation
— general knowledge and improvement of language.

IN-SERVICE ORIENTATION
The in-service orientation course for college teachers nominated by provincial governments was to be residential and last for four weeks. The course was to include:

— the study of innovation in teaching methods, teaching aids and instructional technology
— the semester system, its requirements, evaluation techniques and assessment procedures
— a literature survey, information, documentation and libraries
— college management, public dealings and student assessment.

The three-week course on university teaching methods was intended for teachers with some years' experience and was to be primarily concerned with increasing teaching efficiency.

The academy was also to organize summer seminars, educational workshops, work in the field of curriculum development, have an active research 'cell' publishing reports and monographs in the field of higher education, and provide an information service to universities by maintaining an up-to-date reference library on educational planning.

CONCLUSION
Two important factors, which concern any work in developing teaching, lay behind these proposals: academic respectability and financial restraint.

## 7.4 Nepal

### 7.4.1 Background — geographical limitations

In few countries is geography more relevant to educational development. Nepal's population of nearly 14 million is similar to that of Australia, but it only has an area of 141,577 square kilometres. Its altitude varies from little more than sea level in the Terai to the highest point on earth. The steepness of the terrain, which helped the country's pre-1950 policy of isolation, makes the development of large-scale agriculture difficult, and has allowed the development of only four or five major roads capable of taking heavy motor traffic. Large parts of the country can only be reached on foot, making postal distribution of educational materials slow, difficult and unreliable.

More significantly, the poorly developed transport system has maintained cultural differences within the country. It has 13 languages and 36 distinguishable ethnic groups. Consequently the widespread dissemination of ideas, which may be conceived as part of the social function of a university, is severely hampered. Furthermore few students study in their own language. Only a minority of the population speak Nepali, the national language, and those books that are available are mostly in English, a third language. Thus most students do not read widely and are over-taught.

Rapid improvements in the standards of university education in Nepal will be difficult without a broader educational base and could in any case increase social differences if there is not a comparable programme at primary and secondary levels. There are no reliable figures for the birth rate, but it is obviously high, and infant mortality has been put at over 200 per 1000. The population has increased from 9 million in 1961. United Nations statistics suggest that over 90 per cent of females, and over 70 per cent of males, have been judged as illiterate, although the criterion for this statistic is not clear. For the foreigner, smallpox, cholera, typhoid, tetanus, malaria and hepatitis are to be avoided; and I have seen signs of tuberculosis and infant malnutrition in towns and villages.

These comments are not intended as criticisms. The reader must ask: 'what is the role of academic staff development in this context?' It is part of the background against which the National Education Plan for 1971-76 and the efforts of the Nepali people should be seen as bold and imaginative. Prior to 1950 Nepal was a pre-industrial society and although manufactured goods are now available in Kathmandu and other main towns, and the internal combustion engine is increasingly evident, many of the rural areas are not wholly dependent upon an industrial economy. Goods not produced within walking distance are a bonus to normal life; they are not relied upon; and the country areas could return to a self-sufficient economy if required.

Another question to consider is: 'what is the difference between Nepal and Switzerland?' In terms of resources such as scenery, hydroelectric power, cultural heritage, local self-identity, forestry, and so on, Nepal seems marginally superior. The differences cannot be wholly explained by nearby western economies, or Switzerland's wartime neutrality. Switzerland's standard of living has been consistently higher than that of most of Europe. The answer lies in the skill and cultural sophistication of its people — in short, in its system of education. Thus any programme of university staff development should be seen in the context of the national education system.

### 7.4.2 The National Education System Plan for 1971-76
Against this background it is easy to see why the National Education Plan was conceived as a process of nation building. Several problems were identified:

- Educational policies and objectives are neither well defined nor explicit. This results in the mis-allocation of educational resources.
- Education is based on 'the unproductive values of the society'. Instead of being vocational and practical, concentrating on skills that would increase production throughout the country, education is urban, élitist, a process of selection for higher education, and 'a means of avoiding manual labour'.
- Education needs to be more vocational and related to the National Plan. In particular 'middle-level manpower' is needed.
- There are difficulties in maintaining educational standards. Equipment, visual aids, trained teachers, and standard textbooks are in short supply. The Plan states that the examination system is effective and attributes commercial motives to educational institutions.
- There is high educational wastage. A high proportion of children leave school after one year. Since wastage is greater in remote areas, resulting educational contrasts could create national disunity rather than national self-identity.
- The main weaknesses are diagnosed as administrative.

The aims of the National Education Plan may not be seen as blatantly opposed to the university ideal of India or the West, but they are significantly different:

- to produce a loyal nation with a sense of national identity
- to preserve, develop and propagate the national language, literature, culture and art
- to develop learning, science, technology and skills for national development and
- to inculcate moral integrity, habits of work, self-reliance, creativity, the scientific approach, powers of appreciation, aesthetic awareness and cosmopolitanism.

It was hoped that 64 per cent of children at primary school age would receive schooling, 26 per cent of children would receive lower secondary education, and half this number secondary education. Only 2½ per cent would receive higher education. Although to western eyes these figures may seem less than satisfactory, in Nepalese terms they represent an ambitious programme which it has been impossible to achieve in the stipulated time.

### 7.4.3 The structure of higher education in Nepal

A major task is to establish comparable academic standards throughout the country. Clearly staff development has a role in this. Under the National Education Plan all higher education has been incorporated into a single university, Tribhuwan University. The work of the university has been divided into 16 institutes (British universities would call them faculties) of which 12 have so far been established. There are four levels of higher education: certificate, diploma, degree and research. These are intended to provide low-level, middle-level, high-level and specialized manpower respectively. Thus from the Government's need to produce middle-level manpower it will be seen that courses up to diploma level are particularly important. Students are assessed at the end of their course at each level. They need to be re-selected for succeeding levels for which success at the preceding level is a necessary requirement. This means that academic staff devote considerable time to the selection and assessment of students. Indeed it has been estimated that 30 per cent of a student's time is spent taking examinations. If this appears unnecessarily disruptive, it will be seen that a significant effort in staff development should be made towards the redesign of curricula. Table 7.1 shows that the design of new curricula is particularly required in vocational subjects at diploma level and above. This is part of the work of the Curriculum Development Centre.

Table 7.1 Courses provided in 1971 by the Institutes of
Tribhuwan University (From National Education System Plan 1971-76,
published by the Ministry of Education, His Majesty's
Government of Nepal, 1971)

| | *Certificate* | *Diploma* | *Degree* | *Research* |
|---|---|---|---|---|
| Institute of Nepalese Studies | | | | ● |
| Institute of Asiatic Studies | | | | ● |
| Institute of Public Administration | | ● | | |
| Institute of Law | ● | ● | | |
| Institute of Arts, Humanities and Social Sciences | ● | ● | ● | ● |
| Institute of General Sciences | ● | ● | ● | ● |
| Institute of Commerce and Business Administration | ● | ● | ● | |
| Institute of Sanskrit Studies | ● | ● | ● | ● |
| Institute of Education | ● | ● | ● | |
| Institute of Agriculture | ● | ● | | |
| Institute of Forestry | ● | | | |
| Institute of Engineering | ● | | | |
| Institute of Medicine | ● | | | |
| Institute of Applied Science and Technology | ● | | | |
| Institute of Fine Arts | ● | | | |
| Institute of Veterinary Science | ● | | | |

## 7.4.4 The development of teaching by the Curriculum Development Centre

It is clear that the Curriculum Development Centre could achieve much
very efficiently through the presence of the Director on committees
concerned with the development of curricula of any institute. These
committees also include experts and teachers from the various
disciplines who nominally represent others in campuses scattered
throughout the country. Each curriculum is now being systematically
reconsidered to establish uniform standards throughout the country,
and this should in time lead to a general improvement in teaching.
Nevertheless there is likely to be a long transition period. It is not
always easy to teach an old dog new tricks. Many of the older teachers
are set in their ways. They have well-established teaching methods and,
more important, do not have the facilities and, in many cases, the
ability to teach new curricula. Curricula are considered from an inter-
disciplinary angle. They should be vocationally oriented and not
necessarily theoretical or 'bookish'. It is expected that academic staff
will try to raise standards continuously and, by their own writing, will
strive to improve the supply and quality of books. Inter-disciplinarity

157

requires new patterns of thinking which many academic staff find difficult. The Curriculum Development Centre must assist these developments.

It can do this in a number of ways. It has produced some documents of general educational interest such as *Curriculum Evaluation Guidelines — a Set of Guidelines and Questions for Assessing Curriculum in Higher Education.* Individual members of the Centre may work with groups of academic staff from specific institutes or subject disciplines on any aspect of the curriculum. This work is usually in response to requests either from individuals or small groups, or more commonly from an official committee or body of the University. Thirdly, the Centre conducts courses with the support of external agencies. Fourthly, it has four peripatetic teachers touring the country running workshops to explain and ease the introduction of the semester system. However, their employment seems to be temporary. Finally, the Centre tries to work through the administrative machinery of the University via the deans of the various institutes.

Bearing in mind the size of the problems, the Centre for Curriculum Development is not well staffed, but at least the Government, the Vice-Chancellor and the University Rector recognize the need for its work. In 1977 the Centre had three other permanent staff in addition to the Director, and a number seconded from the institutes for varying periods to carry out specific work. For example, one man was specifically concerned with the modification of the Sanskrit studies curriculum, which is probably the oldest curriculum in the country and has evolved rather than been planned.

A major difficulty in the work of the Centre is the scattered nature of the University. It is on 32 different sites throughout the country. In America each of these would be called a campus but in Nepal the word is used a little differently. A campus refers to the work of an institute on a given site. Thus there may be three or four campuses on one site because three or four institutes teach students there. Thus, throughout Nepal there are over 80 campuses on 32 different sites. Bearing in mind the difficulties of travel it would be quite impossible, given the present level of staffing in the Centre, for one of its members to spend even one day per year at each campus. The minimal effect of such a visit can be imagined.

There is at present no training for university teaching staff and the vast majority of schoolteachers also have no training. His Majesty's Government is making an attempt to provide some in-service training for a small number of schoolteachers who, when returning from a training course at university, are required to pass on their training to colleagues in the same school. It is hoped that local education inspectors will also provide some support, but since they will be unfamiliar with what has been taught on the university courses, it is difficult to know what form this will take. It is unlikely that a comparable scheme could be successfully operated at university level.

### 7.4.5 Problems of Nepali higher education

A recent UNESCO (United Nations Educational, Scientific and Cultural Organization) report (Bligh, 1978) summarizes the problems of Nepali higher education as follows:

— Higher education is in the process of rapid change
— The knowledge/educational base is too narrow to support rapid expansion without lowering standards
— Both teaching and assessment place a heavy emphasis upon learning information to the possible detriment of stimulating thought
— Teaching methods are lecture-dominated
— There is a serious shortage of books
— Campuses are dispersed
— There is a heavy commitment of time by teachers and students to assessment processes
— For many teachers, current teaching methods provide an inadequate feedback on their performance
— Teaching and assessment methods do not satisfactorily monitor students' progress
— Language poses difficulties for students of differing ethnic origins
— Teachers' qualifications and interests are varied
— When students are unmotivated for compulsory first-year courses, the consequent high failure rate decreases the rate of recruitment to central professions (such as medicine)
— While not wishing to produce uniformity, there may at present be too wide a disparity in the content and standards of courses
— Among some teachers morale is low, particularly when they are required to teach subjects and students outside their speciality.

### 7.4.6 Keller courses — a possible solution

All these problems are interconnected. The point I wish to make most strongly is that staff development in Nepal cannot be successful — indeed it can hardly begin — if it adopts the British or Australian model in which a consultant sits and waits for clients. It is a radical process of reconstruction which has to be imposed by those in power. The policy of patiently waiting for teachers to attain self-enlightenment simply will not work in an environment unaccustomed to the adventure of ideas and where imagination is stifled by the poverty of varied experience. If, despite poor transport, there needs to be a central control of standards, some kind of distance learning seems appropriate. The United Nations

Development Programme headed by Professor Zaki, formerly Vice-Chancellor of the People's Open University of Pakistan, has considered the use of radio broadcasts on the British and Pakistani models. Unfortunately the steepness of the mountains will make this difficult if not impossible to accomplish without feats of radio engineering on Himalayan peaks beyond the present capacity of Nepali funds. Many people do not possess a radio, and since sound broadcasts for most listeners will not be in their native language, there may be comprehension difficulties.

A method of instruction using self-pacing within indigenous technical competence seems preferable. An open university system requiring students to purchase books is not feasible — there is a chronic shortage of books. Books from abroad cost foreign currency; they are expensive by western standards because of the cost of transportation and import tariffs; and they are prohibitive in terms of Nepali salaries. A standard American textbook costs about one-fifth of an academic's monthly salary. The shortage of books makes libraries loath to loan them, and this throws the responsibility of presenting basic information in a thorough and systematic way on teachers. This reinforces the domination of the lecture system and the habit of uninspiring regurgitation of factual information by both lecturers and students.

Although the Central Library of Tribhuwan University has an important national function as the major library of the country, it has only 90,000 books and an annual budget of $US 40,000. The Library is particularly short of journals. Sets are only 40 per cent complete. Pilfering and mutilation of books may be no higher than elsewhere, but with limited resources the effects are severe.

Nevertheless Nepal has trees. It can make its own paper. It could print its own books. If the Curriculum Development Centre could develop courses on the Keller principle, based upon indigenously produced books, some of the problems of Nepali higher education could be relieved. Dissemination of information could be improved. The inbuilt thought-provoking problems and testing systems could force teachers in distant rural areas to raise their academic standards; they could provide measures of comparability between centres and could ensure that at least some common teaching objectives were achieved. As with the British Open University's programmes, students could receive some training in observation and experimental techniques. Competence in professional skills to diploma level should be attainable. Since the assessment method is an integral part of the teaching, other time devoted to assessment of students could be drastically reduced.

Is this staff development? No, it is much more. The point to be made in the Nepali context is that the typical British and Australasian approach to staff development is mere tinkering with the problems facing Nepal. There is a tacit belief that if you can 'develop the staff' you can change the system. The Nepali context shows this the other way round. Only if you can develop the teaching will you change the staff.

## 7.5 Conclusion

In one sense this chapter is obviously a descriptive account of staff development in the Indian sub-continent. But it is intended as more than this. It is about the way ostensibly similar situations can lead to very different courses of action. It is about familiar western university practices, traditions and methods interacting with problems and cultural climates very different from the western backgrounds in which they developed. Nepal and Pakistan are adopting centralist solutions. India and Bangladesh anticipate the need for dispersed variety.

# 8: The Netherlands — tertiary teacher training as a growth industry

Geoff Isaacs

## 8.0 Introduction

The Dutch higher education system consists of two sectors (see Table 8.1 for demographic data on the Netherlands and its higher education system). One is the university sector, which comprises 13 institutions — universities and more specialized university-like institutions known as *Hogescholen* (universities of technology for example; all will be included under the generic head 'university'). The other is the higher vocational education sector, which contains numerous rather small institutions (typically 300 or so students) with little in common (Wieringen, 1974). Estimates of the total number of higher vocational institutions vary; one reasonably authoritative source (Wieringen, 1974) puts the number at 386. The higher vocational education institutes educate social workers, school teachers, sub-professional engineers, musicians and other similar groups. Being so small they lack most of the institutional supports available to the universities.

The higher vocational institutions fall under the parliamentary act governing secondary schools (the 'Mammoth Act' of 1968) not, as one might have expected, the act which governs universities. Consequently, most staff employed by higher vocational institutes are trained teachers (usually trained *before* they get their jobs). In contrast, the vast majority of university staff are not trained in teaching. Given their small size and the teaching qualifications of their staff, it is not surprising that staff development activities are almost non-existent in the higher vocational institutes. Given their large size and their staff's lack of teaching qualifications it is not surprising that staff development activities, on a modest scale, are undertaken in all Dutch universities.

### 8.0.1 The universities in the 1970s
The Dutch universities have not had a very peaceful or settled time since about 1968. In 1970 a major act of parliament, the University Administration (Reform) Act, completely reorganized the universities, giving the Government greater power over them and removing from the professors control over research, teaching and staffing and placing it in

162

**Table 8.1 The Netherlands and its higher education system – some demographic data**

| Year | Number in universities | Percentage of these who are female | Number in higher professional education | Percentage of these who are female | Number in higher education | Percentage of 18- to 24-year-olds who are in higher education |
|---|---|---|---|---|---|---|
| | | | The students | | | |
| 1961 | 45163 | – | 55796 | – | 100959 | – |
| 1965 | – | – | – | – | – | 11.4 |
| 1971 | 112932 | 20 | 134562 (80608 full-time) | 34 | 247494 | – |
| 1975 | 127699 | 30 | 139000 (approx) | – | 267000 (approx) | 17.1 |

**Some statistics for 1975**

population of the Netherlands: 13,600,000
number aged 18 to 24 years: 1,560,000 = 11.5 per cent of the population
expenditure on higher education: 4.1 milliard guilders = 2.01 per cent of GNP
the largest universities were: Amsterdam with 18,722 students: Utrecht with 17,612 students
the smallest university was: Twente with 2145 students
The staff : student ratio in the universities was roughly 1 : 8
So there were about 16,000 staff in the universities

*Sources: Wieringen (1974), NUFFIC (1976a, c; 1977). For further data see NUFFIC (1971-78)*

the hands of elected bodies representing students, non-academic staff and academic staff of all grades. Also in the 1970s there were two general elections (1972 and 1977); each resulted in a change of Government. After each election there was a hiatus of more than six months before a Government was formed.

In the midst of these changes the universities were told to shorten their courses considerably (from about seven years to about five years), university fees were increased five-fold (and then halved from that value) and two major planning papers on the future of Dutch education (*Contours of a Future System of Education* and *Higher Education in the Future*) were published (NUFFIC, 1976a, 1976b; OECD, 1976). These reports foreshadowed a merging of the higher vocational institutes into much larger polytechnics (a change which has not yet taken place) and a continued freeze on university funding. A *numerus clausus* for student intake was imposed on more university faculties and an almost complete freeze on staff levels in the universities was implemented. The freeze on university funding was hardly surprising (Kemenade, 1975); education funding had risen from 7.4 per cent of the Government budget in 1960 to 23.4 per cent in 1973, while the share of this amount going to the universities changed from 13.4 per cent to more than 20 per cent. The universities took a very large share of education expenditure but by 1975 did not take any more students than the poorly funded higher vocational institutes (which take significant numbers of part-time students — see Table 8.1).

The universities were in uproar from about 1970 to 1974 as the various reforms were debated, fought over and partially implemented (Daalder, 1975; NUFFIC, 1971-78). Since the reforms have been implemented the chain of control has run as follows: in matters of curriculum (other than length of courses), research policy, mode of instruction and staffing the chain of control is nowadays from department *(vakgroep)* to faculty, to the council of the university, to the Netherlands Universities Council (formally, it advises the Crown), to the Government. Except for rare occasions and for the broadest of policy decisions, most decisions are made, in effect, at faculty level. Faculties bear the responsibility for educational development within them, subject to broad policy guidelines from above. The situation is similar in the case of research.

## 8.1 Staff development — the general picture

There are three main areas of staff development in the Netherlands' universities. Firstly, there are courses in many universities on management and administrative skills, such as meeting and interview techniques, report writing, public speaking. Such courses are usually available both to academic and administrative staff. Secondly, academic staff do seem to manage to develop their research skills; such development is almost invariably achieved by individuals on their own initiative. Rarely is training systematically supplied to university staff; either they gain research skills as students or pick them up by experience, osmosis or apprenticeship in the course of their work. Many professional societies and groups offer recurrent or continuing education, mainly in the field of updating of research skills by means of literature, seminars or conferences. These are not usually aimed specifically at university staff and will not be treated further here. Finally there is the training of academic staff in the skills they need to fulfil their role as educators. Such training is becoming available on an ever-increasing scale although to date it is taken by only a small minority of Dutch academics. The bulk of this chapter is concerned with this last form of staff development.

### 8.1.1 Training in management skills

Apart from the education development units to be discussed in subsequent sections of this chapter there is, in most Dutch universities, at least one other body which runs training courses aimed to some extent at university teachers, but mainly at administrative staff. Here are some examples:

At Utrecht an institute known as OMAVO (*Organisatie en Managementvorming* – Organizational and Management Training) offers courses in such areas as group dynamics, organization development, decision-making and planning, meeting and discussion technique. At the Free University of Amsterdam similar courses are organized by the staff section and generally given by outside consultants. Some courses are also offered at Delft (including a four-hour introduction to the University's administrative structures) and at Tilburg.

At Nijmegen a newly formed (1978) institute, SAT, offers courses on working in groups, meeting and discussion skills, two-person discussions (interviews, advising and consultation discussions and similar face-to-face situations), training and assistance in running groups and a range of other options. The institute runs set courses and is also available to existing groups (eg departments, committees), for training or assistance related to more specific aims or problems.

### 8.1.2 Education development as staff development – the RWO-centres

The history of the introduction of opportunities for Dutch academics to train in teaching skills and be assisted with the problems of their role as educators is mainly the story of the development and changing roles of education research and development units (RWO-centres).

In the 1960s there was a steadily increasing demand for education development in all Dutch universities. In the young, small universities

Table 8.2 Scientific staff establishments of the 13 Dutch RWO-centres in 1974-75 and 1977-78*

| University | Date RWO-centre founded | Staff | | | |
|---|---|---|---|---|---|
| | | 1974-75 | | 1977-78 | |
| | | *number* | *full-time equivalent* | *number* | *full-time equivalent* |
| Eindhoven | 1963 | 4 | 4 | 6 | 6 |
| Utrecht | 1965 | 13 | 11 | 15 | 14.5 |
| Twente | 1965 | 11 | 9.5 | 14 | 10.5 |
| Amsterdam | 1966 | 9 | 7.7 | 15 | 13.2 |
| Nijmegen | 1967 | 9 | 9 | 14 | 14 |
| Groningen | 1967 | 7 | 6.5 | 8 | 7.5 |
| Delft | 1968 | 4 | 3.8 | 6 | 4.7 |
| Erasmus | 1968 | na | 5 | na | na |
| Leiden | 1968 | 6 | 6 | 9 | 9 |
| Amsterdam (Free) | 1969 | 6 | 6 | 9 | 7 |
| Tilburg | 1969 | 9 | 6.6 | 6 | 6 |
| Wageningen | 1969 | 4 | 4 | 4 | 4 |
| Limburg | 1974 | na | 2 | na | na |

* *Foundation dates and some 1974-75 staff levels from van der Klauw and Wagemakers (1975); other data from questionnaire.*

the problems were those of the development of new systems, and the demand for expert help came as much from planners as from students. In the older, larger universities rapid growth, student unrest and criticism of university education seem to have fuelled the demand. The need for educational development gave rise to a new type of institute, the higher education research and development unit. The first such unit in the Netherlands was set up at the University of Technology, Eindhoven, in 1963; it is an academic department of the University *(vakgroep)* and its main concern, since its inception, has been with research into higher education. By the end of 1969 all universities then in existence had such units; details of the units in 1978 are given in Table 8.2.

The units vary in name (various combinations of 'education', 'research', 'development', 'centre', 'institute'), just as they vary in function and, in particular, in the relative emphasis given to the research and the development functions. All units now do significant amounts of development work, although a few units did very little until recently; the division between research and development still varies widely among the units.

In their background paper for the Council of Europe, van der Klauw and Wagemakers (1975, 1976) detail the history of the units and, in particular, the gradual shift in emphasis within their development work from diagnosis and description of problems (at a time — about 1968 — when research was more favoured than development) to prescriptive advice and change-oriented activities largely falling into the area of university teacher-training and assistance (1974).

This trend has continued into the second half of the 1970s. Units have become increasingly disillusioned with innovations that have lapsed and a university education system in which improvements in the quality of teaching have come all too slowly. The growing consensus seems to be: an innovative course or curriculum will not succeed if it is not expertly taught; teachers will not themselves become independent innovators if they lack skills (and the consequent confidence) in teaching; teachers should be trained, and the RWO-centres are the obvious bodies to do the job. At the same time, those who would improve the quality of teaching in the universities are faced with an institutional structure which rewards research achievements but not innovation or excellence in teaching. Most Dutch university staff are tenured civil servants, and most promotions before promotion to reader are automatic; thus even disincentives for poor teaching would be difficult to arrange.

### 8.1.3 Co-operation among the RWO-centres: CBOWO and CRWO

The initials RWO in the name of the RWO-centres stand for Research in

University Education *(Research Wetenschappelijk Onderwijs)*. The units
have been co-operating since 1966 in two structures: a contact group
called CRWO (Contact Group Research in University Education — hence
'RWO-centres') and a Central Bureau, CBOWO, which supports the
Contact Group. The Contact Group had one founding member which
was not (and is not today) located in a university. That member is the
higher education section of SISWO (Inter-university Foundation for
Social Science Research). Today the Contact Group consists of the
higher education section of SISWO, the 13 RWO-centres, one in each of
the 13 universities in the Netherlands, and individuals and various
smaller units doing work similar to that of the RWO-centres, but within
particular university faculties (eg there is such a unit in most medical
faculties).

The Central Bureau is government-funded and part of the Netherlands
Universities Council; it acts as a secretariat for the Contact Group. This
Group meets monthly as a council for the centres; usually each member
unit sends one representative to these meetings (often the director of
the centre). The Bureau and the Contact Group can act as pressure
groups and mediators between individual RWO-centres and Government
departments such as the Ministry of Education and Science. The Contact
Group also performs the function, as implied by its name, of keeping
workers at the various RWO-centres in contact with each other. It does
this in three ways: by organizing study groups or study days in areas of
common interest (in 1975 there was a CRWO study day on the training
of academics as teachers — Blom, 1976), organizing conferences and by
publishing a monthly newsletter for RWO-centre staff — *RWO-contact*.
Since the fifth issue of *RWO-contact* in 1977 the newsletter has also
contained news from the Belgian group VWUD (the Flemish equivalent
of CRWO).

Both the Contact Group and SISWO fulfil definite roles in academic
staff development. SISWO organizes study groups, mainly on various
areas in the sociology of higher education, and these are open to all
academics. CRWO publishes, through CBOWO, a quarterly journal,
*Onderzoek van Onderwijs* (Research in Education), which is distributed
among university staff. The journal is concerned with university
teaching and matters which impinge on university teaching (eg student
workloads). Articles are of various kinds, ranging from formal research
reports through less formal literature reviews to informal articles of
the 'teaching tips' variety.

### 8.1.4 The staff development activities of the RWO-centres
In order to obtain up-to-date information on the individual RWO-centres
a questionnaire was sent to the 13 centres late in July 1978. Usable
replies were received from 11 of the centres. The questionnaire was
unsuited to the special nature of the RWO-centre at the State University,

Limburg. The latter is a new university, having taken its first 50 students in 1974; only the Medical Faculty has started teaching — it is run somewhat along the lines of McMaster University, Canada (Schmidt, 1977; Schmidt and Bouhuijs, 1977; Bouhuijs *et al*, nd). The State University, Limburg will not be treated further here; the interested reader should consult the references given.

It might be thought that the way in which an RWO-centre fits into the administrative structure of its host university could affect the nature of its activities. This does indeed seem to be so, at least to the extent that those units which are academic departments seem to do less teacher-training work than others. Most units are either independent service units (like the library or the student health service) or subsections of the university's central administration. The advantages, disadvantages and consequences of these various set-ups have been canvassed, somewhat inconclusively, in the literature (Hazewinkel, 1974). All the RWO-centres, regardless of their position in the university structure, lay claim to a satisfactory degree of autonomy.

Table 8.3 shows a breakdown of the activities of the RWO-centres for the years 1974-75 and 1977-78. The figures shown are the average percentage of scientific staff time (averaged over units) spent on each of six classes of activity. The range of percentages among the units for each activity are shown in brackets. All percentages should be taken as very rough estimates (especially those for 1974-75).

Two categories in Table 8.3, 'Education research' and 'Other activities' cannot be regarded as staff development work. These non staff development activities took up, on average, about 54 per cent of the RWO-centres' efforts in 1974-75 and about 52 per cent in 1977-78. It can be seen that there is wide variation among the centres in the amount of effort devoted to these activities; this is especially true of research. Five centres devoted 30 per cent or more of their time to this activity in 1977-78 (two devoted 50 per cent). Decreases in research and advisory activities from 1974-75 to 1977-78 are largely offset by a substantial increase in the effort devoted to teacher-training activities. An inspection of the detailed returns for the individual RWO-centres shows that these changes are related; indeed, as we shall see in a later section, the increase in teaching activities is *meant* to bring about a reduction in advisory activities; training courses are thought to be an efficient substitute for advice.

The staff development activities of the RWO-centres fall into four categories: giving formal teacher-training to university teachers; disseminating information on teaching and learning to university teachers; advising teachers, either as individuals or in small groups, on educational matters; working on committees whose aim is to improve teaching or to set about evaluating or designing courses. Most (more

169

Table 8.3 Mean percentage of scientific staff effort on each of six areas of activity (averaged over centres) in the RWO-centres in 1974-75 and 1977-78

| Activity | 1974-75* per cent of effort | | 1977-78† per cent of effort | | change 1974-75 to 1977-78 |
|---|---|---|---|---|---|
| | mean | range | mean | range | |
| Formal courses for university teachers | 2 | (0-5) | 10 | (0-30) | +8 |
| Dissemination of teaching/learning information | 9 | (0-30) | 8 | (0-20) | −1 |
| Educational advising; observing, analysing teaching — small groups or individuals | 20 | (5-35) | 15 | (0-35) | −5 |
| Committee work aimed at: improving teaching; course evaluation and design | 15 | (5-30) | 15 | (6-25) | 0 |
| Education research not tied to the above categories | 28 | (8-50) | 25 | (3-50) | −3 |
| Other activities — staff meetings, conferences, CRWO, maintaining professional knowledge, teaching students etc | 26 | (5-39) | 27 | (10-45) | +1 |

*Data source: replies to a questionnaire sent to the 13 RWO-centres late in July 1978; 11 replies were received.*

\* *Data from 10 questionnaires used*
† *Data from 11 questionnaires used*

than three-quarters) of the effort in the last category is devoted to committee work on course design and evaluation. While it can be argued that such work, by the example it sets and the experiences and feedback it gives to teachers, is an effective (if indirect) means of staff development, it will not be treated further here. Similarly, educational advice and the observation of teaching for small groups of academics is also an effective (if sometimes unsystematic) form of staff development, even if in many cases the intent is rather to solve short-term problems. It is nonetheless essentially a private activity and will not be considered further here. The remaining two activities, information dissemination and teacher-training will be treated, the latter in some detail, the former fairly briefly.

### 8.1.5 Dissemination of information on teaching and learning

All RWO-centres run at least some information dissemination activities. All produce series of technical reports on research or development work carried out by the centre. Many produce monthly or bi-monthly a newsletter for university staff (or a page or two in the university's newspaper). Such newsletters contain articles on teaching and learning, short research reports and publicity for the RWO-centre's activities. Most of the centres have small specialized education libraries open to staff; the largest of these, at the Utrecht RWO-centre, has more than 3000 books, 1000 reports and takes many journals. In 1977 the Utrecht centre offered on-line access to computer-based information retrieval services, including the ERIC data base (O and O van O, 1977a).

## 8.2 Courses in university teaching

Two universities, Eindhoven and Delft, are about to begin offering courses. All other universities except the University of Amsterdam (which is running experimental versions of new self-instructional courses) ran established courses in 1977-78, the numbers of such courses ranging from one to a dozen or so, three or four courses being the norm. Most courses consist of about four to six meetings of a group of academics and one or more trainers (Blom, 1976). Meetings generally last about half a day and there may also be a follow-up meeting some months after the main part of the course. Typical topics for such courses are:

- giving lectures
- giving tutorials
- designing and marking examinations
- writing study materials
- teaching by the project method
- classroom skills
- using audiovisual media
- educational objectives

- writing and using multiple-choice questions
- open-ended questions and essay tests
- designing a course
- working with groups
- teaching large numbers of students.

One further type of course, the most common of all, which goes under names such as basic course in education, or general teacher training course, or introductory seminar in education, is offered at most Dutch universities. In general it is the first course developed by a unit commencing teacher-training activities and usually provides a sample of the more specific courses to come later. The courses are rarely *ad hoc* or once-only events. Generally they have well-defined goals and are carefully prepared. Usually they are run first in an experimental version with a small number of participants, and are then evaluated, discussed and revised before being put into production.

Although some courses (notably the Twente-Nijmegen lecturing course described below) work from and with the actual teaching experiences of participants, they usually do so in a highly structured way. Most courses are of a more conventional kind, involving a certain amount of instruction from the trainer, background reading, homework, and exercises during training sessions; training in group work is usually carried out in small groups. Self-instructional courses are becoming increasingly common, especially for training in areas which are concerned with written materials ('how to write behavioural objectives') rather than classroom interaction. In the following subsections some of the more popular or innovative courses or course types are described in more detail.

### 8.2.1 The basic course in university teaching
A typical example is the course 'Arranging for teaching and learning' (*Onderwijs maken*) run by the RWO-centre at the State University, Utrecht. The course lasts 35 hours (a full working week) and is usually run twice in a year; in 1977 more than 80 university teachers attended this course. Here is the description given in the pamphlet advertising the ten courses offered at Utrecht in 1977 (O and O van O, 1977b; see also Ackers and Rigter, 1976).

> A general introduction to the most important aspects of teaching at a university. Participants in this seminar will gain insight into teaching/ learning processes and learn how to shape and use adequate and effective learning situations. The main themes in this seminar: course design; selecting teaching/learning situations; motivation; classroom skills; educational media and evaluation. Especially suited to new staff at the University, who can at the same time become acquainted with the other services that the Bureau has to offer.

### 8.2.2 The clinical approach — 'giving lectures'

Probably the course most widely used in the Netherlands is the 'giving lectures' course, initially developed at Twente by Smuling and van Hout (1977) and carried on as a joint venture when van Hout became head of the Nijmegen RWO-centre. This course has been strongly influenced by the activities of the Clinic to Improve University Teaching at the University of Massachusetts (van Hout, 1975; Melnick and Sheehan, 1976). It has also been used at Groningen (Knippenberg, 1977b) and at Leiden (Blom and Versfelt, 1977); several other RWO-centres have indicated in their questionnaire responses that they probably will use it in 1979.

The course is described in a document by Wolters (1977b); evaluation reports from Groningen and Leiden are noted above. Nijmegen evaluations are reported in a later section of this chapter (8.2.5). Basically the course consists of the training of pairs of people from the same department in those lecturing skills which they feel they lack. Diagnosis of deficiencies is facilitated by videotaping a lecture by each of the trainees prior to the commencement of training. Training consists mainly of practising the desired skills in the trainees' normal lectures; background is supplied by a course book (Smuling and van Hout, 1977) and feedback and support by the trainees to each other — each attends the other's lectures. The training is completed with a viewing by the trainees of videotapes of their lectures 'before' and 'after'.

In an interview with the author in August 1977, van Hout indicated that each diad training cycle cost at least 50 hours of an IOWO staff member's time and an earlier report (van Hout, 1976) speaks of times of the order of 80 hours; Knippenberg found 125 to 150 hours were needed.

### 8.2.3 Self-instructional packages

The trend towards the development of self-instructional materials for the training of university teachers seems to have followed soon after the introduction of self-instructional materials for students and the PSI schemes — in the early 1970s (Plomp, 1974; van der Klauw and Plomp, 1974a, 1974b; van der Meer and Plomp, 1975; Donders, 1974; Pilot and Kramers-Pals, 1973; Verreck, 1976). Vroeijenstein (1975; see also Rosenboom, 1977) notes that self-study packages were under development at six RWO-centres in 1975, while written materials designed to stand on their own were also available from several units.

The RWO-centre at the University of Amsterdam has chosen to develop all of its university teacher-training courses in a self-instructional format (Mirande, 1977a, 1977b). As Mirande (1977a) points out, self-instructional materials are best suited to a 'tools of the trade' approach to teacher-training, as against an 'attitude change' or interactive approach. The Amsterdam courses are therefore backed up with an optional guidance service, the possibility of interaction training, training in the use of audiovisual media and access to a 'mini-library' for teachers. It is hoped that these ancillary options will compensate for possible deficiencies inherent in the self-study approach. The courses being developed at Amsterdam comprise the most ambitious attempt at self-instructional teacher-training courses in the Netherlands; some are now ready, and all have passed through one or two experimental versions.

Many other self-instructional packages are reviewed by van Dorp in an annotated bibliography published in *Onderzoek van Onderwijs* (van Dorp, 1977b).

Several other units, Tilburg among them, have foreshadowed the development or use of self-instructional materials in the near future. It should not be long before these widespread developments in the Netherlands will begin to provide hard evidence as to which areas of university teacher-training can be covered adequately by self-instructional materials; certainly the evidence is not in yet.

### 8.2.4 The 'sourcebook for university teacher training'

In the year 1976-77 eight newly developed courses were run by the RWO-centre at the Catholic University at Tilburg. The materials for these courses — statements of objectives, exercises, teaching materials, references to the literature and test items — have been assembled under the editorship of Elsinga and van Dorp (1977) into ten volumes, each about 100 pages long. Volume 9 is a manual for users of the *Sourcebook* and volume 10 consists of the questionnaires used to evaluate the courses (the 1976-77 evaluation is discussed in the next section of this chapter — 8.2.5).

> The sourcebook is a half product: it has no pretensions other than to offer building blocks — albeit as solid ones as is possible — for the preparation, execution and/or evaluation of university teacher training courses. The course leaders themselves will have to look after introductions, discussions, other ways of working, summaries and the like, as well as the assembly of all the elements into a well-constructed course.

Each of the eight course volumes is divided into four blocks. The first block contains global goals (useful raw materials for propaganda for the course) and specific objectives; the second contains learning materials and a bibliography; the third part consists of exercises and homework assignments, and the last of test items. Each goal in part one is linked to relevant specific objectives; objectives are linked by references to exercises, homework and test questions in other sections, as well as to the bibliography. Test items are supplied with item analyses from actual courses and completion items are supplied with typical (correct) answers. Items are keyed to facilitate the construction of parallel tests. The eight 'course volumes' are: 'Teaching and learning principles', 'Curriculum construction', 'Giving lectures', 'Leading educational groups', 'Media in education', 'End results', 'Written tests with open questions', 'Tests'.

### 8.2.5 Evaluation of training

University teacher-training in the Netherlands has two main strengths. One is the wide dissemination of information within the Netherlands both by personal contact and by publication. The other, connected with the first, is the tendency to evaluate courses systematically. The publications of the group at Tilburg University provide a useful framework in which to set evaluation data. This group points out that the goals of university teacher-training can usefully be classified on four levels (van Dorp, 1977a; Rosenboom, 1977). The four levels of goals are *process goals* (the course itself runs smoothly both from the trainers' and the trainees' points of view), *direct goals* (the trainees learn something from the course), *intermediate goals* (the course, directly or indirectly, favourably influences the trainees' teaching) and *ultimate goals* (the course, through improvements in the trainees' skill as educators, results in enhanced student learning and/or satisfaction).

At Tilburg an evaluation of seven courses run in 1976-77 has been carried out (Rosenboom, 1977). This evaluation was of outcomes on the direct and intermediate levels and showed that academics did learn from the courses; substantial transfer of skills and attitudes from the course to participants' teaching was not shown conclusively. As has been pointed out by both van Dorp and Rosenboom, while the relevance of the goals increases as one moves from the process level to the ultimate level, the ease of assessment of outcomes *decreases*. The research paradigm used by the workers at Tilburg, a quasi-experimental research design (Campbell and Stanley, 1963) with statistical tests of significance, development of valid and reliable measures and careful control of irrelevant variables, presents formidable difficulties — especially in the measurement of higher level outcomes. Nonetheless it does hold out the hope of measuring such outcomes.

The group at the RWO-centre at the Catholic University, Nijmegen, while also paying careful attention to evaluation of its courses, does not adopt the Tilburg approach. New courses are subjected to formative evaluation (Scriven, 1967) on both the process and direct levels (Wolters, 1977a; Dousma, 1977a); fully developed courses are subjected to 'long-term product evaluation' (van Dorp's intermediate level). The spirit of the Nijmegen evaluations is very much exploratory, especially when courses are under development. Courses under development are repeatedly tried out with small numbers of participants, variations being allowed in the course on each occasion to suit the varying needs of the participants and to take account of the results of previous trials. As much emphasis is put on *after care* of former participants (such as help with teaching problems) as on long-term evaluation of course effects — requests for after care will be made into opportunities for evaluation, if possible (Dousma, Hupkens and Wolters, 1977). Finally, there is overt rejection of the crucial point of the Tilburg model — that the ultimate goal of university teacher-training, the enhancement of student learning, is achievable by this means and success is measurable. It is argued that many other factors play important roles in improving the quality of students' learning — organizational and financial factors, for example — and to attempt to attribute such improvements to teacher-training (alone) is to go too far. The aim of teacher-training should be (and is at Nijmegen) to 'professionalize' academics as educators. This view of the aims of training is the dominant one in the Netherlands at present.

Most evaluation of teacher-training carried out by RWO-centres is, as noted by Rosenboom, process evaluation. On the whole the methods used tend towards the less formal Nijmegen model. Extensive evaluations have been carried out by Knippenberg at Groningen; among others the courses evaluated include an adaptation of the Twente-Nijmegen lecturing course (Knippenberg, 1977b) and a course in discussion skills for meetings (Knippenberg, 1976a). Blom, who is based at Leiden, has also evaluated an adaptation of the Twente-Nijmegen lecturing course (Blom and Versfelt, 1977) and a course in microteaching (Blom, 1977f, h). Almost all courses are favourably evaluated by almost all participants. This would appear to be clear evidence that clients' self-perceived needs are being met.

## 8.3 Reasons for change

When, in the space of four or five years, no less than 13 institutes (and 13 out of 13 at that) proceed either to introduce teacher-training courses or to expand the set of courses they offer, one is tempted to look for a reason or cause common to all. Questionnaire replies and evidence in the literature all indicate that this development was not initiated by the Government, nor by the CBOWO, nor by the Contact Group CRWO nor indeed by the individual universities as corporate bodies. In fact several RWO-centres echo the spirit of the times when they point out that the running of courses, once started, was encouraged by the University, but 'without any consequences (financial, staff)'.

All units noted, in one way or another, that the decision to start training courses originated *within the unit itself.* Beyond this point respondents fell into three groups: those who gave as one reason that the teaching staff expressed a need (often rather vaguely) for courses; those who felt the teaching staff needed to have such courses; and those who were swept along by the other units. Some units gave more than one of these reasons. An influential document establishing that staff *felt* a need for training was the survey conducted in 1976 at Nijmegen (Bevers and Wolters, 1976). It has been used by several RWO-centres to justify running training courses (see, for example, Knippenberg, 1976b, 1978). Similar survey results were obtained by van de Water (1973) and by Knippenberg (1976c) in his discussions with 11 educational committees at the University of Groningen. The needs revealed were for courses in the usual areas (curriculum construction and, in particular, choice of teaching methods; classroom teaching to both large and small groups of students; using audiovisual media; grading methods). The survey also revealed the need for *information* on many educational questions.

Two other reasons, given by many units, shine out as the major reasons for starting courses, however. The first is *efficiency* (see, for example, the Preface to Dousma, 1977d). So many of the problems which individual staff bring to the RWO-centres are similar to each other and fall into three or four well-defined areas that giving courses in these areas is a more efficient way of solving the problems. Indeed, it leaves more RWO-staff time free to answer more complex individual problems. The second reason is that *innovative curricula,* often sponsored or developed by the RWO-centres, were failing either because of poor teaching or lack of support in the department teaching them (see, for example, Plomp and van der Meer, 1977). As one unit director put it: 'Experience with course construction projects is one thing — to give the new course in a right way is another!' Hence, the introduction of teacher-training courses.

### 8.3.1 Do university teachers want teacher-training? Why?

We have just seen that many RWO-centres justify their running training courses on the basis that academics need and want them (Bevers and Wolters, 1976). It should be noted, however, that if demand is to be measured by enrolments in formal courses, then demand is not overwhelmingly large. Typical enrolment figures for the courses offered at Utrecht, which is more active in this area than any other Dutch unit, are of the order of 20 per course, though their introductory course attracted more than 80 people. But there seems to be a larger group of Dutch academics interested in getting teacher-training than there was in the past (in the 1960s, say). In particular, in many RWO-centres (Utrecht among them), there is a large amount of less formal teacher-training activity in the form of 'one off' short-term specific purpose training sessions for groups of clients with other problems. The problem may be 'my biology practicals just don't work', and the answer may then be 'let's run a group-work training course for your demonstrators and their students.' Such courses are rarely reported in the published literature.

If it is accepted that there is a demand for training, what is the reason for this change? Stef Blom in his comprehensive planning paper for teacher-training courses at Leiden (Blom, 1977e) attempts an explanation. He first asks 'why didn't training come sooner?'; after all it is not generally the case 'that there is rejoicing over the quality of university education. On the contrary, poorly planned and poorly executed classes are taken for granted.' What is his explanation? Firstly, academics see themselves mainly as intellectual investigators (*wetenschapsmensen*); teaching is a nuisance that consumes good research time; good students have never learned from teaching — what they need is an intellectual climate in which they will (inevitably?) realize their potential. Secondly, what should we teach teachers? 'There is still too little known about such a complex task as teaching to permit statements as to what components add up to good teaching.'

What has changed, if this analysis is correct?

> The universities have grown a lot in the last ten years. With that growth has come a new group of students whose reasons for studying have often lain in a somewhat different direction. Putting it rather strongly: schooling has changed from a socially usable upbringing for an élite to a practical vocational training for a much broader group. Because of this growth teaching has occupied a much larger part of the lives of university teachers, and because of the changed composition of the student population the question of the efficiency of education has grown greatly in importance. Also social development and cost aspects have played a greater role.

> In summary, it could be said that the academics themselves have become more aware of their role as teachers and that the demands made of education have become heavier.

## 8.4 The institutional context of staff development

In their paper on the RWO-centres van der Klauw and Wagemakers (1976), under the heading 'Educational climate', wrote:

> Within the universities education as a rule has little status. The career of university staff is generally exclusively based on their performance in the field of research and they are not trained for their teaching functions. Therefore the teaching staff is neither concerned nor interested in teaching.

This is an important statement, implying as it does that attempts to improve teaching in Dutch universities will be severely hampered by a lack of institutional incentives. In particular, it implies that the careers of academics who devote themselves to teaching are unlikely to be successful (in so far as success is dependent on extrinsic rewards).

In order to test current (1978) opinion on this matter the statement was broken into four components and included in the questionnaire sent to RWO-centres. The format of the question included the published form of the statement (and a reference to its source) followed by the question:

> To what extent do you feel that this statement is true for your university now? Please comment separately on each of the points made in it; evidence in support of your comments would be most useful.
>
> — Within the universities education, as a rule, has little status.
> — The career of university staff is generally exclusively based on their performance in the field of research.
> — They are not trained for their teaching functions.
> — The teaching staff is neither concerned, nor interested, in teaching.

Eleven replies to this question were received, and it rapidly became clear that most respondents could not give unqualified assent to all four of the points in the question. There was general agreement, subject to a few qualifications, with the first three points, but eight of the 11 replies disagreed with the claim that 'the teaching staff is neither concerned, nor interested, in teaching'; the three in agreement all felt the proposition overstated the facts. Independent corroboration of the substance of the questionnaire responses can be found in Plomp and van der Meer's (1977) account of problems they encountered in implementing an individualized course:

> We agree with Vroon (1975) who, writing about Dutch universities, states that intensive concern with teaching problems is inhibited rather than stimulated. Scientific achievements are rated higher than didactical skills; one does not make a name by improving one's teaching but by writing a highly specialized dissertation and by adding to one's list of scientific publications.

Accordingly, teachers often are (or want to be) interested in teaching techniques and problems, but the values implicit in the reward system in Dutch universities make it difficult to turn *interest* into *practice*. Discouragement of teaching excellence goes beyond the individual level, moreover; in the same paper, for example, Plomp and van der Meer speak of 'the lack of financial support for innovations in teaching'.

### 8.4.1 An emerging philosophy of staff development

It is by no means clear that one can speak of 'the philosophy' of staff development in Dutch higher education. There are one or two pointers in the 'Higher education in the future' planning paper as to what the now defunct den Uyl Government might have had in mind (NUFFIC, [1976a], p 11; see also van Eijk and Kleijer [1977] and references cited there), but that memorandum has not become law. There is an indication that the governing bodies of the universities would like to see a more efficient processing of student input into academic output — see, for example, Utrecht's Rector Magnificus Verhoef, quoted in

Ackers and Rigter (1976). There are signs among the RWO-centres that they would like to see university teachers armed with a larger arsenal of teaching skills and, in most cases, a more humanitarian approach to teaching. By promoting student evaluation of courses and teachers the RWO-centres are supporting implicitly the line that students should be part of the development process (a trend reinforced by the democratizing process of the 1970 University Administration [Reform] Act).Equally there are signs (for example, their patronising of the services offered by the RWO-centres) that some staff at least are willing to contemplate being developed.

However, as the Netherlands Science Policy Research Council pointed out in its 1976 report on mobility among Dutch research staff (reported in *Higher Education and Research in the Netherlands,* NUFFIC, 1977, p 23), there is a mobility problem for Dutch academics. In the aftermath of the expansion of the universities in the 1960s there are few new posts and most existing staff are young, promoted automatically and are in tenured posts which they are unlikely to leave. Most academics' careers are therefore predetermined to a large degree. Were the incentive structure within the universities to be changed (as it may well be) to provide more balanced rewards for excellence in either research or teaching, it is likely that the impact would be minimal. There are signs that the van Agt Government is about to take a tougher line with the academics (see, for example, the article 'Academics face time clock control of working hours' in the *Times Higher Education Supplement* of 24 March 1978). The philosophy of staff development that emerges may well be one with its roots more firmly in the hard soil of 'efficiency' and 'accountability' than in the harmonious, heavenly pastures described by Piper and Glatter (1977).

*Acknowledgements*
Much of the initial research for this chapter was carried out during the six months from July to December 1977 when I was on study leave at the Department of Research and Development in Higher Education, State University, Utrecht. I also visited the RWO-centres at Nijmegen, Maastricht, Rotterdam and the Free University, Amsterdam. My thanks to the staff of all of these centres, and for special help with this chapter to Pierre van Eijl (Utrecht), Cees van Dorp (Tilburg) and Ernest Roe (Brisbane).

# 9: New Zealand — working with teachers towards course improvement

John C Clift and Bradford W Imrie

## 9.0 Introduction

In New Zealand, higher education is available in a range of institutions comprising the universities, technical institutes, and teachers' colleges. As yet it has not been considered necessary to produce specific definitions of the roles or functions of any of these institutions. All are involved in contributing to the further education of the school-leaver and to vocational education, as well as in responding to the needs of professions, commerce and industry. Although this flexibility is desirable, it nevertheless contributes to some ambivalence of attitudes of staff, within these institutions, to their role as teachers and to expectations of society.

Another feature of higher education in New Zealand is the public's expectation that, as for primary and secondary education, most of the finance for capital and running expenses of the tertiary level institutions should come from public funds. It is also expected that bursaries should be generally available to enable students to attend and that there should be easy access to university, with a minimal selection or low threshold entry policy. This relatively open entry into higher education presents problems for teaching and, in the universities, results in high failure rates particularly in the initial years of study, although giving opportunity to a wider range of school achievement.

Miller (1970, p 19) commented on some comparisons:

> Selection does not appear to be as rigorous as in Britain. If a wider range of ability were allowed to enter first year courses it would be possible to give a fighting chance to the highly motivated though *apparently* less able candidates, who might have been rejected in a less open system.

The relation of entry qualifications to failure rates was also reported on to the National Development Conference in 1969. The report considered the position of all the tertiary institutions in suggesting that improvement in the quality of teaching could help deal with the problem of failure. Clearly, appropriate policies and programmes of staff development would have some significance for the quality of teaching at the tertiary level.

In institutions of higher education, staff development is conceived in terms of in-service training. The appointment conditions and criteria used by these institutions preclude pre-service training except, perhaps, for the incidental teaching qualification which most teachers' college lecturers will have before appointment. Because of the particular nature and traditions of the different groups of institutions, each group tends to approach staff development differently.

## 9.1 Universities

Prior to 1961, New Zealand had one Federal University with four constituent colleges and two agricultural colleges. The University Act, in 1961, granted autonomy to each of the constituent colleges at Auckland, Wellington, Christchurch, and Dunedin. Since then, two additional universities have been created: the University of Waikato (1964) in Hamilton and Massey University[1] (1964) in Palmerston North.

By international standards, New Zealand universities are not large; Table 9.1 shows the number of staff and students in 1978.

#### Table 9.1 Number of students and academic staff at New Zealand universities in 1978

| University | Full-time students | Part-time students | Staff |
|---|---|---|---|
| Auckland | 7760 | 3294 | 757 |
| Waikato | 1797 | 1388 | 186 |
| Massey* | 3758 | 1197 | 475 |
| Victoria | 4483 | 2503 | 390 |
| Canterbury | 5167 | 2232 | 444 |
| Otago** | 5419 | 1451 | 617 |
| Lincoln College | 1293 | 93 | 156 |

   * *Also 6029 extra-mural students*
 ** *Including full-time staff of the Clinical Schools of Otago University Faculty of Medicine located at Christchurch and Wellington.*

The 'teaching climate' within these universities has been affected significantly, first by expansion and then by the end of expansion; the effects have been compounded, in some respects, by fluctuations in the popularity of various courses of study. The 1960s saw a demand for science, which was replaced by a swing to the social sciences, and now seems to be changing into an increasing interest in vocational courses related to commerce and administration.

Since the majority of university staff have tenure of appointment, universities have real difficulty in responding to the changes in staffing required to meet these fluctuating demands. Unfortunately, this has frequently resulted in unequal distribution of resources between departments in relation to student numbers. For example, staff : student ratios can vary from 1 : 6 in one department to 1 : 22 in another.[2]

In selecting staff for teaching positions, academic excellence is still the principal criterion. While the last decade has seen a greater recognition of the need to improve the general level of teaching in the universities (Educational Development Conference, 1974, p 106), previous teaching experience and qualifications are of minor importance in the appointment stakes (National Council of Adult Education, 1977, p 17).

In the 1960s in New Zealand, as in Australia, Britain and elsewhere, the expansion of higher education brought in its wake a growing pressure on the universities to consider their relationships with the other tertiary institutions and to reconsider how and what they teach, and how they might evaluate their effectiveness (Advisory Council on Educational Planning, 1974, p 86). The sources of pressure are difficult to identify. Certainly, the growth and development of other tertiary institutions has caused the universities to scrutinize their role; the move towards accountability in education has had its effects on the universities and, without doubt, student activity made the universities more conscious of the inadequacies of much of their teaching (*Salient,* 1962a, 1962b). Evidence of this concern about the quality of teaching students experience is to be found in at least one university as far back as 1962, when the editor of the student newspaper asked the university for permission to evaluate all first-year classes. The university responded by setting up a committee to investigate how teaching standards might be improved. Permission to evaluate lectures was not given.

To appreciate the present situation, it is necessary to consider the roles of students, staff, and institutions with reference to moves to improve the general quality of university education, of which staff development is part. One early attempt by students to improve the quality of teaching and examining in their university has already been mentioned. In 1968 the national student body entered the scene and, in collaboration with their Canterbury University branch, attempted to establish guidelines for the role of students in evaluating courses or staff. The evaluation questionnaire associated with this initial exercise was used on a trial basis in 1968. Since then the New Zealand University Students' Association has striven continually, by publication and direct action, for improvements in courses, presentation, and examining (New Zealand University Students' Association, 1971; Bassey, 1971).

The Vice-Chancellors of the New Zealand universities meet at regular intervals to exchange views on all aspects of university development. This committee has, for many years now, approved the holding of inter-university subject conferences in each discipline on a triennial basis. The prime purpose of these conferences is 'discussion of academic and administrative problems, such as curricula development, course structures, teaching, examining and assessing' (New Zealand Vice-Chancellors Committee, 1976, p 5). While, arguably, such activity could be claimed to contribute to staff development, its impact is questionable since discussion tends to centre around existing systems and traditions and there is little, if any, new information from outside sources.

At a meeting of the New Zealand universities held in 1969, there was consideration of the quality and performance of students. As a result, the New Zealand Vice-Chancellors Committee now provides an annual report on the academic progress of students at New Zealand universities (New Zealand Vice-Chancellors Committee, 1969-74). This led to individual universities producing their own statistics and, in many cases, these have acted as a stimulus for debate about university education.

Apart from these activities, there has not been the visible support for staff development in New Zealand universities, by the Vice-Chancellors Committee or by the University Grants Committee, that there has been both in Australia and the UK, where national committees and conferences have been established and funds made available to support efforts to improve the quality of university education. As yet there have been no moves for co-operation between universities at the national level, and there is no New Zealand equivalent to the UK Co-ordinating Committee for the Training of University Teachers (see Section 2a.1.2). The universities feel that little can be gained by national co-operation and, in fact, consider that it might divert attention from the need for each university to accept responsibility for staff development.

At the local level, co-operation exercises have been introduced in at least two areas. In Christchurch, the Tertiary Education Liaison Committee has established a sub-committee on teaching procedures. In November 1977, this sub-committee, 'in response to a longstanding and often repeated demand for some sort of teacher training in tertiary institutions in Christchurch', prepared a proposal for a joint local training programme. The proposed programme required a year's part-time commitment by participants, with partial release from duties, and acknowledgement of successful completion by the awarding of a certificate. To date, no final decision has been taken in regard to the proposal.

In Wellington, with the assistance of the Department of University Extension, the University Teaching and Research Centre, in conjunction with the Wellington Polytechnic and the Wellington Teachers College, mounted a series of minicourses for those teaching adults. While the programme is directed at a more general audience, it is nevertheless seen as being suitable for those teaching in tertiary institutions. The first series of courses was run in 1978, and the response has warranted a further programme for 1979, in which the Tutor Training Unit (see Section 9.2) will also be involved.

The NZ Association of University Teachers, through its local branches and often in co-operation with lecturers associations, has provided what might be described as 'informational' programmes. As early as 1961, the University of Canterbury Branch of the Association of University Teachers had introduced biennial one-day seminars which incorporated a number of lecture/discussion sessions about the teaching/learning process. Such programmes do not, however, provide the conditions necessary for systematic development of individual skills of course design, presentation and assessment. These objectives call for a regular series of activities in which the emphasis is on practice rather than listening.

In a submission to a nationwide conference on educational priorities, the Association of University Teachers stated that it was 'not prepared to accept that provision for the training of university teachers is a luxury that can be treated lightly' (Association of University Teachers of New Zealand, 1972, p 1). Its submission urged the University Grants Committee to make adequate allowance in its funding to the universities to further the development of suitable staff development programmes. There is no evidence to suggest that this plea was successful.

These groups have made various attempts over the years to improve the quality of university education, by identifying problems, gauging student reaction to course and teaching, and making staff better informed about matters related to teaching and learning.

It was with this background and with hopes of progress that the universities looked to the establishment of units for staff development and education research.

### 9.1.1 University of Canterbury

In New Zealand, the first higher education research unit was established at the University of Canterbury in 1969. This unit, the Educational Research and Advisory Unit, was the executive arm of the University's Professorial Board's Standing Committee on Educational Policy.

The first full-time appointment to the unit was made in 1970, when Dr Sally Hunter was appointed as Research Officer. At this stage, the main objective of the unit was to

> provide the fullest information possible as a background for discussions and decisions on academic developments arising from the day-to-day operations of the University.[3]

In 1972 a full-time Educational Advisory Officer, Mr Roderick McKay, was appointed to provide educational services to assist staff in the improvement of teaching practices and examining techniques.

Since then, in addition to its task of providing information to facilitate academic decisions, the unit has had the responsibility of mounting courses for academic staff on teaching practices and examining techniques, and of providing an advisory and consultative service to individual staff members seeking assistance to improve the quality of their teaching.

Courses are offered during term time rather than in the vacation periods, and the spaced out format of several sessions rather than the concentrated commitment over two or three days has been found to be the more successful. Initially, 'how to' programmes were popular, but the trend now is towards deeper professional exploration of topics:

> I can foresee more use of the study group approach in which lecturers with common interests and enthusiasm enter into peer teaching and mutual development exercises. I would certainly like to see my role as a catalyst for self-help groups continue to expand. There will always be a place for basic practical techniques courses; perhaps these can become more effective by keeping them specific and pragmatic in their aims, rather than attempting to emulate our early offerings in which the practical impact was perhaps diluted by attempts to include discursive and philosophical material which I now think is better and more professionally treated by the 'study group' approach.[4]

In 1977 Dr Tuan Emery was appointed full-time director of the Educational Research and Advisory Unit. The unit receives administrative support from the university's administrative services.

### 9.1.2 Victoria University of Wellington

Following discussions which started in 1969, the McKenzie Education Foundation offered a generous 'seeding' grant to the university to establish a university teaching and research centre. This offer was accepted and in June 1973 Professor John C Clift took up the position of founding director. In addition to the director, the centre now has a staff of senior lecturer (Mr B W Imrie), junior lecturer (Mrs Christine Leong), secretary, and part-time research assistant.

The centre is an autonomous academic entity within the university, with the director responsible to the University Council through the Vice-Chancellor for the satisfactory administration of the centre. The director has full professorial status and centre staff are appointed within the academic structure. The centre has a close association with a professorial board committee on teaching and learning.

The centre was envisaged as

> providing a service to teaching staff and becoming a source of help and

advice to those departments and members of staff who might wish to consult with it on aspects of course planning, organization of teaching programmes, lecture preparation and presentation, the conduct of seminars and other teaching and learning situations, the working out of examination objectives and techniques and, in general, the range of teaching methods including the use of teaching aids.

It was envisaged also that the centre would

through its accumulation of information and its library and data service, act as an information centre and clearing house, enabling university staff to keep in touch with developments in university teaching practice and academic course developments in the other New Zealand universities and in universities overseas.[5]

The organization and structure of the centre was influenced greatly by the guidelines prepared by the Australian Vice-Chancellors Committee's Report on Higher Education Research Units (see pp 248-54). This was possibly inevitable since the director of the centre, prior to taking up his appointment, had been a member of the working party which produced that report.

In carrying out its task, the centre has found it convenient to group staff development activities under three headings: teaching, advisory, research (Figure 9.1). The teaching programme (Figure 9.2) is aimed at helping staff to develop their skills of course design, presentation, assessment and evaluation, to widen their knowledge of the range of appropriate techniques available, and to provide opportunities for them to gain confidence in the use of these techniques and skills. While some of these programmes are designed to cater for participants from a wide variety of academic departments, other programmes are provided at the request of specific departments. In both cases the centre attempts to involve university staff in the preparation and presentation of such programmes.

For those who wish to study the discipline of higher education, the centre offers three courses as part of the Diploma in Educational Studies and the Bachelor of Educational Studies.

Seminars are also organized in collaboration with other university committees to provide the opportunity for the university community to discuss and debate its own policies, activities and effectiveness.

The teaching programme is seen as only one step towards the goal of improving the quality of teaching and learning. Just as important is a strong advisory or consultation service (Figure 9.3) and a research programme. While the centre may generate its own research projects, most proposals stem from department and faculty demands. This is particularly true of evaluation studies. A major problem in university teaching stems from the fact that staff and students often do not appreciate how to make the most of the resources for teaching and

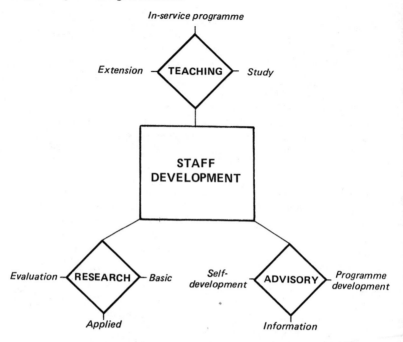

Figure 9.1 Provisions for staff development, University
Teaching and Research Centre, Victoria University

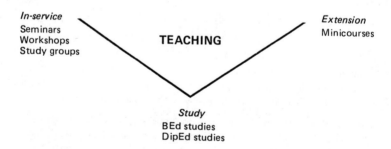

Figure 9.2 The teaching programme of the University Teaching
and Research Centre, Victoria University

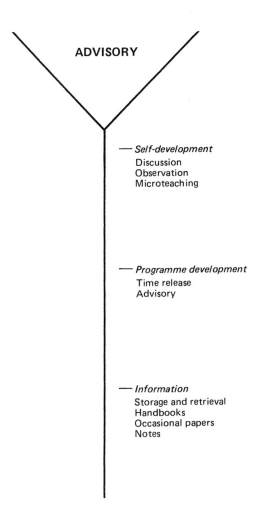

Figure 9.3 Advisory services of the University Teaching and
Research Centre, Victoria University

learning available to them. To this end evaluation studies, involving staff and students working together, have been found to be an important in-service activity for improving the educational quality of a course and the professional competence of teachers (Clift and Imrie, 1977).

In all its activities, the centre emphasizes the importance of the principle of working with rather than for people; there is more benefit if departments or individual staff members or students work on their own problems, supported by advice and resources from the centre. The centre has no supervisory role and, in all its work with individuals, departments or faculties, confidentiality is rigorously observed.

### 9.1.3 University of Auckland

Since 1970 there have been courses in teaching methods for academic staff. These courses were initially the responsibility of the Centre for Continuing Education but in 1974 they became the responsibility of the newly established Higher Education Research Office (HERO). This office is staffed by a Higher Education Research Officer, Dr John Jones, supported by research and secretarial assistance. In making the initial appointment, the university saw the duties of the Higher Education Research Officer as being primarily research oriented:

> As a result of research and other activities, the Higher Education Research Officer will be expected to improve the quality of University education in Auckland. He will be required to respond to requests from Departments to investigate and report on such matters as: the basis and methods of students' selection where enrolment is restricted; specific teaching and examining problems including innovations and experiments in teaching and examining methods; the effectiveness of various pedagogical aids; the effective use of student and staff time in various learning and teaching contexts; the causes of success and failure of various student groups; the reliability of examining and course assessment procedures; the effectiveness of various courses as training for the professions; and many other matters related to the teaching and examining functions of the University.[6]

At the time of the establishment of the Higher Education Research Office, the university already had an audiovisual centre.

In 1978 the university approved plans for a teaching methods and research centre (TMRC) which will be responsible for the area of overlap in the activities of HERO and the audiovisual centre. As is the case at present for HERO, TMRC will be responsible to the University Senate and Council through the Academic Committee of Senate. Currently the Higher Education Research Office runs a series of short courses primarily for new/inexperienced staff to introduce them to some basic teaching skills and to help them make contact with other 'new' members of staff and the resources available for teaching. Other courses dealing with specific themes, such as assessment, cater for both new and more experienced staff. A paper in higher education is available also in the undergraduate degree programme.

### 9.1.4 University of Otago

With the establishment of two staff development agencies, the
University of Otago is rather unique on the New Zealand scene. One of
these agencies, the Audio Visual Learning Centre (AVLC) has a major
commitment to educational technology, with emphasis on audiovisual
media. Even so, it has as a major aim the task of 'improving and
advising academic staff on teaching methods and course evaluation'.

The Centre was established in late 1973 with the appointment of
Dr David Teather as the founding academic director. Even though the
centre has a relatively large staff of nine, including a librarian,
technicians and secretaries, the directorship remains the only
academic post.

Also in 1973 the university invited applications for the 'newly created
position of Director of Research Unit in Higher Education'. The
position was seen as an advisory one with a research framework:

> the Director to initiate studies which are relevant to the problems of
> teaching and examining within the University and to make available
> to staff information or practical guidance which may contribute to
> the quality of teaching.[7]

The position has not yet been filled. In 1976 the Higher Education
Research and Advisory Centre (HERAC) was established with the
full-time appointment in 1978 of Dr Terry Crooks as lecturer-in-charge,
supported by a half-time research assistant.

Both the AVLC and HERAC are funded through the university budget,
and are responsible to the University Senate through its Academic
Services Committee. The two centres combine to provide a
comprehensive series of seminars and workshops throughout the year.
Dr Teather and Dr Crooks teach papers within the university's
Department of Education Diploma in Education and help teaching
staff in a consultative role.[8]

### 9.1.5 Waikato University, Massey University
###        and Lincoln Agricultural College

These institutions have not as yet established full-time staff
development units. Nevertheless, they do have very active committees
responsible to their professorial boards for co-ordinating and
organizing staff development activities.

### 9.1.6 General

As mentioned in the introduction to this chapter, the universities have
no clear single role. If anything, in their efforts to meet the
accountability challenge, they have moved more towards those tasks
that appear to have public approval. This is particularly so in the
provision of multi-disciplinary courses for graduates who find

employment in business, industry or teaching. Green (1969) suggests that such a shift is seen by many as a lowering of academic standards. Certainly, those students entering such programmes appear to be more concerned with obtaining their qualifications than with scholarship. Whether this attitude stems from the nature of the programmes, or from the teaching and attitudes of the teachers, it is hard to judge. It is also true that staff tend to display an ambivalence towards this more generalized teaching. Such teaching is seen by some as requiring the 'mere communication of known truths' (Wilson, 1967), which reduces teaching to the level where it is viewed as a trivial task.

This 'mechanical' concept of teaching was encouraged in the 1960s when, partly in response to student demands for improved teaching, a number of the universities made a considerable investment in audiovisual aids and, in particular, in television. This investment was supported by courses, seminars and workshops run to motivate and instruct lecturers in the use of such equipment. Such programmes catered for the enthusiast but were seen by many as being of a trivial nature, which reinforced their views of teacher-training.

It was soon appreciated by those involved that a worthwhile programme of staff development should include serious study of matters pedagogical and androgogical (Knowles, 1970), and should also be identified with ethics and standards commensurate with the continuing evolution of higher education.

Perhaps the above developments are some of the 'causes' which led to the 'effect' described by Sir Zelman Cowen[9] (1972, p 23) when, in writing about the Australian scene, he suggested that:

> There has been a persistent downgrading of undergraduate teaching. Staff say that there is no adequate recognition of teaching performance.

And, in talking about the changing attitudes of senior and often distinguished university teachers:

> Research, postgraduate studies, extra-university activities involving substantial absences from the university, are seen as preferred activities.

In the UK, similar remarks have been made by observers such as Dainton[10] (1974):

> Perhaps the most disappointing feature of the universities for the young is the learning experience itself.

> . . . most (university teachers) have never received in their careers any kind of preparation for the tasks of encouraging student learning and assessing students' progress, nor will they do so if they look for their rewards and promotions through achieving status accorded to them by research.

> There are many students whose motivation is weakened by the feeling their teacher ranks his teaching of them lower in priority to the research which he hopes will lead to his promotion.

There is no evidence to suggest that the situation in New Zealand is any different. Whatever the reasons, be they the status of teaching, lack of professionalism, inadequate recognition for tenure and promotion, or the lack of valid criteria to judge teaching competence (Hore, 1973), there does appear to be substantial resistance by university staff to engaging in a worthwhile programme of staff development.

## 9.2 Technical institutes and community colleges

Within New Zealand there are several institutes which developed out of the secondary school system to provide further education directly related to or in preparation for a trade or profession (Lee, 1970). These are the technical institutes. Two, the Central Institute of Technology (CIT) and the Technical Correspondence Institute, are national institutes; in addition there are 15 regional institutes. Of more recent development are the community colleges, of which there are now four.

While the New Zealand universities are autonomous institutions, the technical institutes and community colleges are governed by bodies representative of outside community interests, and are subject to State control through the Department of Education. As mentioned, the majority of the work in the institutes is vocationally directed although, in recent years, more students have been taking courses for cultural or recreational reasons. Indeed, the community colleges are concerned mainly with cultural and community studies. The courses offered by the institutes are generally day-release or block or sandwich courses.

Tutors within the institutes and community colleges have a wide variety of qualifications, ranging from trade certificates to doctorates. Few tutors have had any form of teacher-training, and many are employed only on a part-time basis.

In 1973 the State Department of Education was authorized by the New Zealand Government to establish a national 12-week initial training course for tutors entering the technical institutes. A Tutor Training Advisory Council was formed, and a Tutor Training Unit established within the Central Institute of Technology. The Head of the Tutor Training Unit is Mr A B Carter and he is supported by a staff of nine, including two technicians and a secretary. Associated with its main function of providing initial tutor training, it also provides a consulting service for tutors, conducts research into the needs of tutors and students in technical institutes, and provides courses on special topics of interest to tutors.

All new tutors, unless they have had previous teacher-training, are required to undertake the 12-week course, which is divided into three short block courses each of a month in length. The first block of training is focused on the class and, in particular, those skills and techniques associated with the preparation and presentation of lessons, the assessment of students, and classroom management. The second block extends these skills while introducing more theoretical material associated with student learning and the aims of education. The third block course provides opportunities for personal development through assignments and individual projects.

Once the tutors have returned to their home institution, they are supposed to become involved in further staff development activity. In at least four of the regional institutes, special provision has been made for this continuing staff development.

### 9.2.1 Auckland Technical Institute
The Teaching and Learning Resource Centre was established in March 1975, and a full-time director, Mr A Johnson, was appointed in February 1976. The director is responsible directly to the principal of the institute, and is assisted by a graphics technician. The centre's task is to act as an organizer and planner of workshops, courses and seminars for tutors, to provide an advisory service to staff seeking assistance, and to develop an audiovisual media resource centre.

### 9.2.2 Central Institute of Technology (CIT)
As a result of a recommendation from the CIT's Board of Studies, an educational resources unit was established in October 1977, with Mr J Upritchard as tutor-in-charge. The unit is required to co-ordinate existing teaching resources and to provide staff with assistance in course planning, material presentation and student assessment.

### 9.2.3 Christchurch Technical Institute
With the appointment of Mr M Pentecost in February 1975, the Learning Resources Centre at the Christchurch Technical Institute was historically the first staff development centre to be established in a technical institute. The director of the centre is at senior tutor level, and he is responsible to the Staff Education and Development Standing Committee, which acts as a controlling committee. While the main thrust of the centre has been towards the development and use of audiovisual aids, a considerable effort is now made to provide a more balanced staff development programme. Recently the centre has taken over responsibility for running the Tutor Training Unit's second block course for local tutors.

### 9.2.4 Manukau Technical Institute
The Institute has an educational resource centre which aims to improve teaching standards within the institute and to develop skills that tutors have learned at the Tutor Training Unit in Wellington. There is one full-time tutor, and the centre provides a range of activities, including

such topics as lesson planning and assessment techniques, use of overhead projectors and other teaching aids.

### 9.2.5 Otago Polytechnic
In 1976 the services provided by the library were extended to include a tutor resource centre, which is responsible for non-book resources. The centre also provides courses on the use of audiovisual aids.

### 9.2.6 Wellington Polytechnic
A teaching resources unit was initially established on an experimental basis within the School of General Studies. At the beginning of 1976 the unit became responsible directly to the deputy principal, and independent of any one school. Initially, the emphasis of the unit was towards the provision of audiovisual aids, but it has now become increasingly involved in staff development activities.

### 9.2.7 Other institutes
The remaining regional institutes, mainly because of their size, have been unable to establish formal staff development units. They have coped by selecting an appropriate tutor to act in a part-time capacity as the Tutor Training Unit Liaison Officer.

### 9.2.8 Other staff development activities
It was the intention of the Tutor Training Advisory Council that a certificate or diploma programme would be introduced to follow on from the initial 12-week training course. It was to be based on a correspondence strategy with associated block or in-service courses. However, approval for such a programme has been deferred by the New Zealand Government. In addition to the tutor training courses and institutional in-service programmes, tutors are encouraged to attend national and regional courses organized by the State Department of Education. Tutors are also entitled to industrial refresher leave, which is a period of paid leave after five years' service, to enable tutors to obtain appropriate experience in industry.

### 9.2.9 New Zealand Association of Teachers in Technical Institutes (ATTI)
The ATTI first established a policy for teacher-training of tutors in 1971, and this policy has been updated recently. In addition to supporting the 12-week initial training programme, the Association believes that

☐ Tutor resource centres should be established in each institute to provide for voluntary participation by both full-time and part-time tutors. The emphasis of the centres' programmes should be on learning and teaching attitudes.

☐ New tutors should have a reduction in class contact time.

☐ Study leave should be available for
  − attending in-service training courses, conferences, seminars, etc
  − tutors to complete qualifications
  − refreshment.

☐ Training needs to be provided for principals, heads of departments, and course supervisors.

## 9.3 Teachers' colleges

There are two secondary teachers' colleges and six primary teachers' colleges in New Zealand. These colleges are involved in the training and education of schoolteachers and, at the tertiary level, are responsible for the vocational and subject studies of adolescents and adults. Some primary teachers' colleges, such as Dunedin, Palmerston North, and Hamilton, are associated with local universities in BEd programmes. Auckland and North Shore Teachers' Colleges are collaborating with Auckland University in providing a BA programme of studies for primary school college students. There are similar arrangements for students at the Secondary Teachers' College, Auckland.

Many teachers' colleges are developing continuing education, in-service programmes for teachers, and are also becoming involved in pre-service training for other professions, eg, certificate courses provided at the NZ Library School will be transferred to the Wellington Teachers' College from the beginning of 1980.

A normal requirement for appointment to the staff of a teachers' college is recent and successful experience in schoolteaching. College staff are usually made up of senior people in the profession or younger people who are making very able and rapid progression. However, further professional development is required for teaching at the tertiary level.

> Because we are a teachers college, there is also further point to staff training. Whatever we do must be seen to be the best model we can produce, regardless of what we are teaching or why.[11]

While most of the teachers' colleges have established committees to organize staff development activities, there has been no move by any of the colleges to establish a unit or centre, or to make a full-time appointment in this area. Lecturing staff are encouraged to improve the quality of their teaching by obtaining evaluation information about their courses from their students, and from the schools at which the students undertake teaching practice.

In most of the colleges, staff may attend staff development programmes, many of which are run within the subject departments. Colleges also encourage staff to attend local and national in-service courses and to share these experiences with their colleagues. At Palmerston North Teachers' College, where there is a declining student roll and a stable teaching staff,[12] the college intends to handle retraining or staff development on an individual basis, a procedure which they have found successful in the past.

## 9.4 The future

What of the future? There can be no argument that over the last decade in New Zealand there has been an ever-increasing awareness by the institutions, both staff and students, of the need to consider the quality of teaching and learning in our tertiary institutions. The impetus started with student and staff associations, and their efforts brought to the surface the dissatisfaction felt by many. In this atmosphere it was not surprising that the quality of tertiary education should be debated and become a topic for comment by a number of working parties and committees established to consider various aspects of education in New Zealand. Of the reports prepared by these various groups, that published by the New Zealand Advisory Council on Educational Planning (ACEP) is probably the first significant report to comment on the quality of teaching and learning at the tertiary level. The report (Advisory Council on Educational Planning, 1974) resulting from the extensive Education Development Conference held in 1973 stated that (p 85): 'more attention needs to be paid to the continuing education of those who teach in tertiary institutions.' The report goes on to 'note with approval' the move by universities to review their educational programmes and to develop programmes aimed at improving the quality of university teaching.

A second significant report was that prepared by the Marshall Committee on the Registration and Discipline of Teachers (1978). This report recommends a diploma in teaching as the basic teacher qualification for registration. In discussing who should be required to register as teachers the committee concluded that for those teaching in technical institutes:

> While the registration of tutors would be in the public interest it is not feasible to recommend registration at present. The Committee recommends, however, that in the meantime, tutors with the requisite qualifications should be encouraged to register, and that suitable teacher training should be provided so that registration is ultimately available at least to all full-time tutors (p 20).

The committee's findings in regard to university staff were somewhat similar:

> registration should not be a requirement for university teachers at this stage but that those who wish should be permitted to register if they are qualified. For lecturers who have teaching responsibilities, the Committee believes that provision should be made within the university for teaching

skills programmes to be made available and that the teachers' registration authority should investigate, in consultation with the university authorities, the introduction of a system of registration for university teachers (p 20).

Finally, a third important document will be the report from a working party established in November 1977 by the Minister of Education to review teacher-training in New Zealand. At the time of writing, the final report is not available but the Working Party Paper, considered at a National Conference held in August 1978, contained a number of themes related to the training of tertiary teachers:

- greater emphasis on teaching ability of staff in all tertiary institutions
- the provision of opportunities by way of time release from teaching, and a teaching commitment limited in range and depth of responsibility to encourage probationary staff to take advantage of professional development programmes in teaching
- the requirement of evidence of contribution to teaching and administration and, in the case of universities, as criteria for promotion
- a system of study leave to be instituted for teachers' college staff
- the system of tutor training for technical institutes to be evaluated
- courses to be available on the complexity of dealing with students of other ethnic origins
- provision of induction courses for new staff.

These documents would indicate that the interest in teacher education has not abated.

In June 1979 the second triennial conference on staff development in universities will be held at Victoria University. Such conferences of specialists in a particular field or discipline are funded by the Vice-Chancellors Committee to enable exchanges of experience and view to take place. The Vice-Chancellors Committee has asked this particular conference to report on the following extract from a report[13] prepared by the Committee's representatives at the Review of Teacher Training Conference (1978):

> One matter to the side of the main themes of the conference gave us concern. This was the critical and negative attitude that found expression in various ways at the conference, including some statements in the report of the Working Party itself, towards the manner in which the universities are responding, or seen to be responding, to their responsibilities as teaching institutions. Arising out of this concern we *recommend that the Vice-Chancellors' Committee take initiative in the convening of a gathering of appropriate persons from each university, to examine and report on developments in each university with respect to a range of issues involved*

*in the teaching functions of the universities.* The major purpose of such a gathering would be to report on the progress being made in each university to strengthen its teaching activities, with a view to encouraging improved methods of teaching and providing for cross fertilisation of different developments in the separate universities. A minor purpose would be the tactical one of enabling it to be seen that the universities, collectively, are taking seriously their teaching functions and, further, of being able to provide a documented account of what is taking place for the information of interested persons and groups.

Both the Association of University Teachers and the Association of Teachers in Technical Institutes are reviewing current policy, and the NZ University Students Association has given notice of its intention to apply pressure continually to have additional resources made available to provide more organized training for university staff.

Talk and good intentions, however, are not enough. They may well create a climate favourable to some form of teacher-training or staff development, but effective professional development has little to do with attendance at courses. What is critical is the attitude of teaching staff to their task. A major objective of any in-service programme must be to create, within the institution, an atmosphere receptive to educational principles and practices: an atmosphere in which the quality of teaching is seen as the intentional product of a number of considered decisions made by people at all levels within the institution. Such an objective places the emphasis on the institution as a centre of learning in which faculty and students are seen as partners in the processes of learning; the teacher knowledgeable in content and competent in managing the conditions of learning; the students knowledgeable about their responsibilities in the learning situation and sharing the relevance of the learning experience.

With this as an overall aim for improving the quality of tertiary education, the aim of staff development must then shift from its narrow concern with teaching methods to finding ways of working with teachers to help them solve particular educational problems related to specific situations. By researching and considering teaching and learning in this way, the professional teaching task may eventually be seen as more than just the mere imparting of known facts, and be given equivalent scholarship status to research, when applications for appointments and promotions are being considered. This latter situation will require those responsible for staff development to find solutions to the four factors associated with 'promotion through teaching' (Hore, 1973):

— establishment of criteria against which teachers can be judged
— the development of instruments to provide an assessment
— the provision of some agency to administer the assessment devices

 — the cultivation of an environment to act upon the information derived from the instruments.

*Notes*

1. Massey University was formed by the merger of Massey Agricultural College (founded 1926) and the Palmerston North branch of Victoria University of Wellington.

2. As reported in the 1980-85 Quinquennial Submission of Victoria University.

3. 'Aims and Objectives' of the Educational Research and Advisory Unit.

4. Correspondence between McKay and Clift, July 1978.

5. Both statements appear in the conditions of appointment prepared by the University.

6. From the newspaper advertisement for the vacancy.

7. From the advertisement for the position which appeared in *The Australian*, 24 March 1973.

8. *Editor's note:* In November 1978 the Otago University Council approved the merging of the Audio Visual Learning Centre and the Higher Education Research and Advisory Centre into one unit. This is now known as the Higher Education Development Centre.

9. Sir Zelman Cowen, Vice-Chancellor, University of Queensland (1970-77).

10. Sir Frederick Dainton, Chairman of the University Grants Committee (1973-78).

11. In response to an inquiry about staff development provisions at Christchurch Teachers' College.

12. This is typical of all the other colleges.

13. Report by Professor P S Freyberg (Waikato) and Professor W G Malcolm (Victoria) to the Vice-Chancellors Committee, September 1978.

# 10: Sweden — strong central provision complementing local initiatives

Hans Jalling

## 10.0 Background

Up to the end of World War II the major part of university teaching was given by professorial staff (in Sweden holders of chairs). It is true that the professors' teaching was supplemented by junior staff (*docents*), particularly in introductory courses, but owing to the increase of students — 75 per cent between 1918 and 1938 — and the minimal teaching obligations of the junior staff, this picture did not change much during the inter-war period. From 1945 onwards, however, the tendency has been to create a series of new academic positions of non-professorial rank with undergraduate teaching as their main concern.

The five public commissions entrusted to review the university system between 1938 and 1968 have shown considerable interest in undergraduate teaching; no commission has, however, dealt with the problem of how to acquire the desired competence as a university teacher. The early 1950s saw a growing concern about the undergraduate situation, particularly in the faculties of arts and sciences. An unacceptable drop-out rate was reported and the students complained about the lack of teaching competence on the part of their tutors. The remedies proposed included the creation of new teaching positions but no training for potential candidates.

Although the Swedish universities have undergone dramatic changes during the last decades — not only regarding numbers and qualifications of their students but also as far as organization and staffing are concerned — it should be pointed out that the question of staff training was never considered by the politicians.

## 10.1 The Committee for University Teaching Methods

One of the organizational changes of the 1960s was the creation of a central governmental agency for the supervision of universities and other institutes of higher learning. The Office of the Chancellor of the

Universities came into existence in 1964 and it is interesting to see that one of its first initiatives was to call a committee of experts to review the need for the training of academic teachers. It is true that the brief of the Committee laid emphasis on the younger members of staff — speaking about professors and *docents* the brief states that 'it can be assumed that by and large they master the pedagogical part of their duties' — but for the first time the issue of teacher-training of academic staff was given serious consideration.

The Committee started its work in April 1964 under the chairmanship of Professor Torsten Husén who had been an influential expert in the reforms of the Swedish school system. However, the Committee soon found its task impossible: 'more definite proposals for a teacher training programme for university teachers must be founded on considerations of the intensity, forms, contents and methods of academic teaching', which were not included in the brief of the Committee.

The problem was solved by the creation of a committee with a broader frame of reference, the Committee for University Teaching Methods. Under the chairmanship of the Vice-Chancellor of Uppsala University, Professor Torgny Segerstedt,[1] the Committee spent five years on a thorough review of academic teaching, during which time it also initiated a series of experiments on teaching and learning. From 1966 it had public funds at its disposal for such experiments.

As is only natural considering the background of the Committee, the possibility of teacher-training for academic staff was one of the central issues. University initiatives were backed financially and the Committee also arranged a series of pilot courses for staff from several universities, usually on a discipline basis. Although it would be an exaggeration to say that these first attempts were a roaring success, it was obvious to everybody that the Committee had an attentive audience — the situation at the universities was chaotic with an ever-increasing number of students, and any help in mastering the problems was gratefully accepted.

At the suggestion of the Committee, the post of 'educational consultant' was established at every university in 1969. Apart from being a specialist in education at the disposal of departments with educational problems, the educational consultant was in charge of the training of new teachers. Thus since 1969 each university has had the mechanism and funds for a more systematic training of teachers.

In its final report, which was presented to the Office of the Chancellor in April 1970, the Committee proposed a two-week introductory training course for new university teachers. It bears an unmistakable resemblance to the provisional proposal of the preceding

Committee (for contents, see Table 10.1) but has the undeniable merit of being a revised edition of the courses offered at the universities.

Table 10.1 Two-week teacher-training course for new
academic staff as proposed by
the Committee for University Teaching Methods

| General part | | |
|---|---|---|
| Lectures | 10 hours | *Contents* Analysis of objectives, |
| Seminars | 20 hours | diagnosis and evaluation, educational planning |
| **Discipline-oriented part** | | |
| Lectures | 5 hours | *Contents* Counselling, planning |
| Seminars | 15 hours | of lectures, audiovisual aids, examinations, oral practice |
| Visits to classes | 8 hours | Under the supervision of the |
| Microteaching | 10 hours | Director of Studies |

NB The course should be spread throughout one semester.

The report was very favourably reviewed by the universities. It is true that there was some doubt even at that time whether the reviews represented the true opinion of the academic staff or whether the universities found it in their interest to go along with more emphasis on teaching. However, the basis for a national programme now existed.

## 10.2 The First National Programme

It rested with the Office of the Chancellor to submit proposals for university development to the Government, and it became the task of the Staff Training Unit — the creation of which was another visible effect of the work of the Committee for University Teaching Methods — to prepare the proposal on the training of university teachers. When analysing the findings of the Committee it was felt, however, that the Committee's proposal was not far-reaching enough.

On the one hand, the Committee proposed the creation of 'senior lecturers', who should be in charge of sections of undergraduate teaching, and increased responsibilities for the Directors of Studies, who should be the departmental experts on educational technology; on the other hand, only courses for *new* staff were proposed. Surely also the older and more experienced academics could learn more about educational methods and planning?

In April 1971 the Office of the Chancellor presented a four-year plan for the training of Swedish university teachers comprising three elements:

  — a two-week introductory course for *all* teachers irrespective of rank
  — a six-week course for future 'senior lecturers'
  — a four-week administrative course for Directors of Studies on top of the course for 'senior lecturers'.

While the introductory courses were to be arranged at each university, the longer courses were the responsibility of the Staff Training Unit of the Office of the Chancellor and should draw participants from all universities. At the end of the four-year period approximately 8000 persons should have attended the introductory courses and each of the 600 departments should have one senior lecturer and one Director of Studies who had taken part in the longer courses. The cost was estimated at approximately 20 million Sw Kronor (US \$4.5 million) plus another 50 million Sw Kronor (US \$11 million) to cover the cost of replacement teachers while the regular staff attended courses.

The Government accepted the plan with one vital exception: it was not prepared to accept the need for replacement teachers. The Swedish school system had established an extensive in-service training programme in the 1960s where the activities took place outside the teachers' 'regular hours', mainly in the vacation periods. Like teachers in the schools, university teachers should devote their spare time to training activities. This position led to a long argument between the Ministry of Education and the Office of the Chancellor; however, both parties refused to yield.

It is true that the proposed training programme resulted in more money being made available for training purposes. It is also true that the then budget system of the Swedish universities made it possible for the Office of the Chancellor to compensate the universities for costs incurred by the need for replacement teachers. However, the fact remains that the programme was never accepted by the Government as a way of making university teaching more efficient.

### 10.2.1 A pilot training course

To the Staff Training Unit money or official blessing was not the most pressing problem. It had proposed a six-week national course for senior lecturers and it now had to develop this course. It was decided that the first pilot course would take place in April 1972, leaving a little less than a year for the development work.

The unit was fortunate in securing the help of a group of interested and experienced university teachers,[2] and there can be little doubt that the future development to a very large extent stemmed from the ideas presented in this group. As the Committee for University Teaching Methods had been dominated by the views of educational technology, it was only natural to produce a course with analysis of objectives and evaluation as the central points. However, the developmental group imposed two restrictions on themselves: (a) the course should deal with matters relevant to higher education, ie only examples of successful projects for academic professions should be included, and (b) the course should not be *about* educational technology, but itself be a model course *in* educational technology.

It soon became evident that these restrictions made life very difficult; while it was, for example, relatively easy to find examples of stringent analysis of objectives in a number of courses for mechanics and firemen, the group was not able to find a single instance of analysis for an academic course which could be accepted by everyone in the group. The gospel of educational technology started to fade away and alternative approaches were sought.

In the end the course turned out to be something quite different from that anticipated at the start. It was not a six-week course at all: it was a training programme stretching over two semesters with the motto 'look after your department'. It was an inter-disciplinary programme beginning with a two-week residential period during which problems of relevance and attitudes were studied and the participants, alternating as teachers and students, experimented with means of communication.

After this initial period the participants returned to their own departments for two weeks, during which they were free from their normal duties. They analysed the way their departments worked in the light of the discussions with their colleagues during the residential period, and they also tried to find remedies for what they considered needed changing.

During a second residential period of one week the various analyses of departmental problems were discussed in the old inter-disciplinary groups, and projects for the following semester were initiated. At this point inter-faculty relations and relations with the administrations became a point of central interest: how could one convince one's fellow professors that they should change the lecture programmes, or examination procedures, or whatever the case may be?

During a final week, six months after the first residential period, the participants met again for comparison of results and discussion on new ideas and projects.

The pilot course was an obvious success.[3] It also proved beyond reasonable doubt that experienced university teachers would benefit from training. During the next few years three such courses were given each year and more than 350 experienced university teachers participated.

### 10.2.2 A pilot course on the administration of educational development

The next step was to develop a course on educational administration for Directors of Studies. Although it was of a more traditional nature than the course for senior lecturers, organizational development was an important part of the curriculum,[4] and it may be of interest to note that the first power game seminar ever held in Sweden was included in the pilot course in spring 1973.

However, the main objective was to make the Directors of Studies so familiar with administrative principles of university management that they could fight the bureaucracy on its own ground. The mere existence of this course seemed to contribute to a better understanding between faculty and administration, as the course became a natural platform for discussions on how universities should be run. The course directors who were the heads of the educational administration from different universities have underlined this aspect; they have learned to respect the work carried out within the departments and come to see the problems of the departments in a different light. The same seems to be true of the national administration represented by the Office of the Chancellor: issues under debate were included in the course programme to make discussions possible between the person responsible at national level and the Directors of Studies.

No Director of Studies was admitted to the course without first having participated in the pedagogical training course. It was not the objective to create a new bureaucratic level but to make the organizational structure of the universities more attentive to and suitable for innovation. Consequently, only people who have already formed ideas about university teaching may attend; their obvious starting point is not to refine an administrative system but to find such administrative techniques that promote progress and development.

Two national courses have been organized every year since 1973. (Table 10.2 shows an example of a course programme.) From 1979 the national courses will be superseded by regional courses with a new national course on management as a supplement.

### 10.2.3 Changes in the reward system

No matter how good and efficient the training programmes may be, unless the teachers are rewarded in terms they find important, the scheme will fail. Having developed the courses proposed in the training programme and having proved their usefulness to both academics and administrators, the next obvious step was to start a debate on promotion policies. As student numbers now started to

Table 10.2 General programme for the course on
educational administration for directors of studies

---

**Part 1:** The work of the administration of a university (three days); this
part of the course is organized by the different universities.

**Part 2:** Educational administration: residential course (nine days)

| *Thursday* | *Friday* | *Saturday* | *Sunday* |
|---|---|---|---|
| Introduction Swedish higher education policy (Dep Chancellor of the Swedish universities) | The public Commission on the duties of academic staff (Secretary to the Commission) | Planning the work of a university — simulation of the University of Y-stad (Administrative officers from the National Board and two universities) | University of Y-stad (cont) |
| *Monday* | *Tuesday* | *Wednesday* | *Thursday* |
| Analysis of the University of Y-stad Civil Service Code (Lord Justice) | The two roles of Directors of Studies — managerial and educational (Ed consultant, Univ of Göteborg) | Research and undergraduate teaching (Head of Dept, Regional Board) Committee work (Course director) | Question time — discussions with the Chancellor of the Swedish universities |

*Course director for Part 2: Vice-Chancellor of Borås College*

**Part 3:** Improving the educational administration of departments; this
part of the course is organized at the participants' departments
(five days)

**Part 4:** Reporting on and discussions of proposed projects for the
development of the participants' departments: residential course
(five days)

*Course director for Part 4: Vice-Chancellor of Borås College*

---

drop and the overwhelming majority of Swedish university teachers
were not tenured, it was an issue of concern to most academics.

Although lip service was paid to candidates' teaching records, every
academic knew that his research work was the prime criterion as far as
tenure and promotion were concerned. Even those who wanted to
take teaching competence into account were at a loss: how should
one grade academic teaching?

With the aid of the same group of active university teachers that had
assisted in the development of the national courses, the Staff Training
Unit referred a memo on university teacher competence (Table 10.3)
to the universities for consideration. It would be an understatement
to say that it was hotly debated; however, more and more faculties
started to apply the suggested criteria and it became evident that a good
research record was not enough.

### Table 10.3 Criteria for assessing competence
### in university teaching

In December 1973 a memorandum on criteria for promotion and tenure for university lecturers which had been prepared by the Staff Development Unit of the Office of the Chancellor was referred by the Government to the universities for comments. As a result of this memorandum the statutes were changed in favour of more note being taken of the candidates' competence as teachers.

Teaching competence was still undefined, however. The memorandum suggests that the following criteria could be used:

The concept of teaching competence comprises:
— teaching skills
— educational planning and administration
— teacher-training
— experience of university teaching.

The assessment of candidates should include:
— concerning teaching skills:
   (a) the ability to co-operate with the students and to arrange learning situations in which the students' creativity and capacity for critical and constructive analysis is fostered
   (b) the ability to develop the contents of the teaching
   (c) the ability to develop the format of the teaching

— concerning educational planning and administration:
   (a) experience of educational planning at departmental level, eg as head of department or Director of Studies
   (b) experience of educational planning at university level, eg as member of educational boards or university committees

— concerning teacher-training:
participation in formal training organized by the Office of the Chancellor or the Board of Education, or diploma courses in education

— concerning experience of university teaching:
the range within the candidates' discipline and the degree of responsibility should be taken into account in the first place.

The university statutes were also changed. While research still would count as the first criterion for professorships, teaching competence should be given more weight than research for teaching positions. Although it is true that these statutes have been somewhat arbitrarily applied, there can be little doubt that a demonstrated interest in university teaching and university development nowadays is taken into account in matters of promotion and tenure.

## 10.2.4 Teacher-training becomes staff development
Even when the first national programme was being discussed in early 1971, there was a feeling that the exclusion of categories of staff other than researchers/teachers would be harmful in the long run. At the request of the Staff Training Unit its brief was therefore extended to include all kinds of staff employed at the universities, non-academic

as well as academic, from the academic year 1971-72. Thus, the prerequisites for a comprehensive staff development programme came into existence.

It is quite clear that this opened new perspectives. It was not only possible to organize joint training activities for several categories of staff, eg the course for Departmental Boards (see below), but it was also possible to promote interest in educational development among staff members who undeniably play an important role in the life of a department, eg study counsellors and departmental secretaries.

Staff development should promote understanding between various kinds of staff and different levels of administration. Another obvious advantage is that people are put in communication situations where communication — and indeed the need to influence other people — matters to the participants and where, consequently, they are in a learning mood. Though many academics would never dream of attending a course on how to teach students more effectively, they may be highly interested in learning how to get the better of local or central bureaucrats. More often than not, they will find that just the same sort of skills are required.

Whatever teaching occurs is necessarily a reflection of the organizational structure of the university. Staffing policies, administrative divisions and examination procedures are not the property of the teachers, so changes which may have far-reaching effects on classroom behaviour, eg the introduction of problem-oriented courses, need the consent and understanding of a much larger body. The readiness of the principal administrative officers to support unconventional ideas, the efficiency of the media services or the attitudes of the secretarial staff to new concepts, are just as important for innovation as the feelings of the academic teachers.

Since 1972 national courses have been provided for a great variety of staff. Study counsellors have discussed educational theory as well as the theory of guidance and information; administrators and supervisors have been trained as instructors; engineers and technicians have studied principles of middle management as well as electronics and mechanics of materials; personnel officers have been trained in negotiation techniques and staff development.

Perhaps one of the more interesting courses has been the departmental board course. Five departments from five different universities make up one course, and each department is required to send the head of the department, the Director of Studies, a study counsellor or a junior lecturer, one secretary, one technician and one student, ie six people with varying functions and responsibilities, from each department. They mix with a course staff which includes senior administrative officers from one or two universities and the central university administration, and people representing the general public. The main core of the course consists of running a mini-university where the participants make up all the ruling bodies of the university and have to solve the sort of problems that universities face, from students revolting because of bad teaching to the recruitment of staff and next year's budget. At regular intervals the proceedings of the mini-university are stopped to see if the analyses made and the decisions taken are reasonable ones. (For course programme, see Table 10.4.)

## 10.3 Programmes offered by individual universities

The national courses should be seen as a supplement to the diversified staff training activities offered by the individual universities. From a modest start under the auspices of the Committee for University Teaching Methods local staff training now extends over a wide variety of topics.

As is only natural the organizational patterns differ. Some universities, eg Uppsala and Stockholm, have maintained the division between an educational development unit responsible for teacher-training and a unit responsible for the training of other categories of staff, while other universities, eg Lund and Göteborg, have created a staff development section within the personnel departments. However, at each university or college there are one or more persons responsible for staff development (see pp 315-17).

The successor of the Office of the Chancellor, the National Board of Universities and Colleges, provides funds for local staff training and development each year from the State grant for the development of university staff. In addition to this, the universities and colleges may — and normally do — direct some part of the State grant for undergraduate education to staff training purposes. The new university budget system also makes it possible to cancel other activities, eg teaching or research, in favour of such staff development activities the university or college considers necessary.

However, the only compulsory training is the introductory programme. Each university or college is obliged to provide an annual course on 'the university (college) as my place of work' for all newly appointed staff (including university teachers) which comprises five days and, apart from a general introduction to the research and teaching interests of the university, deals with the legal framework of the Civil Service (to which university staff belong in Sweden). For newly appointed teachers without previous experience of university teaching — normally assistant and junior lecturers — this is followed by a two-week teacher-training programme and guidance and supervision by the departmental

**Table 10.4 General programme for departmental board courses organized by the National Board of Universities and Colleges**

| Monday | Tuesday | Wednesday | Thursday | Friday |
|---|---|---|---|---|
|  | Planning in Y-stad (cont) | Planning in Y-stad (cont) | Planning in Y-stad (cont) | Who should do what in a university department? |
| Lunch | Lunch | Lunch | Lunch | Lunch |
| Team training | Modern principles of personnel administration | University administration and the Democracy of Work Act | Meeting of the Senate of the University of Y-stad | Is there a place for a head of department? |
| Welcome to the University of Y-stad |  |  | Analysis of the simulated university |  |
| Dinner | Dinner | Dinner | Dinner |  |
| Planning in Y-stad | 'Meetings, bloody meetings' (film on committee work) | Planning in Y-stad (cont) | Formal and informal power structures in a university |  |

Director of Studies during their first term. The training should concentrate on the new teacher's duties during his first term: thus, if he is going to lecture he will get lecture training; if he is going to supervise laboratory work, he is trained in laboratory group work, etc.

The introductory programme was made compulsory from 1 July 1976 as one part of the Second National Programme (see Section 10.4 below). However, the small number of newly recruited teachers in the last few years has made it impossible to divide this initial teacher-training into as many sub-groups as originally intended, and there has been a tendency to provide a comprehensive course on general principles rather than the job-oriented training envisaged. This has, of course, led to less interest in the training from the heads of department who have to budget for a full year's salary but have to grant the newly appointed teachers leave of absence for three weeks during their first semester.

However, recent developments seem to indicate a growing interest in the initial training. One reason for this may be closer co-operation between the staff development units and the departments concerned in the general framework of the programme. It is also interesting to note that several universities now combine pedagogical and linguistic training for their new staff; the most striking example is perhaps the new introductory course at the University of Stockholm which is, in fact, a joint Staff Development/Department of Scandinavian Languages programme.

211

**Table 10.5 Staff training and staff development activities
organized by the University of Uppsala
for the autumn term, 1978**

| Title | Participants | Duration |
|---|---|---|
| Welcome to the university | All newly appointed staff | 5 days |
| Elementary didactics | Newly appointed teachers | 10 days |
| The work of departmental boards | Members of departmental boards | 1 day |
| The role of the secretary of a departmental board | Secretaries of departmental boards | 1 day |
| Committee work | New members of boards and committees | 2 days |
| Administration | New heads of departments and new Directors of Study | 3 days |
| Write better Swedish | Open to all staff | 4x3 hours |
| Filing techniques | Departmental secretaries | 1 day |
| Offset printing, duplication and copying | Departmental reprographic staff | 2 days |
| University account system | Departmental secretaries | 2 days |
| Laboratory toxicology | Laboratory assistants | 8x3 hours |
| Biochemical methods of separation | Laboratory assistants | 8 days |
| Safety regulations in chemical laboratories | Laboratory assistants | 40 hours |
| Injections on laboratory animals | Laboratory assistants and animal attendants | 30 hours |
| Modern electronics | Technicians | 40 hours |
| Technical aids for cleaning and servicing | Cleaning inspectors | 20 hours |
| Spectrophotometry | Technicians | 1 day |
| Galvanic surface treatment | Technicians | 2½ days |
| Modern lacquering and enamelling techniques | Technicians | 2 days |
| Protection against radiation | Technicians | 2 days |
| Seminars for teachers of biology | Open to all teachers of biology | 5 days |
| Be a better teacher | New teachers in the medical faculty | 5 days |

Although the universities and colleges provide a great number of courses every year (Table 10.5 lists relevant activities organized by one university during one term), the most important difference between local and national efforts for staff development is found in the departmental approach. For obvious reasons it is not possible to invite all staff of a department — or even all teachers of large departments — to national seminars and workshops. University-based developmental work does not suffer from this restriction, and recent years have seen an increase in the number of organizational development projects that aim at departments as a whole rather than individual members.

About 50 per cent of the funds for staff development available to the National Board is distributed to the universities and colleges for local staff development programmes. The rivalry between university and national programmes of the early 1970s seems to have passed away, and the various programmes are nowadays co-ordinated on an annual basis.

## 10.4 The Second National Programme

The First National Programme aimed at a relatively quick improvement of teaching through a series of courses for existing staff. For financial reasons it was not possible to organize the large number of courses needed — it is, of course, also doubtful if it would have been possible to find a sufficient number of competent course directors — and it became obvious that a new approach was called for.

It seemed reasonable to suggest that recurrent education is a valid idea not only for the ordinary citizen but also for university staff. After consultation with the participants in the national training programme and a thorough review by the universities, the following progression was proposed to the Government in the estimates for 1976-77:

| | |
|---|---|
| — newly appointed teacher *without* experience of university teaching | three weeks' introductory programme (see Section 10.3) aiming at the teacher's first term at the university |
| — after 3 to 4 years' teaching experience | the teacher should make up his/her mind on important educational issues — two-week inter-disciplinary course on creative teaching |
| — after 7 to 9 years' teaching experience *and* after 10 to 12 years' teaching experience | the teacher should be prepared to assist in curriculum development — one-week discipline-oriented review course to update him/her on recent developments outside his/her own research field |
| — every year | three-day seminar with fellow teachers in the department — topic to be chosen by the department |

It was proposed that the programme should be made compulsory for teachers appointed after 1 July 1976.

The government responded in a positive way, and the introductory programme was immediately made compulsory for all newly appointed teachers without previous experience of university teaching. However, the old disagreement on the need for replacement teachers remained, and in 1977 a public commission was appointed to review the work conditions of faculty. This commission is expected to present a report in 1979.

To a large extent, the new budget system which was introduced in connection with the university reform of 1977 has made the question of replacement teachers insignificant. Staff development costs fall into two categories: salaries for the participants that must be covered by the universities and costs for particular activities (eg travel, residential accommodation, course staff) for which special grants may be available. However, the fact that an agreement has been reached in principle means, of course, that staff development now is a recognized and important part of university development.

During the preparation for this proposal it became evident that the formerly successful 'look after your department' programme was disintegrating and that a new approach was needed. With the help of some participants who were particularly dissatisfied with the programme,[5] a new course on creative teaching was developed. While the residential periods of the older course had been unstructured and in themselves an example of participant steered education, the course on creative teaching deals with problems that have been decided in advance.

For the first course four problems were selected: (a) teacher authority, (b) discipline v project studies, (c) examinations, and (d) inter-faculty relations. The participants who represented a variety of disciplines were given actual learning tasks[6] and subjected to varying teacher behaviour. After each learning period the experiment was discussed and questions asked such as 'how did I react as a student?', 'what kind of knowledge did I get?', 'what were my expectations of the teacher?' and 'did I find examination procedures relevant and fair?' Other components of the course are a 'mini-project' and two days of interpersonal relations training (Table 10.6).

At the request of the universities a new unstructured course on creative teaching has also been developed and from 1978-79 teachers can choose between two different kinds of courses.

The first discipline-oriented course will take place in spring 1979. Each course should contain three elements: (a) a review of relevant research,[7] (b) a comparative study of curriculum on an international basis, and (c) discussions on teaching and learning. To facilitate the international aspects of the course the Staff Development Unit has sought the co-operation of similar agencies outside Sweden and several of the pilot courses are organized with bi-national participation.

Table 10.6 General programme for the structured, inter-disciplinary, creative teaching course organized by the National Board of Universities and Colleges (first residential period)

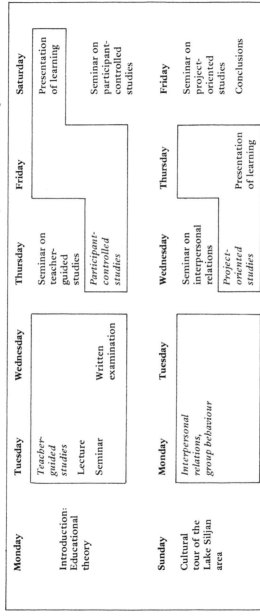

| Monday | Tuesday | Wednesday | Thursday | Friday | Saturday |
|---|---|---|---|---|---|
| Introduction: Educational theory | *Teacher-guided studies*<br>Lecture<br>Seminar | Written examination | Seminar on teacher-guided studies<br><br>*Participant-controlled studies* | | Presentation of learning<br><br>Seminar on participant-controlled studies |

| Sunday | Monday | Tuesday | Wednesday | Thursday | Friday |
|---|---|---|---|---|---|
| Cultural tour of the Lake Siljan area | *Interpersonal relations, group behaviour* | | Seminar on interpersonal relations<br><br>*Project-oriented studies* | Presentation of learning | Seminar on project-oriented studies<br><br>Conclusions |

*Examples of learning tasks*

— teacher-guided studies: The Nazi assumption of power
— participant-controlled studies: Sweden at the outbreak of World War II
— project: Health care in the Siljan area

Although the departmental seminar may not be called — and perhaps not even felt as — staff development, such activities exist in the overwhelming majority of Swedish university departments. The role of the programme therefore has been to legitimize rather than initiate such seminars.

## 10.5 Seminars in the developing countries

In January 1972 the Office of the Chancellor appointed a committee chaired by Mr Bertil Östergren[8] to investigate the possible need for an internationalization of Swedish higher education. The Committee found that the Swedish universities had not adapted themselves to the global process of internationalization, and in its final report (1974) the Committee proposed a series of measures to improve the situation. Staff development should, of course, play an important part, and the Committee pointed to the need for other kinds of international contacts than those normally established through participation in research and international conferences.

Since 1975 the Staff Development Unit has therefore organized seminars in the developing countries in co-operation with the Swedish International Development Authority. The aim of the seminars has been to stimulate appreciation of international problems and development efforts by offering the participants 'unusual' or 'unexpected' experiences in inter-disciplinary groups.

The first of these seminars, which took place in Kenya, studied the problems of planning at different levels of administration. The participants worked in groups of four, each group comprising a human geographer, a sociologist, an economist and a political scientist. As was only to be expected, the groups found that some of the research models they were used to handling — and that consequently are taught in the undergraduate courses — were not applicable to the problems encountered. This has given an incentive to the revision of research programmes and undergraduate education.

Similar seminars with participation from other disciplines have been held in a number of countries. It is important to stress that the academic teachers are not going to these seminars expecting to play the roles of experts; on the contrary, they are there to study problems and conditions of which they know very little.

It is evident that these seminars are only a poor substitute for the full experience of actually working in a developing country for a longer period. However, the majority of Swedish university teachers have chosen not to work in developing countries for a variety of reasons, and the seminars are seen as a chance to get at least some impression of vital international problems without damaging family life, etc.

A seminar is a six-month programme comprising three to four preparatory conferences in Sweden, individual studies of the problems under consideration, a four-week field programme, and one or two follow-up conferences where the seminar is evaluated and proposals for future changes of curriculum are discussed. For 1979 a more ambitious seminar is planned in which rural development in Indonesia and Sweden will be compared by a group of Indonesian and Swedish academics. During the field studies — four weeks in Indonesia and four weeks in Sweden — the participants will be working as members of university projects on area development.

## 10.6 Bi-national and tri-national courses

One way of evaluating training programmes is to present the programme for international scrutiny, preferably through foreign participation. At the same time there is a danger in mixing too many educational systems at once; a training programme is then easily transferred into a conference where everybody talks about the merits of his/her system. The Staff Development Unit has therefore initiated a series of bi-national and tri-national workshops which have been practical demonstrations of staff training or development activities in different countries.

The first tri-national workshop was held in Sweden in 1976. With the same number of colleagues from Britain and Holland respectively, eight Swedish university teachers participated in the first two residential weeks of the 'look after your department' programme. The only deviation from the 'normal' programme was that of language: English instead of Swedish. Similar workshops were held in Holland in 1977 when Dr Peter Veltman of the Rijksuniversiteit in Utrecht presented a Dutch model for university teacher-training and in Britain in 1978 when Dutch and Swedish staff participated in the Kent/Surrey course.

In co-operation with the Ontario Universities Program for Instructional Development two Canadian/Swedish training courses have also been organized. The 1977 workshop in Ontario was an example of university teacher-training in Canada while the 1978 workshop in Sweden was the first presentation of the new course on creative teaching to a wider audience.

The next logical step, obviously, is a joint production of seminars and workshops. Through extended co-operation with the Co-ordinating Committee for the Training of University Teachers in the UK there will be three jointly organized events in 1979: a discipline-oriented course for university teachers of biology, a creative teaching course, and a course on research and creative teaching. All courses will have bi-national participation and will be directed by British/Swedish teams. Similarly in 1979 a bi-national seminar will be organized in Ontario, in co-operation with the Ontario Universities Program for Instructional Development, on the problems of recurrent education; a German/Swedish seminar on the role of universities in modern society, in co-operation with the Westdeutsche Rektorenkonferenz, will also take place in 1979.

There can be little doubt that the bi-national and tri-national programmes have been of great importance as stimuli not only for the development of further staff development activities but also for educational development within the participants' departments.

## 10.7 Prospects for the future

While staff training is a way to elucidate educational policy, ie it should fortify the signals of the governing systems, staff development may be seen as an invitation to the members of the system to participate in the formulation of policies. Staff training is designed to make people conform; staff development, on the other hand, aims at increasing the readiness to accept and promote innovation. The present Swedish programme tries to cover both these aspects. Thus, in addition to the activities described above, several specialized courses and workshops are arranged every year both at the universities and as part of the national programme (Tables 10.5 and 10.7).

**Table 10.7 National courses organized in the academic year
1977-78 by the Staff Development Unit
of the National Board of Universities and Colleges,
in addition to courses that are part of the Second
National Programme** (*bi-national and tri-national courses
and seminars in developing countries are excluded from this list*)

|  | Number of courses | Duration |
|---|---|---|
| **Administrative courses** | | |
| — departmental boards | 2 | 1 week |
| — heads of departments | 1 | 1 week |
| — maintenance engineers | 1 | 1 week |
| — evaluation of universities | 4 | 1 week |
| **Management courses** | | |
| — middle management | 1 | 1 week |
| **Teacher-training courses** | | |
| — special education | 2 | 3 days |
| — teachers of medicine | 1 | 1 week |
| — teachers of dentistry | 1 | 1 week |
| — study supervisors in schools of journalism | 1 | 3 days |
| — practical social studies | 1 | 1 week |

Table 10.7 *(cont)*

| | Number of courses | Duration |
|---|---|---|
| **Courses for study counsellors** | | |
| — theory and methods of guidance | 1 | 2 weeks |
| — guidance concerning the labour market | 2 | 1 week |
| **Other courses** | | |
| — laboratory animal care | 3 | 3 days |
| — plain Swedish in education | 1 | 1 week |
| — job rotation for teachers in schools of economics | 1 | 6 weeks |
| — dissemination of information | 2 | 3 days |

In Sweden, as in most other countries, universities seem to be moving towards a stage where more and more people become involved in the process of decision-making ('democratization'). As this necessarily means increased communication between different ideas and interests, the role of staff training and staff development tends to become indistinct, particularly as no one person, or group of persons, can claim a monopoly on staff training and development measures.

It seems reasonable to assume that the *staff training programme* will become more and more the responsibility of parts of the administrative system other than a special staff development unit. The old system of ruling by ordinance is changing in favour of the idea of more participatory rule which necessitates frequent and closer contacts between people and which presupposes a common ideology. There is a growing tendency to conduct seminars and workshops on issues of contention, ie staff training methods are used as regular elements of governance.

However, it will also be necessary to vitalize the 'creative' powers of the universities, and this will probably be the most important objective of staff development in the 1980s. The Swedish experience seems to suggest that innovation can be enhanced through experience outside one's own department, and one of the tasks of staff development units — at the universities as well as in central administration — will be to provide opportunities for 'unexpected' learning.

*Notes*
1. The other members were Professor Carl Gustaf Andrén, University of Lund, Mr Folke Haldén, the Association of Swedish Employers, Professor Bertil Hallert, Royal Institute of Technology, Professor Kjell Härnquist, University of Göteborg, Dr Arne Nordlander, University of Umeå and Mr Carl Tham, the National Union of Students.
2. The Committee of Experts comprised Drs Bengt-Eric Bengtsson (electronic engineering), Ingvar Carlsson (English), Gunnar Höglund (physiology), Dick Mårtensson (education) and Arne Nordlander (mathematics).

Dr Nordlander was also the representative of the National Union of University Teachers.

3. For a description of the first courses, see Grahm *et al*, 1974.

4. The same group of university teachers assisted the Staff Training Unit in the development of the administrative course with Mrs Anne-Marie Rydell, Head of Undergraduate Administration, Stockholm University, as an additional member.

5. The members of the planning groups were Dr Göran Behre, University of Göteborg, and Dr Reidar Larsson, University of Stockholm, who later directed the first courses, and Drs Björn Larússon, University of Lund, Germund Michanek, University of Uppsala, C G Ribbing, University of Uppsala, and Lieut-Col Håkan Wahlström, the Military Academy.

6. The learning tasks are chosen by the course directors from their own disciplines. Examples are 'The Nazi assumption of power in Germany' (directors: an historian and a political scientist) and 'Manipulation of genes' (directors: a chemist and a biologist).

7. One obvious problem in undergraduate teaching today is the distance between the research front and the undergraduate curriculum. The hypothesis is that the researcher has an active research interest in only a portion of the undergraduate programme and therefore would benefit from reviews of research areas other than his own.

8. The other members were Mr Mathias Berg, National Union of Students, Professor Sune Carlsson, University of Uppsala, Mr Anders Forsse, Swedish International Development Authority, Mr Helge Hane, Alfa Laval Corporation, Professor Lennart Holm, The National Board of Urban Planning, and Mr Tore Tallroth, Foreign Office.

# 11: Switzerland
# — largely non-institutionalized instructional development activities

Marcel L Goldschmid

## 11.0 Introduction

Perhaps it is appropriate first to define the meaning of staff development in the context of this review. Given its more narrow focus in Switzerland, *instructional* development might have been a more adequate term. In other words, issues specifically dealing with teaching and learning have been in the foreground rather than more general ones, such as career planning, recurrent education, promotion of suitable organizational structures, etc, which one could include in staff development (Piper and Glatter, 1977). Instructional development, on the other hand, is interpreted rather broadly here and refers not only to courses for faculty, but also to consultations, student-oriented work (eg counselling), activities of reform committees, evaluation of teaching, development of instructional materials (written and audiovisual), and educational research.

As an earlier review of staff development practice in North America has already demonstrated (Alexander and Yelon, 1972), some activities are found on most campuses (eg occasional seminars on teaching for faculty) whereas the origins, organizational structure, and particular orientation and services offered differ widely from one institution to another. Switzerland is no exception: every university has followed a unique pattern in addressing itself to issues in staff development.

On the whole, staff development has evolved very slowly in Switzerland, at least as far as institutionalized efforts are concerned. As a matter of fact, at the present time there exists only *one* university institute directly and principally concerned with faculty development in higher education in Switzerland: it is the chair in Lausanne to which the author is affiliated. In at least some of the other Swiss universities[1] there are occasional and mostly informal opportunities offered to the faculty for staff development.

In line with the actual state of affairs, this review will first briefly describe the efforts elsewhere, based largely on a recent report by a study reform committee of the Swiss Conference of Universities and

Rectors (*Commission pour la réforme des études,* 1977), and then present in more detail the activities of the *Chaire de Pédagogie et Didactique* in Lausanne.

## 11.1 Staff development in Swiss universities

The Swiss Federal Institute of Technology (ETH) in Zürich has, since 1974, offered its faculty the opportunity of attending an annual two-week course on instruction in higher education, specially organized for them at the University of Klagenfurt, Austria. It includes an introduction to psychology, basic principles of instruction and teaching in engineering, public speaking and training in group work. It is composed of a theoretical and a practical part (each lasting one week) and is limited to 15 participants. Probably because of scheduling problems (eg overlap with exam period and the length of the course), the number of faculty who enrol is rather small, ie, just about all those who apply can be accommodated.

Since 1968, furthermore, the ETH in Zürich has organized a yearly weekend seminar on instruction for its faculty. These external seminars are devoted to a different topic each year, which is usually introduced by a guest speaker and then pursued in small groups. Discussions over the past years have centred on traditional and innovative teaching methods, the relation between objectives and instruction, participation of students, 'heuristic instruction', motivation, examination and visualizing in instruction. Usually because of practical constraints, such as available space, the participation is limited to 60, but indications are that the interest is much more widespread.

Both the course and the seminar are entirely financed by the ETH and are organized by its *Subkommission für Studiengestaltung* (Committee for the organization of studies).

The University of Zürich has recently also introduced courses for its faculty on the formulation of objectives and microteaching. Both courses are practically oriented and offer the participants the opportunity to exercise their skills and receive individual consultations and feedback. These short courses organized by the University's *Hochschulreform Kommission* (Committee for university reform) have been favourably evaluated by the participants. They were based on those held at the University's Dental Institute where they have been declared mandatory for all junior teaching staff.

The University of Berne does not yet offer courses on teaching to its faculty, but a working party has been constituted to plan such activities. On the other hand, the *Institut für Ausbildungs- und Examenforschung* (Institute for research on training and examinations) and the *Abteilung für Unterrichtsmedien* (Department of instructional media), both

associated with the Faculty of Medicine, have been involved in staff
development activities. For example, the former has been involved in
efforts to reform medical exams and training, in consultations, tutor
training and instructional research. It also offers regular seminars
(usually led by a guest speaker) to the medical faculty. The latter
institute has been particularly active in establishing a media resource
centre. Its holdings include over 160 (self-produced and bought)
video and tape-slide programmes which are on loan to medical students
on a 24-hour basis including weekends. The department is also involved
in developing the University's independent study programme, training
tutors, and offering consultations and courses on instruction to the
medical teachers (for example to general practitioners).

The *Institut für Wirtschaftspädagogik* (Institute for the pedagogy of
economics) at the University of St-Gall has offered occasional courses
to the faculty in the past several years on such topics as course
planning, objectives and microteaching.

The *Centre d'enseignement médical et de communications
audiovisuelles* (Centre for medical teaching and audiovisual
communications) in Lausanne and the *Zentrum für Lehre und
Forschung* (Centre for teaching and research) in Basel, both associated
with the medical faculties of their respective universities, have recently
begun their operations. Like the department of instructional media in
Berne, they have focused their efforts on developing media resource
centres.

At least some of these centres have expressed interest in expanding
their role beyond the medical faculty and/or the technological
orientation towards more general staff development activities.

At the University of Geneva, a *commission d'enseignement*
(committee of teaching) has recently been established under the
chairmanship of one of its *vice-recteurs*. Its mandate includes the
study of ways to improve the effectiveness and efficiency of university
instruction. The University's rather large Faculty of Psychology and
Education represents at least a potential resource for staff development.

The preceding descriptions of activities in teaching and learning in
various Swiss universities do not represent an exhaustive list. They
constitute only the more visible and formal ones. A number of other
informal and sporadic efforts in staff development, either by specific
departments, associations, eg the *Gesellschaft für Hochschule und
Forschung* (Society for higher education and research) or the Swiss
Educational Research Association, or individuals, have been made, all
of which cannot be enumerated here. The activities of the national
Study Reform Committee, which began its work in 1971, however,
should be singled out. Although its main task was the stimulation and

co-ordination of discipline-specific reform projects (eg in architecture, psychology, biology, etc), it also attempted to deal with more general issues, such as problems faced by students who begin their study, and how to work with student groups, as well as how to introduce innovations in higher education. It organized and co-ordinated a number of working parties, courses, seminars and workshops, but because of internal and external tensions its activities came to an end in 1977 (Gut, 1978).

Finally, it should be mentioned that the management faculties of the French Swiss universities decided to centre their one-year graduate programme, in 1978-79, on the systems approach in management training in the university and private enterprise, thereby making a concerted effort to improve instruction.

Given the present embryonic staff development in Switzerland, it would be desirable if individuals, actively involved, could establish closer contacts and begin to form a network of communication, information and materials exchange and perhaps later on try to co-ordinate some of their activities. The sixth international IUT (Improving University Teaching) conference which will be held in Lausanne in 1980 may represent an additional impetus for such a national endeavour.

## 11.2 The 'Chaire de Pédagogie et Didactique' in Lausanne

Before reviewing the activities of the Chair, it is necessary first to describe briefly its institutional context. The Chair is part of the Swiss Federal Institute of Technology in Lausanne which, together with our sister institute (ETH) in Zürich, is the only technical university in Switzerland. The Institute is one of the smaller Swiss universities with about 2000 students, 100 professors and 700 research, teaching and administrative staff. It was founded over 125 years ago and is composed of nine departments (essentially in the physical sciences, engineering and architecture).

The Chair was founded in 1973 largely through the initiative of the University's president. Its primary aims are to develop an instructional development programme, conduct research in psychology and higher education, and teach psychology to students in architecture and engineering. It is an independent unit and its director reports directly to the University's president.

Its regular staff, at present, comprise the following positions: a professor and director of the unit (PhD in psychology), an educational psychologist (MA), a psychologist (MA, half-time), an instructor for public speaking (quarter-time), an audiovisual technician, a documentalist (MA, half-time), a secretary, an office apprentice, and teaching and student assistants (part-time).

### 11.2.1 Courses for faculty

The Chair regularly organizes courses, seminars and workshops for the teaching staff. Occasionally it sponsors debates for faculty and students. The topics typically deal with important issues of teaching and learning, such as evaluation of students and courses, the lecture method, formulation of objectives, individualized instruction, the development of written and audiovisual instructional materials, the project method, teaching in the laboratory, etc. (For a complete list, see Goldschmid, 1978a.) The programme of activities offered is largely based on suggestions by the teaching staff and oriented towards issues that actually concern the faculty, the students and the administration. A seminar on constructive ways to adapt to a new examination policy adopted by the University, which we recently organized in collaboration with the Committee on Teaching, illustrates this orientation.

A more general remark might be in order here. A staff development unit can be largely inspired, for example with respect to its programme content, by external developments and diverse publics (eg issues in educational literature and staff from other universities) or can concentrate on local concerns and serve primarily its own campus. One can find units with either orientation in some countries (eg in Britain or Sweden). Clearly both entail advantages and risks. For example, the former, while offering more flexibility, may make it difficult or impossible to create a solid following and rooting on one's own campus. The unit may subsequently face severe problems when the university has to cut its budgets.

Most seminars in Lausanne are of short duration and usually consist of one or several half-day sessions. Given the timetable constraints, it is very difficult to schedule longer periods, say one or two weeks, where a sufficient number of faculty would be available for training courses.

Another important issue concerns the *format* of the courses. We have found that different approaches attract different faculty. In other words, some will prefer the workshop approach, others the seminar style and still others the debates.

All our courses are regularly evaluated at the end by the participants and results so far have been very encouraging. We need to know, however, what the long-term effects are or, more specifically, whether the principles and new ideas that were presented in the courses are being applied in the participants' instruction. There are at least three ways to ascertain what the practical effects of such courses are: individual consultation, evaluation of the courses by the students and videotaping classes. Each of these will be described in turn.

### 11.2.2 Consultation

The Chair offers consultations on a variety of instructional problems, such as the selection and development of audiovisual materials, the evaluation of students and courses, the pedagogical training of teaching assistants, and innovative teaching methods.

Occasionally, the Chair collaborates with groups of faculty (eg members of an institute or a committee). The Chair has been particularly active in helping to develop individualized instruction in a number of courses. The results of these innovations have been very gratifying (see Section 11.2.9).

We are about to introduce a new approach in consultation which will focus on course planning and course development. The idea is to provide concrete help and guidance on the level of individual courses in order to increase the likelihood of actual changes in the classroom. Thus, this procedure is to help us move beyond the discussions which occur at seminars and conferences to practical considerations. Additional resources will be made available to the faculty, notably assistance by students, who have previously passed the course with distinction, and who are specially trained by the Chair for their course development work. The steps involved in the course planning consultation include: the analysis of needs, the definition of objectives, the selection and development of teaching and learning methods and the evaluation of the students and the course.

### 11.2.3 Evaluation of courses by students

In order to facilitate the evaluation of courses by the students, we have developed a 40-item computer-scored questionnaire (*Chaire de Pédagogie et Didactique,* 1978). The first section deals with the student's own behaviour and preparation and general features of the course (instructional materials, difficulty of the subject matter, etc). Subsequent sections deal with the lecture, examinations, practical and laboratory work. The instructor can delete any question he finds inappropriate and add up to seven of his own. A comment sheet allowing the students to make personal and detailed remarks about any one aspect of the course accompanies the questionnaire. Finally, a manual (Champagne, 1978) is made available to the teacher, the purpose of which is to help him interpret the results and guide him in his efforts to improve the quality of his instruction.

The questionnaire has met with considerable success, ie a majority of the teaching staff have been using it without any administrative obligation or pressure. In fact, our whole procedure is designed solely to contribute to the improvement of teaching rather than to the evaluation of faculty for promotional purposes (Goldschmid, 1978b).

### 11.2.4 Videotapes of teaching
A further approach we use to provide feedback to instructors on their teaching is to videotape lectures, seminars and laboratories upon the faculty's request (Champagne, 1977).

Afterwards the teacher can view the tape individually, with his teaching assistants, with some of the students and/or with some of the staff of our unit. For individual viewing we recommend to the instructor the use of a checklist (*Chaire de Pédagogie et Didactique,* 1976) which will help him focus on important issues. Practically all teachers who have had their lectures taped prefer to analyse their classroom behaviour together with a team from the Chair (usually including an instructor in public speaking). For this purpose, we produce a montage composed of important extracts which we review critically with the teacher. Our experience shows that, on the whole, faculty members find this analysis very helpful, since it gives them the opportunity of obtaining immediate and concrete feedback on their performance, as well as guidance on how to remedy deficiencies.

### 11.2.5 Audiovisual services
In collaboration with the teaching staff, the Chair produces short films, tape-slide shows and video-recordings for various courses and institutes. Examples of such productions include a series of instructional films for the lab work in introductory physics, a descriptive film for the Institute of Energy Production, video-recordings of on-site illustrations for students in architecture and translation into French and adaptations of American films in psychology.

Several workshops are also offered by the Chair each year to train staff in the use of audiovisual equipment and the preparation of software. Given our very limited resources in technical personnel, we have no other choice but to decentralize the services as much as possible and help staff acquire skills to produce the simpler audiovisual materials themselves, thus leaving the specialist some time to concentrate on more difficult productions.

Recently a well-furnished audiovisual centre has been added to the Chair on our new university campus. It contains film, television and sound recording studios and equipment and materials for recording and playback in all major media, as well as for graphics, film editing and animation.

### 11.2.6 Services to students
Since 1974 the Chair, in collaboration with individual professors and students as well as with the student association, has helped organize and evaluate a system of peer counselling called *parrainage* (Goldschmid and Burckhardt, 1976).

Briefly, second-, third- and fourth-year students *(parrains)* volunteer to assist a small group of freshmen (two to four) in their own department in finding solutions to practical problems, such as transportation and housing, as well as to help them with their preparation of courses and exams. In addition, they provide valuable information about the curriculum, optional courses, practical work and vocational choices.

In general we would like to expand the student services along the lines proposed in Goldschmid and Goldschmid (1976). In particular, establishing a student learning centre, developing a simple manual on study skills (in French) and a permanent student tutoring system are possibilities we are contemplating at the moment.

It should be noted in this connection that there have been a number of initiatives to develop student services in several Swiss universities. Most often they have come from student counselling centres (for example, at the Universities of Berne and Zürich) or an individual faculty or institute (eg in economics and medicine at the University of Berne). They have focused on the new student, on ways to help him settle down at university and orient him in his discipline. Other attempts to help students (for example in the law faculties of the Universities of Zürich and Geneva) have concentrated on producing rather detailed handbooks and study guides for freshmen.

Although these endeavours to reduce anonymity and anxiety and increase efficiency are not themselves staff development activities, they are nevertheless part of instructional development and intimately related to issues such as orientation and organization of (usually large) introductory lectures, teacher-student contacts and relationships, and the planning and structure of the curriculum.

### 11.2.7 Library and documentation
The Chair has been able to constitute a small but specialized library of some 2000 books, 100 journals and several hundred articles in higher education and psychology. Besides its own productions, the Chair has also acquired a number of films, video-recordings and cassettes. All this material is available on loan to faculty and students, as well as to borrowers from off-campus.

A system of perforated cards, 'Swifta' (De Marchi, 1977), and key words (Champagne, 1974a) permits a rapid search of all available materials on any given topic.

Normally the Chair produces a special working document for each of its training activities (courses, seminars, etc). These documents (see Goldschmid, 1978a, for a complete list) represent a short review of the literature and practical suggestions. Bibliographies are produced for similar occasions and in connection with research projects, as well as longer and more specialized papers for conferences and international meetings. Altogether we have now prepared over 130 documents (books, monographs, chapters, articles, bibliographies, etc) which are classified according to the following main headings (Goldschmid, 1978a): trends in and principles of university instruction, teaching methods (general), individualized instruction, written and audiovisual materials, student learning methods, peer teaching and evaluation of student learning and teaching.

### 11.2.8 Psychology courses

Besides the seminars, workshops, etc which it organizes for the faculty, the Chair also offers a course in introductory psychology (2nd year — required) and a course in environmental psychology (3rd year — optional) to students in architecture. This teaching experience is important, since it provides a direct and continuous contact with students, their problems and their views on teaching and learning. Besides, these courses offer the Chair an opportunity to experiment with innovative instructional methods.

### 11.2.9 Research and surveys

Assisted by a grant from the *Fonds National Suisse de la Recherche Scientifique* (Swiss National Research Foundation), the Chair was able to carry out a major research project on individualized instruction, from 1975 to 1977 (Goldschmid and Brun, 1979). For several courses in physics, civil engineering, architecture and psychology at the Federal Institute of Technology and the University of Lausanne, the teaching format was radically altered from a classical lecture approach to the Personalized System of Instruction (PSI), modular instruction, case study or project method. The results indicate significant gains in student learning and greater satisfaction for staff and students, especially in physics and engineering.

Encouraged by these findings, there are now other teachers who are planning to individualize their instruction.

In addition, the Chair has collaborated in a number of research projects in developmental psychology.

As a future project, it is proposed to study the conception and use of instructional texts in the context of various student characteristics. The theoretical framework adopted is that of ATI (Aptitude-Treatment-Interaction), the multiple interactions with the learning process being the main focus of the study.

The Chair has also carried out surveys in order to identify faculty and student experience and opinions. In 1974, for example, practically all professors of the Federal Institute of Technology were interviewed individually on 11 topics ranging from their teaching load, instructional objectives, teaching and evaluation methods to their pedagogical training (Champagne, 1974b). Several surveys have been carried out by the Chair to assess the *parrainage* (described in Section 11.2.6) and the students' needs and opinions about various forms of assistance in the development of learning skills.

### 11.2.10 Future plans

Projects for a research study and a student learning centre have already been mentioned. In addition, we intend to publish a number of our workshop and conference papers in the form of a practical guide for faculty (Goldschmid, Champagne and De Marchi, 1979). This guide will also provide the instructional material for a basic one-week course on the systems approach in higher education which we would like to add to our seminars and workshops.

Furthermore, we are planning a master's programme for teachers in higher education and training officers in public administration and private enterprise. Based on the credit system and the mastery learning approach, it too will focus on the systems approach and be composed of courses (eg needs analysis, definition of objectives, instructional strategies and methods, and the evaluation of learning and teaching), practical work (teaching with feedback) and a thesis (based on research in the participants' area of instruction). It is hoped that this programme, which will be individualized (modular and peer teaching and emphasis on formative evaluation), will help close a gap which exists at present in most graduate programmes.

The Chair has also been asked to provide training for instructors who will teach in a new engineering school in Africa. Thus, we are called upon to respond to the challenge of meeting the specific needs of developing countries.

Finally, since our University has launched a fair number of post-diploma courses, the Chair also plans to offer seminars on instructional approaches in adult education.

## 11.3 Conclusion

As has become obvious, staff (or instructional) development in Switzerland, at least in institutionalized form, is only beginning. Although most universities are showing signs of concern, there has been no commitment yet — with the exception of the Federal Institute of Technology in Lausanne — to establish special units specifically designed to help teachers improve their instruction. Nor have there been — apart from medicine — noticeable efforts by academic disciplines to provide resources for this purpose. Even in medicine, the emphasis has been largely on providing instructional resources rather than staff training.

On the other hand, there have been a number of individual initiatives in every Swiss university ranging from courses for faculty to structural reform efforts, from tutor programmes to student handbooks, and from evaluations of teaching to curricular changes.

What will the likely developments be in the future? Budget restrictions loom rather large. The continuous high enrolment and the fear of a *numerus clausus* (quota system), especially in medicine, are factors which must be taken into account. On the one hand, these developments are cause for pessimism. Given the lack of new resources and the pressure on the university, it is unlikely that other staff development units will be created. On the other hand, as the example of the University of Geneva shows, the very fact that the budgets are getting smaller and the demands for higher education remain strong, may mean that universities will want to explore possible ways to make more effective and efficient use of available personnel and resources. Staff development in that case may provide one means to accomplish this. In fact Centra (1977) as well as Rose, Nyre and Marantz (1977) have cited the 'steady state' condition of higher education as being one of the principal factors responsible for the great increase of staff development units in the United States.

In any case, in Switzerland it appears highly desirable at the present time to consolidate efforts already accomplished and to create a network of communication among those actively at work to facilitate contact and future co-operation.

*Note*
1. There are 10 universities in Switzerland. All of them are public; eight are cantonal (the Universities of Basel, Berne, Fribourg, Geneva, Lausanne, Neuchâtel, St-Gall and Zürich) and two are national (the Swiss Federal Institutes of Technology in Lausanne and Zürich).

# 12: The United States of America — toward the improvement of teaching

Jerry G Gaff

## 12.0 Introduction

Staff development in the field of higher education in the United States is focused mainly on faculty members, by far the largest professional group and the group most directly responsible for the quality of education. Professional development for faculty is not new; it has been customary for colleges and universities to assist instructors to complete degree programmes, provide sabbatical leave, pay for travel to gatherings of academic specialists and support research and scholarship. These various practices have been designed to help professors upgrade or update their knowledge of academic specializations. It has been an article of faith among academics that just as training to conduct research in one's academic discipline — certified by a doctoral degree — prepares one to teach, the acquisition of additional knowledge and the conduct of research improves teaching. While the need for instructors to know what they are talking about cannot be disputed, there has been increasing recognition that professors' scholarly competence does not automatically translate into teaching effectiveness. It is a necessary but not a sufficient condition.

Conditions affecting post-secondary education during the 1970s have led many to think that these traditional approaches to staff development are inadequate.

Faced with the prospects of levelling student enrolments, declining faculty positions, and becoming 'tenured in', leaders of most colleges and universities are beginning to realize that in the years ahead they will have to rely on their current faculty to provide fresh perspectives, infuse new ideas, and give leadership to innovative programmes if they expect to maintain vigorous educational climates. Faculty members, too, find the going tough. In the midst of the tightest job market in memory, they are finding it difficult to get jobs, to change jobs, or even to obtain tenure at their own institutions. Increasingly, faculty careers will be confined to one institution, and they will have to look to that school to provide the enriching experiences they need in order to grow professionally and personally. Changes in student clientele, educational settings and instructional methods require many faculty members to alter their usual teaching practices and adopt new relationships with students. New student groups, such as ethnic minorities, older adults and part-time students, have required instructors to adjust their usual practices and in many cases to acquire special sensitivities and techniques to suit them. New structures, such as external degree programmes, living-learning centres or inter-disciplinary programmes, have required faculty members to range beyond familiar specializations and relate to colleagues and students in new ways. Traditional lecture and seminar methods have been supplemented by self-paced learning, use of media and technology, and individualized education in which few faculty members are experienced.

In response to these new conditions, many colleges and universities have established programmes to facilitate the development of faculty, particularly in their teaching roles. In the process of fashioning these programmes, new concepts of instructional improvement have been devised, new organizations have been established to apply the concepts, and new approaches to the improvement of instruction have been advanced. Each of these is discussed below.

## 12.1 Changing concepts of professional development

First, let us consider the changing concepts. New pressures on colleges and universities have led many faculty members and administrators to re-examine traditional concepts of professional development. Academic folklore holds that 'a teacher is born, not made' and that 'teaching is an art, not a science', implying that little can be done to facilitate the instructional improvement of professors. This folk wisdom is given expression in the standard prescription to 'hire good people and get out of their way'. Such negative injunctions are interwoven with the tradition of academic freedom, and faculty have come to feel that 'a professor's classroom is his castle', that it is somehow unprofessional for a faculty member to criticize, interfere with, intrude upon, or even observe another instructor in his classroom. These proscriptions make it difficult for instructors to learn from their colleagues and to improve their teaching competencies. In their more candid moments, most faculty members readily confess that they learned to teach by being thrown into the classroom and either swimming or sinking; almost all will testify to thrashing about considerably before learning how to swim, and some do go under. Given the new realities of higher education, this 'do nothing' approach is not sufficient. Whatever its merits may have been, the call to hire good people and get out of their way becomes a hollow slogan when student enrolments dip, faculty positions are trimmed, and the very survival of some institutions is threatened.

As these traditional conceptions have been called into question, new concepts of professional development for faculty have emerged.

Because the primary professional activity of most faculty members centres around their teaching role, the improvement of instruction is a central part of this concept. The basic assumptions are that the instructional behaviour of faculty members is a learned complex of knowledge, attitudes, values, motivations, skills and sensitivities, and that faculty members may learn to improve these instructional competencies. The focus is directly on the improvement of instruction, and the aim is to help faculty develop in the several aspects of their instructional roles. Efforts are now being made to assist faculty members to reconsider their traditional conceptions about teaching and learning, expand their instructional repertoire, sharpen their sensitivities and skills in working with students and colleagues, and work effectively with new techniques, new programmes and new students. In short, attempts are being made to help faculty members become more competent teachers.

The new concept of faculty development for instructional improvement may be better understood by an examination of the conceptual framework that underlies the work of new programmes in this area. A close reading of the documents produced by these programmes reveals a distinctive configuration of inter-related assumptions and propositions. Although no individual programme necessarily incorporates all these propositions, and many fail to make their basic assumptions explicit, the following is a list of the most important components of the conceptual framework that characterizes the new approach to professional development:

— Faculty members are the most important educational resource of a college or university, and just as material resources must be given special care and attention to retain or enhance their value, so must the talents, interests and skills of faculty be systematically cultivated.

— Teaching is the primary, though by no means the only, professional activity of most faculty members. A major reason why professors choose to work in a college or university is their commitment to teaching, and most faculty members are interested in excelling in this activity.

— Scholarship and research — another major professional activity of many faculty members — need not be antithetical to effective teaching. Ways can and should be found by which research enriches and complements teaching.

— Teaching is much neglected by academic tradition. In most schools this neglect is not due to the lack of interest in teaching among individual faculty members. Rather, the neglect can be traced to factors pervading the general academic culture, such as the lack of preparation for teaching roles during graduate education, the relative absence of in-service education which is found in other professions, and the paucity of academic policies (eg promotion, salary increases or tenure) which provide incentives and support for effective teaching.

— Although there is little systematic evidence about how good the quality of teaching and learning actually is in most institutions, there is a general feeling, shared by many within and outside academia, that it can be improved.

— Improving teaching requires working with administrators and students — perhaps even members of the larger community — as well as with faculty members. All of these groups have legitimate interest in and responsibility for making the instructional programme work well.

— Just as faculty members receive little preparation for their instructional roles, administrators have little training for the leadership, policy formulation, administrative and managerial roles of their work. Department chairmen, deans, vice-presidents and presidents — no less than faculty members — need to develop and, furthermore, they need to encourage and support the growth of the individuals in their charge.

— Teaching involves a complex set of attitudes, knowledge, skills, motivations and values. The improvement of teaching and learning requires an awareness of the complexities involved in faculty, students and institutions and hence the avoidance of simplistic solutions.

— Effective teaching involves helping students to attain desired learning objectives. Faculty members can be assisted in specifying learning objectives, choosing learning experiences designed to achieve those outcomes, and evaluating their attainment. These procedures can make instruction more systematic, thereby increasing the probability that desired competencies will be attained.

— There is no single model of effective teaching or learning; proposals advanced as panaceas with a doctrinaire approach are suspect and to be avoided.

— There is great diversity among students. Their various learning styles, which are based on differences in ability, interest, educational background, future aspirations and personality orientations, call for different kinds of learning experiences.

— Faculty members, too, are a diverse lot. They vary on such key factors as age, field of specialization, teaching experience and educational philosophy. Because diversity is one of the greatest strengths of any faculty, every effort should be made to assist individual faculty members in ways consistent with their diverse values, needs and personal styles and with student needs and institutional goals.

— An individual's professional work is intimately connected with his/her personal life; the quality of work may be affected for good or ill by family, health and personal habits. An instructional improvement programme may require efforts to promote the personal growth of individuals as well as their professional development.

— Intrinsic interest rather than extrinsic demand is what leads individuals to seek improvement. Lasting change can best be brought about by stimulating, supporting and reinforcing positive efforts by faculty members. When external motivation is used by instructional improvement programmes, the carrot — not the stick — is the most common form of incentive.

— The willing involvement of faculty members and others in the various programmes is seen typically as a necessity if enduring improvement is to be obtained.

— Every institution contains many persons with expertise and experience, who may be included in instructional improvement programmes. Faculty members with the ability to assist their colleagues are generally willing, often eager, to do so. These people may be used to develop a rich pool of talent at an institution which may be used by individuals with various needs.

— Teaching and learning are individual but not solitary activities; they occur within a social context. The climate of the institution, the relationships between faculty, administrators and students, and the policies and practices of the school affect the character of teaching and learning. The improvement of instruction requires attention to these social and institutional factors as well as to individuals.

These items represent a radical new view of teaching and of how its quality may be enhanced. This conceptual framework, containing assumptions that have no empirical aspects as well as propositions that may be tested scientifically, provides the intellectual substratum on which new approaches to the professional development of faculty rest.

## 12.2 Organizations for professional development

Special organizations have been established at many institutions to implement these new concepts of instructional improvement. Centres, offices, divisions, programmes and projects that provide services variously referred to as faculty development, teaching improvement, instructional development, learning resources, professional development, or educational development, have been created to assume responsibility for facilitating the improvement of instruction. Such organizations have a separate identity, a small staff often drawn from among the current faculty from a variety of academic disciplines, a separate budget and a responsibility to be an active proponent of the improvement of teaching and learning. These organizations have been established in all kinds of institutions — public and private universities, state colleges, liberal arts colleges, community colleges, professional schools, consortia, state systems and educational associations. They are found in all regions of the country, probably in every state, and are growing in number, size and significance.

In an ideal world a special instructional improvement programme perhaps would not be necessary — the work it does would be done by the various members of the academic community as a regular part of their jobs. However, the Group for Human Development in Higher Education (1974, p 46) points out the realities of the situation on most campuses:

> In theory, professors could individually arrange for students, friends, widely admired teachers, or consultants on pedagogy to evaluate their work in detail and discuss their reactions. Some of this is already happening, but not to any great extent. In theory, too, groups of professors and students could simply get together in order to share and deepen their knowledge about learning as an activity. Some of this happens too, but few structures exist to intensify and draw others into these conversations. Departments could, and some do, offer training to their own graduate students about the very demanding job of being a college teacher, apart from the disciplinary knowledge that must be mastered. But even where an effort is made, we know of few departments in which programs on pedagogy call forth the same intensity and sophistication as ordinary course work. As a result, few institutions benefit from a rich pedagogical culture that would support the improvement of teaching.

It is for this reason that special organizations with a specific responsibility for improving teaching and learning have been created.

## 12.3 Approaches to the improvement of instruction

Not only have new concepts and new organizations been created, but new approaches have given rise to quite different services and activities. Three quite different viewpoints have characterized the work of teaching improvement programmes: instructional development, faculty development and organizational development. These different approaches draw upon different intellectual traditions, make different analyses about what is wrong with teaching and learning and lead to different improvement activities. Descriptions of some of these innovative approaches follow.

### 12.3.1 Instructional development

The focus of instructional development is on the design of conditions of learning, particularly as provided by courses. The intellectual roots of this programme lie in fields of curriculum and instruction, learning theory, educational media and technology, and systems theory.

The instructional developer helps a faculty member, or a team of teaching faculty, to specify measurable cognitive and affective objectives of student learning, design learning activities and materials relevant to the objectives, measure student accomplishment and revise the instructional sequence and procedures in light of the evaluation.

One of the major strengths of this approach is that it enables the faculty to tailor its instruction around the outcomes of learning for students rather than merely to cover the course content. In addition, the objectives, learning experiences and evaluation of students' attainment of objectives are more systematically related, thus increasing the probability that the objectives will be attained.

Because it is easier to apply these concepts and techniques to a structured discipline, instructional development tends to be more readily accepted by faculty members in the natural sciences. Although the faculty in the humanities and softer social sciences generally is less attracted to the systematization of its courses, there are numerous cases where this approach has been profitably used in those fields as well.

### 12.3.2 Faculty development
The focus of faculty development programmes is faculty members, rather than the courses they teach. In this case, the intellectual roots lie in those disciplines that study human development over the life span, particularly developmental, clinical and social psychology and psychiatry. The major emphasis of these programmes is development of different aspects of the instructional competencies of faculty; many different kinds of activities are carried out, including the following:

*Knowledge about higher education.* It is commonly asserted that faculty members lack knowledge about education and that they need to be exposed to the professional literature and diverse practices of higher education. Some faculty development programmes help faculty to acquire this knowledge by inviting lecturers to analyse contemporary educational issues, provoking formal and informal discussion groups among interested faculty members, acquiring a collection of books, articles and reports, publishing a newsletter, or working with interested departments to incorporate substantive educational discussions into their faculty meetings.

*Teaching skills.* Some critics maintain that faculty members lack various skills involved in effective teaching both in and out of class, and several programmes are directed to help faculty acquire these skills and sensitivities. Workshops, videotaping of teaching episodes, and classroom visitations have been used to help faculty develop specific communication skills such as listening or questioning, develop sensitivities to such factors as affective tone and interpersonal dynamics in a classroom, improve common instructional strategies such as preparing and delivering lectures and leading discussion groups, and adopt new instructional approaches such as preparing learning contracts or serving as resource persons.

*Feedback about their own teaching behaviour.* Most people in any walk of life have only partial knowledge about how they are seen by others, and some believe that faculty might become better teachers if they had accurate and useful feedback from their students, colleagues and administrators about their teaching behaviour. It is not uncommon these days for faculty members to have students rate them on general qualities that are presumed to be indicative of effective teaching, but other techniques also have been used. Faculty members have recorded their classes with either video or audiotapes and have discussed the tapes with students and/or colleagues, rating scale items have been developed by individuals and/or departments which reflect specific concerns of those involved in teaching, and classroom visitations provide a basis for obtaining useful feedback.

*Affective development.* Some critics argue that the main problem with teaching is that faculty has not examined its attitudes, values and assumptions with respect to what constitutes effective teaching, desirable relationships with students, or productive relationships with colleagues. Since these attitudes have often been derived from the faculty members' previous training, they may work in opposition to the needs of their current students, and even to their own satisfaction. Some institutions have held workshops for faculty to explore its attitudes and values about teaching and learning by means of task-oriented sensitivity groups, simulations and games, or mutual interviewing.

*Awareness of other disciplines and the community.* A common charge levelled against academics is that they are encapsulated in narrow academic specializations and unaware of important relationships with other fields of knowledge and of the realities of the larger world. In order to promote contact among faculty members from different disciplines, cross-disciplinary seminars have been held, various kinds of inter-disciplinary programmes have been formed, team teaching has been encouraged and experimental colleges have been created.

*Learning rather than teaching.* Some analysts assert that the problem is not to have faculty work on improving teaching but to become more sensitive to the learning of students. Distribution of written materials, seminars and workshops, often with cognitive, affective and skill development components, has been developed to acquaint faculty with the needs of students who vary on such factors as intellectual ability, social background, learning style and personality orientation.

### 12.3.3 Organizational development
The focus of organizational development is the organization within which faculty, students and administrators work. The intellectual roots of this approach are found primarily in organizational theory, organizational change and group dynamics, and because the application of organizational development has received its greatest impetus in the world of business, it has become intertwined with concepts of management.

One aspect of this approach is the development of administrative and interpersonal competencies among leaders of the organization. Central administrators, department chairmen, and faculty who play leadership roles are seldom prepared to administer or manage organizations, and they must learn a variety of concepts, skills and techniques relevant to this kind of professional responsibility. Discussions, workshops, and consultations are provided to help those persons responsible for operating the organization (a) clarify their attitudes, (b) identify various leadership styles and develop those consistent with their personalities and the needs of the organization, (c) clarify and establish organizational goals, (d) plan and conduct meetings effectively and expeditiously, and (e) manage conflict among individuals in a creative and productive manner.

A second aspect of this approach is the development of policies which support teaching improvement. When instructional improvement programmes are established, one of the first things encountered is the fact that policies within the organization are not entirely supportive of such activities. If any of the above programmes are to succeed, institutions must have policies which provide positive support for faculty efforts since, in the long run, these programmes will succeed only if faculty and other individuals have the assurance that they may advance themselves through their efforts. What this means for most colleges and universities is that they must make sure their policies — particularly with respect to hiring, promotion, salary, tenure, release time and leave — give adequate weight to teaching effectiveness and recognize improvement efforts.

## 12.4 Progress to date

Faculty development, as currently understood, is a product of the 1970s. Prior to the early part of this decade, the term was virtually unheard of, even though a few small-scale and relatively isolated ventures could be found. A great deal has been accomplished since that time. For one thing, many different types of programme and approach have been conceptualized, pilot-tested, and proven to be valuable to faculty members. Many colleges and universities have established faculty development programmes. Centra (1976) estimated that over half the institutions of higher learning in this country have established faculty development programmes. Although some of these consist only of traditional approaches of helping faculty to update or upgrade knowledge of their subject matter, many also incorporate some of the newer approaches such as teaching improvement or career enhancement.

Several private foundations and federal agencies have initiated major funding programmes to provide seed money for experiments in faculty development. The Danforth Foundation, Lilly Endowment, W K Kellogg Foundation, and Fund for the Improvement of Postsecondary Education were among the earliest of these. Although some of them have since withdrawn their support for faculty development, others remain active. And still other such agencies are now moving into this area. But perhaps most significant is the increasing inclusion of faculty development efforts in the individual colleges and universities. Additional support in the form of exercises, activities, and other materials for use with college faculty have been produced. The two volumes of the *Handbook for Faculty Development* (Bergquist, Phillips and Quehl, 1975, 1977) contain the best collections (see below), but a variety of other useful materials is also available including questionnaires, interview forms, summaries of research on teaching and learning, guidelines for designing workshops, video and audio cassettes, simulations and games.

The increased interest in faculty development in the 1970s is well documented by the extensive growth of the professional literature. Not only have several new books been published, but also the journals contain many descriptive, analytic and evaluative articles, and reports from individual campuses are so numerous that one can hardly keep up with them. (For a summary of the literature on this and related topics, see *Professional Development: A Guide to Resources* [Gaff, Festa and Gaff, 1978] .) And conferences on faculty development or teaching improvement have been well attended, as have training workshops for those called upon to provide development services to their colleagues. In addition, a new group of professional academics has emerged to provide development services to faculty and administrators, and predictably they have formed an organization, the Professional and Organizational Development (POD) Network in Higher Education. Although a journal devoted to this new specialization has not appeared, an important communication vehicle is *Faculty Evaluation and Development in Higher Education,* a newsletter published quarterly at the University of Florida (Smith, 1978).

The progress of faculty development, like other fields of endeavour, can be traced in the questions addressed in its literature. Prior to this decade the term was virtually unheard of, except for a few modest experimental programmes. With the publication of *Faculty Development in a Time of Retrenchment* (Group for Human Development in Higher Education, 1974), the concept was brought to the national attention, and the questions on the minds of most were: What is faculty development? Why is it important? What can it do for us?

Subsequently administrators and faculty members began asking more practical questions: How can we do it? What are others doing? How can we get started? Several publications responded to the need for

241

information and materials that could be immediately useful. Bergquist and Phillips (1975) devised a model of faculty development that incorporated personal, teaching and organizational components, and, in collaboration with Quehl (1975, 1977), compiled a set of faculty development activities, exercises, questionnaires, interview forms and related documents in two volumes of the *Handbook for Faculty Development. Toward Faculty Renewal* (Gaff, 1975) conceptualized different types of teaching improvement programmes and provided guidelines about ways to structure, staff, finance and operate them. A more recent set of recommendations for *Designing Teaching Improvement Programs* by Lindquist *et al* (1978) discussed how to devise programmes in different kinds of institutions: liberal arts colleges, universities, community colleges, non-traditional institutions and consortia.

The emergence of new questions now signals yet another stage in what has become a faculty development 'movement'. Having seen the potential of the concept and the ways it has been applied at different institutions, people are now asking: What lessons have been learned? What are the outcomes for individuals and for institutions? Is faculty development actually worth while? These questions can be answered in part by means of the evaluation of the impact of these programmes.

## 12.5 Evaluation of outcomes

While the literature of faculty development is replete with descriptions and analyses of programmes, little evidence has been gathered about the impact of these programmes on participants or on their institutions. The lack of attention to such evaluation of formal programmes is understandable; thus far energies have been focused largely on establishing faculty development programmes rather than on evaluating them. But as more and more programmes are established, it becomes increasingly important to determine what faculty actually gains from these efforts and what benefits the institutions accrue. Such information can help not only in improving the programmes themselves, but also might be a crucial factor in determining their very survival.

Evaluations have been conducted but for the most part they have been rather simplistic. For instance, they include reactions of participants at the conclusion of specific activities, annual reports of programme directors or staff, visits by outside evaluators, and case studies prepared by insiders or outsiders. While each of these kinds of evaluation serves useful purposes, they tell us more about the operation of a programme than its outcome. Further, the generally favourable nature of these evaluations tends to be discounted because of the loose methodologies employed.

More sophisticated research indicating that faculty development does have demonstrable benefits is starting to appear. For instance, Kozma (1978) found that a group of faculty members at the University of Michigan who were given release time and extensive support to redesign a course adopted several instructional innovations. Those who received less support also increased their use of new approaches, but to a lesser degree, and there was no measurable change in teaching techniques among a control group of faculty which was not involved in either programme. Hoyt and Howard (1978) found in separate studies at Kansas State and Wichita State Universities that students rated teaching effectiveness of faculty members who participated in teaching improvement activities significantly higher than that of their colleagues who did not participate. Further, Erickson and Erickson at the University of Rhode Island (in press) found evidence, also from student ratings, that 'volunteer faculty who use the teaching consultation process consider it useful and well worth their time and effort', and that 'it results in significant, positive, and lasting changes in their classroom teaching skill performance'.

The most extensive evaluation of the outcome of faculty development programmes was conducted as a part of the Project on Institutional Renewal through the Improvement of Teaching. This was a three-year enterprise that involved 16 diverse colleges and universities, each of which established an institution-wide teaching improvement programme. A survey in which 479 faculty participants and 442 non-participants returned completed questionnaires was reported by Gaff and Morstain (1978).

Some of the results of that survey showed that participants were drawn from all sectors of the faculty. For instance, 7 per cent were under 30 years of age; 40 per cent between 30 and 39 years; 29 per cent between 40 and 49 and 16 per cent were over 50 years old. (The percentages do not add up to 100 because some of those surveyed did not complete each item and because the results were rounded off.) The largest single group of disciplines represented was in the area of humanities/fine arts, which accounted for 27 per cent of the total; 24 per cent came from the professional fields; 21 per cent from the natural sciences and mathematics, and 15 per cent from the social sciences and history. A little more than half were from the senior academic ranks of professor and associate professor. While this was not a random sample, the faculty participants who were surveyed represented a large and diverse group. They also closely resembled the non-participants surveyed as a group in each of the aforementioned dimensions.

Given the various programmes and activities offered at each of the schools involved in this survey, the particular kinds of events in which those surveyed participated were highly varied. The activities most frequently cited were: attending a one- to two-hour seminar or workshop, talking with a colleague or consultant to analyse or improve one's teaching, developing a new course or substantially revising an old one, and attending a half- to a full-day workshop or activity. From additional sources it has been learned that the content of these activities was also quite varied and included such topics as innovative teaching methods, inter-disciplinary programmes, teaching-learning styles, test construction, teacher and course evaluation, communication, student-faculty relationships, advising and career development. The common denominator of this sample is participation in a variety of teaching improvement activities rather than in any one specific type of activity.

A configuration of responses indicated that, for the most part, the experiences were positive. For example, 84 per cent stated that they would 'recommend that a friend or colleague get involved' in similar activities; only 9 per cent said that they would not recommend such activities. Fifty-three per cent reported that their attitudes towards teaching improvement efforts 'remained about the same, mostly favourable'; 34 per cent reported that their attitudes 'became more favourable' as a result of their participation. Less than 10 per cent became or remained unfavourably disposed towards these teaching improvement activities. Thirty-three per cent stated that they gained 'a great deal' from their involvement, 54 per cent said 'a moderate amount' and 9 per cent 'little or nothing'.

In order to investigate the specific benefits which faculty derived from these activities, a list of possible outcomes was compiled, and faculty was asked to indicate the extent to which it gained each benefit. The most significant outcome was 'contact with interesting people from other parts of the institution'; 58 per cent stated that they had gained 'a great deal' or 'much' as a result of this contact. The second greatest benefit was 'increased motivation or stimulation for teaching excellence', with 48 per cent choosing one of the higher categories. The other top five benefits were 'support or confirmation of your previous ideas or practices', 'greater awareness of *your own* teaching assumptions and practices', and 'personal growth or renewal'.

The thread that runs throughout these responses is that of personal enrichment or renewal which is related to the teaching roles of faculty. Whether through a re-dedication to the vocation of teaching, the discovery of colleagues working towards the same end, finding support for their ideas or clarifying their own assumptions, faculty members seem to be revitalizing their teaching. These benefits were not derived by everyone, and they seldom have the intensity of a religious conversion, but they do appear to be major outcomes of involvement in teaching improvement activities. Other outcomes are discussed in the full report of the study.

The accomplishments cited previously indicate that faculty development is no longer a shiny new concept untarnished by actual experience. The amount of practical experience that has been gained in the practice of faculty development is in fact extensive. On the basis of this accumulated experience and emerging positive evaluations, it is now possible to conclude that, in general, professional development has been put to the test and that it does work. It is time to recognize that faculty development, conceived of as teaching improvement, represents an important new human technology, in the dictionary sense of that term, 'a technical method of achieving a practical purpose'. The practical purposes in this case are educational improvement, individual development and institutional renewal. And the methods consist of the various types of programme that have been devised, the number of programmes that have been created, the financial support that sustains these efforts, the materials that have been prepared, the professional literature that has been published, the conferences and training sessions that have been held and the specialists that have been created in these new arts.

## 12.6 A look ahead

Faculty development, as it has been used recently, has attended largely to extending and enhancing the skills, knowledge and understanding of faculty members as teachers. The realization of the full potential of teaching improvement now faces three major challenges. First, existing programmes, even successful ones, have short histories and are quite fragile. Most have small staffs and modest budgets, operate on the periphery of their institutions and enjoy little institutional commitment. Several were established with the assistance of grants, and face uncertain future support from their institutions. Existing programmes must become institutionalized, understood, accepted and used by the professional staff, if they are to flourish. Second, the benefits available from faculty development should be widely disseminated so that similar programmes can be established at other institutions and aid larger numbers of faculty.

A further challenge is related to the major emphasis of faculty development to date: the improvement of teaching. Since teaching is the single most common activity of professors, it was logical and important that it receive primary emphasis. It will doubtless remain the cornerstone of this new technology, and one may look forward to further advances in the practice and evaluation of teaching improvement programmes. But what is to be done when there are simply not enough teaching positions to go around? Teaching improvement programmes will neither create teaching jobs nor relieve the pressure that the scarcity of jobs places on faculty and institutions. New techniques for career development will be needed to address these issues. Many new approaches of various kinds are already beginning to appear. Some programmes retrain faculty from fields that are in low demand to teach those in high demand. Faculty exchanges permit individuals to gain fresh perspectives outside their institutions. Life and career planning assistance give faculty a variety of future alternatives. Temporary job placements in non-academic settings allow faculty to try out other careers and life styles. Career counselling for faculty members permits them to deal with changing circumstances in their work. Early retirement or part-time work arrangements for those who do not wish to continue full-time employment help to create more job openings. And experimentation has suggested alternatives to traditional employment practices, such as one-term contracts and new evaluation procedures.

These devices point to new directions for faculty development and represent promising endeavours to be shaped by practice.

## 12.7 Conclusion

Some argue that faculty development is a fad that has already peaked. In one sense at least they are correct. The concept has been articulated, pilot programmes have been devised, materials have been prepared, activities have been held, and evaluations are starting to accumulate. It is understandable that those national opinion leaders who want to stay at the forefront of new developments are beginning to lose interest in championing faculty development. But faculty development for individual colleges and universities is far from a passing fad. As Douglas Kindschi, Dean of Grand Valley State College, puts it, 'Many think faculty development has passed its prime, but we haven't seen anything yet in terms of retrenchment compared with what lies ahead. Faculty development will simply have to become even more important in the years ahead' (1978). Although the frontier spirit has passed nationally, each individual college or university constitutes a new frontier when it comes to applying, refining, extending and improving what has already been learned.

At this point, faculty development can be considered not a high-risk experiment but a set of tools that can be used as one component of total institutional renewal. Several years ago, colleges and universities established offices of institutional research; it is now hard to imagine how a modern institution of higher learning can be wisely administered without adequate data concerning its staff, its students and its plant. Faculty development can be expected to take a similarly vital place in contemporary colleges and universities.

*Author's note*
Portions of this chapter have been drawn from two sources: Jerry G Gaff (1975)
*Toward Faculty Renewal,* Jossey-Bass, San Francisco and Jerry G Gaff (ed)
Institutional renewal through the improvement of teaching. *New Directions for
Higher Education,* 24, Winter 1978.

# Key documents in staff development

## 1. Australia: Report on Australian University Centres for Higher Education Research and Development by the Directors of the Existing Centres

A report on Australian University Centres for Higher Education Research and Development was prepared in 1973 for the Sub-committee on Educational Research and Development of the Australian Vice-Chancellors Committee (AVCC). The authors of the report were the directors of the six existing centres, namely:

| | | |
|---|---|---|
| Prof F M Katz | — | Director, Tertiary Education Research Centre, University of New South Wales (Convenor) |
| Mr A W Anderson | — | Director, Research Unit in University Education, University of Western Australia |
| Prof J C Clift | — | Director, University Teaching and Research Centre, Victoria University of Wellington, New Zealand (Previously Director of the Higher Education Research Unit, Monash University) |
| Prof Kwong Lee Dow | — | Acting Head, Centre for the Study of Higher Education, University of Melbourne |
| Dr G R Meyer | — | Director, Centre for the Advancement of Teaching, Macquarie University |
| Prof E Roe | — | Director, Tertiary Education Institute, University of Queensland. |

This report has been influential both within Australia and further afield. It is reproduced here by kind permission of the Secretary of the Australian Vice-Chancellors Committee.

### Foreword

(By Dr K H Star, Research Information Officer, AVCC, and Executive Officer of the Sub-committee on Educational Research and Development)

Most of the Australian universities which do not already have a centre for higher education research and development are currently in the course of setting up such centres or of finalizing plans for their establishment to be included in the triennial

248

submissions to the Australian Universities Commission. The AVCC's Sub-committee on Educational Research and Development is anxious to assist those universities in this task in whatever way it can. One obvious way is to provide information about the existing centres and about the views of the directors of those centres which they have acquired as a result of their experiences. To that end, the Sub-committee requested the directors of the existing centres to prepare this report . . . Of course, the views expressed in this report are not necessarily endorsed by the Australian Vice-Chancellors Committee or by its Sub-committee on Educational Research and Development.

As mentioned in the report, the way in which each of the existing centres has developed has been, to some extent, a function of the personality of the director. It is my view that the qualities of the director are very much more important in determining how a centre of this kind develops than are the qualities of the head of the normal academic department. This is so partly because there are no traditions of long standing to guide the new director or to define the expectations of him held by other members of the university, and partly because his efficacy is so dependent upon his social skills and upon the respect and confidence he can command from other members of the university. Thus the selection of a new director is crucial. Indeed, although some of the centres set up in universities in Britain have gone from strength to strength and are held in the highest esteem in their own universities, recently a small number of centres have collapsed and become defunct, presumably through the selection of an unsuitable director. I believe that the Australian universities have been fortunate in this connection so far, but there is a very real danger that this might not continue. Recently a number of foundation directorships have been advertised and have attracted poor fields of applicants: as more universities decide to establish such centres the selection problem will become more acute.

Where are the new directors to come from? There is no career structure through which they come and it is not even possible to specify the formal academic qualifications required. Although it might not be the whole answer to the problem, the situation might be made easier if there were some sort of training programme for potential directors followed by a period of secondment to existing centres during which 'learning on the job' could take place and some assessment of the individual's suitability for the job could be made. The Sub-committee is thinking about the possibility of mounting such a programme as one of the other ways in which it might be of assistance to those universities planning the establishment of new centres and, in due course, it might make recommendations along these lines to the AVCC.

I must apologise for the length of this foreword but I believe that I have drawn attention to what will be the greatest single problem confronting universities setting up new centres. One could hardly have expected the authors of the report to have discussed the importance of their own personalities and the good fortune their universities had in selecting them.

Finally, on behalf of the Sub-committee I should like to thank the authors of this report.

*Dr K H Star*

## 1. Introduction

1.1      In Australian universities, as in those of many other countries, there is considerable concern about the effectiveness of educational programmes and processes.

     There is now, more than ever before, pressure on administrators to examine their institution critically — its objectives and processes — and to effect changes where these are deemed necessary. There is pressure on teachers to improve their courses of study; to develop effective ways of facilitating students' learning; and to evaluate their own performance as well as that of their students.

1.2 The present concern is in response to conditions which challenge universities everywhere; conditions such as:

- the increased number and diversity of students
- the critical and often articulate student body
- the explosion of knowledge
- the changing community values and expectations
- the changing requirements of professions, of employers of graduates, and of governments
- the institutional characteristics of some universities, their size and emphasis on activities other than teaching.

1.3 In response to these and other emerging conditions, universities have begun to study themselves, applying the processes of scientific inquiry to their own institutions — to the input, process and output of universities. To assist in this process a number of universities have set up special centres, specifically charged with the responsibility of carrying out institutional research and development with the objective of improving our understanding of institutional characteristics, and to facilitate change or improvements. A special task of these centres has been to initiate improvements in instruction to improve the quality of the teaching-learning process.

1.4 The first two such centres in Australia were established, almost simultaneously, at the Universities of Melbourne and New South Wales. Subsequently, other centres were set up at Monash and Macquarie Universities and the Universities of Western Australia and Queensland, and now several other universities are either in the process of planning or actually developing centres. This development is supported by the Australian Universities Commission which in its Fifth Report (p 102) commented:

> Units concerned with improving the effectiveness of university teaching and learning and with conducting research into problems of higher education have been established at nine universities and three universities are proposing to establish them in the 1973-75 triennium. The Commission supports the establishment of such units. Student representatives who met the Commission stressed repeatedly their belief in the importance of such units as contributing to improved teaching. The Commission believes that all universities should operate such units. Their cost is not great in relation to total expenditure on teaching and research and there is evidence that considerable benefits flow from them.

The Australian Union of Students similarly has been very active in advocating the development of such centres as a means of improving teaching.

1.5 The establishment of centres dedicated to research and development and to the facilitation of improvements in the teaching-learning process does reflect, above all else, the emergence of what is essentially instructional accountability, the need to provide evidence to all concerned with university education that serious attempts are being made to make the educational programme as effective and efficient as conditions and present knowledge will allow.

1.6    Since university centres for the study and improvement of the educational process are relatively new in Australia and elsewhere, it is probably premature to assess their effectiveness. However, the experiences gained in the last decade by those working in these centres may provide useful guidelines for universities establishing centres. It is hoped that the information about the organization and functioning of centres will, in itself, enrich the operation of existing centres.

The present report then, based on information supplied by those directing the existing centres, will seek to provide this information by giving:

- a description of existing centres – their organization, resources and activities
- an identification of difficulties or problems which have been or are being experienced and
- finally, some guidelines as to the required resources of staff and equipment and the organizational pattern which is considered most conducive to the effective functioning of centres.

1.7    The report is based on information supplied by the directors of existing centres. Recommendations which emerged during the conference of the directors of the centres are presented as guidelines for the development of new centres.

1.8    Before presenting the information, we wish to emphasize that this report is not evaluative – it is *not* intended to identify strengths or weaknesses of any individual centre, or to compare resources which universities have committed to these centres. Instead, it is our aim to describe the operations and to present views of those engaged in pursuing identified objectives so that this may provide models for others to use if deemed appropriate.

## 2. Description of existing centres

(*Editor's note:* This section, in which the six fully operative centres were described in detail, has been omitted. Of all the sections of the report, this has dated most. A later account of these and other centres in Australasian universities is provided by Hore [1976], and the Tertiary Education Institute [1977 *et seq*] provides a cumulative record of the current activities of higher education research and development centres in Australia and New Zealand.)

## 3. General comments

3.1    The preceding brief description of six university centres dedicated to research and development in higher education is indicative of common approaches, similarity of functions and common problems. It also serves to highlight some differences in operation. By commenting on some of these similarities and differences it may be possible to identify essential functions and essential resources which, in turn, may then guide us in formulating recommendations for future centres.

3.2    It is noteworthy that although the word 'research' appears in the title of several centres, the majority of the centres function as what might best be described as 'change agents'.

There appears to be an emphasis in most of the centres on action research — co-operative involvement with the teaching staff of the respective universities in designing, pursuing and evaluating new educational programmes and practices.

3.3    Most of the centres identify their own objectives as the facilitation of improvements in teaching and learning, the major aims being to assist in the development of improved educational programmes and processes.

3.4    Most of the centres attempt to achieve this aim by: providing information about the teaching-learning process; guiding the activities of the teaching staff in the use of new strategies and new instructional resources; providing such other services as are available in assisting lecturers to gain both the necessary knowledge and skills of teaching and to carry out research projects relevant to the above and other questions, providing the necessary support during the initial phase of introducing new programmes.

3.5    Most of the centres, but especially those which have been established for some time and those with relatively greater resources, report an increasing demand for their services by both administrators and teachers. In general, the centres appear to have gained acceptance by a majority of university staff — certainly by students — and as their effects are recognized so the demand for, and expectation of, service has increased appreciably. This in turn has produced a need for additional resources.

3.6    The differences in operation of the centres, to some extent at least, are a function of the resources available to the centre, but also necessarily reflect the personality of the director and staff, and the autonomy of the centre.

3.7    Half the existing centres are located within a department or faculty of education. The others are autonomous units directly responsible to the Vice-Chancellor or his deputy.

3.8    Two of the centres, namely those at the Universities of Melbourne and New South Wales, have responsibility for some of the instructional hardware and instructional services, such as visual aids. For one centre, namely that at Macquarie University, this provides a major focus of its activities. As will be indicated, the advantage of a close link or co-ordination between units providing instructional aids and those concerned with development cannot be disputed.

3.9    Some centres are now offering to the staff of their universities courses of variable time duration, designed to improve the educational knowledge and skills of lecturers. One centre has held residential workshops of relatively short periods for staff of a department or of one faculty.

Some universities are now offering courses which lead to the award of a degree in higher education.

3.10   Some centres are active in providing services such as the processing of examinations and evaluations of courses and teaching effectiveness, and in this way influence the educational processes.

3.11   Some centres have become involved in curriculum development and definitions of institutional and course objectives.

3.12   Generally, it would appear that problems encountered by the different centres in their development as viable units were fairly similar. Each centre had to establish credibility, to gain acceptance as a unit which is able to provide a service for the improvement of instruction. Some of the research concluded has provided valuable insights into problems of higher education in Australia. However, the dissemination of the findings of such research is often difficult.

Adequately trained people are scarce and centres have had to train their own staff.

Finally, the efforts, and even success, of a centre's operations are not always easily recognizable and hence the staff of centres often experience considerable anxiety if not frustration.

## 4. Guidelines

As a consequence of the meeting on which this report is based, the directors were in most instances unanimous in offering the following recommendations as guidelines:

### 4.1 *Organization*

4.1.1   Centres should be distinct autonomous units — not part of a faculty or department of education. It is recommended that the director of the centre be directly responsible to the Vice-Chancellor or his deputy. Care should be taken to ensure, however, that the centre is seen to be independent from the administration.

(On this recommendation, 4.1.1, the Director of the Centre for the Study of Higher Education, University of Melbourne, is not in agreement.)

4.1.2   It is recommended that staff of centres be accorded normal academic status; that is, that appointments are made at the level of professor or lecturer/senior lecturer level. This would ensure that suitable, well-trained staff members are attracted to the centres and that there is a possibility of persons moving in from other departments and out to their original disciplines.

4.1.3   The centre should be organizationally linked to service units responsible for instructional services.

### 4.2 *Resources*

4.2.1   It is recommended that the director of the centre be appointed at the status of professor or reader (minimum). The director should be a member of committees responsible for educational policy.

4.2.2   It is the view of the directors that the *minimum* staff requirements for a viable unit are one director and one senior academic, plus supporting staff. The number of staff required will necessarily be related to the size of the university.

4.2.3   The provision of staff should take cognizance of the likely increase in demand for services from the centre, and the need to meet this demand in a reasonable time. Hence planning of the establishment should include a growth factor.

4.2.4   Because expertise in a number of different areas is required, eg teaching processes, evaluation, curriculum development and instructional aids, the staff establishment must provide for such different expertise.

4.2.5    There is strong support for a policy of staff release, ie for staff to be seconded to the centre by other departments for variable periods of time. This would have the advantage of avoiding the necessity for all staff of centres to commit themselves to a career shift. It would ensure also that eventually there would be members of staff in different departments who had been actively engaged in educational research and development.

4.2.6    Because much of the work of the centre is difficult to predict, and because there are often periods of sudden pressure, there is need for flexibility in budgeting for staff. A special fund for appointments of short-term or part-time staff should be made available to the director of the centre.

4.2.7    The minimum resources, other than staff, will necessarily be dependent on the functions the centre is expected to perform. It is recommended, however, that adequate data processing equipment and a range of instructional aids including videotape equipment and library facilities be available to the centre.

### 4.3 *Activities*

4.3.1    The operation of each centre will differ but it is essential that they are oriented to the improvement of educational programmes and processes within the institution.

To further this aim the centre will necessarily be involved in:

- providing information about relevant educational principles to be applied in the clarification and definition of objectives, the effectiveness of different teaching strategies and evaluation processes
- providing services which will facilitate the task of the lecturer
- gathering information on problems relevant to the functioning of the institution
- identifying constraints which hinder the development of new programmes and processes
- facilitating communication between students and staff and between the staff at different levels.

4.4    In addition it is recommended that the existing centres and those to be established should co-operate to a much greater extent than hitherto and that they should carry out cross-institutional research.

4.5    It is also desirable that some rationalization of services offered by centres be attempted; for instance, it may be possible that one or two centres use their equipment to facilitate examination processing for other centres.

4.6    The consensus of the directors is that the work of the AVCC Research Information Officer has been very helpful and that this should be further strengthened.

### 5. Concluding remarks

The directors of the existing centres feel that these suggested guidelines will enable those about to set up centres to recognize some of the basic requirements for viability. In addition, staff at existing centres may consider some re-orientation or extension of the services they are presently offering. Centres based on these guidelines, we feel, will go far in dealing with the problems confronting higher education.

## 2. Britain: 'Agreement concerning the procedure and criteria to be used in connection with the probationary period'

In 1974 an agreement between the University Authorities Panel (the 'management' side in salary negotiations) and the Association of University Teachers committed universities in Britain to 'taking the training of probationary academic staff (non-clinical only) much more seriously than they had hitherto' (Piper, 1977). With the kind permission of the secretaries of the UAP and AUT, the full text of the agreement is reproduced below:

### Introduction

The 1971 academic and related salaries settlement included the following agreement:

*Lecturers*
Probationary period to be three years with possible extension to four years in doubtful cases. Training procedures to be improved with thorough review prior to confirmation on the basis of revised and improved procedures and criteria.

In furtherance of this agreement a working party of Committee A (non-clinical academic staff) has been engaged in reviewing the procedures and criteria for assessment of university teachers on completion of probation. The results of that review are set out below. *It should be stressed that the following paragraphs are intended to be applicable only to academic staff appointed to full-time established posts with tenure and to no others.* Furthermore, anything said here is without prejudice to the rights of universities to terminate appointments for 'good cause' or for redundancy.

### The nature of the probationary review

1.  The terms of probation as now laid down in salary agreements have certain precise implications which must be recognized:

    — The probationary period is strictly limited, normally three years and at most four years. In practice and in order to allow a person not being retained time to look elsewhere for employment the experience upon which an assessment has to be based is normally not more than two years.
    — Within the probationary period a decision must be reached either that the appointment shall be terminated at the end of the probationary period or that the person concerned shall be confirmed in his appointment.
    — A judgement has therefore to be made about a person's promise on very limited evidence; and there are no 'in-between' positions. The probationary period may not be extended beyond four years.
    — Probation having been *satisfactorily* completed in one institution, it would not be appropriate for a second probationary period to be imposed by another institution to which the person concerned subsequently moved.

2.  Thus the decisions made on its probationary lecturers are among the most vital staffing decisions that a university can make. At this point, the ability

and energy of a lecturer are both under scrutiny, with termination of employment the sanction against failure on either count. Thereafter, the university is committed by the confirmation of appointment to the judgement that its lecturers are capable at least to the standard for lecturers, which is the career grade. Within that grade, only their energy and application may thereafter be called in question. There are the incentives of promotion to a higher grade, of the regard of one's colleagues, of professional success and eminence. But the only sanction is a halt to salary increments at the efficiency bar except where a member of staff is found guilty of misconduct, incapacity or dereliction of duty under proceedings for termination of his appointment through 'good cause'.

3. In the circumstances, it is essential in the Working Party view that the decision to confirm an appointment at the conclusion of the probationary period must require a *positive act of decision* by the employing university. Such considerations would not apply to temporary appointments, that is, those for a stipulated period of years only.

Thus:

- While there should always be a definite prospect of confirmation of appointment whenever a probationary appointment is made (ie probationary appointments should only be made to established posts) there is no commitment on the part of the employing university to make confirmation of appointment at the conclusion of probation an automatic process.
- At the end of the third probationary year the employing university should have offered confirmation of appointment or taken appropriate steps to end the appointment or offered an extension of the probationary period for a fourth and final year. Where confirmation or extension of probation is offered the probationer must have accepted the offer for it to be effective.
- Extension of the probationary period to a fourth year is without commitment on the part of the university to offer confirmation of appointment. At the end of the fourth probationary year if the appointment is not to be confirmed the appropriate steps must have been taken to end it.
- A temporary appointment in place of an extension of a probationary appointment for a final year may be offered to allow the person concerned a longer period in which to find employment, he having been informed that a confirmation of appointment will not be offered.

### Selection, training and development

4. The Working Party is of the opinion that universities must maintain high standards of selection procedures when they are considering making appointments to their academic staff. Where appointments have a probationary period it is incumbent on universities to provide training for the probationer of a helpful and comprehensive nature. Advice and guidance by a senior colleague nominated for this task and encouragement to attend formal courses of instruction should be included. Attention should be paid to developments in the training of university lecturers at a national level as well as to internal courses of instruction. The probationer should receive a co-ordinated development programme which lasts throughout his probationary period and permits appropriate reports to be made, and remedial action to be taken where necessary, at regular stages. Universities

should also ensure that the day-to-day duties and workload allocated to a probationer are appropriate for a person of his age, standing and experience.

### Criteria

5.    The primary considerations for the employing university in deciding whether or not to retain a person at the conclusion of his probation must be the long-term interests of the university itself, of the other members of its staff, and of its students. But it is recognized at the same time that a university has a responsibility to assist the development of a member of staff in his probationary period, and also some concern for the future of a probationer whom it does not wish to retain. In the light of these general considerations the Working Party has concluded that there are two sets of conditions which should be involved in any decision to offer confirmation of appointment. These are discussed in turn in the next four paragraphs.

6.    The Working Party considers that the conditions to be met first should be as follows:

> For a person to be offered confirmation of appointment following a period of probation, the employing university shall be satisfied that, having regard to his standing, age, experience and the opportunities he has been offered:
>
> — he has satisfactorily engaged in the teaching of prescribed courses and the supervisory and tutorial work assigned to him
> — he has satisfactorily engaged in research towards the advancement of his subject
> — he has conscientiously carried out such examining duties and satisfactorily performed such administrative duties as have been required of him, and
> — he shows promise by his work and enterprise of continuing to develop as a university teacher and scholar.

7.    The first three of these conditions are fairly straightforward and each admit of objective data. The fourth condition is the more difficult in that, like the confirmation of appointment which is at issue, it is concerned with future prospects rather than with past performance. Assessment here depends inevitably upon subjective estimate — the estimate of the person's head of department and other senior colleagues. It is, however, in just this class of assessment, the assessment of academic worth and potential, that senior university teachers are most experienced and most skilled.

8.    Secondly, some forms of behaviour, and they are very exceptional, may seriously harm the capability, good order or morale of a department, a faculty or even a university. For example, a person may be persistently unco-operative or careless or may deliberately make serious breaches in matters of confidentiality.

9.    The Working Party accepts that such behaviour, if proved, may be a proper reason for not confirming a probationary appointment. However, judgements on these aspects of a person's overall academic performance can be more heavily influenced by subjective assessments and irrelevant considerations than judgements on the merit of the person's published work or teaching ability. In some cases, the faults complained of in a probationary lecturer may be traceable, at least in part, to defects of management or personnel relations. Accordingly, it is essential that

unfavourable reports on any matters of personal behaviour be made in such a way that the probationary lecturer has an adequate opportunity to make out his defence. It is further essential that wider consultations and broader inquiries take place than would be carried out in connection with a person's teaching or research ability.

10. The fact that a person holds or expresses views, on any matter, which differ from those of his colleagues or other members of the university is no reason for not confirming his appointment.

11. An employing university which declines to retain a person on grounds of inadequate performance or insufficient promise or personal unsuitability should be able to show (a) that training in university teaching was made available and (b) that continuing advice and help towards improvement were offered and due warning given of inadequacies by the head of department or other responsible person. As part of the 1971 salary settlement universities agreed to improve the standard of training provided for probationers. In the matter of continuing guidance it is important that heads of departments or other designated persons should be conscious of their responsibilities, and that advice and warning where warranted should be given as early as possible and repeated as often as necessary. It should be the responsibility of the university authorities to see that a record of the probationary period is kept. Such a probationary record must be full enough to enable it to be produced in evidence if required. In particular details of the advice given and of warnings given in respect of those matters described in paragraphs 5. and 8. above must be included in the record. Where the probationer's failings are sufficiently serious to justify consideration of non-confirmation of appointment a written warning must be handed to him and a copy placed in the probationary record. A university which is in serious default in respect of (a) or (b) above retains the right not to confirm the appointment on the grounds that the conditions set out in paragraphs 6. to 8. above have not been met, but it may face arguments for the extension of the probationary period or even for confirmation of the appointment.

### Review procedure

12. It is desirable to ensure that the offer of confirmation of appointment following probation is not unreasonably withheld. The Working Party considers that the review procedure should provide safeguards against unreasonable termination. It is the Working Party's view that an employing university should give an explanation of the reasons for not confirming probation to the individual concerned but there should be no obligation to publish the details of the proceedings unless this is required by legal process.

13. The Working Party considers that there should be a specific procedure whereby an individual may appeal to an appropriately constituted body against a decision not to confirm his appointment. This procedure should derive from the ordinances and statutes of individual universities where this is practicable.

# 3. The Federal Republic of Germany: 'AHD — principles of Hochschuldidaktik'[1]

The Committee of the Association for Hochschuldidaktik (AHD) at the closed session at Wieckenberg on 23-24 August 1973

- in the conviction that the present state of Hochschuldidaktik in Germany requires a theoretical as well as a practical exposition
- in the knowledge that the present situation of Hochschuldidaktik has made such an exposition possible
- with the aim of promoting Hochschuldidaktik in Germany
- with the intention of mapping out a field of action and a strategy for the Association for Hochschuldidaktik

unanimously adopted the following 'AHD — principles of Hochschuldidaktik' as the basis for discussion at the Annual General Meeting, to be held at Marburg on 16 and 17 November.

### The frame of reference of Hochschuldidaktik

1. The Association for Hochschuldidaktik believes that pronouncements about Hochschuldidaktik are meaningless without a statement of the frame of reference. Consequently, the meaning of 'Hochschuldidaktik' on which the work of the Association for Hochschuldidaktik has to be based cannot be defined without statements about the basic interpretation of the academic arts and sciences in general, and about the relationship of the arts and sciences to the state and to social structures.

### The relationship of the academic arts and sciences to the state and to social structures

2. The AHD takes the view that the academic arts and sciences, in their relationship to the state and to social structures, should be addressed primarily, as institutions, to the tasks of criticism and innovation. Criticism and innovation within this relationship are defined by the relevant basic principles of the German Constitution.

3. To carry out these tasks of criticism and innovation, it is necessary to have a kind of social sub-system, namely the academic arts and sciences, which is essentially removed from the state and from interest groups of society. The maintenance of this distance between them can traditionally be defined by the word 'autonomy'. Nevertheless, there must be control mechanisms to guarantee the fulfilment of this function (ie criticism and innovation). In particular, this autonomy must not be used by adherents of the disciplines to hold on to individual advantages or group privileges, or to establish new ones, or to conceal irregular actions.

4. At present the claim to autonomy of the academic arts and sciences is disputed in the Federal Republic of Germany. In particular, the orientation of the state — in accordance with that of prestigious social groups — towards supervision in respect of the subject matter of research and teaching and towards possibilities of rigorous intervention has been steadily growing. Not the least important reason for this may be that tertiary institutions have not been entirely trustworthy in their use of this freedom, which has been conceded to them in a rather uncontrolled fashion since 1945.

5. In theory, the autonomous organization of the academic arts and sciences is confirmed by the basic right in Article 5, Section 3 ('Institutional

Guarantee of Academic Freedom') of the *Grundgesetz* (Constitution). Within the historical situation there is an additional necessity for content-based argumentation. Possible arguments can be derived, in the opinion of the AHD, from a theory of systems, and from political and pragmatic concepts:

— State and society create a scrutinizing body which will examine the system 'from the outside' and will identify areas where improvement is possible (justification from a theory of systems);
— in the interests of the democratization of society, those who are concerned with the actual conduct and organization of any work should be the same persons as those who make the relevant decisions about the work and its utilization (political justification);
— those who demonstrate or acquire the essential knowledge of the discipline in question are especially qualified to articulate the rationally necessary grounds for the subsequent decision process (pragmatic justification).

6. The Association for Hochschuldidaktik recognizes that it has to be the responsibility of the state to cater for the interests of all social groups. The state therefore has the power to lay down the boundaries and the basic framework of the area of autonomy of the academic arts and sciences. This happens, on the one hand, through the establishment and administration of laws and regulations, and on the other hand through decisions about resources.

Before laying down these frameworks, however, intensive public discussion has to take place between the academic arts and sciences as an organized system, the social groups concerned, and the state. Continuing middle- and long-term planning, in which the state and the sub-system of academic arts and sciences, on both local and federal levels, should be equal partners with equivalent planning instruments, is an essential for carrying on this discussion in relation to the critical and innovative functions of the academic arts and sciences.

## The relationship of Hochschuldidaktik to the academic arts and sciences, the state, and social practice

7. Hochschuldidaktik cannot act instead of individual disciplines in arriving at a definition of the relationship between individual disciplines and social groups. But as this definition is central to its operation, Hochschuldidaktik should emphasize that this exchange between individual disciplines and social practice should take place.

8. The relationship between the academic arts and sciences and practice is particularly relevant to Hochschuldidaktik in so far as all theory-practice relationships fall within its field, given the nature of its task of academic education. The methodology of Hochschuldidaktik thus consists of analysis, consultation, and planning.

9. Hochschuldidaktik and the autonomy of the academic arts and sciences are interdependent:

— the autonomy of the academic disciplines forms the basis of Hochschuldidaktik, as defined here;
— Hochschuldidaktik forms a basis for argument for the claim to autonomy of the academic disciplines.

**The range of activities in Hochschuldidaktik**

10.  Hochschuldidaktik should not be broken down into component parts, eg theory of knowledge, educational technology, methodology of teaching particular subjects, politics of higher education, economics of education, group dynamics, or research into teaching, although the issues and content of each of these fields (and of others) must be considered. Hochschuldidaktik is therefore necessarily inter-disciplinary.

11.  Hochschuldidaktik is a discipline of action which does not confine itself to the description and explanation of social phenomena, but includes planning and model development and practice. Thus it can succeed only when its practitioners have at their disposal not only hypothetical but actual fields of action.

12.  The action of Hochschuldidaktik takes place at a number of levels: analysis and planning of

- the framework of conditions of teaching and learning in higher education
- curricula
- individual phases of curricula
- individual courses, as well as
- individual phases of parts of activities within courses.

The effectiveness of Hochschuldidaktik depends on the co-ordination of activities on these levels.

13.  Hochschuldidaktik embraces the tasks of research, self-scrutiny, planning, development and practice of models, in-service and further education, documentation, publication, and public promotion.

14.  Research is the foundation of all the work of Hochschuldidaktik. It should not be restricted to attempts to prove hypotheses; above all, it should include communication with those concerned, clarification of interests and concepts, and a consideration of the implications of the practice of Hochschuldidaktik, and should thereby develop starting points for action research. It must also strive for a re-direction of the by-and-large easier to handle methods of inquiry (adapted to cognition categories) towards methods of observation of behaviour to discover how people in fact behave. Research endeavours should be related to premises which are believed to be right, and these should be clearly stated.

15.  Self-scrutiny in Hochschuldidaktik must safeguard the theoretical basis and the limits of the discipline.

16.  Planning in Hochschuldidaktik must state clearly its empirical and normative premises. This applies particularly to the safeguarding of research data and to the explication of aims, as well as to the appropriateness and suitability of the proposed procedure.

17.  The development and practice of models at all levels must be one of the essential tasks of all action within Hochschuldidaktik. It ranges from *ad hoc* innovations in one particular teaching situation to fully developed project study.

18.  In-service and further education in Hochschuldidaktik cannot (at least at present) take the form of a specialized course of study. Rather, it must stand in a close relationship with the actual practice of teaching and learning, and cover the range of all activities in Hochschuldidaktik. Its target group consists of all those involved with teaching as well as other persons

concerned with problems of higher education, especially the rising generation of academics.

19. Documentation, publication and public promotion are vital to the success of Hochschuldidaktik.

### The institutionalization of Hochschuldidaktik

20. Hochschuldidaktik can follow the principles laid down above only if it is institutionalized within the universities, in centres independent of any faculty. A connection with the central administration is to be avoided, as is a tie-up with a particular faculty.

21. All centres for Hochschuldidaktik should be able to be active at all levels and areas of work described above. Supra-regional co-operation and co-ordination is absolutely essential.

22. In their organization, their styles of work and their forms of communication, the centres for Hochschuldidaktik should conform to the requirements they have formulated for others.

### Proposals for action for the Association for Hochschuldidaktik

Within the framework outlined, the Association for Hochschuldidaktik has, in the view of the Committee, to face the following urgent tasks:

23. The AHD must occupy a clearly defined position in the politics of higher education.

24. In its activities, it has to seek partners for an alliance; it must clarify what kind of relationship the internal planning of universities and the work of the centres have to its own work. It must publicize which organizations and institutions are opposed to a progressive Hochschuldidaktik in accordance with these principles.

25. It must seek financial supporters who are willing to promote its aims.

26. If the work of reform through Hochschuldidaktik is impeded, the Association for Hochschuldidaktik must resist this. In this respect, it must adopt a critical standpoint towards the constitutional verdicts of the German High Court concerning the participation of workers and the *numerus clausus*,[2] as well as towards the draft of a Tertiary Education Ordinance.

27. The Association for Hochschuldidaktik should examine models for a supra-regional instrumentality of its own for Hochschuldidaktik (for universities as well as for centres for Hochschuldidaktik), as well as carefully watching the policies of the Assembly of Ministries of Culture, the Federal Ministry of Education and Science, the Commission of the Federation and States, and the German Assembly of University Presidents, to see whether they are favourable or unfavourable to the objectives of Hochschuldidaktik as laid down in these principles.

28. The Association for Hochschuldidaktik must try to the best of its ability — under certain circumstances by soliciting the support of third parties — to disseminate comprehensive and systematic information about issues in Hochschuldidaktik. The establishment of an information centre for Hochschuldidaktik is important. The Association for Hochschuldidaktik should promote this project and actually work on it.

29. It must furthermore adopt a more critical attitude than hitherto to research

and practice in Hochschuldidaktik, in order to promote development according to these principles.

30. It must actively concern itself with efforts to reform teaching; that means supporting and, where appropriate, co-arranging, meetings, symposia, or groups working on study reform, as long as they serve the aims of these principles.

31. The Association for Hochschuldidaktik must stimulate tertiary institutions to work in Hochschuldidaktik, and must seek majority support in the universities for its aims.

32. It must build up its organization in such a way as to encourage the foundation of local branches of AHD groups in individual tertiary institutions, as well as requesting selected members to initiate the establishment of local groups.

33. It must intensify its activities and canvassing in pedagogical universities and technical colleges *(Fachhochschulen)*, and exert itself to attract the membership of tertiary institutions which do not yet belong to the AHD.

34. The Association for Hochschuldidaktik should continue its efforts to establish a journal for higher education research and development.

35. It must improve its production of publications through critical selection, planning of topics, and appropriate selection of authors.

36. The Association for Hochschuldidaktik should develop a far-reaching future perspective, and on the basis of this should propose an overall plan for higher education research and development in the Federal Republic of Germany.

*Notes*
1. Translation by Janet Healey, Office for Research in Academic Methods, Australian National University, Canberra.
2. In the context of a British university, the term *numerus clausus* is best rendered by 'quota system' *(Translator)*.

# Centres and associations concerned with staff development

## 1. Australia

*Higher Education Research and Development Society of Australasia (HERDSA), c/- TERC, University of New South Wales, PO Box 1, Kensington, NSW 2033*

Research and Development Unit
Adelaide College of Advanced Education
46 Kintore Avenue
Adelaide, SA 5000

Mr Robert A Cannon
Acting Director
Advisory Centre for University Education
The University of Adelaide
Box 498 GPO
Adelaide, SA 5001

Mr Ian Burnard
Alexander Mackie College of Advanced Education
PO Box 259
Paddington, NSW 2021

Dr D Anderson
Head
Educational Research Unit (ERU)
Australian National University
PO Box 4
Canberra, ACT 2600

Mr A Miller
Head
Office for Research in Academic Methods (ORAM)
Australian National University
PO Box 4
Canberra, ACT 2600

Mr F Morgan
Director
Instructional Media Centre
Canberra College of Advanced Education
PO Box 381
Canberra City, ACT 2601

Mr Charles Noble
Head
Educational Development Unit (EDU)
Caulfield Institute of Technology
PO Box 197
Caulfield East, Victoria 3145

Mr Frank Warren
Director
Educational Services Unit
Cumberland College of Health Sciences
PO Box 170
Lidcombe, NSW 2141

Mr M P McFarlane
Head
Department of External and Continuing Education
Higher Education Research, Evaluation and Inservice Section (HEREIS)
Darling Downs Institute of Advanced Education
c/- PO Darling Heights
Toowoomba, Queensland 4350

The Director
Educational Research Unit (ERU)
The Flinders University of South Australia
Bedford Park, SA 5042

Mr R L Taylor
Head
Educational Development Department
Footscray Institute of Technology
PO Box 64
Footscray, Victoria 3011

Mr K Smith
Head
Educational Services Division
Gippsland Institute of Advanced Education
PO Box 42
Churchill, Victoria 3842

Dr R A Ross
Director
Centre for the Advancement of Learning and Teaching (CALT)
Griffith University
Nathan, Queensland 4111

Mr H Batten
Head
Department of Educational Resources
Lincoln Institute of Health Sciences
625 Swanston Street
Carlton, Victoria 3053

Dr G R Meyer
Director
Centre for Advancement of Teaching (CAT)
Macquarie University
North Ryde, NSW 2113

Mr Norman W Henry
Head
Education Unit
Royal Melbourne Institute of Technology
GPO Box 2476V
Melbourne, Victoria 3001

Prof D G Beswick
Director
Centre for the Study of Higher Education
University of Melbourne
Parkville, Victoria 3052

Dr Terry Hore
Director
Higher Education Advisory and Research Unit (HEARU)
Monash University
Wellington Road
Clayton, Victoria 3168

Dr R McDonald
Director
Educational Services and Teaching Resources Unit (ESTR)
Murdoch University
Murdoch, WA 6153

Assoc Prof Charles Engel
Chairman
Division of Medical Education and Programme Evaluation
Faculty of Medicine
University of Newcastle
Shortland, NSW 2308

Dr Harry Maddox
Director
Higher Education Research and Services Unit (HERSU)
University of Newcastle
Newcastle, NSW 2308

Dr D Watkins
Educational Research Unit
University of New England
Armidale, NSW 2351

Ms J Lublin
Educational Services Unit
Educational Development Branch
New South Wales Institute of Technology
PO Box 123
Broadway, NSW 2007

Dr John Powell
Acting Director
Tertiary Education Research Centre (TERC)
University of New South Wales
PO Box 1
Kensington, NSW 2033

Mr Derick Unwin
Head
Educational Research and Development Unit (ERDU)
Queensland Institute of Technology
GPO Box 2434
Brisbane, Queensland 4001

Prof Ernest Roe
Director
Tertiary Education Institute (TEDI)
University of Queensland
St Lucia, Queensland 4067

Mr B Hawkins
Head
Education Unit
Swinburne College of Technology
PO Box 218
Hawthorne, Victoria 3122

Mr P Northcott
Head
Educational Practices Unit
Tasmanian College of Advanced Education
GPO Box 1415 P
Hobart, Tasmania 7001

Dr Harry E Stanton
Director
Higher Education Research and Advisory Centre (HERAC)
University of Tasmania
GPO Box 252 C
Hobart, Tasmania 7001

Mr Alan Barton
Head
Research Unit
Torrens College of Advanced Education
Holbrooks Road
Underdale, SA 5032

Mr F Bosch
Head
Education Unit
Warrnambool Institute of Advanced Education
PO Box 423
Warrnambool, Victoria 3280

Educational Development Unit
Western Australian Institute of Technology
Hayman Road
South Bentley, WA 6102

Mr A W Anderson
Director
Research Unit in University Education (RUUE)
The University of Western Australia
Nedlands, WA 6009

## 2. Britain

*Society for Research into Higher Education (SRHE) at the University of Surrey, Guildford, Surrey GU2 5XH*

(a) **Universities:** Only 22 universities are listed. Universities not listed represent cases where no one individual has responsibility for staff development, or where such information is not available.

Dr Ray McAleese
Department of Education
University of Aberdeen
Aberdeen AB9 2UB

Mr Colin Flood Page
Department of Educational Enquiry
University of Aston
Gosta Green
Birmingham B4 7ET

The Director
Educational Services Unit
University of Bath
Claverton Down
Bath BA2 7AY

Dr Desmond Rutherford
Advisory Service on Teaching Methods
University of Birmingham
PO Box 363
Birmingham B15 2TT

Dr Alan Harding
Educational Development Service
University of Bradford
Bradford, West Yorkshire BD7 1DP

Mr Leo Evans
Head
Centre for Educational Technology
The City University
St John Street
London EC1V 4PB

Dr Derick Hoare
Department of Chemistry
University of Dundee
Edinburgh EHB 9YL

Dr Peter Kennedy
Psychiatry Department
University of Edinburgh
Edinburgh EHB 9YL

Dr Donald Bligh
Director
Teaching Services Centre
University of Exeter
Exeter EX4 4QJ

Mr Walter Humes
Department of Education
University of Glasgow
Glasgow G12 8QQ

Dr John Cowan
Civil Engineering Learning Unit
Heriot-Watt University
Edinburgh EH1 1HX

Mr Graham Settle
Department of Computational and Statistical Science
University of Liverpool
PO Box 147
Liverpool L69 3BX

Dr David Mack
Department of Social Sciences
Loughborough University of Technology
Loughborough, Leics

Mr Nick Boreham
Department of Adult and Higher Education
University of Manchester
Oxford Rd
Manchester M13 9PL

Dr Fred Bell
University of Manchester Institute of Science and Technology
Oxford Rd
Manchester M13 9PL

Dr George Brown
Department of Adult Education
University of Nottingham
University Park
Nottingham NG7 2RD

Mr Don Pritchard
School of Education
University of Reading
Reading
Berkshire RG6 2AH

Miss Susan Sayer
Audio Visual Centre
University of Salford
Salford, Lancs M5 4WR

Mr Colin Coles
Department of Teaching Media
University of Southampton
Highfield
Southampton SO9 5NH

Mr Alex Main
Centre for Educational Practice
University of Strathclyde
155 George Street
Glasgow G1 1RD

Prof Lewis Elton
Head
Institute for Educational Technology
University of Surrey
Guildford
Surrey GU2 5XH

Dr Eric Hewton
Department of Education
University of Sussex
Falmer, Brighton
Sussex BN1 9RH

*Co-ordinating Committee for the Training of University Teachers*

Chairman:    Dr Clifford Butler
             Vice-Chancellor
             Loughborough University of Technology
             Loughborough, Leics

Co-ordinating and Research Officer:
             Dr C C Matheson
             The Registry
             University of East Anglia
             Norwich NR4 7TJ

**(b) Polytechnics:** Responsibility for staff development in the polytechnics normally resides in one or more committees of the academic board under the chairmanship of a member of the directorate. The following polytechnics have established units with executive responsibility for at least some aspect of staff development

Ms J Tait
Co-ordinator
Educational Development Unit
Brighton Polytechnic
Moulsecoomb, Brighton BN2 4GJ

Mr J Davidson
Centre for Educational Services
Bristol Polytechnic
Coldharbour Lane
Frenchay, Bristol BS16 1QY

Mr S Cox
Learning Systems Group
Lanchester Polytechnic
Priory Street
Coventry CV1 5FB

Mr A J Tribe
Head of Education
Educational Development Service
The Hatfield Polytechnic
PO Box 109
Hatfield, Herts AL10 9AB

Mr W C Chavner
Head
Educational Technology Unit
Leeds Polytechnic
Calverley Street
Leeds LS1 3HE

Mr J L Clarke
Head
Educational Technology Centre
Leicester Polytechnic
PO Box 143
Leicester LE1 9BH

Mr D J Mortimer
Head
Educational Development Unit
Polytechnic of Central London
309 Regent Street
London W1R 8AL

Dr Penny Griffin
Co-ordinator
Learning Systems Group
Middlesex Polytechnic
Bounds Green Road
London N11 2NQ

Division for Staff and Educational Development
North East London Polytechnic
Livingstone House
Livingstone Road
London E15 2LJ

Mr A George
Head
Educational Development Service
The Polytechnic of North London
Holloway, London N7 8DB

Mr R Thackwell
Education Unit
Polytechnic of the South Bank
Borough Road
London SE1 0AA

Mr G J Grant
Head
Educational Services Unit
Manchester Polytechnic
John Dalton Building
Chester Street
Manchester M1 5GD

Miss B Hollingshead
Head
Staff Development Unit
Manchester Polytechnic
John Dalton Building
Chester Street
Manchester M1 5GD

Mr R Fothergill
Head
Polytechnic Educational Technology Resources and Advisory Service (PETRAS)
Newcastle-upon-Tyne Polytechnic
Pandon Building
Northumberland Road
Newcastle-upon-Tyne NE1 8ST

Mr D Fox
Staff Development Service
Trent Polytechnic
Burton Street
Nottingham NG1 4BU

Mr R S Darby
Co-ordinator
Education Services Unit
Oxford Polytechnic
Headington, Oxford OX3 0BP

Mr W Hopwood
Learning Resources Centre
Plymouth Polytechnic
Drake Circus
Plymouth PL4 8AA

Dr D S Trickey
Educational Development Service
Sheffield City Polytechnic
Pond Street
Sheffield S1 1WB

*Standing Conference on Educational Development Services in Polytechnics (SCEDSIP)*

Chairman:  Trevor Habeshaw
Centre for Educational Services
Bristol Polytechnic
Coldharbour Lane
Frenchay, Bristol BS16 1QY

Secretary:  Dr Penny Griffin
Learning Systems Group
Middlesex Polytechnic
Bounds Green Road
London N11 2NQ

Publications obtainable from:
Richard Fothergill
PETRAS
Newcastle-upon-Tyne Polytechnic
Pandon Building
Northumberland Road
Newcastle-upon-Tyne NE1 8ST

# 3. Canada

*Dr Alexander Gregor, Secretary-Treasurer, Canadian Society for the Study of Higher Education, Department of Educational Foundations, The University of Manitoba, Winnipeg, Manitoba R3J 2N2*

*Dr Bruce M Shore, Comité des Directeurs des Services Pédagogiques du Québec, Centre for Learning and Development, McGill University, 815 Sherbrooke Street West, Montreal, Quebec H3A 2K6*

*Dr George L Geis, Special Interest Group: Instructional Development (SIG:ID), American Educational Research Association (AERA), Centre for Learning and Development, McGill University, 815 Sherbroo Sherbrooke Street West, Montreal, Quebec H3A 2K6*

*Dr Bruce M Shore, Chairman, Teaching Effectiveness Committee, Canadian Association of University Teachers, Centre for Learning and Development, McGill University, 815 Sherbrooke Street West, Montreal, Quebec H3A 2K6*

Dr Dan Coldeway
Director
Instructional Development Unit
Athabasca University
14515 122nd Avenue
Edmonton, Alberta T5L 2W4

Mrs Karen Zanutto
Co-ordinator of Instructional Development Activities
Counselling Centre
Brock University
St Catherines, Ontario L2S 3A1

Mrs June Landsburg
Office of Instructional Development
Room 1513, Arts Tower
Carleton University
Ottawa, Ontario K1S 5B6

Prof Ronald Smith
Director
Learning and Development Office
Concordia University
7141 Sherbrooke Street West
Montreal, Quebec H4B 1R6

273

Dr John Neill
Co-ordinator for Instructional Development
Office for Educational Practice
C/o Audio Visual Services
University of Guelph
Guelph, Ontario N1G 2W1

Dr Barbara Perticaro
Co-ordinator
Teaching and Learning Activities
Room C105
Laurentian University – Université Laurentien
Sudbury, Ontario P3E 2C6

M Jacques Parent
Directeur
Le Service de Pédagogie Universitaire
Bureau 35302
Pavillon de la Bibliothéque
Université Laval
Québec, Québec G1K 7P4

Dr George L Geis, Director
Dr Bruce M Shore, Acting Director (1978-79)
Centre for Learning and Development
McGill University
815 Sherbrooke Street West
Montreal, Quebec H3A 2K6

Dr David Humphreys
Director
Instructional Development Centre
Senior Sciences, Room 101
McMaster University
Hamilton, Ontario L8S 4M1

M Pierre Dalceggio
Directeur
Le Service Pédagogique
Université de Montréal
Chambre ≠830, 5858 Côte-des-Neiges
Montréal, Québec H3S 1Z1

Dr Charles E Pascal
Director
Ontario Universities Program for Instructional Development
130 St George Street
Suite 8039
Toronto, Ontario M5S 2T4

M Paul-André Quintin
Directeur
Service de développement pédagogique
Université du Québec à Trois-Rivières
Pavillon Pierre Boucher, CP 500
Trois-Rivières, Québec G9A 5H7

Ms Sue Pisterman
Co-ordinator and Head
Instructional Development Programme
Queen's University
Kingston, Ontario K7L 3N6

Dr John Kirkness
Co-ordinator
Educational Development
University of Toronto
65 St George Street
Toronto, Ontario M5S 1A1

Dr Christopher K Knapper
Teaching Resource Office
University of Waterloo
Waterloo, Ontario N2L 3G1

Dr Douglas McCready
Director
Office of Instructional Development
Room 2C5-C, Arts Building
Wilfrid Laurier University
Waterloo, Ontario N2L 3C5

Dr Walter Romanow
Co-ordinator
Program for Teaching and Learning
University of Windsor
Windsor, Ontario N9B 3P4

Mr Richard Handscombe
Director
Teaching Skills Programme
York University
4700 Keele Street
Toronto, Ontario M3J 1P3

## 4. Denmark

Department of Further Training and Social Odontology
Dental College of Copenhagen
Universitetsparken 4
DK 2100 Copenhagen Ø

Institute ILF/CTS
Copenhagen School of Economics and Business Administration
Howitzvej 60
DK 2000 Copenhagen F

Institute for Studies in Higher Education
University of Copenhagen
St Kannikestraede 18
DK 1169 Copenhagen K

# 5. The Federal Republic of Germany

*Arbeitsgemeinschaft für Hochschuldidaktik e V (AHD)*
*Rothenbaumchaussee 32, 2 Hamburg 13*

*Arbeitsgemeinschaft Gruppendynamik im Bildungsbereich (AGIB)*
*c/- Chr Grützmacher, Schinkelstr 13, 4006 Erkrath*

*Gesellschaft für Gruppenarbeit in der Erziehung (GGE)*
*c/- Prof Dr Ernst Meyer, Schlittweg 84, 6095 Schriesheim b,*
*Heidelberg*

*Für Hochschuldidaktik der Naturwissenschaften: Gesellschaft für*
*Didaktik der Chemie und Physik (GDCP)*
*c/- Prof Dr H Dahncke, Olshausenstr 75, 23 Kiel*

*Hochschuldidaktische Zentren*

Dr Dietrich Brandt
Hochschuldidaktisches Zentrum der Technische Hochschule Aachen
Büchel 29-31, 5100 Aachen

Dr Johann Nowak
Hochschuldidaktisches Zentrum der Universitat Augsburg
Eichleitnerstr 30, 8900 Augsburg

Dr Brigitte Behrend
Arbeitsstelle Hochschuldidaktische Fortbildung und
Beratung der Freie Universität Berlin
Habelschwerdter Allee 34a, 1000 Berlin 33

Prof Dr Carl Hellmut Wagemann
Institut für Hochschuldidaktik der Technische Universität Berlin
Jebenstr 1, 1000 Berlin 12

Wolff-Dietrich Wedler MA
Interdisziplinäres Zentrum für Hochschuldidaktik der Universität Bielefeld
Postfach 8640, 4800 Bielefeld

Dieter Mützelburg
Organisationsbereich Lehrerbildung der Universität Bremen
Achterstrasse, 2800 Bremen

Jens Pukies
Hochschuldidaktisches Zentrum der Technische Hochschule Darmstadt
Karolinenplatz 5, 6100 Darmstadt

Prof Dr Sigrid Metz-Göckel
Hochschuldidaktisches Zentrum für den Gesamthochschulbereich Dortmund
Rheinlanddamm 199, 4600 Dortmund

Prof Dr Jürgen Klüver
Hochschuldidaktisches Zentrum der Gesamthochschule Essen
Postfach 6843, 4300 Essen 1

Didaktisches Zentrum der Universität Frankfurt
Senckenberganlage 13, 6000 Frankfurt:
Arbeitsstelle II: Prof Dr Egon Becker
Arbeitsstelle V: Prof Dr F Roth
Institut Markt und Plan, Hochschuldidaktik der Wirtschaftswissenschaften:
Prof Dr U P Ritter

Prof Dr Birkenhauer/Frau A Schlösser
Didaktisches Zentrum der Gesamthochschulregion Freiburg
Pädagogische Hochschule Freiburg
Kunzenweg 21, 7800 Freiburg

Prof Dr W Himmerich/Dr Manfred Bayer
Zentrum für Lehrerausbildung Universität Giessen
Karl Glöckner Str 21a, 6300 Giessen

Dr Gudrun Scholz
Hochschuldidaktisches Zentrum der Universität Göttingen
Nikolausberger Weg 11, 3400 Göttingen

Prof Dr Ludwig Huber
Interdisziplinäre Zentrum für Hochschuldidaktik der Universität Hamburg
Sedanstr 19, 2000 Hamburg 13

Dr A Bonnemann
Hochschuldidaktisches Zentrum der Hochschule der Bundeswehr Hamburg
Holstenhofweg 85, 2000 Hamburg 70

Prof Dr Manfred Walter
Zentrum für Rechtsdidaktik an der Technische Universität Hannover
Hanomagstr 8, 3000 Hannover

Dr Dr Dahmer
Arbeitsgemeinschaft Didaktik der Medizin an der Medizin Hochschule Hannover
Bissendorfer Str 11, 3000 Hannover

Jörg Henning
Arbeitsgemeinschaft für Hochschuldidaktik der Universität Karlsruhe
Herzstrasse, Westhochschule, Bau 35, 7500 Karlsruhe

Frau Ayla Neusel
Modellversuch Teilprojekt I, Architektur Gesamthochschule Kassel
Holländischer Platz, 3500 Kassel

Peter Hauswaldt
Projektgruppe für Hochschuldidaktik der Universität Marburg
Biegenstr 22, 3550 Marburg

Prof Dr F W Kron
Senatskommission für die Bildung eines Zentrums für Hochschuldidaktik
Münsterstr 18, 6500 Mainz

Dr A Winteler
Hochschuldidaktisches Zentrum der Hochschule der Bundeswehr München
Werner Heisenberg Weg 39, 8014 Neubiberg

Prof Dr Manfred Sader
Arbeitsgruppe Hochschuldidaktik der Universität Münster
Schlaunstr 2, 4400 Münster

Detlev Spindler
Zentrum für Pädagog Berufspraxis, Universität Oldenburg
Ammerländer Heerstr 6, 2900 Oldenburg

Wolfgang Streffer
Zentrum für Pädagog Berufspraxis, Universität Osnabrück
Ziegelstr, 4500 Osnabrück

Prof Dr Michael Daxner/Dr Ilse Bürmann
Fachgebiet Hochschuldidaktik am Fachbereich III
Seminarstr 20, 4500 Osnabrück

Institut für Hochschulbau
Universität Stuttgart
Kienestr 41, 7000 Stuttgart 1

Dipl Ing Eva-Maria Kreuz
Projektgruppe für Planungsdidaktik
Seidenstr 50, 7000 Stuttgart 1

Prof Dr H Hoffmann
Kontaktstelle für Fachhochschuldidaktik an den Fachhochschulen in Bayern
Fachhochschule Weihenstephan abt Triesdorf
8821 Triesdorf

Gerd Rosenbrock
Zentrum für Hochschuldidaktik der Universität Tübingen
Holzmarkt, 7400 Tübingen

Prof Dr Peterssen
Ausschuss für Hochschuldidaktik der Pädagogische Hochschule Weingarten
Kirchplatz 2, 7987 Weingarten

## 6. The German Democratic Republic[1]

Prof Dr sc Horst Möhle
Chair of University Pedagogics
Karl-Marx-Universität
Karl-Marx-Platz 9
701 Leipzig

## 7. The Indian Sub-continent

*Bangladesh*

Bangladesh Education Extension and Research Institute (BEERI)
Dhanmandi
Dacca-5

Institute for Advancement of Science and Technology Teaching (IASTT)
31 New Eskaton Road
Dacca-2

University Grants Commission
House No 49
Road No 3/A
Dhanmondi Residential Area
Dacca-5

*India*

National Council of Educational Research and Training
Nie Campus
Sri Aurobindo Marg
New Delhi 110016

University Grants Commission
Bahadur Shah Zafar Marg
New Delhi 110001

*Nepal*

Dr Prem Kasaju
Director
Centre for Educational Research, Innovation and Development
Maharajgung
Kathmandu

Dr R K Rongong
Director
Curriculum Development Centre
Tribhuwan University
Kirtipur Campus
Kathmandu

*Pakistan*

University Grants Commission
Sector H-9
Islamabad

# 8. The Netherlands

*Drs P Buis, CBOWO (Central Bureau, including Secretariat of Contact Group), Prinzes Beatrixlaan 428, Voorburg*

*Drs H Kleijer, SISWO (Interuniversity Foundation for Social Science Research), O Z Achterburgural 128, Amsterdam*

*RWO — Centres*

Dr M Mirande
Centrum voor Onderzoek van het Wetenschappelijk Onderwijs
Gemeente Universiteit Amsterdam
Spui 21, Amsterdam

Dr G Bernaert
Afdeling Onderwijsresearch
Vrije Universiteit Amsterdam
De Boelelaan 1105, Amsterdam

The Director
Sektie Onderzoek en Ontwikkeling
Onderwijskundige Dienst
Technische Hogeschool Delft
Mijnbouwplein 11, Delft

The Director
Groep Onderwijsresearch
Technische Hogeschool Eindhoven
Postbus 513, Eindhoven

Drs P Knippenberg
Centrum voor Onderzoek van het Wetenschappelik
Universiteit Groningen
Oude Kijk in 't Jatstraat 13, Groningen

Drs S Blom
Bureau Onderzoek van Onderwijs
Universiteit Leiden
Boerhaavelaan 2, Leiden

Dr W H F W Wijnen
Capaciteitsgroep Onderwijsresearch
Rijksuniversiteit Limburg
Tongersestraat 53, Maastricht

Dr J van Hout
Inst voor Onderzoek van het Wetenschappelijk Onderwijs
Katholieke Universiteit Nijmegen
Oranjesingel 41, Nijmegen

Drs C F van der Klauw
Vakgroep Onderwijs-Research
Erasmus Universiteit Rotterdam
Postbus 1738, Rotterdam

Dr C van Dorp
Onderwijs Research Centrum
Katholieke Hogeschool Tilburg
Hogeschoollaan 225, Tilburg

Drs W Hengeveld
Centrum voor Didaktiek en Onderzoek van Onderwijs
Technische Hogeschool Twente
Postbus 217, Enschede

Drs F Kiela
Afdeling Onderzoek en Ontwikkeling
Universiteit Utrecht
Mailiebaan 5, Utrecht

The Director
Bureau Onderzoek van Onderwijs
Landbouwhogeschool Waginengen
Stadsbrink 389 III, Wageningen

# 9. New Zealand

*Higher Education Research and Development Society of Australasia (HERDSA), c/- TERC, University of New South Wales, PO Box 1, Kensington, NSW 2033, Australia.*

Mr A Johnson
Teaching and Learning Resource Centre
Auckland Technical Institute
Private Bag
Wellesley Street
Auckland

Dr John Jones
Higher Education Research Office (HERO)
University of Auckland
Private Bag
Auckland

Dr T Emery
Director
Educational Research and Advisory Unit
University of Canterbury
Christchurch 1

Mr A B Carter
Head
Tutor Training Unit
Central Institute of Technology
Private Bag
Trentham Camp PO
Upper Hutt

Mr Russell Woolcock
Tutor in Charge of Staff Education
Christchurch Technical Institute
PO Box 22-095
Christchurch

Mr H S Hepple
Chief Staff Training Officer
NZ Technical Correspondence Institute
PO Box 30-335
Lower Hutt

Dr David C B Teather
Director
Higher Education Development Centre
University of Otago
PO Box 913
Dunedin

Professor J C Clift
Director
University Teaching and Research Centre (UTRC)
Victoria University of Wellington
Private Bag
Wellington

Dr Roger Osborne
Department of Physics
University of Waikato
Private Bag
Hamilton

Miss Dorothy Comley
Tutor Education Officer
Wellington Polytechnic
Private Bag
Wellington

## 10. Sweden

There is always at least one identifiable person at Swedish universities
and colleges responsible for staff training (and sometimes also staff
development). It is, however, not easy to find a clear division between
institutions that may be called 'centres for staff training' and other

institutions. A further difficulty is the varying organizational pattern with divided responsibility for academic and non-academic staff. The following list is thus somewhat arbitrary.

## Universities and other research institutions

\*   *Responsible for university teacher training*
†   *Responsible for training of non-teaching staff*

Dr Bengt-Eric Bengtsson\*
Educational Research and Development Unit
Chalmers University of Technology
Fack
S-402 20 Göteborg

Mr Gunnar Jonnergård†
Personnel Department
Chalmers University of Technology
Fack
S-402 20 Göteborg

Dr Airi Rovio-Johansson
Head
Staff Training Unit
University of Göteborg
PO Box 53 261
S-409 10 Göteborg

Mr Dick Mårtensson\*
Educational Research and Development Unit
Karolinska Institutet
Fack
S-104 01 Stockholm

Mr Folke Meijer†
Personnel Department
Karolinska Institutet
Fack
S-104 01 Stockholm

Mr Stefan Bergström†
Personnel Department
University of Linköping
S-581 83 Linköping

Mrs Margareta Koch\*
Undergraduate Teaching Department
University of Linköping
S-581 83 Linköping

Mr Rune Olsson
Head
Educational Research and Development Unit
Luleå Tachnical University
Fack
S-951 87 Luleå

Mrs Eva Falk-Nilsson
Head
Staff Training Unit
University of Lund
Fack
S-221 01 Lund

Dr Matts Håstad*
Educational Research and Development Unit
Royal Institute of Technology
S-100 44 Stockholm

Ms Ewa Rönnbergt
Personnel Department
Royal Institute of Technology
S-100 44 Stockholm

Dr Magnus Håkansson*
Educational Research and Development Unit
University of Stockholm
S-106 91 Stockholm

Ms Catharina Dahlqvistt
Personnel Department
University of Stockholm
S-106 91 Stockholm

Mr Nils-Erik Wedman*
Educational Research and Development Unit
University of Umeå
S-901 87 Umeå

Ms Gunvor Larssont
Personnel Department
University of Umeå
S-901 87 Umeå

Mrs Ingar Hellkvist*/Miss Agneta Ydrént
Educational Research and Development Unit
University of Uppsala
PO Box 256
S-751 05 Uppsala

## Names and positions of persons responsible for staff training at colleges

Nils-Bertil Faxén
Vice-Chancellor
Borås College
PO Box 55 067
S-500 05 Borås

Mrs Barbro Eriksson
Head, Department of Education
Eskilstuna/Västerås College
Runebergsgatan 2
S-723 35 Västerås

Karin Johansson
Administrator
Falun/Borlänge College
PO Box 548
S-791 02 Falun

Gösta Ivarsson
Head
Information Department
Gävle/Sandviken College
PO Box 6052
S-800 06 Gävle

Elisabeth Andreasson
Administrator
Jönköping College
Fack
S-551 01 Jönköping

Bengt Sedvall
Head
Personnel Department
Kalmar College
PO Box 328
S-381 01 Kalmar

Ragnar Adéen
Head
Personnel Department
Karlstad College
Fack
S-650 09 Karlstad

Kaj Björk
Vice-Chancellor
Kristianstad College
S Kaserngatan 6
S-291 31 Kristianstad

Maud Östling
Administrator
Orebro College
PO Box 923
S-701 30 Örebro

Alf Gunnmo
Vice-Chancellor
Östersund College
Fack
S-831 01 Östersund

Dr Erik Blix
Vice-Chancellor
Stockholm Teacher Training College
Fack
S-100 26 Stockholm

Åsa Sundin
Administrator
Sundsvall/Härnösand College
Fack
S-851 01 Sundsvall

Hans Wieslander
Vice-Chancellor
Växjö College
PO Box 5053
S-350 05 Växjö

## Government agency with national responsibility for staff training and development at Swedish Universities

Dr Hans Jalling
Director
Staff Development Unit
National Board of Universities and Colleges
PO Box 45501
S-104 30 Stockholm

Mrs Brita Bergseth
Project Secretary
Special section for Stockholm Colleges of Art
Staff Development Unit
National Board of Universities and Colleges
PO Box 45501
S-104 30 Stockholm

## Agencies outside the jurisdiction of the National Board of Universities and Colleges

Dr Nils Trowald
Head
Educational Research and Development Unit
Swedish University of Agricultural Sciences
S-750 07 Uppsala

Mr Lars Jeding
Director General
Civil Service Training Board
Fack
S-103 80 Stockholm

# 11. Switzerland

*Prof Dr S Portmann, President, Gesellschaft für Lehr- und Lernmethoden (GLM), Postfach 8021, Zurich*

*M W Quenon, President, Groupe de Réflexion et d'Etude sur l'Education et les Techniques d'Instruction (GRETI), 6 rue de la Barre, 1005 Lausanne*

*Prof Dr Marcel L Goldschmid, President, Société Suisse pour la Recherche en Education (SSRE), Chaire de Pédagogie et Didactique, EPFL, Centre Est, 1015 Lausanne*

*Dr A Schraffel, President, Société Université et Recherche (SUR), Talstrasse 83, 8001 Zurich*

Prof Dr H P Rohr
Zentrum für Lehre und Forschung
University of Basel
Hebelstrasse 34
4031 Basel

Prof Dr Hannes Pauli
Institut für Ausbildungs- und Examensforschung
University of Berne
Inselspital 14c
3010 Berne

Dr J Steiger
Abteilung für Unterrichtsmedien
University of Berne
Inselspital
3010 Berne

Prof Dr Jean Posternak
Vice-Recteur
Président de la Commission de l'Enseignement
University of Geneva
Rue Général Dufour 24
1211 Genève 4

Prof Dr M Huberman
Faculté de Psychologie et des Sciences de l'Education
University of Geneva
Rue Général Dufour 24
1211 Genève 4

Dr Pierre-Henri Gygax
Centre d'enseignement médical et de communications audio-visuelles
University of Lausanne
Centre Hospitalier Universitaire Vaudois
1011 Lausanne

Prof Dr Rolf Dubs
Institut für Wirtschaftspädagogik
University of St-Gall
Guisanstrasse 9
9000 St-Gall

Prof Dr Marcel L Goldschmid
Chaire de Pédagogie et Didactique
Swiss Federal Institute of Technology
Centre Est
1015 Lausanne

Subkommission für Studiengestaltung
Swiss Federal Institute of Technology
ETH-Zentrum
8092 Zürich

Dokumentationsstelle
Hochschulreformkommission
University of Zurich
Universitätsgebäude
Rämistrasse 78
8006 Zürich

PD Dr H H Freihofer
Direktor des Zahnärztlichen Instituts
University of Zürich
Plattenstrasse 11
Postfach
8028 Zürich

## 12. The United States of America

*Glen R Erickson, Executive Director, Professional and Organizational Development Network in Higher Education, Instructional Development Program, University of Rhode Island, Kingston, RI 02881*

*Reed Williams, Secretary/Treasurer, Special Interest Group : Instructional Evaluation (SIG:IE), American Educational Research Association (AERA), Southern Illinois University, School of Medicine, PO Box 3926, Springfield, Illinois 62708*

Only some of the more established professional development centres and programmes are given here. (Over 250 centres and programmes are listed in Gaff, J G (1975) *Toward faculty renewal.* Jossey-Bass, San Francisco.)

David Whitcomb
Director
Center for Faculty Development
California State University Long Beach
1250 Bellflower Boulevard
Long Beach, California 90840

Robert C Wilson
Director
Teaching Innovation and Evaluation Services
University of California
Berkeley, California 94720

Frank J Vattano
Director
Office of Instructional Development
Colorado State University
Fort Collins, Colorado 80521

Jeaninne Webb
Director
Office of Instructional Resources
University of Florida
Gainesville, Florida 32611

Charles J McIntyre
Director
Office of Instructional Resources
University of Illinois
Urbana, Illinois 61801

Richard E Owens
Director
Office of Educational Improvement and Innovation
Kansas State University
Manhattan, Kansas 67701

Chester H Case
Professional Development Facilitator
Los Medanos College
2700 East Leland Road
Pittsburg, California 94565

Sheryl Riechmann
Director
Center for Instructional Resources and Improvement
University of Massachusetts
Amherst, Massachusetts 01002

Carol Zion
Director
Office of Staff and Organizational Development
Miami-Dade Community College
11011 SW 104th Street
Miami, Florida 33167

Robert H Davis
Director
Educational Development Program
Michigan State University
East Lansing, Michigan 48824

Wilbert J McKeachie
Director
Center for Research on Learning and Teaching
University of Michigan
Ann Arbor, Michigan 48104

B Claude Mathis
Director
Center for the Teaching Professions
Northwestern University
Evanston, Illinois 60201

Steven R Phillips
Director
Faculty Development Program
University of Puget Sound
1500 North Warner
Tacoma, Washington 98416

288

Robert M Diamond
Director
Center for Instructional Development
Syracuse University
Syracuse, New York 13210

Ohmer Milton
Director
Learning Research Center
University of Tennessee
Knoxville, Tennessee 37916

James E Stice
Director
Center for Teaching Effectiveness
University of Texas
Austin, Texas 78712

John F Noonan
Director
Centre for Improving Teaching Effectiveness
Virginia Commonwealth University
901 West Franklin Street
Richmond, Virginia 23284

## International

*The Secretariat, European Association for Research and Development in Higher Education (EARDHE), University Klagenfurt, A-9010 Klagenfurt, Austria*

*'Improving University Teaching' Conferences, Office of the Chancellor, University of Maryland University College, College Park, Maryland 20742, USA*

---

[1] *Editor's note:* Information on other centres in the German Democratic Republic was not available at the time of going to press.

# References and bibliography

## Chapter 1: Australia

Adams, M (1972) The promotion bar, *Vestes*, 15 (2), 122-6

Australian Universities Commission (1972) *Fifth report*, Australian Government Publishing Service, Canberra

Australian Universities Commission (1975) *Sixth report*, Australian Government Publishing Service, Canberra

Australian Vice-Chancellors Committee (1965) *Teaching methods in Australian universities*, Australian Vice-Chancellors Committee, Canberra

Australian Vice-Chancellors Committee (1973) *A Report on Australian university centres for higher education research and development by the directors of the existing centres*, Australian Vice-Chancellors Committee, Canberra

Boud, D and Pearson, M (1979) The trigger film: a stimulus for affective learning, *Programmed Learning & Educational Technology*, 16 (1), 52-6

Cannon, R (1979) The design, conduct and evaluation of a course in lecturing, *Programmed Learning & Educational Technology*, 16 (1), 16-22

Cumming, G, Macbean, I T, McLaughlin, I L and Woodhouse, D (1976) Aims and methods in university education, *Australian University*, 14 (2), 177-92

Davis, D J (1979) Some effects of PhD training on the academic labour markets of Australian and British universities, *Higher Education*, 5 (1), 67-8

Engel, C E and Clarke, R M (1979) Medical education with a difference, *Programmed Learning & Educational Technology*, 16 (1), 70-87

Falk, B (1970) The Melbourne approach to teacher training for university staff, *Australian University*, 8, 57-66

Falk, B (1977) Evaluation of teaching: decision making about teachers and courses, *South Pacific Journal of Teacher Education*, 5 (1), 41-7

Falk, B and Lee Dow, K (1971) University teaching: reality and change, *Quarterly Review of Australian Education*, 4 (4), 1-58

Fallon, B J (1977) A note on in-service courses for academic staff, *Education Research and Perspectives*, 4 (1), 66-70

Foster, G A (1978) *Attitudes and their effects on learning processes in an engineering course*, Institution of Engineers Australia Conference on Engineering Education, 151-4

Goldschmid, M L (1978) The evaluation and improvement of teaching in higher education, *Higher Education*, 7 (2), 221-45

Hall, W C (1975) Pretending not to be an educational technologist, *Programmed Learning & Educational Technology*, 12 (6), 327-32

Hall, W C (1977) Models for tertiary teaching units, *Australian Journal of Education*, 21 (1), 55-64

Harman, G (1977) Academic staff and academic drift in Australian colleges of advanced education, *Higher Education,* 6 (3), 313-35

Harman, G S and Selby-Smith, C (1976) Some current trends and issues in the governance of Australian colleges of advanced education, *Australian Journal of Education,* 20 (2), 129-48

Henry, N W and Willis, Q F (1975) A non-threatening procedure for the evaluation of tertiary teaching, *Australian Journal of Advanced Education,* 5 (1) (This issue has no page numbers)

Hore, T (1977) Implications for academic staff of the 'steady state', *Vestes,* 20 (3), 21-3

Hore, T, Linke, R D and West, L H T (eds) (1978) *The future of higher education in Australia,* Macmillan, Sydney

Katz, F M and Connor, D V (1975) The Indonesian university lecturers' scheme: a teacher training programme, *Vestes,* 17 (1), 2-10

Labyrinth — see Tertiary Education Institute

McCaig, R (1977) Institutional management in higher education — a professional development tool for college and university administrators, *Australian Journal of Advanced Education,* 6 (3), 9-11

Maddox, H (1975) The assessment of teaching by ratings — a critique, *Australian University,* 13 (2), 139-47

Magin, D (1973) Evaluating the role performance of university lecturers, *Universities Quarterly,* 28 (1), 84-96

Meyer, G R (1979) The development of minicourses (with a basis in educational technology) for the in-service education of teachers and trainers, *Programmed Learning & Educational Technology,* 16 (1), 23-37

Miller, A H (1976) The preparation of tertiary teachers, *Australian University,* 14 (1), 33-42

Miller, A H (1977) Symposium on teacher education for tertiary teaching: an outline of the needs, *South Pacific Journal of Teacher Education,* 5 (1), 5-13

Miller, A H (1977) Improving the facilities for evaluating tertiary teaching: some initial steps, *South Pacific Journal of Teacher Education,* 5 (1), 47-59

O'Neil, W M (1977) Improving university teaching and learning, *South Pacific Journal of Teacher Education,* 5 (1), 14-21

Powell, J P (1977) *Higher education: a select bibliography, Volume 3, 1970-75,* Higher Education Research and Development Society of Australasia, Sydney

Powell, J P (ed) (1978) *Higher education in a steady state; proceedings of the third annual conference of HERDSA,* Higher Education Research and Development Society of Australasia, Sydney

Probert, S (1974) A new direction in improving university and college teaching, *Australian Journal of Advanced Education,* 4 (2), 4-8

Rich, P, Simpkins, W S, Browne, R K and Field, T W (1970) Research on teaching in higher education: student notions of the ideal lecturer, *Vestes,* 8 (2), 187-91

Roe, E (1975) *Using and misusing the materials of teaching and learning,* ANU Press, Canberra

Roe, E (1977) Wasting away in academia, *Education News,* 16 (3), 12-15

Roe, E (1978) *TEDI — the first five years,* Tertiary Education Institute, University of Queensland

Shore, B M (1976) Success and failure of formal teaching improvement efforts in higher education, *Higher Education Bulletin,* 5 (1), 22-34

Singer, G, Wallace, M and Montgomery, R B (1972) How young Newman became an academic eunuch, *Vestes,* 15 (1), 17-23

291

Skertchly, A R B (1975) Department of the university, *Vestes,* 18 (1), 8-17
Skertchly, A R B (1976) Institutional self-renewal in Australian universities, *Vestes,* 19 (1), 14-22
Stanton, H E (1974) Improving university teaching, *Australian University,* 12 (3), 264-9

Tertiary Education Institute (1977 *et seq*) *Labyrinth, Clearinghouse bulletin for higher education research and development units in Australia and New Zealand,* Tertiary Education Institute, University of Queensland
Thomas, A R (1972) Teaching's my problem, *Vestes,* 15 (3), 317-21

Walker, G R (1976) Satisfaction or frustration: the dilemma of university academics, *Vestes,* 19 (1), 35-8
Willett, F J (1977) Quality control of university teaching: the responsibilities of a vice-chancellor, *South Pacific Journal of Teacher Education,* 5 (1), 28-33

## Unpublished materials on staff development

The following list contains a number of items which may be illuminative about staff development activities conducted by research and development units. Copies of many of these documents may be obtained directly from the units named; the list has been abstracted from LABYRINTH (Tertiary Education Institute, 1977 *et seq*) and full addresses are given in that publication.

*Calendar 1978. Minicourses for teachers and trainers,* Centre for Advancement of Teaching, Macquarie University, 1978

Dare, A J *Tertiary teaching: some approaches, a report on a college-based project,* Royal Melbourne Institute of Technology, July 1977

*Evaluation of a series of seminars on 'teaching in a tertiary institution',* Office for Research in Academic Methods, Australian National University, August 1977. Unpublished questionnaires

*HEARU summer workshops, in-service programme,* Higher Education Advisory and Research Unit, Monash University, February 1978

*Other techniques in teaching and learning,* Office for Research in Academic Methods, Australian National University, 27 July 1977. Seminar Outline

Powell, J P *Tertiary teachers learning about learning: a case study of constraints and opportunities,* University of New South Wales, August 1977

*Summary of reasons for attendance at tertiary teaching course,* Office for Research in Academic Methods, Australian National University, June 1977

*Teaching and learning in large groups (lecturing),* Office for Research in Academic Methods, Australian National University, 22 June 1977. Seminar outline
*Teaching in a tertiary institution,* Office for Research in Academic Methods, Australian National University, 1977. Course outline
*Teaching in a tertiary institution,* Office for Research in Academic Methods, Australian National University, 1 June 1977. Seminar outline
*Tertiary teaching: some approaches,* b/w videotape, 1 hour, Royal Melbourne Institute of Technology

# Chapter 2a: Britain — universities

Abercrombie, M L J (1968) The work of a university education research unit, *Universities Quarterly,* 22 (2), 182-96

Association of University Teachers (1968) *In-service training for university teachers,* N 292, April, (Mimeo)

Beard, R (1971) *Research into teaching methods in higher education,* Society for Research into Higher Education, Guildford

Beard, R (1977) Course design, teaching methods and departmental decisions, in Piper, D W and Glatter, R *The changing university,* National Foundation for Educational Research, Slough

Bernstein, R J (1976) *The restructuring of social and political theory,* Harcourt, Brace, Jovanovich, New York (Quoted in Pinar, W F (1978) Notes on the curriculum field 1978, *Educational Researcher,* 7 (8), 5-12)

Bligh, D (1972) *What's the use of lectures?* Penguin, Harmondsworth

Bligh, D A (1976) *Provisions and problems in the training of university teachers,* Co-ordinating Committee for the Training of University Teachers Conference, Birmingham (Mimeo)

Bligh, D (1978) *Policies of acceptance within universities,* a paper discussed at FORUM 78, Co-ordinating Committee for the Training of University Teachers, Norwich

Brown, G A (1976) *Teaching and learning in universities, a course held in the University of Nottingham,* University of Nottingham (Mimeo)

Brown, G A (1978) *Lecturing and explaining,* Methuen, London

Brynmor Jones Report (1965) *Audiovisual aids in higher scientific education,* HMSO, London

Brynmor Jones (1971) *A report of the working group to the Committee of Vice-Chancellors and Principals to consider future arrangements for the provision and co-ordinating of training for university teachers*

Cantrell, E G (1973) Attitudes of junior medical school staff towards a proposed course in teaching, *Social Science Research Council Report HR 1202/1*

Cantrell, E G (1973) *How do medical staff learn to teach?* The Lancet, 11 (29 September) 724-7 (also in *Information from the Department of Audiovisual Communication,* 27, BMA House, London)

Cantrell, T and Abramsky, L (1977) The design of short teacher training courses, *Medical Education,* 11 (5), 311-18

Chilton, J and Bett, B (1971) *A survey of attitudes to training and teaching,* University of Strathclyde (Mimeo)

Coles, C (1977) Developing professionalism: staff development as an outcome of curriculum development, *Programmed Learning & Educational Technology,* 14 (4), 315-19

Committee of Vice-Chancellors and Principals (1976) *Report on the period 1972-76,* London

Co-ordinating Committee for the Training of University Teachers (1974) *Conference and information exchange about the training of university teachers, Manchester, 7-9 June 1974,* Press Release, 10 June

Co-ordinating Committee for the Training of University Teachers (1976) *Training implications of the University Authorities Panel/Association of University Teachers agreement on probation: points for consideration by universities* (Preliminary draft for discussion) CCTUT, Norwich

Creaser, H (1977) Staff development and the fourth revolution, *Journal of Educational Television,* 3 (3), 75-6

Elton, L R B and Kilty, J M (1974) *Courses in higher education at the University of Surrey,* Institute of Educational Technology, University of Surrey (Mimeo)

293

Elton, L R B and Kilty, J M (1975) Courses in higher education at the University of Surrey, in *Issues in staff development,* University Teaching Methods Unit, University of London

Engel, C E (1974) Educational assistants, *The Lancet,* 11 (9 September) 573-5

Evans, L F (1977) *Illustrations, adjuncts and alternatives,* City University, London (Mimeo)

Falk, B and Lee Dow, K (1971) *The assessment of university teaching,* SRHE Monograph 16, Society for Research into Higher Education, Guildford

Fallon B J (1977) A note on in-service courses for academic staff, *Education Research and Perspectives,* 4 (1), 66-70

Fitch, J G (1881) *Lectures on teaching,* Cambridge University Press, Cambridge

Flood-Page, C M (1975) Teasing hamsters in electric cages, *Universities Quarterly,* 29 (3), 318-31

Foley, R, Smilansky, E, Bughman, E and Sajid, A (1976) A departmental approach for improving lecture skills of medical teachers, *Medical Education,* 10 (5), 369-73

Ford, B J (1966) Qualified — but what for? *New Scientist,* 30 May, 452-3

Greenaway, H (1971) *Training of university teachers,* SRHE Pamphlet 2, Society for Research into Higher Education, Guildford

Greenaway, H and Harding, A G (1978) *The growth of policies for staff development,* SRHE Monograph 34, Society for Research into Higher Education, Guildford

Hacquaert, A (1967) *The recruitment and training of university teachers,* International Association of University Professors, Ghent

Hale Report (1964) *Report of the Committee on University Teaching Methods,* under the chairmanship of Sir Edward Hale, HMSO, London

Harding, A G (1974) *Training of polytechnic teachers,* SRHE Pamphlet 3, Society for Research into Higher Education, Guildford

Harding, A G and Sayer, S (1975) The objectives of training university teachers, *Universities Quarterly,* 29 (3), 299-317

Hartley, M G (1964) The summer school on effective teaching, *International Journal of Electrical Engineering,* 1, 615-32

Hearnshaw, T (1977) Staff development: some thoughts on responsibility, *Journal of Educational Television,* 3 (3), 80-2

Kilty, J M (1972) *Preliminary report and course on teaching and lecturing in higher education, 1972,* Institute of Educational Technology, University of Surrey (Mimeo)

Kilty, J M (1973) *Report on the 1972 course on teaching and learning in higher education for lecturers in mathematics, science and engineering,* Institute of Educational Technology, University of Surrey (Mimeo)

Kitchen, K E (1976) The training of university administrators in Britain, *Association of Commonwealth Universities Bulletin of Current Documentation,* 25, 2-6

King, M (1973) The anxieties of university teachers, *Universities Quarterly,* 28 (1), 69-83

McAleese, R (1973a) *Microteaching and the training of university teachers,* paper read at the VIII International Conference on Educational Technology, Brighton, ERIC IR 005 365

McAleese, R (1973b) *The systematic observation of lecturing — its use in training and research,* paper presented at the Social Science Research Council Seminar on Classroom Research held in the University of Leicester, 26-28 September, ERIC IR 005 368

McAleese, R (1973c) *The application of microteaching techniques to the training of university teachers,* paper read at the Education Section of the British Psychological Society's Annual Conference, London, ERIC IR 005 366

McAleese, R (1973d) *The use of interaction analysis in the training of university teachers,* working paper, University of Aberdeen, ERIC IR 005 369

McAleese, R (1974) *The use of closed circuit television in the training of university teachers,* paper read at a meeting of the Co-ordinating Committee for the Training of University Teachers in Aberdeen, 5 March, ERIC IR 005

McAleese, R (1975a) A meta-language of training in higher education, *British Journal of Teacher Education,* 1 (2), 213-20

McAleese, R (1975b) A note on a theoretical approach to training, *Impetus,* 3, 1-3, Co-ordinating Committee for the Training of University Teachers, Norwich

McAleese, R (1976a) *The attitude-knowledge controversy,* University of Aberdeen, ERIC ED 128 347

McAleese, R (1978a) *Changing the perceptions of teachers to their teaching style,* 4th International Conference on Improving University Teaching, Aachen, 28 July

McAleese, R (1978b) *Staff development in the University of Aberdeen: a study of roles,* PhD thesis, University of Aberdeen

Main, A (1975a) The training of university teachers in Britain, *Association of Commonwealth Universities Bulletin of Current Documentation,* 18, 2-4

Main, A (1975b) *The training of university teachers in the United Kingdom — problems and prospects,* Co-ordinating Committee for the Training of University Teachers, Norwich

Malleson, N (1954a) The distressed student, *The Lancet,* 1, 824-5

Malleson, N (1954b) The mental health of the student, *International Universities Bulletin,* 51-8

Malleson, N (1957) The treatment of pre-examination strain, *British Medical Journal,* 2 (3), 551-4

Malleson, N (1958) (as Hopkins, J, Malleson, N and Sarnoff, I) Some non-intellectual correlates of success and failure among university students, *British Journal of Educational Psychology,* 28 (1), 25-36

Malleson, N (1959) Avoiding failure by university students, *The Listener,* 5 March

Miller, G W (1976) *Staff development programmes in British universities and polytechnics,* International Institute for Educational Planning Research Report 18, IIEP, Paris

National Board for Prices and Incomes (1968) *Standing conference on the pay of university teachers,* Report 98, Cmnd 3866, HMSO, London

National Board for Prices and Incomes (1970) *Standing conference on the pay of university teachers,* Report 145, Cmnd 4334, HMSO, London

Nisbet, J (1967) Courses on university teaching methods, *Universities Quarterly,* 21 (2), 186-98

Paulsen, F (1894) *The German Universities,* Macmillan, London (translated by E D Perry)

Piper, D (1975) Like bandaging a broken arm when the patient's spine is shot away, *Times Higher Education Supplement,* 21 September

Piper, D W and Glatter, R (1977) *The changing university: a report on the staff development in universities programme, 1972/4,* National Foundation for Educational Research, Slough

Radcliffe, S (1955) The training of university teachers, *The Universities Review,* 28 (1), 12-15

Richardson, I M (1976) A short course on training for general practitioner trainers, *Health Bulletin,* November, 344-6

Riley, J (1974) University teachers on training courses, *Universities Quarterly,* 28 (3), 450-4

Ritter, U P (1979) Training the trainers for staff development, in Van Trotsenburg, E A (ed) *Higher education: a field of study,* Peter Lang, Frankfurt

Saunders, M (1967) University teaching – a student point of view, in Layton, D (ed) *University teaching in transition,* Oliver and Boyd, Edinburgh

Sayer, S (1977) The relationship between staff development and audiovisual media in British universities, *Programmed Learning & Educational Technology,* 14 (3), 259-64

Sayer, S and Harding, A (1974) Time to look beyond technology to better use of human resources, *Times Higher Education Supplement,* 20 December

Sayer, S and Harding A (1976) Faith, hope and charity, *Impetus,* 4, 14-18, Co-ordinating Committee for the Training of University Teachers, Norwich

Seldin P (1977) *Teaching professors to teach: case studies and methods of faculty development in British universities today,* Blythe-Pennington, New York

Sutherland, A (1975) Whom are we training to teach and how? In University of London Institute of Education, *Issues in staff development,* University Teaching Methods Unit, University of London

Truscot, B (1943) (pseudonym for E A Peers) *Redbrick University,* Faber and Faber, London

University Grants Committee (1972) *Induction course for new members of university staff,* informal survey, August (Mimeo)

University Teaching Methods Unit (1975) *Issues in staff development,* Staff Development in Universities Programme, University of London

Yorke, D M (1976) Staff development: an essay in ambiguity, in *Strategies for staff development,* Manchester Polytechnic

Yorke, D M (1977) Staff development in further and higher education: a review, *British Journal of Teacher Education,* 3 (2), 161-8

# Chapter 2b: Britain – polytechnics

Association of Colleges for Further and Higher Education and Association of Principals of Technical Institutions (1973) *Staff development in further education,* 40 pp, ACFHE, London

Baron, B (1978) *The managerial approach to tertiary education: a critical analysis,* 103 pp, Studies in Education (new series) 7, Institute of Education, University of London

Billing, D E (1977) The nature and scope of staff development in institutions of higher education, in Elton, L and Simmonds, K (eds) *Staff development in higher education,* Society for Research into Higher Education, Guildford

Bristow, A (1973) Staffing and staff development – the present position, *Coombe Lodge Reports,* 6 (1), 2-9

Council for National Academic Awards (1974) *Report of the working party on resources for research in polytechnics and other colleges,* 8 pp, CNAA, London

Department of Education and Science (1967) *Administrative memorandum 8/67,* DES, London

Department of Education and Science (1972) *Education – a framework for expansion,* Cmnd 5174, HMSO, London

Department of Education and Science (1973) *Development of higher education in the non-university sector,* Circular 7/73, DES, London

Department of Education and Science (1976) *A plan for polytechnics and other colleges,* Cmnd 3006, HMSO, London

Department of Education and Science (1977) *The training of teachers for further education,* Circular 11/77, DES, London

Greenaway, H and Harding, A G (1978) *The growth of policies for staff development,* SRHE Monograph 34, 103 pp, Society for Research into Higher Education, Guildford

Harding, A G (1974) *Training of polytechnic teachers,* SRHE Pamphlet 3, 59 pp, Society for Research into Higher Education, London

Miller, G W (1976) *Staff development programmes in British universities and polytechnics,* International Institute for Educational Planning Research Report 18, 159 pp, IIEP, Paris

Mortimer, D J (1975) Marked growth in induction courses, *SCEDSIP Bulletin* 5, Newcastle-upon-Tyne Polytechnic

Piper, D W (1975) The longer reach, in *Issues in staff development,* University Teaching Methods Unit, University of London

Standing Conference on Educational Development Services in Polytechnics (1976) *Register of educational development services in polytechnics,* 56 pp, SCEDSIP, Newcastle-upon-Tyne Polytechnic

Trickey, S (1977) Staff training — a polytechnic perspective, *Impetus,* 6, 15-22, Co-ordinating Committee for the Training of University Teachers, Norwich

Warren, J W L (1977) Institutionalisation of staff development in higher education, in Elton, L and Simmonds, K (eds) *Staff development in higher education,* Society for Research into Higher Education, Guildford

Whitburn, J, Mealing, M and Cox, C (1976) *People in polytechnics,* 212 pp, Society for Research into Higher Education, Guildford

Yorke, M (1977) Staff development in further and higher education: a review, *British Journal of Teacher Education,* 3 (2), 161-8

## Chapter 3: Canada

Annual reports (1969-70 to present) *Centre for Learning and Development,* McGill University, Montreal

Blondin, D, Donald, J G, Gagnon, M, Meunier, J-G and St-Pierre, H (1976) *La pédagogie de l'enseignement supérieur (Teaching strategies in higher education),* Revue des Sciences de l'éducation, Documents, série 4, Méthodologie et technologie de l'éducation, Montréal

Cranton, P A (1979) The McGill faculty and course evaluation system, *The Canadian Journal of Higher Education,* 9 (1)

Davis, R H (1971) International seminar on methods and programmes for the improvement of university teaching, *Learning and Development* 2 (7), 1-4, McGill University, Montreal

Donald, J G (1974) *Staff development: An overview of practices throughout Canada,* paper presented at the annual meeting of the Association of Canadian Community Colleges, Winnipeg, May (available from the Centre for Learning and Development, McGill University, Montreal)

Donald, J G and Shore, B M (1974) *Annotated index to pedagogical services in Canadian universities and colleges,* Centre for Learning and Development, McGill University, Montreal

Foster, S F (1975) Teaching improvement at the university level — some views and some prospects, *Journal of Education of the Faculty of Education*, 21, 63-71, University of British Columbia, Vancouver

Fortin, J-C (1975) La gestion du régime pédagogique de CEGEPs (Running the teaching system at CEGEP), *The Canadian Journal of Higher Education*, 5 (1), 13-24

Furedy, C (1979) Improving lecturing in higher education, *The Canadian Journal of Higher Education*, 9 (1)

Geis, G L (1977) Changing the change agent, *Improving Human Performance Quarterly*, 6 (1), 1-8

Geis, G L (1977) *Instructional improvement and the concept of responsibility, or, who's in charge here?* paper presented at the annual meeting of the Midwest Association for Behavioral Analysis, Chicago, May (available from the Centre for Learning and Development, McGill University, Montreal)

Glasman, N S and Gmelch, W H (1976) Purposes of evaluation of university instructors: definitions, delineations, and dimensions, *The Canadian Journal of Higher Education*, 6 (2), 37-55

Goldschmid, M L (1968) Revolution or evolution at the university, *McGill News*, 49 (6), 11-13, McGill Graduates Society, Montreal

Good, H M (1975) Instructional development — what? why? how? *The Canadian Journal of Higher Education*, 5 (1), 33-51

Good, H M and Trotter, B (1974) Accountability for effective and efficient university teaching, *The Canadian Journal of Higher Education/Stoa*, 4 (1), 43-53

Harris, R S (1976) *A history of higher education in Canada 1663-1960*, The University of Toronto Press, Toronto

Hedley, R L and Wood, C C (1973) Improving university teaching, *University Affairs*, 14 (4), 2-3, Association of Universities and Colleges of Canada

*Inventory of research relevant to higher education in Canada*, survey published annually by the Association of Universities and Colleges of Canada, 151 Slater Street, Ottawa, K1P 5N1

Knapper, C K (1972) Improving teaching effectiveness, *Canadian Association of University Teachers Bulletin*, 21 (1), 9-11

Knapper, C K, Geis, G L, Pascal, C E and Shore, B M (1977) *If teaching is important . . . the evaluation of instruction in higher education*, Clarke-Irwin, Toronto (Canadian Association of University Teachers Monograph Series)

Knapper, C K, McFarlane, B and Scanlon, J (1972) Student evaluation: an aspect of teaching effectiveness, *Canadian Association of University Teachers Bulletin*, 21 (2), 26-9

Konrad, A G (1973) Staff development in western Canadian colleges, *Stoa* (later renamed *The Canadian Journal of Higher Education*), 3 (1), 47-52

Leibu, Y (1976) La qualité de l'enseignement universitaire: essai d'approche systématique (The quality of university teaching: an attempt at a systematic approach), *The Canadian Journal of Higher Education*, 6 (3), 1-11

Marx, R, Ellis, J F and Martin, J (1979) The training of teaching assistants in Canadian universities: a survey and case study, *The Canadian Journal of Higher Education*, 9 (1)

McGill's Office of Educational Development (1977), *Learning and Development*, 8 (3), 1-4, McGill University, Montreal

Parent, J (1979) Le rôle d'un service de pédagogie dans l'évaluation des cours (The role of a teaching support service in course evaluation), *The Canadian Journal of Higher Education*, 9 (1)

Pascal, C E (1974) Pseudo-innovations in higher education, paper presented at International Congress of Applied Psychology, Montreal (available from the Centre for Learning and Development, McGill University, Montreal)

Roid, G H (1971) Research on university teaching: a perspective, *Improving College and University Teaching*, 19, 252-5

Scarfe, J and Sheffield E F (1977) Notes on the Canadian professoriate, *Higher Education*, 6 (3), 337-58

Select bibliography of higher education in Canada, *The Canadian Journal of Higher Education*, an ongoing series in most issues

Sheffield, E F (1973) Approaches (mostly elsewhere) to the improvement of teaching in higher education, *Stoa* (later renamed *The Canadian Journal of Higher Education*), 3 (1), 65-75

Sheffield, E F (1974) Characteristics of effective teaching in Canadian universities — an analysis based on the testimony of a thousand graduates, *The Canadian Journal of Higher Education/Stoa*, 4 (1), 7-29

Sheffield, E F (ed) (1974) *Teaching in the Universities — no one way*, McGill-Queen's University Press, Montreal

Shore, B M (1973) Selected sources of information on research in higher education in Canada, *International Newsletter*, 3, 1-4, Society for Research in Higher Education, London

Shore, B M (1974) Instructional development in Canadian higher education, *The Canadian Journal of Higher Education*, 4 (2), 45-53

Shore, B M (1976) Success and failure of formal teaching improvement efforts in higher education, *Higher Education Bulletin*, 5 (1), 22-34, Lancaster, United Kingdom

Shore, B M and Donald, J G (1974) Pedagogical services: CLD's friends and relatives, *Learning and Development*, 5 (6), 1-4, McGill University, Montreal

Sullivan, A M (1975) Research on teaching, *The Canadian Journal of Higher Education*, 5 (1), 1-11

Summary of publications (cumulative index) (1977) *The Canadian Journal of Higher Education*, 7 (2), 73-8

*The Canadian Journal of Higher Education* (1979) 9 (1), whole issue devoted to instructional development and evaluation (individual articles are listed in this bibliography)

The Educational Development Group 2 (1976) Instructional Development Service, *Learning and Development*, 7 (4), 1-6, McGill University, Montreal

The Educational Development Group 3 (1976) Centre for Learning and Development, *Learning and Development*, 8 (1), 1-6, McGill University, Montreal

## Chapter 4: Denmark

*Aarbog for Koebenhavns Universitet, 1960-1970 (Yearbook of the University of Copenhagen, 1960-1970)* Copenhagen

Fog (1968) *Universitetsproblemer - nu og i morgen (University problems — today and tomorrow)*, Munksgaard, Copenhagen

Güttler, F, Lundstedt, C, Nerup, J and Vejlsgaard, R (1969) Universitetspaedagogik — andet forsøgskursus (University teaching — a second experimental course), *Ugeskrift for laeger*, 1113-16

Koebenhavns Universitet (1967) *Betaenkning om paedagogisk vejledning og bistand for universitetslaerere (Report on guidance and help in teaching for university teachers)*, Copenhagen

Nerup, J and Vejlsgaard, R (1968) Universitetspaedagogik — et forsøgskursus (University teaching — an experimental course), *Ugeskrift for Laeger*, 2037-41

Nerup, J, Vejlsgaard, R and Thomsen, O B (1972) Teaching the teacher to teach, *Danish Medical Bulletin*, 19, 6

Piper, D W and Glatter, R (1977) *The changing university: a report on the staff development in universities programme, 1972/4*, National Foundation for Educational Research, Slough

Rotem, A and Glasman, N (1977) Evaluation of university instructors in the United States: the context, *Higher Education*, 6 (1), 75-92

*Statistisk Aarbog (1977) (Statistical Yearbook, 1977)*, Students at institutions of higher education, senior vocational schools, etc, Copenhagen

Thomsen, O B (1969) Universitetspaedagogik — hvad er det? (University teaching — what is it?), *Nordisk Forum*, 2 (1), 18-34

Thomsen, O B (1971) Universitetspaedagogiske grundkurser — deltages vurderingen og unnovationseffekt (Basic-courses in university teaching — participants evaluation and the effect of innovation), *Dansk Paedagogisk Tidskrift*, 4, 182-91

Va ksten i udvalgte offentlige udgifter, 1969-1970 (The growth of certain state expenditures, 1969-70), *Nationaløkonomisk Tidsskrift*, (1972), No 3.4

# Chapter 5: The Federal Republic of Germany

## SUGGESTIONS FOR FURTHER READING

The best survey about the current field of *Hochschuldidaktik* is given by the series of the *Arbeitsgemeinschaft für Hochschuldidaktik e V (AHD)*, Rothenbaumchaussee 32, 2 Hamburg 13

- *Blickpunkt Hochschuldidaktik* (49 issues to September 1978), concerned more with fundamental problems and methods

- *Hochschuldidaktische Materialien* (65 issues to September 1978), concerned more with experiments and models of teaching and learning in special disciplines

- *Hochschuldidaktische Forschungsberichte* (6 issues to September 1978), detailed reports about larger research projects

- *Informationen zur Hochschuldidaktik* (several issues per year), a kind of newspaper and forum for discussion.

Sader, M, Clemens-Lodde, H *et al* (1973) *Kleine Fibel zum Hochschulunterricht (Small guide to university teaching)*, Beck, Munich. One of the first and most important books about *Hochschuldidaktik*, suggesting practicable models for the improvement of university teaching

Eckstein, B (1978) *Einmaleins der Hochschullehre (The ABC of university teaching)*, Kösel, Munich. The newest basic book about university teaching, covering a wide range of problems, including practical suggestions.

Ritter, U P and Rieck, W (1978) Zur hochschuldidaktischen Ausund Fortbildung von Hochschullehrern: Das Bad Homburger Symposium (The Hochschuldidaktik of in-service education of university teachers: the symposium of Bad Homburg), *Blickpunkt Hochschuldidaktik*, 48, AHD, Hamburg. Report about a symposium of experts in the education of university teachers to improve teaching. Mentions the various kinds of activities and problems.

Prahl, H W (1976) *Hochschulprüfungen – Sinn oder Unsinn? (University examinations – sense or nonsense?)*, Kösel, Munich. Basic book about university examinations. Discusses critically the various purposes and problems.

Zuber, O (1975) *Advisory centres for tertiary education in West Germany*, CAT Education Monograph 11, Centre for Advancement of Teaching, Macquarie University, Sydney. Brief report about the centres in Germany, written in English.

REFERENCES

AHD-Thesen zur Hochschuldidaktik (1973) (AHD-principles of Hochschuldidaktik), *Informationen zur Hochschuldidaktik*, 7, 120-6
AHD-Vorstand (1977) Stellungnahme zum Beitrag 'Hochschullehrer und Hochschuldidaktik' (Reply to the article on 'University teachers and Hochschuldidaktik') *Informationen zur Hochschuldidaktik*, 4, 178-80
Arbeitsgemeinschaft für Hochschuldidaktik (1977) Stellungnahme der Arbeitsgemeinschaft für Hochschuldidaktik eV zur Lage der Hochschuldidaktischen Zentren und zur institutionalisierten hochschuldidaktischen Arbeit (Statement of the Arbeitsgemeinschaft für Hochschuldidaktik eV about the situation of centres for Hochschuldidaktik and work of institutions for Hochschuldidaktik), *Informationen zur Hochschuldidaktik*, 1/2, 20-2

Bargel, T and Bürmann, J (1977) *Hochschulsozialisation und Studienreform (Socialization in universities and study reform)*, Blickpunkt Hochschuldidaktik, 44, AHD, Hamburg
Bargel, T, Framhein, L et al (1975) *Sozialisation in der Hochschule (Socialization within the university)*, Blickpunkt Hochschuldidaktik, 37, AHD, Hamburg
Behrend, B (1969) *18 Jahre Tutorenarbeit an der FU Berlin (18 years of work with tutors at the Free University Berlin)*, Blickpunkt Hochschuldidaktik, 3, AHD, Hamburg
Behrend, B and Schürmann, E (1974) Hochschuldidaktik zwischen staatlicher Planung und Autonomie (Hochschuldidaktik located between government planning and autonomy), *Informationen zur Hochschuldidaktik*, 8, 159-64
Brandt, D (1978) Ein Raster von Aktivitäten zur Aus- und Fortbildung von Lehrenden in Hochschulen (A structure of activities for the in-service education of teachers within universities), in Ritter, U P and Rieck, W (eds) *Zur hochschuldidaktischen Aus- und Fortbildung von Hochschullehrern*, 35-48, Blickpunkt Hochschuldidaktik, 48, AHD, Hamburg
Brauner, Th, Hering, S and Zalfen, M (1976) *Zur Theorie und Praxis des Projektstudiums (The theory and practice of project studies)*, Kassel
Bürmann, J (1978) Gesichtspunkte für die Planung und Durchführung von hochschuldidaktischen Veranstaltungen zur Weiterbildung von Hochschullehrern (Points of view for the planning and performance of seminars for the in-service education of university teachers), in Ritter, U P and Rieck, W (eds) *Zur hochschuldidaktischen Aus- und Fortbildung von Hochschullehrern*, 23-8, Blickpunkt Hochschuldidaktik, 48, AHD, Hamburg

Cohn, R (1974) Zur Grundlage des Themenzentrierten interaktionellen Systems (The basis of the theme-centred interactional system), *Gruppendynamik, Forschung und Praxis*, 5, 150-9

Cohn, R (1976) *Von der Psychoanalyse zur themenzentrierten Interaktion (From psychoanalysis to theme-centred interaction)*, Klett, Stuttgart

Daxner, M (1978) Rechtliche und ökonomische Probleme von Hochschulprüfungen (Legal and economic problems of university exams), *Informationen zur Hochschuldidaktik*, 1/2, 44-8

Eckstein, B (1978) Hochschullehrer und Hochschuldidaktik — Beitrag zu einer Bilanz (University teachers and Hochschuldidaktik — contributions to a balance), *Informationen zur Hochschuldidaktik*, 1/2, 8

Flechsig, K H (1974) Hochschuldidaktik und Fachdidaktik (Hochschuldidaktik and the methodology of teaching in particular disciplines), *Informationen zur Hochschuldidaktik*, 10, 201-4

Flechsig, K H (1975) Handlungsspielräume der Hochschuldidaktik (Possibilities of action for Hochschuldidaktik), *Informationen zur Hochschuldidaktik*, 13, 356-60

Friedrich, H and Tschersig, R (1978) *Das Planspiel als Hochschullehrveranstaltung (Simulation games as a means of university teaching)*, Hochschuldidaktische Materialien, 65, AHD, Hamburg

Gasch, B (1974) Der Stellenwert von Skripten in einem allgemeinen didaktischen Konzept der Hochschule (The importance of student hand-outs in a general education system of university teaching), *Informationen zur Hochschuldidaktik*, 9, 171-8

Gasch, B and Shick, A (1975) Psychologie-Didaktik (Methodology of teaching psychology), in Tack, W H (ed) *Kongressbericht über den 29 Kongress der Deutschen Gesellschaft für Psychologie*, 228-39, Hogrefe, Göttingen

Georgi, W et al (1977) *Kleingruppenarbeit und computerunterstützter Unterricht in der Ingenieurausbildung (Small group learning and computer-assisted instruction in the education of engineers)*, Hochschuldidaktische Materialien, 58, AHD, Hamburg

Götz-Marchand, B and Götz, J (1976) Probleme der Durchführung und Revision eines gruppendynamischen Tutorentrainings in einem naturwissenschaftlichen Fach (Problems of performance and revision of a training in group dynamics for tutors in a scientific discipline), *Informationen zur Hochschuldidaktik*, 18, 620-2

Grochla, E and Thom, N (1975) *Fallmethode und Gruppenarbeit in der betriebswirtschaftlichen Hochschulausbildung (Case study method and group work in the education of micro-economists)*, Hochschuldidaktische Materialien, 49, AHD, Hamburg

Häberlein, F and Nieschmidt, P (1973) Zum Problem von Regelstudium in Studienjahren — Überlegungen zur Funktion eines Hochschuldidaktischen Zentrums im Rahmen eines Studienberatungssystems (The problem of limited study time in study years — reflections about the function of an advisory centre for higher education within a system of study guidance), *Deutsche Universitätszeitung*, 18, 769-71

Heckhausen, H (1970) Zur Bedeutung moderner Lernmotivationsforschung für die Hochschuldidaktik (The importance of modern research in learning motivation for Hochschuldidaktik), in Hentig, H v (ed) *Wissenschaftsdidaktik*, 102 ff, Göttingen

Heinz, H (1977) Die Auszehrung der Marburger Hochschuldidaktik (The decline of Hochschuldidaktik at Marburg), *Informationen zur Hochschuldidaktik*, 3, 117-19

Hering, S and Hermanns, H (1978) *Lernen und Verändern — Zur Theorie und Praxis des Projektstudiums (Learning and changing — the theory and practice of project study)*, Blickpunkt Hochschuldidaktik, 49, AHD, Hamburg

Herz, O, Huber, L and Walther, M (1970) *Organisationsmodelle der Hochschuldidaktik (Organisational models for Hochschuldidaktik)*, Blickpunkt Hochschuldidaktik, 9, AHD, Hamburg

Herz, O, Reif, K H and Sader, M (1972) *Lernen in der Hochschule — Beiträge und Vorschläge aus motivationspsychologischer Sicht (Learning at university — contributions and suggestions from the perspective of the psychology of motivation)*, Blickpunkt Hochschuldidaktik, 22, AHD, Hamburg

Hessischer Kultusminister (1977a) Brief an die AHD (Letter to the AHD), *Informationen zur Hochschuldidaktik*, 3, 115-16

Hessischer Kultusminister (1977b) Brief an das Zentrum für Hochschuldidaktik (Letter to the centre for Hochschuldidaktik), *Informationen zur Hochschuldidaktik*, 4, 185-7

Hoffman, B and Eickhoff, F (1977) *Individuelles Lernen mit audiovisuellen Programmen (Individualized learning by audiovisual programmes)*, Hochschuldidaktische Materialien, 63, AHD, Hamburg

Holtkamp, R (1977a), Bericht über die Versammlung der Hochschuldidaktischen Zentren und Arbeitsstellen am 2.12.76 (Report on the conference of the units and centres of Hochschuldidaktik, 2 December 1976), *Informationen zur Hochschuldidaktik*, 1/2, 24-5

Holtkamp, R (1977b) AHD-Zentrenumfrage (AHD survey on centres), *Informationen zur Hochschuldidaktik*, 3, 109-15

Huber, L (1977) Überblick — Allgemeine Aufgaben und Probleme (Survey — general tasks and problems), *Informationen zur Hochschuldidaktik*, 5, 231-4

Huber, L (1978) Ausgangsprobleme für eine hochschuldidaktische Aus- und Fortbildung von Hochschullehrern (Initial problems for in-service education of university teachers), in Ritter, U P and Rieck, W (eds) *Zur hochschuldidaktischen Aus- und Fortbildung von Hochschullehrern*, 18-22, Blickpunkt Hochschuldidaktik, 48, AHD, Hamburg

Klüver, J (1978) Zur politischen Einschätzung der AHD (The political assessment of the AHD), *Informationen zur Hochschuldidaktik*, 3, 81-5

Klüver, J and Schmidt, J (1977) Brückenkurse beim Übergang Schule/Hochschule (Bridging courses for the transition from school to university), *Informationen zur Hochschuldidaktik*, 3, 93-102

Kochs, M and Dandl, J (1978) *Kontaktstudium in der Bundesrepublik Deutschland (Special admission study in the Federal Republic of Germany)*, Blickpunkt Hochschuldidaktik, 47, AHD, Hamburg

Kultusministerkonferenz (1977) Vereinbarung über die Bildung gemeinsamer Studienreformkommissionen der Länder nach §9 HRG (Contract for the establishment of common state commissions for study reform according to §9 HRG), *Informationen zur Hochschuldidaktik*, 5, 245-53

Leuthold, D, Zechlin, L et al (1977) *Hochschuldidaktische Materialien zur Tutorenausbildung (Hochschuldidaktik materials for the education of tutors)*, Hochschule für Wirtschaft, Bremen

Marburger Autorenkollektiv (1977) *Leitfaden für die Tutorenarbeit (Manual for working with tutors)*, Blickpunkt Hochschuldidaktik, 42, AHD, Hamburg

Mattl, W (1973) *Kleingruppenarbeit in Verbindung mit fernstudiendidaktischem Material (Small group work in relation to correspondence study materials)*, Blickpunkt Hochschuldidaktik, 29, AHD, Hamburg

Meyer, T, Gasch, B et al (1973) *Dozentenbefragung zu Themen der Hochschuldidaktik (Inquiry of university teachers into issues in Hochschuldidaktik)*, Augsburger Studien zur Hochschuldidaktik, 2, HDZ, Augsburg

Meyer-Hartwig, K et al (1975) *1 x 1 zum Entwurf von Diapositiven (ABC of the design of slides)*, Witzstrock, Baden-Baden

Modellversuche im Bildungswesen (1978) (Trials of educational models),
*Informationen zur Hochschuldidaktik*, 1/2, 19-23
Moser, H (1977a) *Praxis der Aktionsforschung (Practice of action research)*,
Kösel, Munich
Moser, H (1977b) *Methoden der Aktionsforschung (Methods of action research)*,
Kösel, Munich

Portele, G (1970) *Intrinsische Motivation in der Hochschule — eine empirische
Untersuchung zum 'forschenden Lernen' (Intrinsic motivation within
universities — an empirical investigation of 'learning by research')*,
Blickpunkt Hochschuldidaktik, 12, AHD, Hamburg
Prahl, H W (1976) *Hochschulprüfungen — Sinn oder Unsinn? (University exams —
sense or nonsense?)*, Kösel, Munich

Quitzow, W (1973) Curriculumforschung als Komponente der Hochschuldidaktik
(Curriculum research as a component of Hochschuldidaktik),
*Informationen zur Hochschuldidaktik*, 7, 133-42

Rauch, M (1978) Studieninformations- und -beratungswoche für Erstsemester
(A week of information and study advice for university freshmen),
*Informationen zur Hochschuldidaktik*, 1/2, AHD, Hamburg
Ritter, U P (1977) *Kleine Fibel zur Prüfungsvorbereitung (Small guide for
preparation for examinations)*, Blickpunkt Hochschuldidaktik, 45, AHD,
Hamburg
Ritter, U P and Diepold, P (1975) *Gruppenarbeit und Tutorenausbildung
in den Wirtschaftswissenschaften (Group work and education of tutors
in the economic sciences)*, Seminar für Hochschuldidaktik der
Wirtschaftswissenschaften, Universität Frankfurt
Ritter, U P and Rieck, W (1977) *AHD-Rundbriefe zur hochschuldidaktischen
Aus- und Fortbildung fon Hochschullehrern (Circulars about in-service
education of university teachers in Hochschuldidaktik)*, U P Ritter,
Universität Frankfurt, Senckenberganlage 31
Ritter, U P and Rieck, W (1978) *Zur hochschuldidaktischen Aus- und
Fortbildung von Hochschullehrern: Das Bad Homburger Symposium (The
in-service education of university teachers in Hochschuldidaktik: The
symposium of Bad Homburg)*, Blickpunkt Hochschuldidaktik, 48, AHD,
Hamburg
Ritter, U P and Thieme, W (1974) Alter und neuer AHD — Rückblick und
Zukunftsperspektiven (The old AHD and the new — retrospective and
perspectives for the future), *Informationen zur Hochschuldidaktik*,
8, 154-6
Röhrs, H (1973) Der Ort der Didaktik im Rahmen der Gesamthochschule
(Heuristisches Modell) (The place of 'didactics' within the Gesamthochschule
[heuristic model] ), *Deutsche Universitätszeitung*, 11, 434-41

Schmid, D (1976) *Abiturnoten, Testverfahren und Prognose des Studienerfolgs
(Final school marks, tests and prognosis of study success)*, Blickpunkt
Hochschuldidaktik, 39, AHD, Hamburg
Scholz, G (1975) *Selbsterfahrungsgruppen in pädagogischen Studiengängen
(Self-awareness groups in the education of teachers)*, Blickpunkt
Hochschuldidaktik, 36, AHD, Hamburg
Schott, E (1973) *Zur empirischen und theoretischen Grundlegung eines
Bewertungsinstruments für Vorlesungen (The empirical and theoretical
basis of an evaluation instrument for lectures)*, Blickpunkt Hochschuldidaktik,
28, AHD, Hamburg
Schott, E and Schott U (1975) *Zur psychosozialen Struktur von Studienanfängern
der Medizin (The psycho-social characteristics of freshmen in medicine)*,
Hochschuldidaktische Forschungsberichte, 2, AHD, Hamburg

Selle, B (1977) Hochschulreform und Studienabbruch (University reform and
drop outs), *Informationen zur Hochschuldidaktik*, 3, 119-28
Senatskommission für Hochschuldidaktik der DFG (1976) *Der
Forschungsschwerpunkt Hochschuldidaktik der Deutschen
Forschungsgemeinschaft (The focus of the Deutsche Forschungsgemeinschaft
supporting research in Hochschuldidaktik)*, Hochschuldidaktische Materialien,
53, AHD, Hamburg
Spindler, D (1968) *Hochschuldidaktik — 25 Dokumente (Hochschuldidaktik —
25 documents)*, Verlag Studentenschaft, Bonn

Thieme, W (1977) Hochschullehrer und Hochschuldidaktik (University teachers
and Hochschuldidaktik), *Informationen zur Hochschuldidaktik*, 4, 176-8
Thomas, W (1974) Die pädagogische Ausbildung der Dozenten bei der IBM
Deutschland (Pedagogical education of teachers of IBM Germany), in
Melezinek, A (ed) *Die Technik und ihre Lehre*, 79-90, Heyn, Klagenfurt

Vopel, K W (1972) *Gruppendynamische Experimente im Hochschulbereich
(Experiments in group dynamics in the university field)*, Blickpunkt
Hochschuldidaktik, 24, AHD, Hamburg

Zuber, O (1975) *Advisory Centres for Tertiary Education in West Germany*,
CAT Education Monograph 11, Centre for Advancement of Teaching,
Macquarie University, Sydney
Zweite Kasseler Hochschulwoche (1975) *Symposium. Die Gesamthochschule
heute (Symposium: The Gesamthochschule today)*, Kassel, Basel, *et al*, 1976

## Chapter 6: The German Democratic Republic

Anordnung zur Verleihung des akademischen Grades Doktor eines
Wissenschaftszweiges — Promotionsordnung A - vom 21 (Ordinance
concerning the conferment of the degree Doctor of an Academic Discipline,
Promotion A) (January 1969), *Gesetzblatt der Deutschen Demokratischen
Republik*, II, 14
Anordnung zur Verleihung des akademischen Grades Doktor der
Wissenschaften — Promotionsordnung B — vom 21 (Ordinance concerning
the conferment of the degree Doctor of Sciences, Promotion B) (January
1969) *Gesetzblatt der Deutschen Demokratischen Republik*, II, 14
Anordnung über das Forschungsstudium vom 1 (Ordinance concerning
research studies) (June 1970) *Gesetzblatt der Deutschen Demokratischen
Republik*, II, 54, p 410
Anordnung über die wissenschaftliche Aspirantur — Aspirantenordnung — vom
22 (Ordinance concerning 'aspirants') (September 1972) *Gesetzblatt der
Deutschen Demokratischen Republik*, II, 60, p 648
Autorenkollektiv (1977, 1978) *Arbeitsmaterial: Einführung in die
Hochschulpädagogik, Teil I Grundlagen der Hochschulpädagogik,
Teil II Aufgaben der kommunistischen Erziehung an Hochschulen,
Teil III Hochschuldidaktik* (Introduction to university pedagogics:
Part I — Fundamentals of university pedagogics; Part II — The tasks of
communist education at institutes of higher education; Part III — University
didactics), Rostock

Bernhardt, G, Möbius, R and Weidemeier, A (1977) Die Weiterbildung leitender
Kader des Hoch- und Fachschulwesens — Ergebnisse, Probleme Aufgaben
(In-service training of senior staff in higher education — results, problems,
tasks), *Das Hochschulwesen*, 2/77, p 32
Böhme, H-J (1977) Aufgaben bei der Herausbildung eines qualifizierten und
politisch gefestigten wissenschaftlichen Nachwuchses (The training of

qualified and politically sound junior academic staff), from a speech given
at a conference in Dresden, May 4/5, 1977, *Das Hochschulwesen*, 7/77, p 162

Böhme, H-J (1978) Referat auf der Konferenz der Rektoren der Universitäten
und Hochschulen der DDR (Speech given at the conference of rectors of
universities and other institutes of higher education of the GDR)

Engel, G (1978) Zur marxistisch-leninistischen Weiterbildung im Hochschulwesen
(Post-experience education in Marxism-Leninism at universities and colleges),
*Das Hochschulwesen*, 5/78, p 108

Goldschmid, M L and Möhle, H (1977) The introduction of educational
technology in higher education, in *Final Document of the International
Seminar on Educational Technology*, pp 112-18, Budapest

Kiel, S (1978) Gemeinsames Seminar UdSSR-DDR zur hochschulpädagogischen
Qualifizierung (USSR-GDR joint seminar on training in university pedagogics),
*Das Hochschulwesen*, 1/78

Kiel, S and Steinhardt, B (1976) Zur weiteren Gestaltung der hochschulpädagogischen Qualifizierung an den Universitäten und Hochschulen (The
further development of pedagogical training in higher education), *Das
Hochschulwesen*, 7/76, p 1

Matthes, B, Panzram, J and Steinhardt, B (1977) Förderung von Beststudenten —
ein hoher gesellschaftlicher Anspruch (Erfahrungen und Wege an unseren
Hochschulen) (The advancement of best students — an important social task),
*Das Hochschulwesen*, 5/77, p 114

Möhle, H (1974) *The role of universities in post-experience higher education*,
contribution at the International Institute for Educational Planning,
UNESCO, Paris

Möhle, H (1974) *Postgraduate studies for university and technical college
graduates as an integral part of the socialist educational system of the German
Democratic Republic*, paper read at the Université de Provence I Marseilles/
Aix-en-Provence

Möhle, H (1975) *The development of university pedagogics in the GDR and the
contribution of Karl Marx University*, paper given at universities in Japan
and Australia

Möhle, H (1977) *Scientific and university development in the GDR*, paper given
at universities in Cuba

Möhle, H (1978) University distance education in the GDR, its place in the
integrated socialist education system, its conception and results, in *University
and Technical College Distance Education in the GDR and in Developing
Countries of Africa*, pp 1-22

Programm der Sozialistischen Partei Deutschlands (SED Party Programme) (1976)
Dietz Verlag, Berlin

Statistiques des effectifs d'étudiants en République Démocratique Allemande
(1978) in *Higher Education in Europe*, May/June 1978, p 22, UNESCO/
CEPES, Bucharest

Verordnung über die Berufung und die Stellung der Hochschullehrer am den
wissenschaftlichen Hochschulen — Hochschullehrerberufungsverordnung
(HBVO) — vom 6 (Regulations concerning the Appointment of Senior Faculty
Staff) (November 1968), *Gesetzblatt der Deutschen Demokratischen Republik*,
II, 127, p 997

Verordnung über die akademischen Grade vom 6 (Regulations concerning
academic degrees) (November 1968) *Gesetzblatt der Deutschen
Demokratischen Republik*, II, 127

Verordnung über die wissenschaftlichen Mitarbeiter an den wissenschaftlichen

Hochschulen — Mitarbeiterverordnung — vom 6 (Regulations concerning university staff) (November 1968), *Gesetzblatt der Deutschen Demokratischen Republik,* II, 127

## Chapter 7: The Indian Sub-continent

Bligh, D (1978) *Nepal. Promotion of the Curriculum Development Centre at Tribhuwan University,* UNESCO

Ministry of Education (1971) *National Education System Plan 1971-76,* His Majesty's Government of Nepal

University Grants Commission (1976) *University teaching methods: Report on seminar and workshop,* University Grants Commission, Dacca (Bangladesh)

University Grants Commission (1975) *Conference of Vice-Chancellors,* University Grants Commission, New Delhi (India)

University Grants Commission (1975) *National Academy of Higher Education,* University Grants Commission, Islamabad (Pakistan)

Zaki, W M (1975) *Education of the people,* Peoples Open University, Islamabad (Pakistan)

## Chapter 8: The Netherlands

Ackers, G W (1979) *University teacher training,* paper presented to the EARDHE Congress, Klagenfurt

Ackers, G W and Rigter, W J (1976) O and O — docentenseminars (O and O university teacher training seminars), *0 and 0 memo,* 3 (1), 1-5

Arnold, C A and Eijl, P J van (1976) *Module: Aanvangsniveau (Module: Starting level),* 50pp, Afdeling Onderzoek en Ontwikkeling van Onderwijs, Rijksuniversiteit, Utrecht

Bevers, J, Dousma, T and Wolters, L (1977) *Doelstellingen in het onderwijs, Inleidend informatie pakket (Objectives in education, Introductory information package),* Memorandum 5-77, Instituut voor Onderzoek van het Wetenschappelijk Onderwijs, Katholieke Universiteit, Nijmegen

Bevers, J and Wolters, L (1976) *Verslag van een inventarisatie van problemen en behoeftes aan onderwijskundige informatie en/of training bij docerend personeel aan de KU ( Report of a stocktaking of problems and needs for educational information and/or training of teaching staff at the Catholic University),* Memorandum 6-76, Instituut voor Onderzoek van het Wetenschappelijk Onderwijs, Katholieke Universiteit, Nijmegen

Blom, S (1976) *Verslag studiedag studiegroep docententrainingen (Report of a study day held by the university teacher training study group),* Memorandum, Bureau Onderzoek van Onderwijs, Rijksuniversiteit, Leiden

Blom, S (1977a) *Over docententrainingen (About university teacher training),* 8 pp, Memorandum 378-77, Bureau Onderzoek van Onderwijs, Rijksuniversiteit, Leiden

Blom, S (1977b) *Simpele visuele hulpmiddelen bij het onderwijs (Simple visual aids in education),* 7 pp, Memorandum 385-77, Bureau Onderzoek van Onderwijs, Rijksuniversiteit, Leiden

Blom, S (1977c) *Docententrainingen ten behoeve van docenten in de propedeuse van de juridische fakulteit (Training for teachers of first year law),* 3 pp, Memorandum 392-77, Bureau Onderzoek van Onderwijs, Rijksuniversiteit, Leiden

Blom, S (1977d) *Doceervaardigheden in werkgroepen (Teaching skills for tutorials)*, 6 pp, Memorandum 393-77, Bureau Onderzoek van Onderwijs, Rijksuniversiteit, Leiden

Blom, S (1977e) *Beleidsplan docententrainingen Rijksuniversiteit Leiden (Management plan for university teacher training at the State University, Leiden)*, 15 pp, Memorandum 395-77, Bureau Onderzoek van Onderwijs, Rijksuniversiteit, Leiden

Blom, S (1977f) *Microteaching voor universitaire docenten (Microteaching for university teachers)*, 22 pp, Memorandum 399-77, Bureau Onderzoek van Onderwijs, Rijksuniversiteit, Leiden

Blom, S (1977g) *Trainingen doceervaardigheden (Training in classroom teaching skills)*, 3 pp, Memorandum 415-77, Bureau Onderzoek van Onderwijs, Rijksuniversiteit, Leiden

Blom, S (1977h) *Evaluatie Microteaching 1977 (Evaluation of microteaching 1977)*, 11 pp + appendices, Memorandum 420-77, Bureau Onderzoek van Onderwijs, Rijksuniversiteit, Leiden

Blom, S (1978) *Handleiding bij de kursus Doceervaardigheden Werkgroepen (Guide for the course Teaching Skills for Tutorials)*, 26 pp, Memorandum 430-78, Bureau Onderzoek van Onderwijs, Rijksuniversiteit, Leiden

Blom, S and Versfelt, W A (1977) *Evaluatie docententraining hoorcolleges (Evaluation of the university teacher training course in lecturing)*, 20 pp, Memorandum 402-77, Bureau Onderzoek van Onderwijs, Rijksuniversiteit, Leiden

Bouhuijs, P A J, Schmidt, H G, Snow, R E and Wijnen, W H F W (nd) *The Development of Medical Education at Rijksuniversiteit Limburg, Maastricht, Netherlands*, 34 pp, Draft Memorandum, Rijksuniversiteit Limburg, Maastricht

Breuker, L (1977) *In kaart brengen van leerstof (Mapping out subject matter)*, docentencursus nr 4, Centrum voor Onderzock van het Wetenschappelijk Onderwijs, Universiteit van Amsterdam, Amsterdam

Buitink, J and Hiemstra, A (nd) *Verslag van de kursus 'Werken met kleine groepen' (Report on the course 'Working with small groups')*, 7 pp, Centrum voor Onderzoek van het Wetenschappelijk Onderwijs, Rijksuniversiteit, Groningen

Camstra, B (1976) *Bouwstenen voor het onderwijs. Een kursus in het construeren van onderwijs (Building blocks for education. A course in the construction of educational experiences)*, docentencursus nr 1 (experimental version), Centrum voor Onderzoek in het Wetenschappelijk Onderwijs, Universiteit van Amsterdam, Amsterdam

Camstra, B (1977) *Evaluatie van COWO-docentencursus nr 1. 'Bouwstenen voor onderwijs' (Evaluation of COWO university teacher training course No 1. 'Building blocks for education')*, Rapport 7705-01, Centrum voor Onderzoek in het Wetenschappelijk Onderwijs, Universiteit van Amsterdam, Amsterdam

Campbell, D T and Stanley, A (1963) *Experimental and quasi-experimental designs for research*, 84 pp, Rand-McNally and Company, Chicago

Daalder, H (1975) The Dutch Universities between the 'New Democracy' and the 'New Management', in Seabury, P (ed) *Universities in the Western World*, 195-231, The Free Press, New York

Dokter, H J and Scheepers, H (1974) *Verslag van een studiereis naar Manchester, 31 maart 1974 — 9 april 1974 (Report of a study trip to Manchester, 31 March 1974 — 9 April 1974)*, Vakgroep Onderwijsresearch, Erasmus Universiteit, Rotterdam

Donders, J M (1974) *Invoering IS Systemen in het curriculum (Introducing ISS systems into the curriculum)*, Onderwijskundig Centrum CDO/AVC, Technische Hogeschool, Twente

Dorp, C van (1972) *Training van medische docenten (Training of medical teachers)*, Rapport nr 6, Dienst Onderwijsontwikkeling, Rijksuniversiteit, Leiden

Dorp, C van (1973) *Systematisch ontwikkelen van multiple choice vragen (Systematic development of multiple choice questions)*, Mededeling 47, Dienst Onderwijsontwikkeling, Faculteit der Geneeskunde, Rijksuniversiteit, Leiden

Dorp, C van (1974) Het Methodisch ontwikkelen van toetsvragen (The systematic development of test questions), *Onderzoek van Onderwijs*, 3 (2)

Dorp, C van (1976) *Een plan voor de docententraining aan de KHT 1976- 77 (A plan for the training of university teachers at the KHT 1976- 77)*, Memorandum 201.76, Onderwijs Research Centrum, Katholieke Hogeschool, Tilburg

Dorp, C van (1977a) Opzet en evaluatie van docententrainingen (Establishment and evaluation of university teacher training), in *Congresboek Onderwijs Research dagen 1977*, 59-64, Amsterdam

Dorp, C van (1977b) Zelfstudiepakketten voor docenten — een bibliographie (Self-study packages for university teachers — a bibliography), *Onderzoek van Onderwijs*, 6 (4), 15-16

Dousma, T (1977a) *Evaluatieverslag docententraining 'Toetskonstruktie' (Evaluation report on the university teacher training course 'Test construction')*, 21 pp + appendices, Memorandum 13-77, Instituut voor Onderzoek van het Wetenschappelijk Onderwijs, Katholieke Universiteit, Nijmegen

Dousma T (1977b) *Kursus toetskonstruktie (Course in test construction)*, 4 pp, Instituut voor Onderzoek van het Wetenschappelijk Onderwijs, Katholieke Universiteit, Nijmegen

Dousma, T (1977c) *Kursus toetskonstruktie. Handleiding voor de kursist (Course in test construction. Guide for participants)*, 9 pp, Instituut voor Onderzoek van het Wetenschappelijk Onderwijs, Katholieke Universiteit, Nijmegen

Dousma, T (1977d) *Toetskonstruktie kursusboek (Test construction course book)*, 90 pp, Instituut voor Onderzoek van het Wetenschappelijk Onderwijs, Katholieke Universiteit, Nijmegen

Dousma, T, Hupkens, E and Wolters, L (1977) *Docententraining. Opzet van nazorg en produktevaluatie op lange termijn (University teacher training. Plan for after care and long term product evaluation)*, 7 pp, Memorandum 26-77, Instituut voor Onderzoek van het Wetenschappelijk Onderwijs, Katholieke Universiteit, Nijmegen

Earl, F A (1976) *The four referrents*, 18 pp, paper presented to the Third National Congress 'Onderzoek van wetenschappelijk onderwijs', 15-16 January, Technische Hogeschool, Delft

Eijk, J van and Kleijer, H (1977) *Studiebijeenkomst over de nota 'Hoger Onderwijs in de Toekomst' en de centra voor onderzoek van het wetenschappelijk onderwijs (Study meeting on the memorandum 'Higher Education in the Future' and the centres for research in higher education)*, 36 pp, Stichting Interuniversitair Instituut voor het Sociaal — Wetenschappelijk Onderzoek, Amsterdam

Eijl, P J van (1975a) *Het schrijven van een module (Writing a module)*, Afdeling Onderzoek en Ontwikkeling van Onderwijs, Rijksuniversiteit, Utrecht

309

Eijl, P J van (1975b) *Het schrijven van operationele doelen (Writing operational goals)*, Afdeling Onderzoek en Ontwikkeling van Onderwijs, Rijksuniversiteit, Utrecht

Eijl, P J van and Odijk, M (1976) *Evaluatiehulppakket (Evaluation help package)*, Afdeling Onderzoek en Ontwikkeling van Onderwijs, Rijksuniversiteit, Utrecht

Elsinga, W J and Dorp, C van (eds) (1977/78) *Bronnenboek docententraining (Source book for teacher training)*, 10 volumes, Onderwijs Research Centrum, Katholieke Hogeschool, Tilburg

Hazewinkel, A (1971) *Hoger Onderwijs-Research als service instituut (Higher education research as a service institution)*, Rotterdam

Hout, J van (1975) *Verslag van een bezoek aan de USA van 29-3 tot 20-4-1975 (Report of a visit to the USA from 29-3 to 20-4-1975)*, Onderwijskundig Centrum CDO/AVC, Technische Hogeschool, Twente

Hout, J van (1976) *Voorstel voor de opzet en uitvoering van onderwijskundige docententrainingen (Proposal for the establishment and execution of university teacher training*, 19 pp, Memorandum 22-76, Instituut voor Onderzoek van het Wetenschappelijk Onderwijs, Katholieke Universiteit, Nijmegen

Hout-Wolters, B H A M, Kramers-Pals, H, Pilot, A and Staak, J L C van der (1975) *Gids voor het schrijven van diktaten door docenten (A guide to the writing of handouts by university lecturers)*, 41 pp, Centrum voor Didaktiek en Onderzoek van Onderwijs, Technische Hogeschool, Twente

Kemenade, J A van (1975) The cost of higher education cannot continue to rise unchecked, *Higher Education and Research in the Netherlands*, 19 (1), 4-11

Klauw, C F van der and Plomp, Tj (1974a) Individualised study systems in theory and practice, *Higher Education*, 3 (2), 213-20

Klauw, C F van der and Plomp, Tj (1974b) The construction and evaluation of a feedback system, in Verreck, W A (ed) *Methodological Problems in Research and Development in Higher Education*, 237-58, Swets and Zeitlinger, Amsterdam

Klauw, C F van der and Wagemakers, J (1975) *Educational research and development at the universities in the Netherlands*, 25 pp + appendices (also available in Dutch), Instituut voor Onderzoek van het Wetenschappelijk Onderwijs, Katholieke Universiteit, Nijmegen

Klauw, C F van der and Wagemakers, J J W M (1976) The Netherlands, in Entwistle, N (ed) *Strategies for research and development in higher education*, 237-48, Swets and Zeitlinger, Amsterdam

Kleijer, H and Kuiper, R (1977) *Verslag van activiteiten van de Studiegroep Theorievorming voor Projektonderwijs (Report on the activities of the Study Group on Constructing a Theory of Project-Based Education)*, Stichting Interuniversitair Instituut voor het Sociaal — Wetenschappelijk Onderzoek, Amsterdam

Knippenberg, P (1976a) *Diskussietraining met docenten en student-assistenten van de sektie taalbeheersing van de afdeling Nederlands, februari - mei 1976. Verslag (Training in discussion with teachers and student assistants of the language skills section of the Dutch Department, February — May 1976. Report)*, 13 pp, Memorandum 76-07PK, Centrum voor Onderzoek van het Wetenschappelijk Onderwijs, Rijksuniversiteit, Groningen

Knippenberg, P (1976b) *Informatieverspreiding, training en begeleiding ten behoeve van universitaire docenten (Information dissemination, training and assistance for university teachers)*, 13 pp, Memorandum N76-12PK, Centrum voor Onderzoek van het Wetenschappelijk Onderwijs, Rijksuniversiteit, Groningen

Knippenberg, P (1976c) *Resultaten van elf gesprekken met onderwijskommissies over de behoeften aan onderwijskundige informatie en/of kursussen ten behoeve van docenten (Results of 11 discussions with education committees about the need for educational information and/or courses for university teachers)*, 7 pp, Memorandum N76-14PK, Centrum voor Onderzoek van het Wetenschappelijk Onderwijs, Rijksuniversiteit, Groningen

Knippenberg, P (1977a) *Onderwijs aan universitaire docenten (Education for university teachers)*, 5 pp, Memorandum N77-01, Centrum voor Onderzoek van het Wetenschappelijk Onderwijs, Rijksuniversiteit, Groningen

Knippenberg, P (1977b) *Collegetraining tandheelkunde (Training in lecturing: Dentistry)*, 4 pp, Internal Memorandum M77-04PK, Centrum voor Onderzoek van het Wetenschappelijk, Onderwijs, Rijksuniversiteit, Groningen

Knippenberg, P (1978) *Werkgroep 'Training van universitaire docenten' (Working group 'Training for university teachers')*, 5 pp, Internal Memorandum, Centrum voor Onderzoek van het Wetenschappelijk Onderwijs, Rijksuniversiteit, Groningen

Krammer, H P M (1976) *Klassikaal vraagstukken oplossen (Classroom work on solving problems)*, 108 pp, Vakgroep Onderwijskunde, Technische Hogeschool, Twente

Krammer, H P M and Smuling, E R (1977) *De ontwikkeling van een Microteaching-kursus; projektverslag (The development of a Microteaching course; project report)*, Rapport nr 32, Onderwijskundig Centrum CDO/AVC, Technische Hogeschool, Twente

Lagendijk, E (1975) *Onderwijsdoelstellingen (Educational objectives)*, Onderwijskundige Dienst, Technische Hogeschool, Delft

Leiblum, M D (1974) Educational technology: an American's perspective on the Dutch university scene, *Educational Technology*, 14 (2), 40-1

Meer, A van der and Plomp, Tj (1975) *Rapport van de begeleidingscommissie ISS (Report of the steering committee ISS)*, Department of Applied Mathematics, Technische Hogeschool, Twente

Meer, Q L Th van der (1976) *Studiewijzer basiscursus onderwijskunde voor docenten (Study guide for the basic course in education for university teachers)*, Bureau Onderzoek van Onderwijs, Landbouwhogeschool, Wageningen

Meestringa, T (1977) *Het enkète — adviesboek in de praktijk; meningen van lezers en gebruikers (The practical questionnaire advice book; comments of readers and users)*, 25 pp, Centrum voor Onderzoek van het Wetenschappelijk Onderwijs, Rijksuniversiteit, Groningen

Melnick, A M and Sheehan, D A (1976) Clinical supervision elements: the clinic to improve university teaching, *Journal of Research and Development in Education*, 9 (2), 67-76

Mirande, M J A (1977a) Principles underlying university teacher courses, in Elton, L and Simmonds, K (eds) *Staff development in higher education*, 14-17, Society for Research into Higher Education, Guildford

Mirande, M J A (1977b) *Achtergronden, opzet en evaluatie van de COWO docentencursussen (Background, establishment and evaluation of the COWO university teacher courses)*, Centrum voor Onderzoek in het Wetenschappelijk Onderwijs, Universiteit van Amsterdam, Amsterdam

Moor, R A de (1976) Adult and part-time education in the Netherlands, in European Centre for Higher Education (eds) *New forms of higher education in Europe*, 125-31, CEPES, Bucharest

NUFFIC (1971-78) *Higher Education and Research in the Netherlands*, volumes 15-22

311

NUFFIC (1976a) Higher education in the future, *Higher Education and Research in the Netherlands,* 20 (3), 4-37

NUFFIC (1976b) Contours of a future education system in the Netherlands, *Higher Education and Research in the Netherlands,* 20 (2), 36-7

NUFFIC (1976c) Student population in 1975-76, *Higher Education and Research in the Netherlands,* 20 (4), 51

NUFFIC (1977) More applications for the 1977-78 academic year, *Higher Education and Research in the Netherlands,* 21 (3), 24

O and O van O (1977a) *Taak en werkzaamheden (Its role and functions),* brochure (also available in English), Afdeling Onderzoek en Ontwikkeling van Onderwijs, Rijksuniversiteit, Utrecht

O and O van O (1977b) *O and O docentenseminars 1977 (O and O university teacher seminars 1977),* brochure, Afdeling Onderzoek en Ontwikkeling van Onderwijs, Rijksuniversiteit, Utrecht

OECD (1976) *Netherlands. Contours of a future education system,* 93 pp, Organisation for Economic Co-operation and Development, Paris

Onderwijs Research Centrum (1976) Individuele studie systemen (1): Twee onderwijsopvattingen (Individual study systems (1): Two educational viewpoints), *ORC-bulletin,* 5, Onderwijs Research Centrum, Katholieke Hogeschool, Tilburg

Philipsen, H (1976) *Teaching methods and practical training in medical schools: the case of Maastricht,* 9 pp, unpublished conference paper, Rijksuniversiteit Limburg, Maastricht

Pilot, A and Kramers-Pals, H (1973) De constructie van een individueel studiesysteem materiaalkunde voor eerstejaars aan de T H Twente (The construction of an individualized study system in materials science for first years at the T H Twente), in Woerden, W M van et al (eds) *Onderwijs in de maak,* Aula 508 Spectrum, Utrecht

Plomp, Tj (1974) *De Ontwikkeling van een Individuele Studie Systeem (The development of an individualised study system),* Tjeenk Willink, Groningen

Plomp, Tj and Meer, A van der (1977) Problems in the context evaluation of individualised courses, *Higher Education,* 6 (4), 437-52

Rommes, A E N (1975) *Beoordelen van studieresultaten (Assessing results),* 3rd revised edition, 74 pp, Onderwijskundig Centrum CDO/AVC, Technische Hogeschool, Twente

Rooij, P G M de (1976) *Development of a management and allocation system in a medical faculty in the Netherlands,* 18 pp, unpublished paper, Rijksuniversiteit Limburg, Maastricht

Rosenboom, J (1977) *Evaluatie van docententrainingen aan de Katholieke Hogeschool te Tilburg 1976/1977 (Evaluation of university teacher training at the Catholic University at Tilburg 1976/1977),* 66 pp + appendices, Internal Report, Onderwijs Research Centrum, Katholieke Hogeschool, Tilburg

Schmidt, H G (1977) *Probleemgeorienteerd Onderwijs (Problem-oriented education),* 2nd revised edition, 61 pp, Kapaciteitsgroep Onderwijsontwikkeling, Rijksuniversiteit Limburg, Maastricht

Schmidt, H G and Bouhuijs, P A J (1977) *Het tutorensysteem (The tutor system),* 2nd revised edition, 57 pp, Kapaciteitsgroep Onderwijsontwikkeling, Rijksuniversiteit Limburg, Maastricht

Scriven, M (1967) The methodology of evaluation, in Tyler, R W, Gagné, R M and Scriven, M (eds) *Perspectives of curriculum evaluation,* American Educational Research Association Monograph Series on Curriculum Evaluation, 1, 39-83, Rand McNally, Chicago

Smal, J A (1977) Machinaal vervaardigen van toetsvragen (Automatic preparation of test items), *Onderzoek van Onderwijs,* 6 (4), 3-8

References and bibliography

Smuling, E B (1977) Diadetraining 'Geven van hoorkolleges'; een rapport over de opzet van een training in doceervaardigheden (The diad training 'Giving lectures'; a report on the establishment of a training course in teaching skills), 34 pp + appendices, Rapport 35, Centrum voor Didaktiek en Onderzoek van Onderwijs, Technische Hogeschool, Twente

Smuling, E B and Hout, J F M J van (1977) Geven van hoorcolleges. Een handleiding bij training in doceervaardigheden (Giving lectures. A guide to accompany training in teaching skills), 96 pp, Centrum voor Didaktiek en Onderzoek van Onderwijs, Technische Hogeschool, Twente

Veltman, P J C (1976) Verslag van de internationale workshop voor universiteitsdocenten, gehouden 1-10 april in Hennickhammer, Zweden (Report on the international workshop for university teachers, held 1-10 April in Hennickhammer, Sweden), Afdeling Onderzoek en Ontwikkeling van Onderwijs, Rijksuniversiteit, Utrecht

Veltman, P J C (1978) International seminar for university teachers: The Netherlands: December 1977, Impetus, 9, 29-32, Co-ordinating Committee for the Training of University Teachers, Norwich

Verreck, W (1976) Instructional programmes and individualization of learning: a review of recent research and development, in Entwistle, N (ed) Strategies for research and development in higher education, 65-83, Swets and Zeitlinger, Amsterdam

Vroeijenstein, A I (1975) Inventarisatie van docententrainingen, ontwikkeld of in ontwikkeling bij de RWO-centra (Stocktaking of university teacher training courses and materials, developed or under development at RWO centres), Centraal Bureau voor Onderzoek van het Wetenschappelijk Onderwijs, Voorburg

Vroon, A G (1975) Onderwijsverbetering, een zaak van onderwijskundigen? (Improving the quality of education; a matter for educationists?), Universiteit en Hogeschool, 22 (2), 92-100

Water, R van de (1973) Resultaten van de enquête naar de behoeften aan medisch-onderwijskundige vorming (Results of the questionnaire on the need for training in medical education), Memorandum 85-73, Rijksuniversiteit, Leiden

Wieringen, A van (1974) Aspirations and identity of vocational colleges in the Netherlands, Higher Education Review, 6 (3), 39-53

Wilbrink, B (1977) Methoden voor het bepalen van de grens zakken/slagen voor studieonderdelen (Methods for setting the pass/fail cut off points in subjects), COWO docentencursus nr 6, Centrum voor Onderzoek in het Wetenschappelijk Onderwijs, Universiteit van Amsterdam, Amsterdam

Wijnen, W H F W (1976) The future of higher education, Higher Education and Research in the Netherlands, 20 (2), 4-11

Wolters, L (1977a) Evaluatieverslag docententraining 'Het geven van hoorkolleges' (Evaluation report on the university teacher training course 'Giving lectures'), 24 pp + appendices, Memorandum 12-77, Instituut voor Onderzoek van het Wetenschappelijk Onderwijs, Katholieke Universiteit, Nijmegen

Wolters, L (1977b) Nadere informatie over de training 'Het geven van hoorkolleges' (Further information about the training course 'Giving lectures'), 5 pp, Instituut voor Onderzoek van het Wetenschappelijk Onderwijs, Katholieke Universiteit, Nijmegen

Wolters, L (1977c) Kiezen van onderwijsvormen (Choosing teaching methods), 88 pp, Instituut voor Onderzoek in het Wetenschappelijk Onderwijs, Katholieke Universiteit, Nijmegen

## Chapter 9: New Zealand

Advisory Council on Educational Planning (1974) *Directions for educational development*, Government Printer, Wellington

Association of University Teachers of New Zealand (Inc) (1972) *Submission to the improving learning and teaching working party of the Educational Priorities Conference on university teaching*, AUTNZ, Wellington

Bassey, M (1971) *The assessment of students by formal assignments*, New Zealand University Students' Association, Wellington

Clift, J C and Imrie, B W (1977) A model of behaviour for evaluating courses in tertiary institutions, in *Curriculum Evaluation, papers of the annual conference of the Australian Association for Research in Education*

Committee on the Registration and Discipline of Teachers (1978) *Report of the Committee on the Registration and Discipline of Teachers*, Department of Education, Wellington

Cowen, Z (1972) The role and purpose of the university, in Harman, G S and Selby-Smith, C (eds) *Australian higher education*, Angus and Robertson, Sydney

Dainton, F (1974) Reported in the *Times Higher Education Supplement*, 9 August

Educational Development Conference (1974) *Improving learning and teaching, report of the working party on improving learning and teaching*, EDC, Wellington

Green, V H H (1969) *The universities*, Penguin, Harmondsworth

Harrison, N (1977) *Centres for the development and improvement of learning and teaching in technical institutes, a record of proceedings of a seminar held 2-3 August 1977 at Wellington Polytechnic*, 40 pp, Wellington Polytechnic, Wellington

Hore, T (1973) Promotion through teaching: some issues and problems, *Notes on Higher Education*, 8, Higher Education Research Unit, Monash University

Knowles, M S (1970) *The modern practice of adult education: andragogy versus pedagogy*, Association Press, New York

Lee, B C (1969) Technical institutes in New Zealand, in *Trends and issues in higher education*, New Zealand Council for Educational Research and the Association of University Teachers of New Zealand, Wellington

Miller, G W (1970) *Higher education research in Australia and New Zealand*, Society for Research into Higher Education, Guildford

National Council of Adult Education (1977) *Report of the working party on the training of continuing educators*, NCAE, Wellington

National Development Conference (1969) *Report of the committee on education, training and research to the National Development Conference*, Government Printer, Wellington

New Zealand Council for Educational Research and the Association of University Teachers of New Zealand (1970) *Trends and issues in higher education*, NZCER/AUTNZ, Wellington

New Zealand Universities Conference (1974) *Co-operation among New Zealand universities in academic planning, advanced studies and research, staff training and the dissemination of information*, a paper prepared by the University of Canterbury for the New Zealand Universities Conference, 13-15 August

New Zealand University Students' Association (1971) *Course and lecture evaluation*, Research Office for the Study of Higher Education, NZUSA, Wellington

w Zealand Vice-Chancellors Committee (1969-1974) *Statistics of University Student Performance*, NZVCC, Wellington
New Zealand Vice-Chancellors Committee (1976) *Information booklet*, NZVCC, Wellington

*Salient* (1962a) Vol 25 (8), 11
*Salient* (1962b) Vol 25 (9), 8

Teather, D C B (1975) A biocommunication centre in embryo, *Journal of Biocommunication*, 2 (1), 10-16
Teather, D C B (1977) The training of university teachers: an integral part of an educational technology centre's activities? *South Pacific Journal of Teacher Education*, 5 (1), 33-41
Teather, D C B (1978) Audiovisual media and educational technology in the traditional university: the working compromise or the grand design? *Higher Education*, 7 (4), 431-42
Teather, D C B and Collingwood, V (1978) Which media do university teachers actually use? A survey of the use of audio-visual media in teaching at two New Zealand universities, *British Journal of Educational Technology*, 9 (2), 149-60

Wilson, O M (1967) Teach me, and I will hold my tongue, in Lee, C B T (ed) *Improving college teaching*, American Council on Education, Washington, DC
Working Party on Review of Teacher Training (1978) *Working paper for review of teacher training conference*, 8-9 August. (Report expected March 1979)

# Chapter 10: Sweden

Abrahamsson, B (1977) *Forskningsanknytning. Om sambandet mellan forskning och grundutbildning (The relation between research and undergraduate education)*, UHÄ-rapport 1977: 10, Stockholm

Behre, G and Larsson, R (1979) The Swedish model — five themes, *Ontario Universities Program for Instructional Development Newsletter*, 22, January
Berg, B and Östergren, B (1977) *Innovationer och innovationsprocesser i högre utbildning (Innovation and processes for innovation in higher education)*, UHÄ-rapport 1977: 1, Stockholm
Berglund, I (1977) *Lärare på kontor. Rapport om utbildning för lärare inom linjen för offentling förvaltning (Teachers in administration. Report on the training of teachers for the civil service degree course)*, UHÄ Personalutbildningsenheten, Stockholm
Behre, G, Jalling, H and Larsson, R (1977) *Teaching teachers to teach? Ten commandments — underlying thoughts and tentative conclusions from a Swedish model for courses*, paper read at the International Conference on University Teaching, McMaster University, Hamilton, June
Björup, K (1972) *Lärarfortbildning i arbetsgrupper (Teacher training in disciplinary groups)*, Rapport, Enheten för pedagogiskt utvecklingsarbete 1972: 1, Lunds universitet

*Den akademiska undervisningen. Principbetänkande avgivet av universitetspedagogiska utredningen (Academic teaching. Report by the Committee for University Teaching Methods )* (1970) Universitetskanslersämbetets skriftserie nr 10, Stockholm

Edén, V (1974) *Universitetets roll — nu och i framtiden (The role of the university — today and tomorrow)*, Rapport från idékonferens (Gotlandsspelet) nov 1973, UKÄ Personalutbildningsenheten, Stockholm

Falk-Nillson, E and Åkesson, E (1972) *Pedgogisk utbildning för studievägledare, rapport fran UKÄ:s försökskurs (Pedagogical training for study counsellors. Report on UHÄ:s pilot course)*, Enheten för pedagogiskt utvecklingsarbete, Lunds universitet

Falk-Nilsson, E and Karlsson, B (1974) *På väg: Från många kurser till en utbildning, rapport från lärardager i biologi (From many courses to a teaching programme. Report from teacher training seminars in biology)*, Enheten för pedagogiskt utvecklingsarbete informerar 1974: 47, Lunds universitet

Grahm, A, Mårtenson, D and Parknäs, L (1974) *Inbjudan till inlärning – (Invitation to learning) – rapport*, UKÄ:s pedagogiska kurser för universitetslektorer/adjunkter år 1973, UKÄ 1974: 6a, Stockholm

Grahm, Å, Mårtenson, D and Parknäs, L (1974) *Inbjudan till inlärning – (Invitation to learning) – dokumentation*, UKÄ:s pedagogiska kurser för universiteteslektorer/adjunkter år 1973, UKÄ 1974: 6b, Stockholm

Grahm, Å, Rovio-Johansson, A and Mårtenson, D (1974) *Rapport från internatkurs i medicinsk pedagogik (Report from a boarding course in medical education) hösten 1973*, Nämnden för pedagogiskt utvecklingsarbete, Karolinska institutet, Stockholm

Jalling, H (1974) *Pedagogisk utbildning av universiteteslärare. Översikt över utvecklingen 1955-1974 (Teacher training for faculty. Review of the development 1955-1974)*, UKÄ Enheten för pedagogiskt utvecklingsarbete, Stockholm

Jalling, H (1974) *Director of studies: new position for departmental instruction development*, paper read at the International Conference on Instructional Development, Amherst, October

Jalling, H (1976) Teacher training or staff development, in *Proceedings of the Second International Conference on Improving University Teaching*, Heidelberg

Jalling, H (1978) *Pedagogisk utveckling (Educational development in staff training)*, 'Statlig personalutbildning' Betänkande SOU 1978: 41, 87-99

Jalling, H (in press) Educational policy and staff development, in *Proceedings of the Fourth International Conference on Higher Education*, Lancaster

Kjöllerström, B (1976) *Universitetesläraren i Näringslivet förnyar sin syn på utbildningen (The teacher with temporary assignment in industry renews his ideas on education)*, PU-enheten vid Lunds universitet informerar 1976: 64, Lunds universitet

Lindholm, K (1976) *Projektorienterad undervisning vid socialhögskolorna, Rapport efter avslutad kurs (Project oriented teaching in Social Work and Public Administration. Report on a teacher training programme)*, UKÄ, Stockholm

Lundén, O et al (Åtta studierektorer, Uppsala universitet) (1975) *Rapport angående studierektorsuppdraget inom filosofisk fakultet vid universitet och högskolor (Report on the position as Director of Studies in the faculties of arts and science)*, Enheten för pedagogiskt utvecklingsarbete, Uppsala universitet

*Pedagogisk utbildning av akademiska lärare (Pedagogical training of university teachers)*, (1965) Universitetskanslersämbetet, Stockholm

Rovio-Johansson, A, Abramson, C and Dahlgren, G (1972) *Lärares och studenters syn på universitetslärarens arbetsuppgifter och behov av pedagogisk utbildning (The views of faculty and students on the tasks of faculty and the need for teacher training)*, BLL-projektet 1, Pedagogiska institutionen, Göteborgs universitet, March

References and bibliography

Rovio-Johansson, A, Abramson, C and Dahlgren, G (1972) *Primärdata från en undersökning rörande lärares och studenters syn på universitetslärarens arbetsuppgifter och behov av pedagogisk utbildning (The views of faculty and students on the tasks of faculty and the need for teacher training)*, BLL-projektet 2, Pedagogiska institutionen, Göteborgs universitet, March

Sandberg, C (1974) *Rapport från personalutbildningskonferens 1974-02-05 (Report from the staff training conference arranged by the office of the University Chancellor)*, UKÄ-rapport 1974: 12, Stockholm

*Statlig personalutbildning, ett principförslag (Staff development in the Civil Service)* (1976) SOU 1976: 61, Stockholm

Söderström, M (1975) *Olika synsätt kring personalutbildning i organisationer (Different views of staff training in organisations)*, FOA rapport A 55002-H8 May 1975, Försvarets forskningsanstalt, Stockholm

Törngren, E and Nordheden, B (1972) *UKÄ:s påbyggnadskurs för studierektorer 1972 – en dokumentation om internatperioderna 1 och 2 (UHÄ's course for directors of studies – report on the 1972 pilot course)*, Psykotekniska institutet rapport 1972: 40, Stockholms universitet

Törngren, E (1973) *UKÄ:s påbyggnadskurs för studierektorer 1972 – en dokumentation om en pedagogisk försökskurs (UHÄ's course for directors of studies – report on the 1972 pilot course)*, Psykotekniska institutet rapport 1973: 52, Stockholms universitet

*UKÄ:s förslag till anslagsäskanden för budgetåret 1972/73: Högre utbildning och forskning (Estimates for the fiscal year 1972/73 submitted by the Office of the Chancellor of the Swedish universities)* (1971) UKÄ:s skriftserie nr 12, Stockholm

*UKÄ:s förslag till anslagsäskanden för budgetåret 1976/77: Högre utbildning och forskning (Estimates for the fiscal year 1976/77 submitted by the Office of the Chancellor of the Swedish universities)* (1975) UKÄ-rapport 1975: 15, Stockholm

*Utbildningens internationalisering. Slutbetänkande från UKÄ:s internationaliseringsutredning (Internationalizing higher education. Final report by the Swedish committee for internationalizing university education)* (1974) Universitetskanslersämbetet rapport nr 21, Stockholm

## Chapter 11: Switzerland

Alexander, L T and Yelon, S L (eds) *Instructional development agencies in higher education*, Michigan State University Press, East Lansing

Centra, J A (1977) Plusses and minuses for faculty development, *Change*, 9 (12), 47-8, 64

Chaire de Pédagogie et Didactique (1976) *Liste de critères pour l'évaluation de cours dans la pratique de l'autoscopie (Checklist for evaluating sequences of teaching recorded on videotape)*, EPFL-CPD, Lausanne, February

Chaire de Pédagogie et Didactique (1978) *Questionnaire d'évaluation de cours (Course evaluation questionnaire)*, EPFL-CPD, Lausanne, January

Champagne, M (1974a) *Liste numérique des mots-clé contenus dans le thésaurus (A numerical list of key words contained in the thesaurus)*, EPFL-CPD, Lausanne

Champagne, M (1974b) *Rapport résumé de l'enquête sur la pédagogie à l'EPFL (Summarised report of an enquiry on teaching at the Swiss Federal Institute of Technology, Lausanne)*, EPFL-CPD, Lausanne, December

Champagne, M (1977) *Procédure pour l'autoscopie: guide pour la collaboration entre les enseignants et la chaire de pédagogie et didactique (Procedures for*

317

videorecording: a guide for collaboration between teachers and the chair of higher education and psychology), EPFL-CPD, Lausanne, December

Champagne, M (1978) *Questionnaire d'évaluation de cours, Manuel d'utilisation (Course evaluation questionnaire, handbook)*, EPFL-CPD, Lausanne, January

Commission pour la Réforme des Etudes (1977) Formation et spécialisation en matière de didactique universitaire en Suisse (Staff development in Switzerland), *Politique de la Science*, August, 3, 208-15

De Marchi, L (1977) *Adaptation du système de classement de la documentation 'Swifta' à la Chaire de Pédagogie et Didactique (An adaptation of the 'Swifta' system of document classification for use by the chair of higher education and psychology)*, EPFL-CPD, Lausanne, October

Goldschmid, B and Goldschmid, M L (1976) Enabling students to learn and participate effectively in higher education, *Journal of Personalized Instruction*, 1 (2), 70-5

Goldschmid, M L (1978a) *Organization and activities of the chair of higher education and psychology*, EPFL-CPD, Lausanne, May

Goldschmid, M L (1978b) The evaluation and improvement of teaching in higher education, *Higher Education*, 7 (2), 221-45

Goldschmid, M L and Brun, J (1979) *The evaluation of different forms of individualized instruction in higher education*, paper presented at the Third International Congress of the European Association for Research and Development in Higher Education, Klagenfurt University, Klagenfurt, 2-6 January

Goldschmid, M L and Burckhardt, C W (1976) Expérience de parrainage dans une école polytechnique (An experiment on peer counselling in a technological university), *European Journal of Engineering Education*, 1 (2), 108-12

Goldschmid, M L, Champagne, M and de Marchi, L (eds) (in press) *Développer les compétences pédagogiques. Guide practique pour enseignants et formateurs (Developing teaching skills: a practical guide for teachers and teacher trainers)*

Gut, W (1978) *Sechs Jahre Kommission für Studienreform (Six years of the Committee for Study Reform)*, Lucerne

Piper, D W and Glatter, R (1977) *The changing university: a report on the staff development in universities programme, 1972/74*, National Foundation for Educational Research, Slough

Rose, C, Nyre, G F and Marantz, L S (1977) *Comprehensive annotated bibliographies: faculty development and evaluation; organizational development and change; instructional development; evaluation*, Education and Training Institute, Los Angeles, California

## Chapter 12: The United States of America

Alexander, L T and Yelon, S L (1972) *Instructional development agencies in higher education*, Michigan State University Continuing Education Service, East Lansing

Bergquist, W H and Phillips, S R (1975) Components of an effective faculty development program, *Journal of Higher Education*, 46, 177-211

Bergquist, W H, Phillips, S R and Quehl, G (1975) *A handbook for faculty development, Volume 1*, Council for the Advancement of Small Colleges, Washington, DC

Bergquist, W H, Phillips, S R and Quehl, G (1977) *A handbook for faculty development, Volume 2*, Pacific Soundings Press, Berkeley, California

Bess, J L (1975) New life for faculty and their institutions, *Journal of Higher Education*, 46, 313-25

Bess, J L (1977) The motivation to teach, *Journal of Higher Education*, 48, 243-58

Birnbaum, R (1975) Using the calendar for faculty development, *Educational Record*, 56, 226-30

Boyer, R K and Crockett, C (eds) (1973) Organizational development in higher education, *Journal of Higher Education* (special issue), May, 44

Brawer, F B (1968) *Personality characteristics of college and university faculty: implications for the community college*, ERIC Clearinghouse for Junior College Information, American Association of Junior Colleges Monograph Series, American Association of Junior Colleges, Washington, DC

Brown, D G and Hanger, S (1975) Pragmatics of faculty self-development, *Educational Record*, 56, 201-6

Buhl, L C and Greenfield, A (1975) Contracting for professional development in academe, *Educational Record*, 56, 111-21

Centra, J A (1976) *Faculty development practices in US colleges and universities*, Educational Testing Service, Princeton, NJ

Centra, J A (ed) (1977) Renewing and evaluating teaching, *New Directions for Higher Education*, 17, Jossey-Bass, San Francisco

Cohen, A M (ed) (1973) Toward a professional faculty, *New Directions for Community Colleges*, 1, Jossey-Bass, San Francisco

Crow, M L, Milton, O, Moomaw, W E and O'Connell, W R Jr (1976) *Faculty development in southern universities*, Southern Regional Education Board, Atlanta

Davis, R H, Abedor, A J and Witt, P W F (1976) *Commitment to excellence: a case study of educational innovation*, Educational Development Program, Michigan State University, East Lansing

DeBloomis, M and Alder, D (1973) Stimulating faculty readiness for instructional development: a conservative approach to improving college teaching, *Educational Technology*, 8, July, 16-19

Dougherty, E A (1974) Should faculty be considered well-educated individuals? *Liberal Education*, 60, 521-30

Eble, K E (1971) *Career development of the effective college teacher*, Project to Improve College Teaching, American Association of University Professors and Association of American Colleges, Washington, DC

Eble, K E (1972) *Professors as teachers*, Jossey-Bass, San Francisco

Erickson, G R and Erickson, B (in press) Improving college teaching: an evaluation of a teaching consultation procedure, *Journal of Higher Education*

Fenker, R M (1975) The evaluation of university faculty and administrators, a case study, *Journal of Higher Education*, 46, 665-86

Francis, J B (1975) How do we get there from here? Program design for faculty development, *Journal of Higher Education*, 46, 719-32

Freedman, M (ed) (1973) Facilitating faculty development, *New Directions for Higher Education*, 1, Jossey-Bass, San Francisco

Gaff, J G (1975) *Toward faculty renewal*, Jossey-Bass, San Francisco

Gaff, J G (ed) (1978) Institutional renewal through the improvement of teaching, *New Directions for Higher Education*, 24, Jossey-Bass, San Francisco

Gaff, S S, Festa, C and Gaff, J G (1978) *Professional development: a guide to resources*, Change Magazine Press, New Rochelle, NY

Gross, A (1977) Twilight in academe: the problem of the aging professoriate, *Phi Delta Kappan*, 58, 752-4

Group for Human Development in Higher Education (1974) *Faculty development in a time of retrenchment*, Change Magazine, New Rochelle, NY

Hammons, J D and Wallace, T H (1976) *An assessment of community college staff development needs in the Northeastern United States,* Center for the Study of Higher Education, The Pennsylvania State University, University Park, Pa

Hodgkinson, H L (1974) Adult development: implications for faculty and administrators, *Educational Record,* 55, 263-74

Hoyt, D P and Howard, G S (1978) The evaluation of faculty development programs, *Research in Higher Education,* 8, 25-38

Jenny, H H and Acton, M A (1974) *Early retirement. A new issue in higher education: the financial consequences of early retirement,* Teachers Insurance and Annuity Association, New York

Kindschi, P D (1978) Personal communication

Kozma, R B (in press) Faculty development and the adoption and diffusion of classroom innovations, *Journal of Higher Education*

Lindquist, J (ed) (1978) *Designing teaching improvement programs,* Council for the Advancement of Small Colleges, Washington, DC

Martin, W B (1975) Faculty development as human development, *Liberal Education,* 61, 187-96

Miller, W S and Wilson, K M (1963) *Faculty development procedures in small colleges,* Research Monograph 5, Southern Regional Education Board, Atlanta

Morstain, B R and Gaff, J G (1977) Student views of teaching improvements, *Educational Record,* 58, 299-308

O'Banion, T (1973) *Teachers for tomorrow: staff development in the community-junior colleges,* University of Arizona Press, Tucson

Sanford, N (1971) Academic culture and the teacher's development, *Soundings*

Smith, A B (ed) (1975 *et seq*) *Faculty development and evaluation in higher education: a quarterly newspaper,* 3930 NW 35th Place, Gainesville, Florida 32605

Smith, A B (1976) *Faculty development and evaluation in higher education,* ERIC/Higher Education Research Report 8, American Association for Higher Education, Washington, DC

Smith, A (ed) (1978) *Faculty development and evaluation in higher education,* School of Education, University of Florida, Gainsville, Florida

Toombs, W (1975) A three dimensional view of faculty development, *Journal of Higher Education,* 46, 701-17

Wergin, J F, Mason, E J and Munson, P J (1976) The practice of faculty development: an experience-derived model, *Journal of Higher Education,* 47, 289-308

## Key documents

Hore, T (1976) *Teaching research units in Australasia.* Draft report of a survey commissioned by the Commonwealth Secretariat, London

Piper, D W (1977) Practical implications of staff development, *Higher Education Review,* 10 (1), 54-64

Tertiary Education Institute (1977 *et seq*) *Labyrinth: Clearinghouse bulletin for higher education research and development units in Australia and New Zealand,* Tertiary Education Institute, University of Queensland, Brisbane

# Subject index

Aberdeen, University of, 9, 10, 268
academic respectability, 33-4, 154, 192
academic staff
— administrative skills, 17, 19, 46, 54, 110, 128, 164, 196, 204, 206, 208
— as educational resource, 234, 236, 238
— assessment of, 208
— associations, *see* Association of Principals of Technical Institutions; Association of Teachers in Technical Institutes; Association of University Teachers; Lecturers' Associations; National Union of University Teachers
— attitude to staff development activities, 17-18, 33, 41, 55, 80, 95-7, 100, 102-3, 113, 117, 129, 176, 179, 192, 202-3, 206, 222, 225, 229, 238, 242-4
— attitude to teaching, 36, 77, 80, 101, 192, 199, 234
— career: counselling, 246; development, 244, 246; enhancement, 240; planning, 221, 246; shift, 254
— demand for training in teaching skills, 47, 99, 113, 129, 177-8, 252
— diversity of, 235
— exchange, 246
— job satisfaction, 36
— limited job opportunities, 36, 180, 206-7, 232-3, 246
— morale, 159
— non-participation in staff development activities, 34, 116-17, 193
— numbers, by country: Australia, 17; Britain, 39, 59; Denmark, 88, 93; GDR, 126; Netherlands, 163; NZ, 182; Pakistan, 151
— participation in staff development activities, 18, 30, 35, 36, 43, 47, 58, 68, 99, 117-18, 122-3, 147, 153, 165, 172, 177, 204-5, 225-6, 243-4
— personal development, 68-9
— political stance, 125, 129-30, 136-7

— probation, 41, 44-5, 198, 255-8
— promotion, 27, 36, 45, 51, 77, 83-4, 113, 117, 126-8, 130-1, 135-6, 138, 167, 178-80, 192-3, 198-9, 206-8, 234, 240, 256
— qualifications, 33, 60, 61, 64, 67, 76, 91, 112, 125-35, 141, 143, 151, 158-9, 162, 178-9, 193, 230
— register of, 152, 197
— regulations, 126, 138
— roles and responsibilities: as teachers, 15, 17, 101, 128, 137, 165, 178, 181, 183, 201, 233-4; of academic staff as a whole, 91, 100-1, 110-11, 117, 127, 143, 145, 150, 156-8, 160, 178, 201, 207, 211, 234, 245; of doctoral candidates, 130; of probationers, 257; of senior academic staff, 42, 56, 60, 64, 128-9, 135, 138, 140, 150, 201, 235, 240, 258, *see also* staff development under senior staff
— salaries, 76, 151, 234, 240
— secondment, 30-1, 61, 249, 254
— selection, 91, 109-10, 126, 129, 135-6, 143, 164, 183, 196, 208, 240
— status, 77, 117
— study leave, 11, 61-3, 67, 77, 83, 113, 138-40, 184, 189, 195-6, 198, 211, 232, 240, 243
— teaching load, 45, 80, 91, 117, 127, 229, 257
— tenure, 27, 77, 83, 91, 167, 180, 182, 193, 207-8, 232, 234, 240, 255
Academies of Fine Arts, FRG, 108
Academy for Further Medical Training, GDR, 139
accountability, 36-7, 83, 85, 180, 183, 250
action research, *see* research
Act on Administration of Institutions of Higher Education, Denmark, 90-1, 100
Adelaide, University of, 10, 31, 264
administrative staff
— conditions of service, 70-1
— courses for, 19, 54, 73-4, 89, 99,

321

# Author index